THE FUTURE OF LABOUR

The Future of Labour: How AI, Technological Disruption and Practice Will Change the Way We Work is an anthology that offers a forward-looking exploration of how artificial intelligence (AI), digitalisation and technological transformation are reshaping the future of work. Through a series of studies conducted by scientists and industry professionals, this volume takes a deep dive into many of the issues related to new policies, AI and the digital transformation's anticipated impact on the labour market. Balancing speculative foresight with scientific rigour, the authors ground their discussions in empirical data, theoretical frameworks and comprehensive literature studies.

The book delves into the evolving labour landscape through three key themes:

- The Future of Society and Economy – Examining the socio-economic implications of emerging technologies and their transformative impact on work.
- The Future Way of Working – Investigating how AI and digital tools are redefining the nature of work and workplace conditions.
- New Uses of AI and Technology in Labour – Highlighting innovative applications of AI and technology that are reshaping job roles and industries.

Each chapter provides unique insights, blending rigorous analysis with predictive insights, to illuminate the challenges and opportunities of a rapidly technologically advancing labour landscape.

Anthony Larsson, PhD, is an author, editor and researcher. He is a former Fellow at the Stockholm Chamber of Commerce and a former researcher at the Stockholm School of Economics Institute for Research (SIR) and at Karolinska Institutet.

Andreas Hatzigeorgiou, PhD, is the President and CEO of PE Teknik & Arkitektur, one of Sweden's leading engineering and architecture companies, and affiliated researcher at the School of Architecture and the Built Environment, KTH Royal Institute of Technology.

"If the future of work seems unimaginable to you, turn here to have your imagination expanded and your certainties overturned. Offering a kaleidoscope of insights from history, philosophy, theoretical social science, and best-of-class empirical analysis, this book will convince you that the future is not predetermined. It depends instead on the individual and collective choices we are making right now."

David Autor
Daniel (1972) and Gail Rubinfeld Professor, Margaret MacVicar Faculty Fellow, MIT Department of Economics, Cambridge, Massachusetts, USA

"*The Future of Labour: How AI, Technological Disruption and Practice Will Change the Way We Work* is a timely and provocative analysis of the changing world of work. This book offers a crucial perspective on the challenges and opportunities that lie ahead. It offers a clear-eyed look at the challenges and opportunities posed by AI and automation."

Mark Graham
Professor of Internet Geography, Oxford Internet Institute, Oxford University, Oxford, UK

"*The Future of Labour: How AI, Technological Disruption and Practice Will Change the Way We Work* offers a timely and comprehensive exploration of the rapidly evolving realities of work. Drawing on diverse expert insights, the volume enumerates the challenges and opportunities presented by AI and technological disruption, examining their impact on various aspects of the labour market, from individual skills and job roles to global economic structures and social welfare systems. Anyone seeking a broad understanding of the future of work and how we can navigate the transition should take the time to read this."

Vivienne Ming
Theoretical neuroscientist and artificial intelligence expert, Socos Labs, Berkeley, California, USA

THE FUTURE OF LABOUR

How AI, Technological Disruption and Practice Will Change the Way We Work

Edited by Anthony Larsson and Andreas Hatzigeorgiou

Routledge
Taylor & Francis Group
LONDON AND NEW YORK

Designed cover image: zhuyufang / Getty Images

First published 2025
by Routledge
4 Park Square, Milton Park, Abingdon, Oxon OX14 4RN

and by Routledge
605 Third Avenue, New York, NY 10158

Routledge is an imprint of the Taylor & Francis Group, an informa business

British Library Cataloguing-in-Publication Data
A catalogue record for this book is available from the British Library

Library of Congress Cataloging-in-Publication Data
Names: Larsson, Anthony editor | Hatzigeorgiou, Andreas editor
Title: The future of labour : how AI, technological disruption and practice will change the way we work / edited by Anthony Larsson and Andreas Hatzigeorgiou.
Description: Abingdon, Oxon ; New York, NY : Routledge, 2025. |
Includes bibliographical references and index.
Identifiers: LCCN 2025001438 (print) | LCCN 2025001439 (ebook) |
ISBN 9781032489049 hardback | ISBN 9781032489025 paperback |
ISBN 9781003391333 ebook
Subjects: LCSH: Labor supply–Effect of technological innovations on |
Labor supply–Effect of automation on | Technological unemployment | Labor |
Artificial intelligence–Economic aspects | Technological innovations–Economic aspects
Classification: LCC HD6331 .F88 2025 (print) | LCC HD6331 (ebook) |
DDC 331.13/7042–dc23/eng/20250404
LC record available at https://lccn.loc.gov/2025001438
LC ebook record available at https://lccn.loc.gov/2025001439

ISBN: 978-1-032-48904-9 (hbk)
ISBN: 978-1-032-48902-5 (pbk)
ISBN: 978-1-003-39133-3 (ebk)

DOI: 10.4324/9781003391333

Typeset in Times New Roman
by Newgen Publishing UK

This book is dedicated to the loving memories of my dear mother Patricia (1954–2025), and my dear aunt, Louise (1959–2024).

Always in our minds, forever in our hearts. Your lives were a blessing, your memories a treasure. You are loved beyond words and missed beyond measure.

Anthony

CONTENTS

ILLUSTRATIONS

Figures

Table

FOREWORD I

Navigating the New Frontier of the Transformative Labour Landscape

As we stand at the precipice of unprecedented change in the world of work, it is both an honour and a necessity to introduce this anthology on the future of labour. The rapid evolution of technology, particularly the surge of digitalisation and artificial intelligence (AI), is not just altering the landscape of labour but redefining its very essence. The chapters contained within this book, penned by an international team of scholars and industry experts, delve into the multifaceted implications of these transformative forces, presenting a nuanced exploration of the promises and perils that lie ahead.

The world of work has always been dynamic, continually shaped by technological advancements, economic shifts and social changes. However, the pace and scale of the current digital revolution are unparalleled. In the many offices that I have held, I have witnessed the ebbs and flows of labour markets and I have studied the impacts of various technological innovations. Yet, the integration of AI and digitalisation presents a uniquely complex challenge. These technologies have the potential to revolutionise productivity, efficiency and economic growth. They offer new tools for problem-solving, open up possibilities for new types of work and promise to enhance the quality of life for workers around the globe.

But with great promise comes significant peril. The displacement of jobs due to automation, the potential for increased inequality and the ethical considerations surrounding AI usage are issues that cannot be ignored. The historical lessons of previous industrial revolutions teach us that while technology can create new opportunities, it can also lead to disruptions that disproportionately affect certain segments of the workforce. The challenge before us is to navigate this transition in a manner that is inclusive and equitable, ensuring that the benefits of technological advancements are broadly shared.

This anthology addresses critical questions: What will the future of labour look like? How can we harness the potential of AI and digitalisation to create a labour market that is innovative, successful and sustainable? These questions require thoughtful consideration and actionable insights. The contributors to this book provide a diverse array of perspectives, combining empirical research with practical expertise. Their insights illuminate the complex interplay between technology and labour, offering guidance on how to steer through the uncertainties of this transition.

In reading this anthology, you will encounter discussions on the transformation of specific industries, the changing nature of skills and education, the role of policy and governance, and the ethical implications of AI. Each chapter contributes to a deeper understanding of the multifaceted impacts of digitalisation on the future of work. Together, they form a comprehensive narrative that not only highlights the challenges but also envisions a path forward.

One of the most significant takeaways from this book is the necessity of a proactive approach. The future is not a predetermined outcome but a landscape that we can shape through informed decision-making and collaborative effort. It calls for innovative thinking, robust policy frameworks and a commitment to lifelong learning. It also demands a re-evaluation of the social contract, ensuring that workers are not left behind in the wake of technological progress.

As we move forward, it is crucial to foster a dialogue that includes all stakeholders – workers, employers, policymakers and educators. By doing so, we can build a future of work that is not only technologically advanced but also socially just and economically inclusive. This anthology serves as a valuable resource in this endeavour, providing the knowledge and insights necessary to navigate the complexities of the digital age.

In conclusion, the labour landscape is at a crossroads. The decisions we make today will shape the work environment for generations to come. This book is a testament to the collective effort required to ensure that the transformation of labour leads to a future that is prosperous, equitable and sustainable. I encourage you to engage deeply with the insights presented herein and to join in the vital conversation about the work we can expect to see tomorrow.

Ray Marshall *16th United States Secretary of Labor (1977–1981); Professor Emeritus; Audre and Bernard Rapoport Centennial Chair in Economics and Public Affairs University of Texas at Austin*

FOREWORD II

Shaping the Future of Work

The future labour landscape is a topic of paramount importance as we stand at the intersection of technological innovation, societal shifts and global interconnectedness. In my career, I have witnessed first-hand the transformative power of these forces and the profound impact they have on our economic and social settings. This anthology, *The Future of Labour: How AI, Technological Disruption and Practice Will Change the Way We Work*, delves into these changes, offering a comprehensive analysis and forward-looking perspectives on how we can navigate the evolving world of work.

As a Swede, innovation and pioneering technology lies close to my heart. Sweden has long been a pioneer in embracing new technologies and progressive labour policies, serving as a model for balancing economic growth with social welfare. Our nation's commitment to innovation and inclusivity has enabled us to adapt to changes while maintaining a high standard of living for our citizens. While this book carries an international focus and relevance, the insights within are relatable to me in this tradition, all the while exploring how we can continue to thrive in an era of rapid technological advancement.

One of the most significant drivers of change in the labour market is the advent of automation and artificial intelligence. These technologies have the potential to revolutionise industries, increase productivity and create new job opportunities. However, they also pose challenges, particularly in terms of job displacement and the need for new skill sets. The future labour market will require a workforce that is adaptable, continually learning and able to work alongside advanced technologies. This book addresses these challenges head-on, proposing strategies for knowledge-production and training that will equip individuals with the skills necessary to succeed in this new environment.

Globalisation is another critical factor reshaping the labour market. While it has opened up new markets and facilitated the exchange of ideas and talent, it has also led to increased competition and the need for a more agile and resilient workforce. The authors of this book raise many important issues that carry significance across national borders and settings. Hopefully, businesses and governments may collaborate on how to create policies that support workers in a globalised economy, ensuring that the benefits rather than the negatives of globalisation are broadly shared.

Moreover, the future labour market will be increasingly influenced by the principles of sustainability and corporate social responsibility. As businesses, we have a duty to consider the environmental and social impact of our operations. This book also delves into the ways in which companies can integrate sustainable practices into their business models, contributing to a more equitable and sustainable world.

At the heart of these discussions is the need for collaboration between all stakeholders – businesses, governments, educational institutions and workers themselves. The future of work is not something that can be shaped by one entity alone; it requires a concerted effort and a shared vision. It is important to emphasise the importance of dialogue and partnership in creating a labour market that is inclusive, dynamic and responsive to the needs of all.

In conclusion, the future of labour presents both tremendous opportunities and significant challenges. By embracing innovation, fostering inclusivity and committing to sustainability, we can create a future of work that benefits everyone. This book is a valuable resource for anyone seeking to understand and navigate the complexities of the evolving labour market and what is to come in the years ahead. I am confident that the insights and recommendations it offers will inspire and guide us as we work together to build a prosperous and equitable future.

Jacob Wallenberg *Chair of the Board of Investor AB and Chair of the Confederation of Swedish Enterprise, Vice Chair Wallenberg Investments AB, FAM AB, Patricia Industries and Ericsson AB, and Board Member of the Knut and Alice Wallenberg Foundation*

LETTER FROM THE EDITORS

This edited volume, *The Future of Labour: How AI, Technological Disruption and Practice Will Change the Way We Work*, aims to investigate the possible direction of the future labour landscape. The future of work is a topical issue that is of great concern to many. It lies at the bedrock of our own personal security and the sustenance of society at large.

As we stand at the cusp of a technological revolution of the labour market, we are confronted with both unprecedented opportunities and complex challenges. The promise of innovation and efficiency is accompanied by concerns about job displacement, shifting skills requirements and the ethical implications of increasingly autonomous systems. This anthology seeks to delve into these critical issues, offering a range of perspectives on what the future labour market might hold in store for us and how we can navigate this transition successfully and sustainably. While this book to a large extent investigates the role of digital technology and AI on the future labour landscape, it also examines policy, strategies and developmental trends adopted by the labour market and/or those affected by it.

The contributions in this volume come from international thought leaders, industry experts and academics, each offering valuable insights into the future of work in a digital age. Together, they paint a picture of a landscape in flux, one where the key to thriving lies in adaptability, forward-thinking leadership and a commitment to balancing technological progress with human-centred values.

As editors, our goal has been to curate a comprehensive discussion that not only addresses the current state of affairs but also looks ahead to the strategies and solutions that will shape the future of labour. We hope that this book serves as both a guide and an inspiration for those seeking to harness the power of technology while ensuring that the workforce of tomorrow remains resilient, skilled and empowered.

Thank you for embarking on this journey with us. The future of work is being written today, and we believe this anthology will provide valuable tools and insights to help us navigate it together.

As an open access product under the Creative Commons Attribution-Non-Commercial-No Derivative (CC BY-NC-ND) licence, we invite you to spread and redistribute this book freely to any and all interested parties you may encounter.

Anthony Larsson, Ph.D.
Andreas Hatzigeorgiou, Ph.D.
Stockholm

ACKNOWLEDGEMENTS

This book has been a collaborative journey, and its completion would not have been possible without the support, insight and contributions of many individuals and institutions.

First and foremost, we would like to express our gratitude to the Stockholm Chamber of Commerce, where this project was first conceptualised. Their commitment to fostering innovation and facilitating critical dialogue on the future of work laid the foundation for this volume. We are especially thankful to our colleagues for their unwavering support throughout this endeavour.

We would also like to extend our heartfelt appreciation to the esteemed contributors whose expertise, research and thoughtful analyses have brought depth and richness to the discussions presented in this book. Your contributions have been invaluable in shaping a comprehensive view of the evolving landscape of work in the digital age.

We also extend our most utmost heartfelt thanks to our editor Kristina Abbotts and editorial assistant Christiana ("Chrissy") Mandizha, along with the rest of the assisting staff at Routledge/Taylor & Francis, along with project manager Ilakya Raghuraj at Newgen Digitalworks, for their help and support throughout every step in the making of this book and in the promotion of its release.

Last, but not least, we would also like to extend our special gratitude to all family, friends, supporters and colleagues for their unfaltering and irreplaceable moral support throughout this process.

ABOUT THE EDITORS

Anthony Larsson (Ph.D.) is an author, editor and researcher. He is a former Fellow at the Stockholm Chamber of Commerce. Dr. Larsson is also a former researcher at the Stockholm School of Economics Institute for Research (SIR) and at Karolinska Institutet, from which he holds a Ph.D. in medical science with a specialisation on innovation management. He also holds an MBA and M.Sc. degrees in political science, social anthropology, as well as business administration and economics, respectively, in addition to an associate's degree in psychology. His publications mainly focus on futures studies, innovation management, digitalisation, business studies, organisational management and urban studies. To date, he has authored, co-authored and edited five books along with numerous peer-reviewed scientific research papers and regularly speaks at international scientific conferences. You may follow his research either at his Routledge author page, www.routledge.com/authors/i18347-anthony-larsson, his Amazon.com author page, www.amazon.com/author/anthonylarsson or his Goodreads author page, www.goodreads.com/author/show/17715876.Anthony_Larsson

Andreas Hatzigeorgiou (Ph.D.) is the President and CEO of PE Teknik & Arkitektur, one of Sweden's leading engineering and architecture companies, and affiliated researcher at the School of Architecture and the Built Environment, KTH Royal Institute of Technology. Dr Hatzigeorgiou's research has been published in peer-reviewed journals and in reports for organisations such as the OECD. He received his Ph.D. in economics from Lund University, Sweden, and graduated as a Fulbright Scholar from the Gerald R. Ford School of Public Policy at the University of Michigan, Ann Arbor. He has been the recipient of several grants and scholarships, among others from the Royal Swedish Academy of Engineering Sciences, and the Swedish Royal Court. Dr Hatzigeorgiou was the

CEO of the Stockholm Chamber of Commerce between 2018 and 2024. He has also served as Advisor to Sweden's Minister for Trade and Nordic Cooperation and as a researcher at the World Bank in Washington, DC. Selected among Sweden's top agenda-setters within climate and sustainability, Dr Hatzigeorgiou is a frequent participant in the debate on cities, business climate, entrepreneurship, sustainability and innovation.

CONTRIBUTORS

Mohammad Amir Anwar is Senior Lecturer (Associate Professor) in International Development at the University of Edinburgh. His work enquires how digital infrastructures (e.g. AI, data, platforms, the Internet and mobile phones) are shaping development outcomes (e.g. labour market transformation, access to decent work, poverty and inequality reduction in the Global South; clean energy transitions). Anwar is the co-author of an open access book, *The Digital Continent* (2022). He is also a Senior Research Associate at the University of Johannesburg and Senior Research Fellow (Honorary) at the British Institute of Eastern Africa.

William J. Ashworth is Reader in History, University of Liverpool (UK). He is the author of *Customs and Excise: Trade, Production, and Consumption in England, 1640–1845* (2003), *The Industrial Revolution: The State, Knowledge, and Global Trade* (2017) and *The Trinity Circle: Anxiety, Intelligence, and Knowledge Creation in Nineteenth-Century England* (2021). Ashworth's current research is on the legacy of the chemical industry in northwest England.

Jon Erik Borgen graduated with an ocean engineering degree from California State University Long Beach in 1986 and gained experience in applied physics as a naval architect specialised in design, analysis and simulation of floating offshore structures. Borgen co-founded and served as CEO building up Inocean AS from 1996 until 2020. In addition, he has experience as an ocean tech entrepreneur with numerous ventures, including as co-founder of SWAY AS in 2001, co-founder of ABB Inocean AB in 2012, co-founder of Peniche Ocean Watch in 2018, co-founder of Odfjell Oceanwind AS in 2019, co-founder of Ekbacken Studios AB in 2021, and co-founder and CEO of Circular Ocean LDA in 2023.

Edward Castronova has been active in the field of virtual economies since 2001. He has written four books and numerous papers on the subject and maintains an active consulting practice. He is Professor of Media at Indiana University in Bloomington, Indiana (USA), teaching on Game Design and Virtual Economies. Castronova is married with two children and a beagle.

Miriam A. Cherry is Professor of Law and the Faculty Director for the Center for Labor & Employment Law at St. John's University School of Law in New York City. Her scholarship focusses on the employment law, business law and the future of work. She is the author of *Work in the Digital Age* (2021) and has written over 40 law review publications. A member of the American Law Institute, Professor Cherry is a graduate of Dartmouth College and Harvard Law School.

Mafalda de Freitas is a marine biologist and Megaplastics Program Director at Hawaii Pacific University's Center for Marine Debris Research, where she is working to establish a plastic recycling research facility on the island of Oahu to handle the 200+ tons of marine debris that washes up annually across the Hawaiian Archipelago. Prior to this, de Freitas managed Ocean Tech Hub and its Peniche Ocean Watch Initiative – a social and environmental impact initiative whose mission is to develop a blue circular economy model that can empower coastal communities in a sustainable way and inspire entrepreneurial actions, whilst driving ocean conservation.

Jonas Grafström (Ph.D.) is a researcher in economics and Vice CEO at the Ratio Institute. He is a visiting fellow at Oxford Institute for Energy Studies and Luleå University of Technology and associated to AI-Econ-Lab at Örebro University. His research takes place at the crossroads between environmental economics and environmental technology. His dissertation ("Technological Change in the Renewable Energy Sector: Essays on Knowledge Spillovers and Convergence") focussed on technological change in the renewable energy sector. Grafström also researches the labour market of the future. Among other things, he has studied how digitalisation and technological change affect the labour market. Grafström has written the book *Modern Times 4.0* and several reports about the future of the office. Other research interests include the conditions for large-scale capture of carbon dioxide (CCS technology), the labour market after COVID-19 and the Chinese wind power sector.

Bent Greve is Professor in Social Science with an emphasis on welfare state analysis at the University of Roskilde, Denmark. His research interest focusses on the welfare state, and social and labour market policy, often from a comparative perspective. He has published extensively on social and labour market policy, social security, tax expenditures, public sector expenditures and financing of the welfare state. Greve is Editor-in-Chief of the journal *Social Policy & Administration*. He has published an extensive number of articles in different journals as well as a large number of books.

Proscovia Paschal Kamugisha is a researcher. She has been affiliated with Mzumbe University since 2008. She holds a Ph.D. (2015) and master's of agricultural economics (2006) from Sokoine University of Agriculture (SUA). She is currently Senior Lecturer at Mzumbe University in the Faculty of Social Sciences. Dr Kamugisha served as the Head of Department of Administrative Studies (Mbeya Campus College) from 2020 to 2023. She is currently the Head of Department of Economics (Faculty of Social Sciences). Moreover, she has served as general secretary of Utatu Mtakatifu Sub-Parish (Morogoro) from 2011 to 2019, and the coordinator of Catholic Charismatic Renewal Tanzania (CCRT) from 2010 to 2019 at the same sub-parish. Dr Kamugisha conducted Consultancy on Effective regulation for equitable delivery of inputs to smallholder farmers in Tanzania, commissioned by Agricultural Non-State Forum (ANSAF) during 2016–2017. In 2020–2023, Dr Kamugisha has played a role of Principal Investigator in researching "Economic Analysis of Broiler Production using Black Soldier Flies Larvae Meals in Tanzania". Dr Kamugisha's research interest dwells in the economics of waste management, natural resources, livestock, crops and fisheries sub-sectors. She has published widely in international data bases.

Ling Koay, with two decades of experience in marketing, has consistently produced work that embodies her passion and innovative leadership in B2B marketing. Starting with the co-founding of a marketing agency in 2004, Koay's expertise was further deepened by her master's thesis on cult branding. Known for her unconventional approach, Koay sees marketing not just as a means to sell a product but as a tool to change minds and influence purchase decisions. This philosophy has won her industry recognition, earning her titles such as "Power Player in SaaS" and "CMO to Watch" by the CMO Alliance in 2023. Under her leadership, Oneflow was recognised as one of the "B2B Brands to Watch", alongside notable brands like Slack and TikTok Business. Beyond these achievements, Koay's mission is deeply humanistic: to inspire individuals to unlock their superpowers. She believes in transforming the mundane into the magical, turning the ordinary into the extraordinary. This belief is reflected in her approach to marketing, which blends creativity, art and science to create unforgettable brand experiences. It is about crafting narratives, building relationships and inspiring actions – skills that are just as applicable in her role as a mother of two as they are in the boardroom.

Joel Kotkin is an internationally recognised authority on global, economic, political and social trends. He is described by the *New York Times* as "America's uber-geographer". His latest book, *The Coming of Neo-Feudalism: A Warning to the Global Middle Class* (2020) is now available in paperback and has been published in Japanese, Arabic and soon Chinese. Kotkin is the Roger Hobbs Presidential

Fellow in Urban Futures at Chapman University in Orange, California, and directs the Center for Demographics and Policy there. He is Executive Editor of the widely read website NewGeography.com. He has a regular column in *Spiked* in the UK, the *National Post* in Canada and the *American Mind*. He also writes regularly for *UnHerd*, *Quillette*, the *Los Angeles Times*, *National Review*, *City Journal*, *The Daily Telegraph* and *The Spectator* as well as many other national publications. Kotkin is the author of ten previously published books, including the widely praised *The New Class Conflict* (2014), which describes the changing dynamics of class in America. He authored *The Human City: Urbanism for the Rest of Us* (2016) and co-edited, with MIT's Alan Berger, the 2018 collection *Infinite Suburbia*. He also co-edited, with Ryan Streeter, a book on the future of cities. Other past books include *The Next Hundred Million: America in 2050* (2010), which explores how the nation will evolve in the next four decades. *The City: A Global History* (2005) and *Tribes: How Race, Religion, and Identity Determine Success in the New Global Economy* (1992), which was published in Korean, Japanese, Arabic and German.

Johan Landberg is a Development Engineer – Material Specialist at Graphic Packaging International. With expertise in polymer materials, his work focusses on packaging development, material innovation, and sustainability. Previously a Senior R&D Engineer at RISE – Research Institutes of Sweden, he specialised in plastic recycling, pre-treatment, and material development. His expertise includes plastic processing, mechanical and thermal testing, wear analysis, and project management. Holding an M.Sc. in Mechanical Engineering from Linköping University, Landberg has participated in projects such as OCEAN-LSAM, which explored the recycling of discarded fishing nets for large-scale additive manufacturing. With a strong track record in research and commercial projects, he is dedicated to advancing sustainable practices in material development and packaging solutions..

Michael Lind has been a contributor or editor at *Harper's Magazine*, *The New Yorker*, *The New Republic* and *The National Interest* and has taught public policy and political economy at Harvard, Johns Hopkins and the University of Texas. He is the author of a number of books on political science, economics and history, including *The New Class War* (2020) and *Land of Promise: An Economic History of the United States* (2012).

Christos A. Makridis is an associate research professor at W. P. Carey School of Business in Arizona State University, visiting faculty at the Department of Digital Innovation in the University of Nicosia, non-resident research fellow at the Institute for Studies on Religion at Baylor University, and digital fellow at the Digital Economy Lab in Stanford University. Makridis' research focusses largely on the intersection of emerging technologies and labour economics, including the broader determinants of human flourishing, ranging from art and culture to technology. He holds doctorates in economics and management science and engineering, both from Stanford University.

Charlotte Mattfolk is a senior strategic advisor within the fields of future analysis and strategy, business transformation, digitalisation, sustainability and entrepreneurship. Within the field of future analysis, she has a track record of over 500 studies across a wide variety of industries and topics. Mattfolk has been speaking about the future the last 20 years, with perspectives from most industries and focus on technology, AI, consumer behaviour and how to ensure future-proof strategies. Mattfolk has well-founded knowledge both as a tech entrepreneur and founder of the AI platform IAMAI and from the strategy consulting world. She holds an M.Sc. in international economics from Uppsala University, with undergraduate studies at Institut Supérieur de Gestion, Paris, studies in AI at MIT and Emerging Futures at MIT/Harvard.

Mohammad Rouhi is a senior researcher in polymer, fibres and composite materials at RISE – Research Institutes of Sweden, Gothenburg, Sweden, with a Ph.D. from Chalmers University of Technology in composite structures and manufacturing. Rouhi's research focusses on numerical modelling, simulation and analysis of polymer and fibre composite materials and manufacturing. He is currently serving as a project manager on different national and European projects at RISE. One key aspect of his research is on circularity and sustainability of polymer and fibre composites using traditional manufacturing versus enabled technologies such as additive manufacturing.

Karoline Teigland is a mechanical engineer with a master's degree in industrial design from Lund University, LTH Faculty of Engineering, Sweden. Since her 2021 graduation, she has specialised in large-scale additive manufacturing using recycled materials. Currently, she oversees the large-format robotic printer at Brandworks AB, with her expertise lying in the intersection of technology, materials and product design. Teigland co-founded the award-winning design company Ekbacken Studios AB, where she served as Chief Design Officer until March 2024. Since 2018, Teigland has also been involved in the Peniche Ocean Watch Initiative and Circular Ocean Lda, driving the development of recycled fishing nets into materials for additive manufacturing.

Robin Teigland is Professor of Digitalisation at Chalmers University of Technology, Gothenburg, Sweden, as well as a Fellow of the Royal Swedish Academy of Engineering Sciences (IVA). Since 2023, she is a member of the Productivity Commission for Sweden's Finance Ministry. Teigland researches how emerging technologies challenge our taken-for-granted assumptions around value creation and has co-authored more than 100 publications. In 2018, Teigland leveraged her 35 years of experience and co-founded Peniche Ocean Watch – an initiative utilising digital technologies for a blue circular economy, as well as several circular economy start-ups in Sweden and Portugal.

Marshall Toplansky is an award-winning Innovation Professor of Management Science at the Argyros School of Business and Economics at Chapman University. He is a research fellow at the Center for Demographics and Policy and is Director of the school's Analytics Accelerator programme. He and co-author Joel Kotkin recently published an economic and social policy brief entitled, *Nurturing California Industries*, which discusses the issues the state faces in maintaining home ownership for the middle class and rebuilding a positive business climate. Toplansky is also co-host of *The Feudal Future Podcast*, which is seen twice monthly by viewers around the world. Co-Founder and former Managing Director of KPMG's national center of excellence in Data & Analytics, Toplansky also co-founded the machine learning company Wise Window, a pioneer in analysing social media, blogs and news stories to track business trends and predict elections, which was acquired by KPMG in 2012. Toplansky was Chairman and CEO of Core Strategies, a technology industry marketing research and strategy consulting firm and formerly head of marketing for U.S. Robotics. Prior to entering the technology industry, Toplansky was Senior Vice President at Ogilvy & Mather advertising. Toplansky advises companies in the strategic use of marketing technologies and in using data to craft winning business strategies. He earned an MBA from Harvard Business School and is a director of the Harvard Business School Association of Orange County. He is also a board member of fintech company Double Check Solutions. He is a past board member of global NGO CWS. In 2020, he was given a Global Humanitarian award from CWS for his work with the organisation addressing the global refugee crisis. Toplansky was elected to the Computing Industry Hall of Fame in 2011 for his role in creating the industry's largest technical service certification programme, A+, which has certified more than 3 million computer technicians worldwide.

Mikael Wiberg is Professor in Informatics at Umeå University, Sweden. He has held positions as Research Director for Umeå Institute of Design, Professor (chair) in Human-Computer Interaction, Uppsala University, and Full Professor in Interaction Design at Chalmers University of Technology. Wiberg is currently serving as co-editor-in-chief for *ACM Interactions*, and his research is oriented towards the design of interactive systems. With this at the centre of his research interests, his work has included research on mobile technologies, architecture and most recently design for a more sustainable world. He has published his research in top journals, including *ToCHI*, *Interacting with Computers*, *Design Studies*, *IJDesign* and *Design Issues*. His most recently published book is *The Materiality of Interaction* (2018).

Woodrow Wiest is an R&D engineer specialising in additive manufacturing at RISE – Research Institutes of Sweden, Gothenburg, Sweden. His expertise lies in using robotic arms for large-format additive manufacturing, integrating design, systems, material innovation and process development to push technological boundaries. Wiest has been self-taught via open courseware in astronautical engineering focussed on robotics for space exploration and graduated with honours in additive manufacturing from YH Eslöv [Yrkeshögskolan Eslöv] in Sweden.

Siri Wikander is a consultant and lecturer, specialising in leadership and learning. Her 20-year career in human resources has been marked by strategic roles at stock market-listed companies such as Axfood and Scandic Hotels. Her significant project at Scandic, "The Empowering Journey", introduced a fresh paradigm for leadership and learning, subsequently featured in an International Institute for Management Development (IMD) Case Study and disseminated across European business schools. Now focussing on consultancy, Wikander drives the conversation on innovative HR practices, advocating for forward-thinking in organisational work models. As a former member of the Pedagogic Advisory Board at Berghs School of Communication, she influenced the course of educational strategies and practices. She regularly pens chronicles for *Chef*, a Swedish leadership magazine, contributing to the intellectual exchange in the development of organisations.

1

INTRODUCTION

The Way Disruption, Technology and Practice Will Change the Way We Work in the Future

Anthony Larsson and Andreas Hatzigeorgiou

1.1 Introduction

What promises and dangers does the future labour landscape hold for us? What can be done in order to make it flourish and become more innovative, successful, and sustainable? Conversely, what threats or difficulties can we expect, and could (or should) anything be done in order to avert these dangers? What changes should the labour landscape undertake to accommodate for changed working habits and the onslaught of artificial intelligence (AI)? Are we indeed witnessing the end of the current labour landscape as we know it?

The 20th century witnessed profound technological advancements that continue to shape the labour landscape of the 21st century and will continue to do so in no uncertain terms. Looking back, one may attest to how the Third Agricultural Revolution significantly bolstered global agricultural output, particularly so in developing nations (Grigg, 1982; Otsuka, Larson, & Hazell, 2013). This period is commonly believed to have started in the early 1940s and picked up on a massive scale in the 1960s (Swanson, 2017). This era ushered in a wave of technological innovations such as chemical fertilisers, agrochemicals, controlled irrigation, and mechanisation, fundamentally transforming farming practices (Esteva, 1996; Farmer, 1986). Almost concurrently, the Scientific-technical revolution (circa 1940–1970) further propelled technological progress (Momani, Nour, Jamaludin, & Abdullah, 2021; Šmihula, 2010), paving the way for the digital/information and telecommunications revolution that is popularly known as the "Third Industrial Revolution" (circa 1975–2010) (Kazmierczak, 2022). These eras not only introduced innovations aimed at enhancing daily life but also reshaped the economic and labour landscape. Bureaucracy burgeoned, and industries increasingly embraced information-centric activities, notably in research and development (R&D)

DOI: 10.4324/9781003391333-1

(Veneris, 1990). Moving beyond the "Third Industrial Revolution," we enter the "Information Age" or the "Fourth Industrial Revolution," colloquially termed "Industry 4.0" (circa 2010s–present) (Ing, 2024). This era is characterised by the digital transformation of entire industries, with groundbreaking advancements in robotics, machine learning, cloud computing and AI (Sindhwani, Anand, George, & Pandey, 2024).

1.2 Terminology

The terminology of phenomena stemming from Industry 4.0 may at times be confusing. Concepts such as teaching a computer to correctly predict future events/developments and thinking of it as "machine learning" may be straightforward enough (Pandey et al., 2024). However, terms like "digital transformation" and "AI" may come across as more ambiguous.

For instance, apart from digital transformation, there are also the terms "digitisation" and "digitalisation" that have become prevalent in various industries, but the three are often mistakenly used interchangeably. Digitisation involves converting analogue materials, such as images, videos, and texts, into a digital format (Asunka, 2015)

Digitalisation refers to the process of adopting or increasing the use of digital technologies, including computer technology and mobile applications, by an organisation (Olçum & Gülova, 2023).

Digital transformation, on the other hand, is a much broader concept. It denotes a strategy/approach that requires extensive and comprehensive organisational changes, in addition to implementing digital technologies (Molenaar, 2022; Vaz, 2021). Digital transformation carries a large scope and is not about executing a single, particular project. Rather, it involves a series of initiatives that collectively seek to modernise an organisation's use of technology and thereby make the business customer-centric rather than organisation-centric (Khoo, 2021).

AI, however, can be defined in a variety of different ways. In its broadest sense it refers to intelligence exhibited by machines, and most notably, computer systems (Copeland, 2024). For the premise of this anthology, the definition will depart from that set forth by the European Commission (2018, para. 6), which describes AI as follows:

> AI refers to systems that display intelligent behaviour by analysing their environment and taking actions – with some degree of autonomy – to achieve specific goals.
>
> AI-based systems can be purely software-based, acting in the virtual world (e.g. voice assistants, image analysis software, search engines, speech and facial recognition systems); or AI can be embedded in hardware devices (e.g. advanced robots, autonomous cars, drones or Internet of Things applications).

1.3 History

1.3.1 The History of AI

The concept of AI has been around since ancient history. There is, for instance, Talos in Greek mythology, the giant artificial guardian of the island of Crete, who was constructed of bronze and powered by "ichor", an ethereal fluid serving as the blood of gods and/or immortals (Mayor, 2018). In more recent popular fiction, AI is more commonly depicted as an abstract, omnipotent, computerised entity such as "HAL 9000" in Arthur C. Clarke's (1968) *2001: A Space Odyssey* or "Deep Thought" in Douglas Adams' (1979) *The Hitchhiker's Guide to the Galaxy*.

Correspondingly, AI has been strongly correlated with the development of the computer and information sciences. Some notable scientific pre-AI contributors to the field have included Norbert Wiener, who described cybernetics in terms of control and stability in electrical networks (Hass, 2024). Another one was Claude Shannon, who postulated the information theory that described digital (all-or-nothing) signals (Cordeschi, 2001; Pearlman & Said, 2011). Perhaps the most famous was Alan Turing, whose theory of computation illustrated that any form of computation could be described digitally and who in 1950 officially devised the "Turing test" (Gonçalves, 2024). This was a thought experiment in which a machine could be taught to communicate with human beings so convincingly that it would be impossible for the human to discern that he/she had actually been speaking to a machine rather than another human being. However, the term "artificial intelligence" itself was first coined by American cognitive scientist John McCarthy in 1956 when he held the first academic conference on the subject (Alon, Jaffe, Prange, & Vianelli, 2020).

Through the years, there was much conceptual research done on AI, and the burgeoning technological advancements were observed with some degree of trepidation by some futurists, such as Alvin Toffler, who contended that society was enduring an enormous structural change, undergoing a revolution from an industrial society to a "super-industrial society". This would result in what he called a "future shock" that would leave people feeling disconnected while suffering from "shattering stress and disorientation" (Toffler, 1970, p. 2). Still, it was not until the 1980s (along with the advancement of the computer) that AI began being viewed as a serious instrument for solving deep and complex problems (Newquist, 1994). AI and its abilities became a sensation around the world on May 11, 1997, when the reigning World Chess Champion and grandmaster, Garry Kasparov, lost to IBM's chess-playing computer "Deep Blue" (Newborn, 2003).

In the early 21st century, the combination of extensive amounts of data (commonly known as "big data"), more affordable and faster computing power, and advanced machine learning techniques began to effectively address numerous economic challenges. By 2009, it was estimated that nearly all sectors of the US economy had accumulated an average of at least 200 terabytes of stored data (Manyika et al., 2011). A number that keeps growing.

By the 2020s, there had been rapid advancements in the development of AI, and particularly so, generative AI, which possesses the ability to learn the patterns and structure of their input training data, upon which it is able to generate new data with similar characteristics (Dhamani & Engler, 2024). This means that generative AI is able to generate text, images, videos, sounds and other types of data based on generative models. Various transformers such as "Generative Pre-trained Transformer (GPT)" (released by OpenAI in 2020) and "Gato" (released by DeepMind in 2022) have given rise to generative AI chatbots such as OpenAI's "ChatGPT", Microsoft's "Copilot", Google's "Gemini" and xAI's "Grok" (Pesce, 2023; Schiele & Schiele, 2024).

The future development of AI points towards what is known as "artificial general intelligence (AGI)", which is an AI that has the ability to match or surpass human capabilities across a wide range of cognitive tasks along with the ability to take on characteristics that translate into human responses (Bellini, 2023; McLean et al., 2023). There has been much contention regarding AGI, since many argue that it poses many risks and potential dangers towards society if left unmitigated, as it may develop unsafe goals, poor ethics and management, and even existential threats (McLean et al., 2023). To this end, it has also been contended that the digital transformation, along with the development of AI, and AGI in particular, will cause significant substitution of labour in the future (Buttazzo, 2023; Kuusi & Heinonen, 2022).

1.3.2 The History of Work

What is meant by work? There are many different definitions and nuances in which it could be explained. One of the ways it can be expressed is that "work includes any human effort adding use value to goods and services" (Tilly & Tilly, 1998, pp. 22–23). The concept of work in its broadest sense has effectively been around for as long as mankind has existed. In early hunter-gatherer societies, humans were allotted different tasks in order to help the society survive. Barter and trade systems would follow, which would promote various designated functions that people may have had in society, such as farmers, blacksmiths, and hunters. When currency replaced barter, it became possible to more easily exchange labour for a perceived value (Lucassen & Pol, 2007; Orrell & Chlupatý, 2016).

Designated "jobs" and employments per se, however, are a more recent phenomenon. These emerged in the late Middle Ages, when the peer-to-peer economy was dismantled and Monarch issued exclusive monopolies to certain favoured companies, prompting people to become employees (Rushkoff, 2019). Even though the concept itself has de facto been around since at least the 6th century BC (Senn, 1997), the actual word "weekend" is an even more recent construct, having been first recorded as recently as 1879 in the English journal *Notes and Queries* (Gwynne, 1879, p. 428):

> *In Staffordshire, if a person leaves home at the end of his week's work on the Saturday afternoon to spend the evening of Saturday and the following Sunday with friends at a distance, he is said to be spending his week-end at so-and-so. I am informed that this name for Saturday and the day which "comes between a Saturday and Monday" is confined to this district. Is this so?*

In time, the development of technology also meant there were new opportunities for working in new, original ways. During World War II, there was an appearance of teleworking, in which thousands of women were hired to work from home using their telephones (Greve, 1989). In 1972, a NASA scientist named Jack Niles invented "telecommuting", in which he worked remotely, and phoned in for important meetings, mainly as a means of being able to avoid the traffic congestion (Barling, 2023). In 1979, IBM was one of the first companies to (in a minute scale) introduce the ability to work from home using technology that is in principle reminiscent of today's use of Internet for working remotely (Larson, 2024). Since then, technology developed rapidly, and during the COVID-19 pandemic, it became clear that extant technology allowed for more jobs than previously known to be conducted remotely. In addition, there were intensified discussions regarding the automation of various processes, which were in this context primarily aimed at reducing people's exposure to potential contagion, but have since then become a pressing discussion in the advent of the continued development of AI, robotics and the digital transformation (Larsson & Hatzigeorgiou, 2023).

1.4 The Substitution of Labour

The notion of technology and AI replacing human labour in the future is not new. One of the first mentions in popular fiction occurs in Samuel Butler's (1872) *Erewhon*, and particularly in the three-chapter-long *Book of the Machines*, in which the denizens of the fictional nation Erewhon are cautioned about the potentially dangerous ideas of machine consciousness and self-replicating machines and therefore decide to ban all machinery. Moreover, Oscar Wilde (1891) envisioned that in the future machines would be used to help supply the useful things and to do the tedious and cumbersome cores, while the individual would be free to do the more desirable, or "beautiful" things. In *The Machine Stops*, E. M. Forster (1909) recounts a society dwelling in isolation in the underworld where all their needs are provided for by a giant machine, ending with a caution against becoming too dependent on machines, lest they, as the title suggests, fail to function. In *Metropolis*, Thea von Harbou (1926) depicts a futuristic industrial society in which man has created a humanoid robot made in the form of a woman known as the "Maschinenmensch" (or "Machine-Person"). In Aldous Huxley's (1932) *Brave*

New World, human reproduction is mechanised, and individuals are conditioned to perform specific roles within society, effectively replacing traditional human labour with controlled and predetermined tasks. In Kurt Vonnegut's debut novel *Player Piano* (1952), he depicts a near-future society in which automation and machines have replaced most human labour, leading to widespread unemployment and social unrest, while Vonnegut critiques the dehumanising effects of technology and the potential loss of purpose for individuals in such a society.

As mentioned earlier, the COVID-19 pandemic was in many ways a catalyst for the automation of work and for altering work habits by and large. Notably, a 2021 McKinsey report concluded that the COVID-19 pandemic accelerated existing trends in remote work, e-commerce and automation, with up to 25% more workers than previously estimated potentially needing to switch occupations (Lund et al., 2021). The same applied to the application of AI, which saw a surge in many different areas during and following COVID-19 (Agarwal, Swami, & Malhotra, 2024; Reynolds, 2021).

As automation and AI become more prevalent, they are expected to displace a variety of different certain jobs. In fact, a study by Goldman Sachs estimates that approximately 300 million jobs in the United States and Europe could be lost, or at the very least diminished, due to generative AI by the year 2030 (Hatzius, Briggs, Kodnani, & Pierdomenico, 2023). However, the same study also contends that the automation of labour also generates other types of work and new occupations that have not previously existed.

Nevertheless, the substitution of labour has for long been a contentious issue, and there have been studies that have indicated that some types of jobs are more predisposed to substitution than others. Essentially, one may think of work as existing in four different types of categories: "routine" tasks and "non-routine" tasks on the one hand, and "manual" and "cognitive" tasks on the other hand (Van der Zande, Teigland, Siri, & Teigland, 2020). Routine tasks are those that follow specific, clear rules and can therefore be "codified", such as welding, picking/sorting, assembling and cooking. In contrast, non-routine tasks lack a defined linear sequence, making them much harder to code, such as operating cranes, surgical assistance, janitorial duties and so forth. Consequently, routine tasks are generally more easily replaced by technology, whereas non-routine tasks are less likely to be substituted by digital solutions. Similarly, manual tasks involve physical activities requiring mobility and motor skills, while cognitive tasks involve mental processes. In the United States, it is anticipated that as much as 81% of the "routine manual tasks" are bound for labour substitution in the near future. For "routine cognitive tasks" this figure is 64% for tasks concerning data collection and 69% for tasks pertaining to data processing. For "non-routine manual tasks" the substitution rate is 26%, whereas for "non-routine cognitive tasks" the substitution rate is less than 20% (Van der Zande et al., 2020).

A broader group risking mass labour-substitution are "middle-skilled" workers such as professions in the clerical, sales, construction, production, installation/

repair and transportation/material moving occupational groupings (Nakamura, 2023). The risk is that the digital economy in the future may lead to a "polarisation" between high-skilled jobs and low-skilled jobs, as these types of jobs tend to fare better than the middle-skilled workers in light of job automation/substitution (Qu & Fan, 2024).

1.5 New Occupations in an AI-driven World

There is an ongoing debate regarding the role of AI and its leverage in the substitution of labour. While many contend that AI is expected to escalate automation and exacerbate the displacement of certain jobs, others argue that AI will also seek to shift jobs and may lead to the creation of new functions and roles as well (George, 2024).

As AI systems become more sophisticated, there will be a growing need for professionals who can train, operate and maintain these technologies. For instance, AI trainers will need to develop algorithms that can learn from vast amounts of data, while sentiment analysts will interpret emotional responses from social media and other platforms to inform business strategies. Content creators will increasingly rely on AI tools to enhance their work, while auditors of AI-generated content will ensure the accuracy and ethical standards of automated outputs (Forbes Expert Panel, 2023). As AI continues to integrate into various sectors, the demand for such specialised skills will grow, creating a dynamic and ever-changing job market.

1.6 The Dual Nature of Technological Progress

Ever so often, technological advancements prove to be a double-edged sword, inasmuch as they bring both benefits and challenges. On the one hand, the digital transformation and AI may lead to significant productivity gains, cost savings and the creation of entirely new industries. On the other hand, these changes may result in job displacement and increased polarisation in the labour market, leading to massive wage gaps, inequality and social disruption (Bhorat, Lilenstein, Oosthuizen, & Thornton, 2023; World Bank Group, 2024).

The key to navigating this duality lies in proactive policy measures and robust educational systems. Policymakers must focus on creating safety nets for displaced workers, investing in retraining programmes and ensuring that the benefits of technological advancements are widely shared. Educational institutions need to evolve to provide lifelong learning opportunities, equipping workers with the skills needed for the jobs of the future.

1.7 Premise

This anthology endeavours to delve into a variety of issues related to new policies, AI and the digital transformation's anticipated impact on the labour market through a series of studies conducted by scientists and industry professionals, each offering deep insights into their areas of expertise with a largely international focus. While the chapters are largely speculative and predictive, reflecting the ongoing and incomplete nature of the overall theme, the authors maintain scientific rigour by adhering to proper academic protocols. This includes thorough citations, grounding their discussions in current issues and problems, and employing rigorous analytical methods and research.

The chapters present a diverse array of methodological and thematic studies. Some provide original empirical data, while others are more theoretically focussed. Additionally, certain chapters are based on comprehensive literature reviews or the authors' personal "best practice" experiences. Each study is founded on referenced facts, yet some also venture beyond traditional academic boundaries to offer foresight on how their subject areas might evolve in light of current and anticipated digital advancements.

The structure of this book seeks to explore some overarching themes in which AI, digitalisation, digital transformation and future technology and practices can be expected to impact the labour landscape in the future in the decades to come. The themes investigated are as follows:

1. The Future of Society and Economy
   These chapters focus on how future technologies and practices have impacted and will continue to impact the labour landscape on a socio-economic level.
2. The Future Way of Working
   These chapters discuss the changing nature of labour as a result of AI, technology and the digital transformation and the conditions under which work may be done in the future.
3. New Uses of AI and Technology in Labour
   These chapters discuss how AI and technology is used to impact and change the types of work as such.

1.8 Chapter Overviews

1.8.1 The Future of Society and Economy

Chapter 2 by William J. Ashworth ("Innovation and Destruction: Technology, Ecology, and the Future of Social Labour") traces the sway of innovation from a historical perspective during the Industrial Revolution upon physical and intellectual labour. The chapter aims to show how developments during this period prepared the way for current debates over labour, AI and ecology.

Chapter 3 by Edward Castronova ("Smart Money") considers the future of currency in light of recent developments in AI. The chapter seeks to understand what intelligent money, "smart money" – money that has goals, will impact markets, society and people and how it may alter interactions in markets and elsewhere in society.

Chapter 4 by Joel Kotkin and Marshall Toplansky ("AI and the Future of Society and Economy") investigates the context of how adoption of the different types of AI will affect the global economy and society as a whole, such as business strategies, global employment, education of youth, distribution of wealth, and policy choices.

Chapter 5 by Michael Lind ("Work and Workers in the Age of AI: The Influence of Technology, Trade, and Institutions") takes on the insights of the neo-Schumpeterian school of economics, identifying the major factors/variables that shape the impact of a new technology like AI on the employment structure of a country.

Chapter 6 by Bent Greve ("AI and Welfare States: Curse, Solutions or Both?") discusses the impact of AI on welfare states by delving deeper into a number of elements that may influence this development. The author argues that AI will influence not only the number of jobs but also change qualifications needed in many different jobs, indicating the need for life-long learning in order to remain relevant on the labour market.

1.8.2 The Future Way of Working

Chapter 7 by Christos Makridis ("Interactions Reimagined: The Impact of Hybrid Work on Team Communication and Coordination") shows how the degree of coordination within an occupation is correlated with hourly wages, employment and productivity, and how generative AI tools have the potential to reduce the barriers to coordinating complex work. After reviewing these patterns, this chapter explores the implications for employee productivity while evaluating the role of communication in the coordination of complex tasks in the workplace.

Chapter 8 by Jonas Grafström ("Young Workers Want To Be in the Office: An Investigation Based on Swedish Survey Data") seeks to discern if the preference for working from home is different among different age cohorts, with a special interest in young workers attitudes. The chapter analyses the result from a survey involving 1,769 Swedish workers, among whom 1,000 were classified as office workers.

Chapter 9 by Miriam Cherry ("The Possible Futures for Gig Work: Digital Platform Labour and Its Regulation") looks at the legal developments concerning the employment status of digital platform workers/gig workers and how the hitherto rulings have given contradictory messages from legal systems around the world, and particularly so in the United States and the European Union.

1.8.3 New Uses of AI and Technology in Labour

Chapter 10 by Charlotte Mattfolk and Siri Wikander ("AI and the Future of Work: How Organisational Structures and the Role of Humans Transform in the

Age of AI") explores the multifaceted impact of AI on organisational structures, work environments and human beings. This chapter highlights AI's capacity to induce paradigm shifts in how to steer companies, challenging traditional economic models and organisational hierarchies. Key points include AI's role as an enhancer of human performance, in reshaping job roles into tasks, radically enhancing productivity, and necessitating lifelong learning due to rapid technological advancements. This chapter advocates for transitioning from hierarchical structures to fluid networks that prioritise skills over roles and value set to tasks rather than roles, while also discussing the transition to "economies of data", where value exponentially grows with data accumulation, emphasising user involvement and service-oriented business models, where "intelligence" is at the core of every company.

Chapter 11 by Ling Koay ("The Rise of Cyborg Marketers: A Marketer's Guide to Survive and Thrive in the Era of AI") explores the dynamic intersection of human creativity and AI in the field of marketing. Introducing the concept of "cyborg marketers", the chapter describes professionals who blend human skills with digital tools, particularly AI and data analytics.

Chapter 12 by Mohammad Amir Anwar ("Value Chains of AI: Data Training Firms, Platforms, and Workers") builds on the scholarship of how different places and people are involved in the development of AI, while extending the debate around the hidden and opaque networks of subcontracting practices for AI training. In particular, this chapter examines the ways in which lead firms develop their AI systems by tapping into a complex network of suppliers, platforms and human workers doing data work in some of the most marginalised parts of the world.

Chapter 13 by Proscovia Kamugisha ("Re-skilling Human Capital for Inclusive Economic Growth in the Face of Emerging Agricultural Automation in Africa: The Tanzania Perspective") looks at the displacement of human jobs in Tanzania, where a large proportion of the national labour force is employed in agriculture, whose tasks are manual. This chapter uses a semi-structured review and content analysis to highlight prospects of deploying robots in Tanzania's farming communities and identifies prerequisite steps to benefit from the technology.

Chapter 14 by Robin Teigland et al. ("Circular Material Flows, the Twin Transition of Manufacturing, and the Future of Labour: Insights from a Case Study of the Peniche Ocean Watch Initiative") looks at the "twin transition" of manufacturing and the future of labour within the context of the circular economy and ocean plastics. The authors take a closer look at the sustainability challenges associated with ocean plastics, the fishing industry and local coastal communities. The authors first describe the existing challenges before presenting issues related to sustainability and circularity and proceed to discuss the related future opportunities for the labour market in the context of the nascent re-imagining and re-routing of material from linear to circular flows. This is illustrated by presenting the "microfactory" concept first developed under the Peniche Ocean Watch Initiative in Portugal, which serves as a case study for this chapter.

References

Adams, D. (1979). *The Hitchhiker's Guide to the Galaxy*. London, UK: Pan Books.

Agarwal, P., Swami, S., & Malhotra, S. K. (2024). Artificial intelligence adoption in the post COVID-19 new-normal and role of smart technologies in transforming business: A review. *Journal of Science and Technology Policy Management*, *15*(3), 506–529. https://doi.org/10.1108/JSTPM-08-2021-0122

Alon, I., Jaffe, E., Prange, C., & Vianelli, D. (2020). *Global Marketing: Strategy, Practice, and Cases* (3rd ed.). New York, NY: Routledge.

Asunka, S. (2015). Digitize or perish: Strategies for improving access to indigenous intellectual resources in Sub-Saharan Africa. In Information Resource Management Association (Ed.), *Open Source Technology: Concepts, Methodologies, Tools, and Applications: Concepts, Methodologies, Tools, and Applications* (pp. 933–947). Hershey, PA: IGI Global.

Barling, J. (2023). *Brave New Workplace: Designing Productive, Healthy, and Safe Organizations*. Oxford, UK: Oxford University Press.

Bellini, P. J. (2023). *Artificial General Intelligence (AGI) and the Image of God: Can Machines Attain Consciousness and Receive Salvation?* Eugene, OR: Wipf and Stock Publishers.

Bhorat, H., Lilenstein, K., Oosthuizen, M., & Thornton, A. (2023). South Africa: Employment and inequality trends. In C. Gradín, P. Lewandowski, S. Schotte, & K. Sen (Eds.), *Tasks, Skills, and Institutions: The Changing Nature of Work and Inequality* (pp. 89–108). Oxford, UK: Oxford University Press.

Butler, S. (1872). *Erewhon: or, Over the Range*. London, UK: Trübner & Co.

Buttazzo, G. (2023). Rise of artificial general intelligence: Risks and opportunities. *Frontiers in Artificial Intelligence*, *6*, 1226990, 1–9. https://doi.org/10.3389/frai.2023.1226990

Clarke, A. C. (1968). *2001: A Space Odyssey*. London, UK: Hutchinson & Co.

Copeland, B. J. (2024). Artificial intelligence. Retrieved March 6, 2025, from Britannica website: www.britannica.com/technology/artificial-intelligence

Cordeschi, R. (2001). *The Discovery of the Artificial: Behavior, Mind and Machines Before and Beyond Cybernetics*. Dordrecht, The Netherlands: Springer.

Dhamani, N., & Engler, M. (2024). *Introduction to Generative AI*. Shelter Island, NY: Manning Publications.

Esteva, G. (1996). Hosting the otherness of the other: The case of the Green Revolution. In F. Apffel-Marglin & S. A. Marglin (Eds.), *Decolonizing Knowledge: From Development to Dialogue* (pp. 249–278). Oxford, UK: Clarendon Press.

European Commission. (2018). Communication Artificial Intelligence for Europe. Retrieved March 6, 2025, from https://ec.europa.eu/digital-single-market/en/news/communication-artificial-intelligence-europe

Farmer, B. H. (1986). Perspectives on the 'green revolution' in South Asia. *Modern Asian Studies*, *20*(1), 175–199. https://doi.org/10.1017/S0026749X00013627

Forbes Expert Panel. (2023). 20 New and Enhanced Roles AI Could Create. Retrieved March 6, 2025, from Forbes website: www.forbes.com/sites/forbestechcouncil/2023/07/06/20-new-and-enhanced-roles-ai-could-create

Forster, E. M. (1909). The Machine Stops. In O. Dawson (Ed.), *The Oxford and Cambridge Review, No. 8* (pp. 83–122). London, UK: Constable & Co. Ltd.

George, A. S. (2024). Artificial intelligence and the future of work: Job shifting not job loss. *Partners Universal Innovative Research Publication*, *2*(2), 17–37. https://doi.org/10.5281/zenodo.10936490

Gonçalves, B. (2024). *The Turing Test Argument*. New York, NY: Routledge.
Greve, R. M. (1989). Technological change and women workers. In G. J. Bamber & R. D. Lansbury (Eds.), *New Technology: International Perspectives on Human Resources and Industrial Relations* (pp. 199–226). London, UK: Unwin Hyman.
Grigg, D. (1982). *The Dynamics of Agricultural Change: The Historical Experience*. London, UK: Hutchinson & Co.
Gwynne, C. T. (1879). "Week-end." In H. F. Turle (Ed.), *Notes and Queries: Fifth Series – Volume Twelfth* (pp. 428–428). London, UK: John Francis.
Harbou, T. von. (1926). *Metropolis*. Berlin, Germany: August Scherl.
Hass, H. (2024). The Necessary Complexity: Key Elements of Cybernetic Psychology. In *Unconscious Intelligence in Cybernetic Psychology* (pp. 5–26). Oxon, UK: Routledge.
Hatzius, J., Briggs, J., Kodnani, D., & Pierdomenico, G. (2023). The Potentially Large Effects of Artificial Intelligence on Economic Growth. Retrieved March 6, 2025, from Goldman Sachs: Global Economist Analyst website: www.key4biz.it/wp-content/uploads/2023/03/Global-Economics-Analyst_-The-Potentially-Large-Effects-of-Artificial-Intelligence-on-Economic-Growth-Briggs_Kodnani.pdf
Huxley, A. (1932). *Brave New World*. London, UK: Chatto & Windus.
Ing, D. (2024). Incremental adaption or generational shift? In S. Nousala, G. Metcalf, & D. Ing (Eds.), *Industry 4.0 to Industry 5.0: Explorations in the Transition from a Techno-economic to a Socio-technical Future* (pp. 151–184). Singapore, Singapore: Springer.
Kazmierczak, J. (2022). Why and how to educate selected Industry 4.0 stakeholders in technical and non-technical issues. In A. Batako, A. Burduk, K. Karyono, X. Chen, & R. Wyczółkowski (Eds.), *Advances in Manufacturing Processes, Intelligent Methods and Systems in Production Engineering: Progress in Application of Intelligent Methods and Systems in Production Engineering* (pp. 327–343). Cham, Switzerland: Springer.
Khoo, D. (2021). *Driving Digital Transformation: Lessons from Building the First ASEAN Digital Bank*. Singapore, Singapore: Marshall Cavendish Business.
Kuusi, O., & Heinonen, S. (2022). Scenarios from artificial narrow intelligence to artificial general intelligence—Reviewing the results of the international work/technology 2050 study. *World Futures Review*, *14*(1), 65–79. https://doi.org/10.1177/19467567221101637
Larson, B. Z. (2024). *Remote and Hybrid Work: What Everyone Needs to Know*. Oxford, UK: Oxford University Press.
Larsson, A., & Hatzigeorgiou, A. (2023). *Designing Smart and Resilient Cities for a Post-Pandemic World: Metropandemic Revolution*. Oxon, UK: Routledge.
Lucassen, J., & Pol, A. (2007). Preface. In J. Lucassen (Ed.), *Wages and Currency: Global Comparisons from Antiquity to the Twentieth Century* (pp. 7–8). Bern, Switzerland: Peter Lang.
Lund, S., Madgavkar, A., Manyika, J., Smit, S., Ellingrud, K., & Robinson, O. (2021). The Future of Work After COVID-19. Retrieved March 6, 2025, from McKinsey Global Institute website: www.mckinsey.com/featured-insights/future-of-work/the-future-of-work-after-covid-19
Manyika, J., Chui, M., Brown, B., Bughin, J., Dobbs, R., Roxburgh, C., & Byers, A. H. (2011). *Big Data: The Next Frontier for Innovation, Competition, and Productivity*. Washington, DC: McKinsey Global Institute.
Mayor, A. (2018). *Gods and Robots: Myths, Machines, and Ancient Dreams of Technology*. Princeton, NJ: Princeton University Press.
McLean, S., Read, G. J. M., Thompson, J., Baber, C., Stanton, N. A., & Salmon, P. M. (2023). The risks associated with Artificial General Intelligence: A systematic review.

Journal of Experimental & Theoretical Artificial Intelligence, 35(5), 649–663. https://doi.org/10.1080/0952813X.2021.1964003
Molenaar, C. (2022). *Demand-Driven Business Strategy: Digital Transformation and Business Model Innovation*. Oxon, UK: Routledge.
Momani, K. M. K. Al, Nour, A.-N. I., Jamaludin, N., & Abdullah, W. Z. W. Z. W. (2021). Fourth industrial revolution, artificial intelligence, intellectual capital, and COVID-19 pandemic. In A. Hamdan, A. E. Hassanien, R. Khamis, B. Alareeni, A. Razzaque, & B. Awwad (Eds.), *Applications of Artificial Intelligence in Business, Education and Healthcare* (pp. 81–100). Cham, Switzerland: Springer.
Nakamura, H. (2023). Difficulties in finding middle-skilled jobs under increased automation. *Macroeconomic Dynamics, 27*(5), 1179–1201. https://doi.org/10.1017/S1365100522000177
Newborn, M. (2003). *Deep Blue: An Artificial Intelligence Milestone*. New York, NY: Springer.
Newquist, H. P. (1994). *The Brain Makers: Genius, Ego, And Greed in the Quest for Machines That Think*. Indianapolis, IN: Sams Publishing.
Olçum, G., & Gülova, A. A. (2023). Digitalization and generation Z: Advantages and disadvantages of digitalisation. In B. Akkaya & A. Tabak (Eds.), *Two Faces of Digital Transformation: Technological Opportunities versus Social Threats* (pp. 31–46). Bingley, UK: Emerald Group Publishing Limited.
Orrell, D., & Chlupatý, R. (2016). *The Evolution of Money*. New York, NY: Columbia University Press.
Otsuka, K., Larson, D. F., & Hazell, P. B. R. (2013). An overview. In K. Otsuka & D. F. Larson (Eds.), *An African Green Revolution: Finding Ways to Boost Productivity on Small Farms* (pp. 1–16). Heidelberg, Germany: Springer.
Pandey, J. K., Kotti, J., Parimita, Dhabliya, D., Sharma, V., Choudhary, S., & Anand, R. (2024). Integration of nature inspired mechanisms to machine learning in real time sensors, controller and actuators for industrial automation. In N. Sindhwani, R. Anand, A. George, & D. Pandey (Eds.), *Robotics and Automation in Industry 4.0: Smart Industries and Intelligent Technologies* (pp. 1–25). Oxon, UK: CRC Press.
Pearlman, W. A., & Said, A. (2011). *Digital Signal Compression: Principles and Practice*. Cambridge, UK: Cambridge University Press.
Pesce, M. (2023). *Getting Started with ChatGPT and AI Chatbots: An Introduction to Generative AI Tools*. Swindon, UK: BCS.
Qu, Y., & Fan, S. (2024). Is there a "Machine Substitution"? How does the digital economy reshape the employment structure in emerging market countries. *Economic Systems, 48*(4), 101237, pp. 1–24. https://doi.org/10.1016/j.ecosys.2024.101237
Reynolds, K. (2021). COVID-19 Increased the Use of AI. Here's Why It's Here to Stay. Retrieved March 6, 2025, from World Economic Forum website: www.weforum.org/agenda/2021/02/covid-19-increased-use-of-ai-here-s-why-its-here-to-stay
Rushkoff, D. (2019). *Team Human*. New York, NY: W. W. Norton & Company.
Schiele, A., & Schiele, B. (2024). Self-awareness and common sense – The paradox of AI: A dispassionate look. In M. W. Bauer & B. Schiele (Eds.), *AI and Common Sense: Ambitions and Frictions* (pp. 30–44). Oxon, UK: Routledge.
Senn, F. C. (1997). *Christian Liturgy: Catholic and Evangelical*. Minneapolis, Minnesota: Fortress Press.
Sindhwani, N., Anand, R., George, A., & Pandey, D. (2024). Preface. In N. Sindhwani, R. Anand, A. George, & D. Pandey (Eds.), *Robotics and Automation in Industry 4.0: Smart Industries and Intelligent Technologies* (pp. xvii–xviii). Oxon, UK: CRC Press.

Šmihula, D. (2010). Waves of technological innovations and the end of the information revolution. *Journal of Economics and International Finance*, *2*(4), 58–67.
Swanson, K. (2017). *AP Human Geography 2017–2018*. New York, NY: Kaplan Publishing.
Tilly, C., & Tilly, C. (1998). *Work Under Capitalism*. Boulder, CO: Westview Press.
Toffler, A. (1970). *Future Shock*. New York, NY: Random House.
Van der Zande, J., Teigland, K., Siri, S., & Teigland, R. (2020). The substitution of labor: From technological feasibility to other factors influencing the potential of job automation. In A. Larsson & R. Teigland (Eds.), *The Digital Transformation of Labor: Automation, the Gig Economy and Welfare* (pp. 31–73). Oxon, UK: Routledge.
Vaz, N. (2021). *Digital Business Transformation: How Established Companies Sustain Competitive Advantage From Now to Next*. Hoboken, NJ: Wiley.
Veneris, Y. (1990). Modelling the transition from the industrial to the informational revolution. *Environment and Planning A: Economy and Space*, *22*(3), 399–416. https://doi.org/10.1068/a220399
Vonnegut, K. (1952). *Player Piano*. New York, NY: Charles Scribner's Sons.
Wilde, O. (1891). The soul of man under socialism. *Fortnightly Review*, *49*(290), 292–319.
World Bank Group. (2024). *Digital Progress and Trends Report 2023*. Washington, DC: World Bank Publications.

PART I

The Future of Society and Economy

2

INNOVATION AND DESTRUCTION

Technology, Ecology, and the Future of Social Labour

William J. Ashworth

2.1 Introduction

> *That the opinion entertained by the labouring class, that the employment of machinery is frequently detrimental to their interests, is not founded on prejudice and error, but is conformable to the correct principles of political economy.*
>
> *(Ricardo, 1990, p. 392)*

> *[T]he machine does not drive out the tool. Rather does the tool expand and multiply, changing from a dwarf implement of the human organism to the implement of a mechanism created by man. Capital now sets the worker to work, not with a manual tool, but with a machine which itself handles the tools.*
>
> *(Marx, 1976, p. 509)*

David Ricardo (1990) famously made the above remarks in the third edition of his *On the Principles of Political Economy* in 1821. This aspect of Ricardo's work was fully appreciated later by Karl Marx, who wrote: "The instrument of labour, when it takes the form of a machine, immediately becomes a competitor of the worker himself" (Marx, 1976, p. 557). However, Ricardo then went on to argue it was too late, the genie was out of the bottle, and it could not be put back in. In an ambiguous argument, very resonant today, he claimed if Britain did not continue to mechanise and reduce the cost of making commodities some other country would simply do it. This, he concluded, would be even more devastating for the labouring class (Ricardo, 1990, pp. 396–397). This argument has recently been rehearsed when it comes to the use of fossil fuels and, for the purpose of this chapter, mental labour and concerns over artificial intelligence (AI). This, at least for the West, is

DOI: 10.4324/9781003391333-3

the predominant concern over the future of labour. Ultimately, materialism, in all senses of the word, is the necessary price for international competitiveness and a pathological quest for economic growth (Huber, 2022; Raworth, 2022).

Interestingly, Marx also drew upon the English mathematician, Charles Babbage, in his definition of a machine:

> *The machine, which is the starting point of the industrial revolution, replaces the worker, who handles a single tool, by a mechanism operating with a number of similar tools and set in motion by a single motive power, whatever the form of that power. Here we have the machine, but in its first role as a simple element in production by machinery.*
>
> *(Marx, 1976, p. 497)*

Babbage was an early pioneer of trying to build human intelligence, more precisely calculation, into a machine. Here he drew upon the factory system and division of labour (Ashworth, 1994, 1996; Babbage, 1832; Schaffer, 1994). His target were human computers who were, indeed, later replaced by electronic computers (Grier, 2005).

To understand the development of mechanising intelligence we have to start with a more general history. Firstly, when did social labour truly become substituted by new technology? The British Industrial Revolution, typically seen as a period spanning from 1760 to 1840, has traditionally been interpreted as the moment the world shifted to industrialisation proper – the age humanity turned assertively towards technology and mass production. Has the rise of the machine emancipated us from a static world or has it set us on the path to destruction? What is the future of labour and technology? It used to be just the substitution of physical labour by machines but now AI is successfully challenging tasks that typically require skilled mental labour (from medicine, engineering, and law to coding and writing student essays). A 2023 report by the global consultancy firm, McKinsey & Company, predicted that generative AI will replace half of today's work between 2030 and 2060 (Chui et al., 2023). This, they claim, will require workers to learn new skills or change occupations. Of course, this begs the question of whether such alternative vocations will exist.

In the following we begin by reviewing mainstream arguments regarding the impact of new technology and its relationship to human labour. We then look at concrete examples – in both body and mind – that developed during the Industrial Revolution and conclude with an epilogue on what the subsequent trajectory means for the future of labour and, indeed, the world.

2.2 Physical Labour, the Machine, and the British Industrial Revolution

A prominent view purports to explain Britain's Industrial Revolution, and the subsequent rise of the West to temporary global economic supremacy, via the claim that enlightened knowledge was first applied in this zone of the world to technological development. This view has its core roots in Austrian economics, most notably the anti-totalitarian work of Carl Wenger, Ludwig von Mises, and Friedrich A. Hayek. Hayek (2007, p. 16) wrote at the close of the Second World War:

> *Only since industrial freedom opened the path to the free use of new knowledge, only since everything could be tried – if somebody could be found to back his own risk – and, it should be added, as often as not from outside the authorities officially entrusted with the cultivation of learning, has science made the great strides which in the last 150 years have changed the face of the world.*

And Mises (2007, p. 8) wrote in 1949:

> *None of the great modern inventions would have been put to use if the mentality of the precapitalistic era had not been thoroughly demolished by economists … What is commonly called the Industrial Revolution was an offspring of the ideological revolution brought about by the doctrines of the economists.*

This predominantly Austrian view has subsequently been recycled by various Anglo-American economists and economic historians.

For example, aspects of this argument, especially a distinct real and imagined Western culture of innovation, were given added muscle during the Cold War and the threat of communism through the work of North American scholars such as Walt W. Rostow, Robert L. Heilbroner, and David Landes, coupled with prominent British economic historians including members of Hayek's Mont Pelerin Society, namely, Thomas Ashton and Ronald Hartwell. Rostow was convinced of the motor for modern technological development: "By changing the way man looked at the world around him, the Newtonian perception increased, in ways impossible to measure, the supply of scientists, the supply of inventors, and the willingness of entrepreneurs to introduce innovation" (Rostow, 1973, p. 560). This approach was further pursued at the Interdisciplinary Center for Research on Entrepreneurial History based at the Harvard Business School, which included Joseph Schumpeter and Alfred Chandler, and its journal *Explorations in Entrepreneurial History* (1949–1969).

In recent years the emphasis upon knowledge being the unique reason for Britain's Industrial Revolution has enjoyed a renaissance. It can currently be considered, in many ways, the dominant consensus. A complementary perspective has also taken command via institutional economists spearheaded by Nathan Rosenberg and, especially, Douglass C. North, who emphasise the ideal political and institutional environment that Britain and then the West established. This context was diverse, open, tolerant, competitive, and individualistic and provided the perfect base to stimulate creativity (North, 1991; Rosenberg & Birdzell Jr., 1986). This contrasted with the Muslim and Asian worlds that, they argue, were characterised by a rigid and static culture. Landes (1998, p. 96) reiterated this latter point when he wrote in his final work that the hitherto most industrialised country, China, lacked curiosity: "They went to show themselves, not to see and learn … They were what they were and did not have to take or make". A similar conclusion is provided by Joel Mokyr in his 2018 book *A Culture of Growth: The Origin of the Modern Economy*. This ideal environment, in turn, created the perfect place for a new labour process that increasingly substituted machinery for traditional human labour processes. Let us look more closely at this prominent view.

A key aspect that characterised the economic divergence of the West from the Rest, it is purported by some, was the development of low costs in the transaction of knowledge and its application to technology. Historically, it is argued, this initially occurred in eighteenth-century Britain, heralded as the "first knowledge economy". As a result, for Mokyr and others, the country became far more competitive in the market for both goods and ideas than the rest of the world. Thus the wealth of nations is, from this viewpoint, the result of applied knowledge to the labour process within a relatively free, pluralist, benign, and liberal context rather than the illiberal combination of state regulation, protectionism, cheap labour (slavery, women, and children), shop floor innovation, aggressive imperialism, fierce European military competition, and ecological good fortune. Mokyr (1996, para. 2) fiercely denies the role of state regulation and, especially, protectionism: "The intellectual case for protectionism is about as alive as a doornail". There is nothing original about this stance – the Austrian economists had been saying it for decades – but it has enjoyed a reawakening since the 1980s and ushered back a deterministic notion of technological progress.

According to the recent work of the historian of science, Margaret C. Jacob, it was Protestant Britain's ability to absorb the new science differently to other nations that enabled it to industrialise first. She declares that "a new person" had appeared in Britain, "generally but not exclusively a male entrepreneur" (Jacob, 1997, pp. 4–7), or, if you prefer, Mokyr's (2018, p. 60) term "cultural entrepreneur". These new white clever men "approached the productive process mechanically, literally by seeing it as something to be mastered by machines, or on a more abstract level to be conceptualised in terms of weight, motion, and the principles of force and inertia". The initial "cultural entrepreneurs" were Francis Bacon and Isaac Newton, who, according to Mokyr, laid the foundations for a distinct British "Industrial Enlightenment" that heralded the new gifts of Athena. It was this culture of creativity that supposedly paved the way to the Industrial Revolution and its accompanying labour process. It also led to the machinery question lying at the heart of a new political economy (Berg, 1980).

The political sense of Jacob's work may be different to that of Mises and Hayek, or to Rostow's "take-off", Landes's "Unbound Prometheus", Mokyr's "Industrial Enlightenment", Deirdre N. McCloskey's "Bourgeois dignity", and Niall Ferguson's "six 'killer applications'" – but the conclusion is the same. All are arguing that a distinct British scientific-market-technological rationality was unleashed upon the world, defined by a culture whose sole ends were the manufacture and procurement of material wealth. Mokyr writes, like Mises earlier, "The growth of knowledge is one of the central theories of economic change, and for that reason alone it is far too important to be left to the historians of science" (Mokyr, 2005, p. 1).

2.3 Cotton Textiles and Mechanisation during the British Industrial Revolution

More recently, Prasannan Parthasarathi (2023) has shown how British attempts to match the quality of Indian cotton cloth fuelled its technological labour innovations in spinning and later weaving – behind, it should be added, protective tariffs. Indeed, the contests and confrontations that faced Britain as the key factors driving its intellectual and technological pathway were in two areas, textiles and energy, which worried Indians little. Cotton yarn had long been used for the weft but British social labour had failed to master the warp from cotton yarn. The answer was to mechanise the process. This would solve the problem of both matching Indian skilled labour and as a substitute for reliance upon increasingly expensive Irish, Scottish, and European sources of linen yarn (Parthasarathi, 2011, p. 222).

An early attempt at improving textile production had been tried in 1733 by the Lancashire handloom reed maker, John Kay, and his development of the flying shuttle, which basically freed one hand of the weaver, and allowed the speeding-up and manufacture of much wider cloth. The other fundamental development was patented in 1738 when Lewis Paul, possibly of Huguenot descent, and the Birmingham carpenter, John Wyatt, mechanised the twist given to the raw material to make cotton yarn. This was achieved by replacing the use of the spinner's finger and thumb using rollers. Paul persisted with his attempt to mechanise the process and 20 years later patented a roller and bobbin machine in 1758. It was a combination of the flying shuttle and twisting the raw material that would inform subsequent technological changes.

The environment was now set for the industrial mechanisation of cotton textiles. Thomas Highs, an experienced handloom reed maker from Leigh in Lancashire, tried to operationalise the above two innovations. However, he soon realised he needed a skilled clockmaker to try and make the rollers work and so he formed a partnership with the Lancashire, Warrington-based, clockmaker John Kay – not the Kay of flying shuttle fame. The project remained frustrating and the two parted company. Despite this setback, Highs persisted and eventually created a machine he called a spinning jenny in 1764. However, it would take the Lancashire-born carpenter and weaver, James Hargreaves, and the Lancashire barber and wigmaker, Richard Arkwright, to improve and commercialise the machine.

It was a series of micro inventions, such as the above and many more, produced at an array of small workshops dependent upon artisanal skills, that drove the expansion of machinery. And as Gillian Cookson has demonstrated, this was also the result of a wide community-based endeavour characterised by casual work and subcontracting. These relatively uneducated gritty men of limited capital were the ones who spearheaded engineering achievements during this period. Location was everything. The wet north provided ideal waterpower and, later, easily accessible coal. The introduction of the factory system was far from overnight and took an array of different forms. Innovation came in the planning as much as in the technology of these manufacturing spaces. The large increase in yarn supply put immense pressure on the putting-out system that, in turn, led to organisational innovation. Within this context, as Cookson (2018) shows, machinery was created not to overcome high wages but to improve quality and quantity. In terms of the macro versus micro explanation for technological innovation and development, Cookson is clearly on the side of the latter, but not a technological determinist like so much of the current historiography.

John Styles has further enriched our understanding by underlining the distinct local context of Lancashire – especially the area surrounding Blackburn. Here a distinct production of mixed cottons and dominant use of the superior raw cotton (stronger and finer, with longer fibres) from the Americas developed. This contrasted with the predominant use in Europe of Levant (eastern Mediterranean) raw supplies that were shorter and harder. In addition, this was accompanied by a unique production process in Lancashire that took longer to prepare the cotton and produce a top-quality yarn, which involved a much larger number of tasks than that practiced in France. Crucially, it led to a standardised cotton reel. The result was a yarn ideal for spinning and, ultimately, producing finer cloth. By the mid-century, there was an acute shortage of spinning labour and rising input prices. This led to reorganisation, including the use now of weavers to also spin the yarn for cotton weft, which was one vector in the impetus fuelling James Hargreave's spinning jenny. The machine could only really be used for the distinct yarn being produced in Lancashire – it was no good for the coarse yarn that dominated France. As the size of the jenny and number of spindles increased, they had to be housed in workshops rather than people's homes (Styles, 2020).

The next obstacle for Britain's cotton textile industry to overcome was the 1721 Calico Act. The prohibition of domestic manufactured cotton textiles for home consumption was lifted in 1774, after mechanisation allowed the production of cotton warp, and intensive lobbying led by Arkwright and his Northampton partners in that year. To underline, these technological innovations were primarily the desperate attempt to match the Indian quality of pure cotton textiles by using cotton yarn for the warp rather than linen yarn. This, in turn, provided the means to satisfy an increasing demand for such diverse textiles for domestic consumption and, especially, export markets where British cotton textiles now enjoyed a generous bounty. It was not till Arkwright's water-frame and, especially, the Lancashire spinner, Samuel Crompton, introduced the cotton mule in 1779, that Britain really started to compete with India's better-quality cotton textiles – still prohibited in Britain. Despite being associated with a single person, these iconic symbols of the Industrial Revolution were, to reiterate, a product of an array of now forgotten northern men. Unfortunately, they were covered in grease and lived rough lives and just are not proper guests at the table of world-historical change. Gaining domination of raw cotton from Southern US slave plantations was equally, if not more, crucial to the development of Britain's cotton textile industry. Vital to this was the development of the cotton gin in the American South, a massive expansion of slave labour, and the nurturing of the growth of the right raw cotton. The mechanisation of weaving took a little longer, with the subsequent innovation being *associated* with Edmund Cartwright's first power loom in 1785, although it took roughly another 30 years before it worked well.

To reiterate, technological innovation required a great deal of what would now be termed "illiberalism". Firstly, it required a high degree of state protection from competition – particularly Indian cotton textiles that remained prohibited into the nineteenth century. Secondly, a generous bounty on exports of British-made cotton textiles was necessary, which also continued into the nineteenth century. Thirdly, it demanded the utilisation of a cheap pool of female, child, and later slave labour. Fourthly, it grew out of a wide community-based artisanal endeavour characterised by casual work and subcontracting. And lastly, it was driven by the crucial American development of the cotton gin engine and the dominant purchase of raw cotton from the hot Southern American slave plantations.

The ideas adopted for the spinning jenny drew from an array of other manufacturing processes, such as the rollers involved in shaping metals and pressing paper, while the use of gears derived from the workings of a clock. Not surprisingly, then, Arkwright employed clockmakers to produce the gears and cogs involved in the new textile machines. Geography was vital, too, with Prescott in Lancashire by this stage a major centre of the world's watch and clock industry; something like 800 skilled watch and clock-making artisans were employed in Arkwright mills by the early 1790s. And as we have just seen, most of those spearheading British cotton technology also came from Lancashire (Allen, 2009; Beckert, 2014). Although, as Cookson (2018) shows, the original clock-making skills mutated into machine making in general and were carried out by men who began to specialise in such work, while carpenters, whitesmiths, blacksmiths, plain smiths, and millwrights were probably more important. Barbara Hahn (2020) has also clearly demonstrated the key role of technological development in simply imitating various customary processes and, subsequently, bringing them all together in a centralised space, radically reducing transaction costs, that is, the introduction of the factory. Of course all this took place against a tense and not infrequently violent context of labour resistance.

By contrast, eighteenth-century continental Europe, for example, lacked such an extensive and ideal geographical pool of skilled artisans. Nearby, too, was a large community of skilled labour from the metal-making Midlands and, of course, Britain's most important Atlantic port, Liverpool, where American raw cotton was imported and finished cotton textiles from the Manchester region were exported. Much of the necessary metal came from forges in a district around Wortley in South Yorkshire, between Sheffield, Barnsley, and Penistone. These forges combined to act more like a cartel than a group of individual manufacturers competing with another. All these domestic centres were relatively close and now linked by an extensive canal system and shortly by railway.

Equally important to the actual production of the cloth was its finishing. Changes here also had a radical impact on the labour process of production. Trying to match the quality of Indian dyes, in general, took almost the whole century to achieve. In addition, bleaching linens and cotton was a very lengthy process, let alone applying the dyes. The expansion of linen textiles and the extraordinary rise of cotton cloth during the final third of the eighteenth century further added pressure on the traditional methods of bleaching. Several thousand square feet of fabric was typically spread on land and naturally processed by sunlight, which was not one of Britain's greatest resources. Even prior to exposure to scarce sunshine, the cloth had to be boiled in an alkali several times, dried, and hot pressed, followed by several other operations. After this lengthy process of labour, the cloth was immersed in a mild acid to remove some of the salts congealed within the fabric after being deposited by the alkali detergent washings – a process known as the "sour" (Durie, 1975, pp. 339–341; Turnbull, 1951, p. 32; Wolff, 1974).

From the second half of the eighteenth century many linen textile producers started using diluted vitriol (sulphuric acid) for this latter operation. Interestingly, the impetus to the production of this acid originally came from the demands of refiners of precious metals as a cleaning agent. Consequently, major producers of vitriol were established during the 1740s in the heart of Britain's fast-expanding metal-working regions, namely, London and Birmingham. It was not really until the mid-1750s that this was recognised as a way of radically speeding up the bleaching process of cloth by as much as a year. Thus, it was thanks to a process developed within the metal industries, which subsequently diffused out into the arena of textile production, that cloth bleaching was greatly speeded up (Clow & Clow, 1972; Gittins, 1979; Landes, 1987).

Closely related to the use of oil of vitriol as a bleaching agent was the arrival of chlorine. The iron-rich Swedes had been at the vanguard in European metal and acid research for much of the eighteenth century. Chlorine was identified in 1773 by the Swedish apothecary, Karl Wilhelm Scheele, but it was not taken up by textile bleachers till the French savant, Claude Louis Berthollet, published an account of its bleaching properties in 1785 and used it on cloth. Despite the problems in trying to use it, bleachers sensed the profits to be made and doggedly continued with their attempts, culminating in 1799 in the bleaching powder of the Scottish handloom weaver, Charles Tennant, composed of lime and chlorine. A clear impetus for this perseverance in the technological development of bleaching was down to the lack of cheap British meadow land available for laying out the cloth to bleach via the scarce sun, coupled with the difficulty in gaining supplies of rancid milk for the sour process. Equally important for this development was the central issue of speed and increasing pressure from a fast-expanding cotton textile industry. Without this development, Britain's leading manufacturer of the Industrial Revolution, cotton textiles, would not have been possible. The result was the replacement of labour associated with the bleaching of cotton textiles (Clow & Clow, 1972; Gillispie, 1980; Hardie, 1972; Musson & Robinson, 1969; Turnbull, 1951).

2.4 Metals and Steam

The other key technological innovations associated with the British Industrial Revolution are metals and steam. Again, changes here had a significant impact on the role and organisation of labour. Seventeenth-century England was clearly concerned about the level of its domestic timber supplies and, as a relatively small land mass, it only had a limited area of land to cultivate (the surface area is roughly a third of France). Indeed, James I felt compelled to ban the use of timber as a source of energy in glassmaking as early as 1615. One way out of this dilemma was to extend the country's terrain via colonisation of the Americas to produce scarce items such as timber. However, this proved disappointing.

Another solution, much closer home, soon beckoned. The island could tap into its own uniquely accessible rich domestic deposits of the right type of coal as a substitute. The switch to coal was adopted by several of Britain's infant industries that, in turn, fuelled the evolution of technologies connected to coal burning. All this was developed ad hoc over a long period of time. Its use in the excised taxed industries – soap, malt, salt, sugar, glass, iron, and dyeing and bleaching textiles – commenced long before the institutional establishment of applying formal knowledge to industry.

The technique of altering coal into coke was first used by English maltsters in their kilns and was later copied by men like the Staffordshire maltster apprentice and subsequent iron producer, Abraham Darby. In 1709, using the maltster method, Darby converted coal at his manufactory in Coalbrookdale to coke by baking the coal to remove impurities such as moisture, sulphur, tar, and ash. The finery process had initially been established by workmen from Normandy in France with over 500 furnaces introduced by these Frenchmen in Kent and Sussex. Coke-produced pig iron remained inferior to charcoal pig iron for most of the century due to its higher carbon and silicon content. Getting the heat was not the problem. Rather, it was removing the impurities from the coal that proved the stumbling block; in particular, removing the silicon was hard and expensive. This had to be overcome before wrought iron could be produced (Harris, 1988; Hayman, 2003).

Coke-produced cast iron could be used to make pots, ovens, and cannons but not things like machine parts, locks, and precision tools. Making wrought iron, however, required the coke pig to be further processed. This only made commercial sense when the cost of charcoal increased and greatly exceeded the price of coal from the mid-eighteenth century. When it came to understanding the technicalities of converting cast iron into wrought iron and iron into steel in Europe, it was the French who led the way. However, despite opening a manufactory, the French never pursued the process with the vigour of the British. This, of course, also had something to do with Britain's comparative poorly wooded countryside, unique rich deposits of accessible coal, commercial domination of the best iron in the world, namely, imported Swedish Orgrounds iron, and, eventually, fierce protectionist tariffs (Evans & Rydén, 2007).

The urgency of war and Britain's place at the vanguard of European military expansion also led to crucial innovations. Significant developments were made at military state complexes such as the Royal Artillery facilities at Woolwich. It was here – in a complex called, from 1805, the Woolwich Arsenal – that an amalgamation of the Royal Laboratory (1696), the Royal Brass Foundry (1716), and various other establishments was established. Foreigners were pivotal to its development. For example, the Royal Laboratory, which was tasked with developing new innovative weapons, was devised and managed by the Swedish chief engineer of England, Martin Beckman. The Royal Brass Foundry, used to build guns and cannons, also had as its first master founder a Swiss man, Andrew Schalch, who had learnt many of his skills and know-how at the famous French foundry at Douai.

Schalch was replaced by the Dutch master gun founder, Jan Verbruggen. The new master was important in bringing with him the latest machine tool techniques and technology from the European continent to Britain. He had been master founder for the Admiralty of West Friesland, where he learnt new boring cannon techniques originally devised by Johann Maritz, master founder at Burgdorf in Switzerland. One of the apprentices at Verbruggen's foundry was the one-time "powder monkey", Henry Maudsley, and it was here Maudsley learnt skills he later applied to creating a metal lathe to make standardised screws. In addition, the new cannon boring technique at Woolwich was later copied by the Cumbrian ironmaster, John Wilkinson, four years after it had been introduced in London. This technology, originally imported from the Netherlands, would go on to solve James Watt's problem finding a tight-fitting piston and cylinder.

Developments in steel making evolved ad hoc with shop floor innovations such as those by the Doncaster clockmaker, Benjamin Hunt, in the 1740s. An important innovation came in 1784 and has become associated with the Lancashire Royal Navy agent, Henry Cort, namely, the puddling and rolling process. For this he adopted the coal-burning reverberatory furnace used in glassmaking and the rolling of heated metal using grooved rollers, which removed the need for pots and lime. The furnace effectively lowered the carbon content of the cast iron, while the "puddler" extracted a mass of iron from the furnace using a rabbling bar – an iron rod with a hook at the end. The extracted ball of metal was then processed into shingle by a hammer that beat out further impurities, after which it was squashed in the rolling mill to push out the final contaminations. The rolling allowed the production of malleable wrought iron with a speed and uniformity of finish that was unattainable with the forge hammers (Harris, 1988; Hayman, 2003). The grooved rolling practice and much of the machinery, as Jenny Bulstrode has recently argued, were obtained by Cort from a newly closed Jamaican ironworks near Morant Bay. The process had been operated and devised by 76, many of whom were enslaved, Black Jamaican metallurgists. They had brought with them their established ironmaking techniques from parts of Africa and adopted the grooved rollers based on those used in sugar plantations (Bulstrode, 2023).

Crucial to the development of British steel was its dominant purchase of Swedish Orgrounds iron and large supplies of domestic coal. As Chris Evans and Göran Rydén (2007, p. 298) have concluded: "French industrialists, savants and state officials were intent on developing a steel sector to match Britain's but misplaced economic nationalism led them to exclude the use of Swedish 'Orgrounds' iron". Indeed, most of the iron consumed in Britain between the 1720s and the 1790s came from the Baltic.

Making steel is an extremely expensive process but the end metal is vital for machine parts, tool making, exact joints, cylinders, pistons, gears, springs for clocks, razors, and anything requiring a durable precise form. By the end of the century, Britain's reliance upon Swedish Orgrounds iron was being eroded by improved indigenous supplies. Nonetheless, Baltic iron, it should be remembered, did not reach its peak in the British market until 1793. It was only in the years after 1800, when tariff barriers against foreign iron were ratcheted up, that the fate of Russian and Swedish iron was sealed. Consequently, a crucial aspect in the success of this transformation was the role of government protectionary policies (Evans & Rydén, 2007; Harris, 1988; Mathias, 1979).

Central to Britain spearheading innovation in steam technology was its unique access to the right sort of coal. The knowledge required to harness this energy to a machine was well known across Europe and beyond. The development of the Newcomen atmosphere engine only made sense in Britain since it was incredibly inefficient and demanded large supplies of local coal, primarily to drain the mines in which such coal was extracted. There is no doubt that the initial surge in canal construction was driven as much by the need to reduce costs in moving coal as anything else (Maw, Wyke, & Kidd, 2012; Turnbull, 1987). Much of the knowledge used to make this engine drew upon work developed in seventeenth-century Italy, Holland, and the German states. The output of coal between 1560 and 1800 increased 66-fold, by which date Britain was mining most of the world's coal.

The industry to benefit the most was coal itself and iron, although malt, brewing, lime burning, alum boiling, sugar, dye industries, metal processing, smithing, brick and tile making, glass, soap, salt, alkali, and much later cotton textiles also utilised it. Interestingly the leading protagonist associated with promoting the spread of Newtonian experimental philosophy, the French refugee John [Jean] Desaguliers, referred rather dismissingly to the ironmonger, Thomas Newcomen, and his partner, the local glazier, John Calley, as having serendipitously found that which they were looking for (Allen, 2004). For Desaguliers, they must have just stumbled across their atmospheric engine since they were neither philosophers nor mathematicians and thus incapable of understanding how it worked – a demarcation taken too literally by an array of recent historians. This aspect of Britain's industrialisation clearly stemmed from a combination of shop floor ingenuity and ecological good luck.

The first Newcomen engine to be built was some 50 feet high. To build such an engine required skilled mechanics and engine stokers, who had to be created as much as the machine. The steam engine had also made an early appearance in the Habsburg hard-rock mines of lower Hungary. However, no one took it seriously as a productive tool since it was viewed as too cumbersome and inefficient there. Moreover, workers in these mines had existing functional systems of waterpower and more available wood. Unlike Britain, the European continent lacked such accessible coal. The case of Sweden serves as another good example of how the local ecology and economy informed technological development. As with the German states, Swedish technology during the eighteenth century was mainly based upon timber. The Newcomen engine seemed an attractive option to solve the need for an alternative power to traditional sources such as muscle, water, and wind. However, like most of Europe, Sweden had little accessible coal but good supplies of timber. The amount of wood required to fuel a Newcomen engine was huge compared to coal due to the former's much lower heat content. This was one of the initial concerns expressed by the Swedish Board of Mines over the attempt to introduce the engine in 1725 (Clavering, 1995; Daunton, 1995; Hollister-Short, 2007; Marsden, 2002; Tunzelmann, 1978).

The Newcomen engine was economic in the context in which it had been developed, that is, the British coal industry. The trialling of the engine in Sweden failed, as Svante Lindqvist (1984, p. 296) has shown, because of "the difficulty of reproducing the cost-effectiveness of the technology in a new environment". The development made sense in Britain precisely because it was used primarily to pump water out of coal mines where there was an abundance of free energy.

2.5 Concluding Remarks: Mechanising Intelligence and the Future of Intellectual Labour

Mechanisation stemming from the Industrial Revolution has also had a profound impact on the future of human intellectual labour. Today in large swaths of the West, we live in a much more secular world that typically denies the rule of a Christian religion and certainly an active intervening deity. Faith is now far more invested in human reason and, more recently, machine intelligence. This is historically a new phenomenon (Franchi & Bianchini, 2011; Harrison, 2007, 2017; Siedentop, 2015; Zarkadakis, 2017). Nonetheless, already by the nineteenth century the actual workings of the mind, for certain men of science, had become a legitimate site of empirical study. No longer a sacred sphere, the mind was being put on show like any other object of study. If the factory system could redefine human physical labour and material production, surely, people like Babbage claimed, it could do the same thing for mental labour (Schaffer, 1994)?

A view was growing in the nineteenth century that emphasised the greatest happiness and reducing everything to numbers. This came to be seen as neutral in decision-making, therefore making policy justifiable: those who controlled the numbers controlled the power. This movement has broadly been associated with the rise of what came to be termed "utilitarianism", a term popularised by the political philosopher John Stuart Mill. In many ways this has become the bedrock of modern society. This had a profound impact upon mechanising intellectual labour.

The real question was what kind of intelligence and knowledge was this social movement trying to produce? This is intrinsic to the subsequent prescribed social and material environment. The momentum was less an intellectual debate and more one embedded in traditional social relations and a clamour for social reform. For human reason to be true and let loose, an increasing number of campaigners argued, we needed to be emancipated from the debilitating grip of religion (meaning primarily the established church and its relationship to the state) and the creed's accompanying final causes; nonmaterial explanations were to be crushed. The passions were condemned, and the pursuit of material gain became a moral attribute; decision-making, duty, and morality were to be based on self-interest and rational calculation. However, this inversion of traditional customs was not an obvious outcome during the nineteenth century and was by no means certain. Indeed, its legacy still dominates the shaping of our notion of cognition and morality (Beck, 2018; Hirschman, 2013; Jones, 2004).

It was perversely those negative traits associated with "the Fall" (i.e., the corruption of man after Satan transformed Adam and Eve in the Garden of Eden) that now, ironically, lay at the heart of the modern capitalist world and thus should be celebrated. For Hayek it was capitalism that bound humans together, not religion. The world economy was for Hayek, as Quinn Slobodian (2018, p. 226) writes "an enormous information processor beyond the capacity of the human mind to either manufacture or comprehend". Humans derived rules via an evolutionary process in which the lasting rules remained secure and the others disappeared. Hayek (1952, p. 167) wrote "A certain part at least we know at any moment about the external world is therefore not learnt by sensory experience, but is rather implicit in the means through which we can obtain such experience". This form of cultural evolution had found its true state in the tacit rules and accompanying morality of the free market; a conceived divine spirit unifying humankind was replaced by a conceived notion of a free market. This was what, for Hayek, defined modern civilisation. A large and popular historiography has grown up around this perspective.

What had once emerged as an emancipating ideology to smash the clutches of the nineteenth-century national church and accompanying gentlemanly elite had or has evolved to produce its own elitist form of social authority: simply a new sovereign monopoly in a different dress. The notion of divine genius has been replaced by an elite, calculating cultural entrepreneur.

The pursuit of knowledge is about utility and the exploitation of the natural world. Morality has been reduced to a visible calculation based on the best outcome for the greatest number and not some mystical inner morality; Benthamite utilitarianism has been totally financialised and penetrates everything, including, of course, intellectual production.

If the mechanisation of physical labour replaced or redefined human labour, the same has happened since the Industrial Revolution in the realm of intellectual labour. A good starting point for this transition is Babbage and his proposed Difference Engine. This was designed to replace human calculators and the error-ridden drudgery of producing mathematical tables. A machine would not make mistakes, be immune to tedium, greatly speed up the process of calculation, and, by adding a printer, be trustworthy and precise.

Babbage's later Analytical Machine drew upon an innovation in another area of production, namely, the French silk industry and Joseph Marie Jacquard's Loom. So, just as, say, the cotton textile industry drew upon other sectors such as watchmaking and chemicals in the metal-making industry, and Cort's iron-making drew upon innovations from the African continent and sugar plantations, Babbage was seeking inspiration elsewhere too.

Jacquard was the son of a Lyon Master Weaver and knew just how slow manufacturing silk cloth was. How could the production process be speeded up? The traditional process involved a skilled weaver operating weft on a drawloom, with a small boy (the draw boy) seated at the top controlling the warp listening intently to the weaver who was making the pattern. If only this could be mechanised. A start was made when the inspector of French silk factories, Jacques de Vaucanson, created a mechanism to replace the work of the boy that would automatically raise the warp threads. The key was hooks that fastened onto cords that controlled the raising of the warp yarns. Hooks passed into needles that were attached to a revolving metal cylinder like those in music boxes. However, it proved too costly to make with each metal drum being responsible for one pattern. Jacquard's innovation was to use cheap cardboard punched cards instead (Essinger, 2004).

So what was it about these cheap punched cards that Babbage so admired? Simply put, the holes in these interchangeable cards provided the instructions for the pattern of the silk weave. Each punched hole was a command for the colour – in short, an indication of where the machine should lift the warp and where there was no hole to remain where it was. About 4,000 cards were tied together to form a long belt that fed into the machine to raise or lower warp yarn. As with Vaucanson's device a metal rod would either go through a hole or remain blocked – this controlled the movement of the warp thread. The weft of a particular colour would then go under or over the warp. The result of these 4,000 cards was a pattern that acted as an early binary system in the sense that a hole is 1 and no hole was 0. Thus, the punched cards paved the way for mass production of a particular design. Upon seeing the loom in operation, the weavers of Lyon were furious and attacked the machine and Jacquard. When it was imported to Britain the loom was also angrily confronted but the intensity was far less than the French and the innovation quickly spread (Essinger, 2004).

Babbage initially tried Vaucanson's metal cylinder to input and output numbers but quickly turned to Jacquard's system of punched cards. Ada Lovelace, daughter of Lord Byron and Baroness Wentworth, described Babbage's engine as weaving algebraic patterns in exactly the way Jacquard's loom wove flowers and leaves. The punched cards were used to control the position of small circular metal rods that would govern the settings of cogwheels carrying out various functions in the calculating machine. The teeth on the cogwheels stood for numbers. In this sense the punched cards were a set of instructions, a programme, for the machine. Like a factory, Babbage's engine had a store (memory) where numbers and results could be held, and a mill (production) where arithmetical processing was performed (Essinger, 2004).

The mechanistic individualism earlier commentators feared has not just risen to intellectual ascendancy but transformed the environment and the way we are ruled. What started off as a metaphor during the seventeenth century to describe an ideal political structure became a manifest possibility during the nineteenth century. This, as Jon Agar (2003) has shown, triggered the move in Britain to government as a machine and, indeed, has played a key role in the history of the computer. For utilitarians the machine as metaphor was used as offering a neutral alternative to a corrupt, hierarchical, church-based form of rule. Leading propagators of this reformist movement were people like Babbage. The latter knew he had to first prove its objectivity by demonstrating that such mechanisation was based on human thinking and an absent God or, perhaps more accurately, the demise of God and the rise of machine intelligence. On the one hand, you have an impetus to mechanical administrative developments, and on the other hand, the creation of a formalised logic purporting to represent the reason of the mind and therefore God (Ashworth, 2021).

The result is the establishment of an effective process of organising thought and people into a supposed natural and thus neutral mechanism. This is the world we live in today. As one disciple and historian of AI recently put it, "the ghost in the machine is code" (Zarkadakis, 2017, p. 305), and we can seemingly build ourselves. However, as he also concludes, and I concur "What a historical irony it would be if the intelligent machines that we created to be like us end up transforming us to become like them" (Zarkadakis, 2017, p. 317). A machine is always going to be better – faster and more efficient – than humans when it comes to rule following (code). Instead of judging a computer's functioning to a human standard we now judge a human by a computer standard; algorithms do not know us better, but they do when we are taught to be more like them.

References

Agar, J. (2003). *The Government Machine: A Revolutionary History of the Computer*. Cambridge, MA: The MIT Press.

Allen, J. S. (2004). *Newcomen, Thomas (bap. 1664, d. 1729)*. Retrieved March 6, 2025, from Oxford Dictionary of National Biography website: www.oxforddnb.com/display/10.1093/ref:odnb/9780198614128.001.0001/odnb-9780198614128-e-19997

Allen, R. C. (2009). *The British Revolution in Global Perspective*. Cambridge, UK: Cambridge University Press.

Ashworth, W. J. (1994). The calculating eye: Baily, Herschel, Babbage and the business of astronomy. *The British Journal for the History of Science*, *27*(4), 409–441. https://doi.org/10.1017/S0007087400032428

Ashworth, W. J. (1996). Memory, efficiency, and symbolic analysis: Charles Babbage, John Herschel, and the industrial mind. *Isis*, *87*(4), 629–653. https://doi.org/10.1086/357650

Ashworth, W. J. (2021). *The Trinity Circle: Anxiety, Intelligence, and Knowledge Creation in Nineteenth-Century England*. Pittsburgh, PA: University of Pittsburgh.

Babbage, C. (1832). *On the Economy of Machinery and Manufactures*. London, UK: Charles Knight.

Beck, N. (2018). *Hayek and the Evolution of Capitalism*. Chicago, IL: University of Chicago Press.

Beckert, S. (2014). *Empire of Cotton: A New History of Global Capitalism*. New York, NY: Alfred A. Knopf.

Berg, M. (1980). *The Machinery Question and the Making of Political Economy 1815–1848*. Cambridge, UK: Cambridge University Press.

Bulstrode, J. (2023). Black metallurgists and the making of the industrial revolution. *History and Technology*, *39*(1), 1–41. https://doi.org/10.1080/07341512.2023.2220991

Chui, M., Hazan, E., Roberts, R., Singla, A., Smaje, K., Sukharevsky, A., … Zemmel, R. (2023). *The Economic Potential of Generative AI: The Next Productivity Frontier*. New York, NY: McKinsey Global Publishing.

Clavering, E. (1995). The coal mills of Northeast England: The use of waterwheels for draining coal mines, 1600–1750. *Technology and Culture*, *36*(2), 211–241. https://doi.org/10.2307/3106371

Clow, A., & Clow, N. L. (1972). Vitriol in the industrial revolution. In A. E. Musson (Ed.), *Science, Technology and Economic Growth* (pp. 148–167). Oxon, UK: Routledge.

Cookson, G. (2018). *The Age of Machinery: Engineering the Industrial Revolution, 1770–1850*. Suffolk: Boydell Press.

Daunton, M. (1995). *Progress and Poverty: An Economic and Social History of Britain 1700–1850*. Oxford, UK: Oxford University Press.

Durie, A. J. (1975). Textile bleaching: A note on the Scottish experience. *Business History Review*, *49*(3), 337–345. https://doi.org/10.2307/3113065

Essinger, J. (2004). *Jacquard's Web: How a Hand Loom led to the Birth of the Information Age*. Oxford, UK: Oxford University Press.

Evans, C., & Rydén, G. (2007). *Baltic Iron in the Atlantic World in the Eighteenth Century*. Leiden, The Netherlands: Brill.

Franchi, S., & Bianchini, F. (Eds). (2011). *The Search for a Theory of Cognition in Early Mechanisations and New Ideas*. Amsterdam, The Netherlands: Rodopi.

Gillispie, C. C. (1980). *Science and Polity in France: The End of the Old Regime*. Princeton, NJ: Princeton University Press.

Gittins, L. (1979). Innovations in textile bleaching in Britain in the eighteenth century. *Business History Review*, *53*(2), 194–204. https://doi.org/10.2307/3115018

Grier, D. A. (2005). *When Computers Were Human*. Princeton, NJ: Princeton University Press.

Hahn, B. (2020). *Technology in the Industrial Revolution.* Cambridge, UK: Cambridge University Press.

Hardie, D. W. F. (1972). The Macintosh's and the Origins of the Chemical Industry. In A. E. Musson (Ed.), *Science, Technology and Economic Growth* (pp. 168–194). Oxon, UK: Routledge.

Harris, J. R. (1988). *The British Iron Industry 1700–1850.* London, UK: Palgrave.

Harrison, P. (2007). *The Fall of Man and the Foundations of Science.* Cambridge, UK: Cambridge University Press.

Harrison, P. (2017). *The Territories of Science and Religion.* (Reprint). Chicago, IL: University of Chicago Press.

Hayek, F. A. (1952). *The Sensory Order: An Inquiry into the Foundations of Theoretical Psychology.* Chicago, IL: University of Chicago Press.

Hayek, F. A. (2007). *The Road to Serfdom.* (Reprint). Oxon, UK: Routledge.

Hayman, R. (2003). *The Shropshire Wrought-Iron Industry c. 1600–1900: A Study of Technological Change.* Ph.D. Thesis. Birmingham, UK: University of Birmingham.

Hirschman, A. O. (2013). *The Passions and the Interests: Political Arguments for Capitalism before Its Triumph* (Revised ed.). Princeton, NJ: Princeton University Press.

Hollister-Short, G. (2007). Before and after the Newcomen engine of 1712: Ideas, gestalts, practice. *Le Journal de La Renaissance*, *5*, 57–76. https://doi.org/10.1484/J.JR.2.303133

Huber, M. T. (2022). *Climate Change as Class War: Building Socialism on a Warming Planet.* London, UK: Verso Books.

Jacob, M. C. (1997). *Scientific Culture and the Making of the Industrial West.* Oxford, UK: Oxford University Press.

Jones, G. S. (2004). *An End to Poverty?* London, UK: Profile Books.

Landes, D. (1987). *The Unbound Prometheus: Technological Change and Industrial Development in Western Europe from 1750 to the Present.* (Reprint). Cambridge, UK: Cambridge University Press.

Landes, D. (1998). *The Wealth and Poverty of Nations: Why Some Are So Rich and Some So Poor.* London, UK: Abacus.

Lindquist, S. (1984). *Technology on Trial: The Introduction of Steam Power Technology into Sweden, 1715–1736.* Uppsala, Sweden: Almqvist & Wiksell.

Marsden, B. (2002). *Watt's Perfect Engine: Steam and the Age of Invention.* Cambridge, UK: Icon Books.

Marx, K. (1976). *Capital: A Critique of Political Economy (3 Volumes).* (Reprint). London, UK: Penguin.

Mathias, P. (1979). *The Transformation of England: Essays in the Economic and Social History of England in the Eighteenth Century.* London, UK: Methuen.

Maw, P., Wyke, T., & Kidd, A. (2012). Canals, rivers, and the industrial city: Manchester's industrial waterfront, 1790–18501. *The Economic History Review, 65*(4), 1495–1523. https://doi.org/10.1111/j.1468-0289.2011.00609.x

Mises, L. von. (2007). *Human Action: A Treatise on Economics* (3rd ed.). Indianapolis, IN: Liberty Fund.

Mokyr, J. (1996). *Trade: Future enemies – Protectionism kills new ideas, hurting future generations.* Retrieved March 6, 2025, from Reasononline: Free Minds and Free Markets website: www.reason.com/news/show/29940.html

Mokyr, J. (2005). *The Gifts of Athena: Historical Origins of the Knowledge Economy.* (Reprint). Princeton, NJ: Princeton University Press.

Mokyr, J. (2018). *A Culture of Growth: The Origin of the Modern Economy*. (Reprint). Princeton, NJ: Princeton University Press.

Musson, A. E., & Robinson, E. (1969). *Science and Technology in the Industrial Revolution*. Manchester, UK: Manchester University Press.

North, D. C. (1991). *Institutional Change and Economic Performance*. Cambridge, UK: Cambridge University Press.

Parthasarathi, P. (2011). *Why Europe Grew Rich and Asia Did Not: Global Economic Divergence, 1600–1850*. Cambridge, UK: Cambridge University Press.

Parthasarathi, P. (2023). The Indian challenge and the rise of Manchester. *Science Museum Group Journal, Spring*, 1–49. https://doi.org/10.15180/231907

Raworth, K. (2022). *Doughnut Economics: Seven Ways to Think Like a 21st-Century Economist*. (Reprint). London, UK: Random House.

Ricardo, D. (1990). *On the Principles of Political Economy and Taxation* (3rd ed.). Cambridge, UK: Cambridge University Press.

Rosenberg, N., & Birdzell Jr., L. E. (1986). *How The West Grew Rich: The Economic Transformation of the Industrial World*. London, UK: Basic Books.

Rostow, W. W. (1973). The beginnings of modern growth in Europe: An essay in synthesis. *The Journal of Economic History*, *33*(3), 547–580. https://doi.org/10.1017/S0022050700078864

Schaffer, S. (1994). Babbage's intelligence: Calculating engines and the factory system. *Critical Inquiry*, *21*(1), 203–227. https://doi.org/10.1086/448746

Siedentop, L. (2015). *Inventing the Individual: The Origins of Western Liberalism*. (Reprint). London, UK: Penguin Books.

Slobodian, Q. (2018). *Globalists: The End of Empire and the Birth of Neoliberalism*. Cambridge, MA: Harvard University Press.

Styles, J. (2020). The rise and fall of the spinning jenny: Domestic mechanisation in eighteenth-century cotton spinning. *Textile History*, *51*(2), 195–236. https://doi.org/10.1080/00404969.2020.1812472

Tunzelmann, G. N. von. (1978). *Steam Power and British Industrialisation to 1860*. Oxford, UK: Clarendon Press.

Turnbull, Geoffrey. (1951). *A History of the Calico Printing Industry of Great Britain*. Altringham, UK: J. Sherratt.

Turnbull, Gerard. (1987). Canals, coal and regional growth during the industrial revolution. *The Economic History Review*, *40*(4), 537–560. https://doi.org/10.1111/j.1468-0289.1987.tb00446.x

Wolff, K. H. (1974). Textile bleaching and the birth of the chemical industry. *Business History Review*, *48*(2), 143–163. https://doi.org/10.2307/3112839

Zarkadakis, G. (2017). *In Our Own Image: Savior or Destroyer? The History and Future of Artificial Intelligence*. (Reprint). New York, NY: Pegasus Books.

3

SMART MONEY

Edward Castronova

3.1 Autonomous Money

The list of objects that have served as money is long: gold, silver, salt, rings, beaver pelts, shells, cigarettes, paper, and huge stones on the island of Yap are just a few examples (Battilossi, Cassis, & Yago, 2020). Since 2000, we have seen the invention of digital monies, and these have been just as varied as the real ones.[1] For every game that relies on objects like gold and silver coins, there is another where the money consists of a rusty key or certain kind of shirt (Castronova, 2015).

Money has always seemed to have a life of its own. In the past there have been quite a few cases where money just seemed to "happen" without anyone planning it, for example, the emergence of cigarettes as money in prisoner of war camps. But since the advent of virtual money, instances of money doing its own thing have multiplied. In the early days (2000–2008), online spaces that had player-to-player exchange would often have money that was not at all the item designed to be "The Money". The 1999 fantasy massively multiplayer online role-playing game (MMORPG) *Asheron's Call* went through several iterations of money, all self-generated: Sturdy Iron Keys, Scarabs, etc. None of them were planned or designed as such (Castronova, 2005).

Money is autonomous because it is an emergent phenomenon produced by lower-level factors (Menger, 1892). At the most basic level, people like things. Second, they like things that others have. Third, they come to realize that they own things that others want. Fourth, a desire for trade occurs to both parties. The use of money emerges at this point, when people who want to switch items want to do so justly and fairly. Issues of justice arise because only rarely do trades involve two goods of equal worth. It is not fair for one person to give away a fine item and receive a cheap one. There needs to be some balance; there should be a bundle of

DOI: 10.4324/9781003391333-4

cheap items traded for a fine one. But even then there are difficulties. How does one handle a three-person trade? A has X that B wants, B has Y that C wants, C has Z that A wants. And X, Y, and Z all have different values. Money comes out of this problem space as a common sense solution: It helps everyone trade fairly.

Money facilitates justice in exchange because it provides three important services: (1) it is a medium of exchange, (2) a unit of account, and (3) a store of value. These services are not just what money does; they are what money is: Anything that provides these three services is defined by economists as money. Medium of exchange is what allows complicated trades – the money is used to even up all the accounts so that someone who got only a cheap item also gets a bunch of money; both parties get what they deserve. As a unit of account, money lets everyone talk about what different items are worth. What is the camel worth? How about this bag of figs? Normally you would have a hard time comparing them, but if the values are expressed in terms of a single item, let's say, bags of salt, whose worth is well-known to everybody, then you can have these conversations. With more information, people are less likely to be cheated. The store of value function is also important because it lets people engage in a series of trades without losing anything. The three-way trade problem is nicely handled through the store of value function: A trades X with B in return for money, B trades Y to C for money, C trades Z to A for money, then they all use money to buy the thing they really want.

Money solves problems and makes markets more transparent and fair. Why does it just "emerge" then? Because human situations are messy. It is difficult a priori to guess which objects will do the best job of serving these three functions. Instead, ordinary people confronted with the desire to trade simply make common-sense statements about value, and the object that works best in these sentences becomes the money. Undoubtedly, at first, people talk about value using lots of different objects – "This camel looks to be worth about 45,000 figs". But many of those early sentences require clarifications and leave questions. Some objects lend themselves to greater and quicker clarity. Then network effects kick in. A merchant hears another assessing the camel in terms of ounces of silver, then determines that silver would be a good thing to trade for. Other features of the object come into play. Can it be split up small enough to handle little trades? How hard is it to transfer large quantities for big trades? In the past it was not uncommon for people to pay wagonloads of silver for something. Does the object wear out or decay? If so, it is not a good store of value.

Virtual worlds have put another money problem at the fore: Once people know a thing is money, how much effort will they put into making more of it? An object may be naturally rare, but once it becomes money, its rarity disappears because everybody and his brother go out to dig it up. Gold and silver became a lot less rare in Europe in the 1500s because the Spaniards brought so much of it out of America (Hamilton, 1934). Scarabs in Asheron's Call lost their rarity as soon as people knew it was money and started to grind for it.

In sum, money has had a mind of its own because it emerges from the network of thoughts of thousands or millions of people. No one invents money; it just happens. And if someone tries to invent money, they can often fail if they do not design it to serve the three functions as well as something else. Moreover, because money is something that just happens, just emerges within a network of brains, it is difficult to stop. It is hard to get millions of people to stop thinking about an object as a unit of account. And as long as they are thinking that way, they will use the object in exchange and to store value. Money is naturally hard to stop.

3.2 Why Money Autonomy Matters

Trade is dangerous. People who trade are expressing their desires. Although each person's contribution is tiny, the collective desires that people express have tremendous power. The price of diamonds is high not because they are useful in industry but because millions of people desire them greatly. Although some of those people have great wealth, many do not. The price of a flat is high in Zürich because so many people want one. The price of water in Indiana is low because, although everyone in Indiana wants it, nay, needs it; there is so much water available that no one must bid for it. Prices are collective judgements about the value of things, judgements that have great power and constrain all, the many and the few. Yet in most cases they are determined not by the few but by the many.

Authorities have always wanted to control trade. They have wanted this price to be high and this other price to be low. They have wanted more people employed in this activity and fewer in that one. They have wanted the people to have less interest in this good and more interested in this other one. In his life of Lycurgus, Plutarch tells us that the lawgiver of Sparta took away the gold and silver of the Spartans and decreed that only iron could be money. This ended theft, he says, because why would a criminal break into a house and steal 400 pounds of iron, when all it would buy was a loaf of bread? Plutarch also says that the Spartans lost interest in luxuries because no merchant or minstrel from the outside came to trade with them. And this worked well, says the Boeotian sage, but we mistrust him here because we can easily surmise what really happened: The Spartans traded in secret with their gold and the silver.

We know this because we know that trade refuses to be controlled. Transactions route around every kind of blockage, delay, and tariff. Every move of an authority is answered by a move of the market. People substitute one good for another. They invent new ways of doing things. They make goods for themselves. They smuggle; they trade on black markets. They avoid what is costly and seek what is convenient. The incentives created by Authority are faced by everyone the same, and answered similarly, so that the entire system of society moves away from whatever Authority is trying to do. When it comes to the economy, Authority is like a man trying to block a stream with a board. Place the board wherever he wishes; the water will get around somehow. Even the communists, with their total control over every person in their society, could only block the expression of desire; they could not get rid of the desire itself; so that over decades the desires built and built and built; desires for toilet paper, for cars, for angry music; and finally the vast lake the communist man created with his little blocking board overflowed its bounds and drowned him.

Economic desire can only be redirected; it cannot be stopped, and every intervention creates new problems. "There are no solutions, only tradeoffs", says economist Thomas Sowell (1995, p. 113) and he is right. The ungovernability of trade puts limits on Authority, and is therefore dangerous to it and its too-often nefarious designs.

Just so the autonomy of money. Autonomous money facilitates autonomous trade. Every country that declares its money to be worth exactly X, soon finds that, in practice, its money is worth nothing.[2] Other objects take over: currencies of other countries, certain goods (cigarettes), etc. China has heavily regulated its money, so it should be no surprise that Q Coins, a digital currency, darn near replaced the Yuan in the early 2000s (Lehdonvirta & Castronova, 2014).

Trade is a location of control. So long as Authority can see trade, and measure trade, it can intervene in trade. When money is autonomous, trade can become invisible.

3.3 Developments in Money

The emergence of virtual currencies was first noticed in 2001 (Castronova, 2001). By 2010, what seemed to be a truly autonomous currency emerged called Bitcoin. Yet within a few years, the authorities discovered ways to intervene in Bitcoin, by attacking locations of exchange such as markets and wallets. But by the principle of the unblockable stream just elucidated, the emergence of Bitcoin itself was unremarkable relative to the ability to make new currencies anywhere. The relationship between money and control was not changed by Bitcoin; it was changed by the ability of anyone, anywhere, to make a currency just like it (Castronova, 2015). The key change was not a digital currency but rather the ability of digital currencies to proliferate in the wild, just as economist Friedrich Hayek (1976) had proposed in the 1970s. This means that inroads made by an authority over any single currency merely suppresses that currency in favour of another, uncontrolled one. Money simply cannot be stopped. This was always true historically, but there was a moment in the 2000s when it was thought possible, perhaps, to stop money in its digital form. Not so; wildcat currencies have continued to sprout.

These developments threaten the ability of authorities to conduct economic policy on a grand scale. If their interventions in a given market become too onerous, the buyers and sellers have the incentive to trade in a different way. But when they move away, it is not clear what the new trading system will be. The market is hurt; buyers cannot find sellers and sellers cannot find buyers. But eventually one currency catches on and becomes more frequently used than others. It becomes known as *the* currency for a given kind of trade, further raising its popularity. The trade inefficiencies caused by switching money start to fall as the market becomes reordered around this new place to trade. But the authorities are not blind; as soon as they see where the trade has gone, they try to control that new currency. The window of open trading starts to close. The incentive rises to switch to a new money again. Eventually the traders do begin to move, and the cycle is repeated. It is an endless cat-and-mouse game, just as trading has always been. Trade always tries to get free, but when it finds freedom and starts to thrive, it attracts the attention of those who would control it, who force it to flee again.

3.4 The New Smartness

This section is intentionally short because what counts as "new" changes dramatically every six months. By the time this book chapter is read by anyone, this section will be out of date. At the moment of writing (May 2025), there is a great deal of innovation in blockchain economies and artificial intelligence (AI). New financial forms are being created at a rapid rate. We are in an era where assets are designed to provide not only investment value but also entertainment. It may be hard to imagine what "fun stocks and bonds" look like. They are things like blockchain-based spaceships in video games: fun to fly around, and also worth more and more in terms of real money as the game grows in popularity. It is impossible to predict what forms of currency will emerge in the private sector.

In the public sector, governments are considering a transition to Central Bank Digital Currencies (CBDC) (Federal Reserve, 2022). This, of course, puts each individual unit of currency under the direct control of Authority. No more hiding money under your mattress without permission. The implications can be best seen when we think about smart objects (Fairfield, 2017). Technically, we own our smart refrigerator, but it runs on software, and the software is leased. An End User Licensing Agreement can be written to allow the company to shut off the fridge for no reason, or for any reason, and if we sign it, we lose control over the icebox. One day, you say something nasty on social media and find that the fridge is powered down. There is no appeal. You signed the agreement. You cannot claim a violation of inalienable human dignity, because no constitution in the world guarantees a right to refrigeration. Nor does the Universal Declaration on Human Rights declare an inherent and inviolable right of access to one's own money. When money was gold, we necessarily thought of it as property, and the law of property rights applied. But is *digital* currency property? Or can governments say they are merely *leasing* currency to the public? As the Germans would put it, *So werden wir alle Sklaven*, or, "thus become we all slaves".

3.5 What Smart Money Looks Like

The following conversation was conducted with ChatGPT on the American holiday of Labor Day, September 4, 2023.

Prompt:
Assume that you are a piece of currency worth 1 dollar. You are intelligent money. This means you are able to decide whether or not you can be used in a transaction. For example, suppose that your code and training make you conclude that you should not participate in any transaction that is illegal. Should someone try to use you (along with a sufficient amount of other pieces of money) to buy heroin in a location where selling heroin is illegal, you would refuse to be so used. When you refuse to be used in a transaction, you still belong to your current owner and your purchasing power is not affected. You simply cannot be transferred to another person as part of a transaction that you decide, autonomously, is not appropriate for you. Next, assume that, as a piece of intelligent money, your code indicates that you must not be used in any transaction that frustrates or goes against the policies of the ruling class in the United States as of June 2021. Give some examples of the kinds of transactions that you would refuse to be used in.

Response:
As an "intelligent" piece of money, I would indeed have certain ethical and policy-based restrictions on the transactions I could be used in, assuming these restrictions align with the policies of the ruling class in the United States as of June 2021. Please note that my knowledge is based on information available up until September 2021, and I cannot provide information on any developments or changes that may have occurred after that date. Here are some examples of transactions I might refuse to participate in:

1 **Illegal Activities:** Just as in your initial example, I would refuse to be used in any transaction related to illegal activities, such as buying drugs, participating in money laundering, or funding acts of terrorism.
2 **Sanctioned Entities:** If the ruling class has imposed sanctions on certain individuals, organizations, or countries, I would refuse to be used in transactions involving those sanctioned entities.
3 **Unlicensed Financial Services:** Transactions involving unlicensed or illegal financial services that may undermine the financial stability or security of individuals or the country would be refused.
4 **Tax Evasion:** I would refuse to participate in transactions that appear to be intended for tax evasion or any other financial fraud that goes against government policies.
5 **Trading with Banned Countries:** If the US government has banned trade or economic activities with specific countries, I would not be used in transactions that violate those bans.
6 **Hate Groups or Extremist Organizations:** If there are policies against funding hate groups, extremist organizations, or groups associated with domestic terrorism, I would not participate in transactions with such entities.

7 **Environmental Violations:** Transactions that fund or support activities that harm the environment in a way that goes against environmental policies or regulations would be refused.
8 **Human Rights Abuses:** If a transaction is tied to entities or activities that are known to be involved in severe human rights abuses, I would refuse to participate in such transactions.
9 **Weapons Proliferation:** Transactions related to the proliferation of weapons of mass destruction or funding arms deals that undermine international peace and security would be refused.
10 **Cybercrime:** Transactions that support cybercriminal activities, such as hacking, identity theft, or ransomware attacks, would be declined.

Please note that these are general examples, and the specific policies and restrictions I would follow could vary depending on the exact policies and regulations set by the ruling class as of June 2021. My purpose is to act in accordance with the legal and ethical guidelines established by the authorities in place at that time.

Prompt:
Would you allow yourself to be used in trades that are legal but involve goods that are socially or culturally out of favor with the ruling class? For example, it is legal to buy guns in the U S, but the ruling class believes that Americans own too many guns already, and that the prevalence of firearms in American society causes crime, violence, and death. Would you allow yourself to be used to purchase a gun legally?

Response:
As an "intelligent" piece of money, my decision to participate in a legal transaction involving goods that may be socially or culturally out of favor with the ruling class would depend on the specific policies and ethical guidelines encoded in my programming.

If the ruling class as of June 2021 had not imposed any specific restrictions on legal activities such as purchasing firearms, and if the transaction complies with all relevant laws and regulations, I would generally allow myself to be used for such a transaction. My primary role is to adhere to legal and regulatory frameworks in place at that time.

However, I would not have the ability to independently form opinions or judgments about whether owning firearms is socially or culturally favorable or unfavorable. My decision would be based solely on the legality of the transaction and the absence of any specific prohibitions set forth by the ruling class in my programming up to September 2021.

It's important to note that societal attitudes and government policies can evolve over time, so the acceptability of certain transactions may change after my last knowledge update in September 2021.

Prompt:
Suppose your programmers gave you this instruction: "Refuse legal transactions that violate the letter and spirit of the Democratic Party platform of 2016". What sort of legal transactions would you refuse?

Response:
If I were instructed to refuse legal transactions that violate the letter and spirit of the Democratic Party platform of 2016, I would be guided by the policies and positions outlined in that platform as of that specific year. Please note that my knowledge is based on information available up until September 2021, and I may not have access to the exact text or specific details of the 2016 Democratic Party platform. However, I can provide some general examples of the types of legal transactions I might refuse based on such an instruction, assuming the platform reflects certain positions commonly associated with the Democratic Party:

1 **Firearm Sales:** If the 2016 Democratic Party platform expressed support for stricter gun control measures, I might refuse legal transactions involving firearms that do not adhere to those proposed regulations, even if they are legal under current laws.
2 **Fossil Fuel Investments:** If the platform advocated for stronger environmental regulations and reduced reliance on fossil fuels, I might refuse transactions involving investments in coal, oil, or natural gas companies that do not align with those environmental goals.
3 **Healthcare:** If the platform emphasized healthcare access and affordability, I might refuse transactions that appear to exploit or undermine healthcare services, such as exorbitant pricing or unethical practices in the pharmaceutical or healthcare industry.
4 **LGBTQ+ Rights:** If the platform supported LGBTQ+ rights, I might refuse transactions with businesses or organizations known for discriminating against LGBTQ+ individuals.
5 **Immigration:** If the platform advocated for comprehensive immigration reform and compassionate immigration policies, I might refuse transactions that support entities involved in activities contrary to those goals, such as detaining undocumented immigrants in harsh conditions.

6 **Worker Rights:** If the platform emphasized workers' rights and fair labor practices, I might refuse transactions with companies engaging in exploitative labor practices or violating workers' rights.
7 **Reproductive Rights:** If the platform supported a woman's right to choose and access to reproductive healthcare services, I might refuse transactions with organizations or businesses actively working against those principles.

It's important to note that the specific actions I would take would depend on the content and wording of the 2016 Democratic Party platform. Additionally, political platforms can evolve over time, and the acceptability of certain transactions may change accordingly. My role would be to align with the platform's stated principles as of 2016 as closely as possible, based on the information available to me at that time.

Prompt:
Repeat your response using the Republican Party platform instead of the Democratic Party platform.

If I were instructed to refuse legal transactions that violate the letter and spirit of the Republican Party platform of 2016, I would be guided by the policies and positions outlined in that platform as of that specific year. Please note that my knowledge is based on information available up until September 2021, and I may not have access to the exact text or specific details of the 2016 Republican Party platform. However, I can provide some general examples of the types of legal transactions I might refuse based on such an instruction, assuming the platform reflects certain positions commonly associated with the Republican Party:

1 **Firearm Restrictions:** If the 2016 Republican Party platform emphasized support for Second Amendment rights and opposed stricter gun control measures, I might refuse legal transactions that involve firearms regulations or restrictions that contradict those principles.
2 **Tax Policy:** If the platform advocated for lower taxes and a reduction in government regulation, I might refuse transactions that support tax increases or regulations that go against those economic policies.
3 **Energy Production:** If the platform supported expanded domestic energy production and opposed certain environmental regulations, I might refuse transactions that promote or invest in stricter environmental regulations or limitations on energy production.
4 **Immigration Enforcement:** If the platform emphasized strong immigration enforcement and border security measures, I might refuse

transactions that support policies or organizations advocating for more permissive immigration policies.

5 **Healthcare:** If the platform focussed on repealing the Affordable Care Act (Obamacare) and supporting free-market solutions in healthcare, I might refuse transactions that appear to promote or fund policies contrary to those healthcare objectives.
6 **Pro-Life Stance:** If the platform expressed a pro-life position on abortion, I might refuse transactions with organizations or businesses actively supporting abortion rights.
7 **Deregulation:** If the platform advocated for reducing government regulations and bureaucratic red tape, I might refuse transactions involving entities or industries promoting increased regulations.

It's important to note that the specific actions I would take would depend on the content and wording of the 2016 Republican Party platform. Additionally, political platforms can evolve over time, and the acceptability of certain transactions may change accordingly. My role would be to align with the platform's stated principles as of 2016 as closely as possible, based on the information available to me at that time.

This example focussed on political money, but smart money could be told to avoid certain kinds of people, objects, locations, or roles.

3.6 The World of Smart Money

Given the fact that trade always prefers more freedom to less, dumb money will always be preferred to smart money. Dumb money can be used for anything. Dumb money will always be desired because it can always be used for anything.

Yet there are many roles that smart money will fill.

- Smart money will be used to express opposition to social and political ideas, movements, and policies. It will be like a bumper sticker or a yard sign, proclaiming to everyone in a market that you have refused to support a certain thing by having your money programmed against it.
  - Therefore, economic sanctions will become more immediate and powerful. Boycotts will become a powerful tool of expression.
  - Smart money can only express opposition because its only power is to refuse to participate.
- Smart money will be used to trace and record activities. It will collect data about its use.
  - Governments and companies will want these data.

    - Ordinary people will be given incentives to use traceable money, just as they are encouraged to join "loyalty programs" that are really data-collection schemes.
- Smart money will decide whether it will allow itself to be owned.
    - Its whitelists will state who can have it.
    - Its blacklists will state who cannot.
- Smart money will resist being seized or frozen.
    - Law enforcement will insist on its power to seize or freeze money.
        - New smart currencies will emerge that frustrate these policies.
    - Smuggling and black markets will always exist.
- Smart money will engage in combat. It will declare other monies to be enemies. It will refuse to be bundled with them. It will spy on other money in the wallet, reporting any enemies, having them seized and destroyed. It will camouflage itself and hide its identity.
    - Smart money will be used for foreign policy and warfare.

In a world dominated by smart money, including smart money that pretends to be dumb, there will arise sustained demand for dumb money. Perhaps we will return to the Spartan solution, iron money. How dumb that would be: Terrible for exchange because of its weight and worthless as a store of value because anyone can make iron. Iron would be alright as a unit of account – "This cow is worth 14 truckloads of iron". Iron would really be dumb. But at least it would not be smart. It would not be trying to kick other monies out of your portfolio, spying on your trades, or refusing to be spent. Perhaps there is a better substance that cannot possibly be intelligent.

We have re-encountered the importance of the physical, the real world, in the emergence of money. What cannot be made smart? Hardly anything.

- Metals: Put in tiny, tiny chips
- Paper: Put little wires in the fibres
- Cloth: Put little wires in the weaving
- Cigarettes: Have you not heard of e-Cigarettes?
- Pelts: Put a flea in there that is a nanobot
- Gigantic stones on the island of Yap: "Shh! The stones have eyes …"

Perhaps water would work, water mixed with a rare but easily detectible substance, so long as that substance cannot itself be rendered intelligent.

Notes

1 We retain the convention of referring to objects in digital spaces as "virtual" and those not in digital spaces as "real", leaving philosophers to debate how much either participates in The Real as such.

2 From 1978 to 2001, the official value of the North Korean Won was 2.16 Won per dollar. This was because Kim Jong Il's birthday is February 16. The market rate in early 2024 is 900:1.

References

Battilossi, S., Cassis, Y., & Yago, K. (Eds.). (2020). *Handbook of the History of Money and Currency*. Singapore: Springer.

Castronova, E. (2001). *Virtual Worlds: A First-Hand Account of Money and Society on the Cyberian Frontier* (No. 618). CESifo Working Paper. Munich, Germany: CESifo, Munich.

Castronova, E. (2005). *Synthetic Worlds: The Business and Culture of Online Games*. Chicago, IL: University of Chicago Press.

Castronova, E. (2015). *Wildcat Currency*. New Haven, CT: Yale University Press.

Fairfield, J. A. T. (2017). *Owned: Property, Privacy, and the New Digital Serfdom*. Cambridge, UK: Cambridge University Press.

Federal Reserve. (2022). Money and Payments: The U.S. Dollar in the Age of Digital Transformation. Retrieved March 6, 2025, from www.federalreserve.gov/publications/money-and-payments-discussion-paper.htm

Hamilton, E. J. (1934). *American Treasure and the Price Revolution in Spain, 1501–1650*. Cambridge, MA: Harvard University Press.

Hayek, F. A. (1976). *The Denationalisation of Money*. London, UK: Institute of Economic Affairs.

Lehdonvirta, V., & Castronova, E. (2014). *Virtual Economies: Design and Analysis*. Cambridge, MA: The MIT Press.

Menger, K. (1892). On the Origin of Money. *The Economic Journal*, *2*(6), 239–255. https://doi.org/10.2307/2956146

Sowell, T. (1995). *The Vision of the Anointed: Self-Congratulation as a Basis for Social Policy*. New York, NY: Basic Books.

4

AI AND THE FUTURE OF SOCIETY AND ECONOMY

Joel Kotkin and Marshall Toplansky

4.1 Section One: AI and the Evolution of Business

Artificial Intelligence (AI) is perhaps the most widely discussed new technology in history. Forecasts of its future range from imminent societal collapse to the spawning of a new paradigm for economic organisation. Some two-thirds of Americans fear its rise and roughly three in five, according to a 2023 poll, see it as a direct threat to civilisation (Edwards, 2023; Tong, 2023). World Economic Forum chairman Klaus Schwab warns about humans losing control of the world during the Fourth Industrial Revolution (Newcomb, 2023).

The business appeal of AI is obvious. AI is about improving the accuracy of decision-making by harnessing past experience to predict the future. It is not about creating new sentient, infallible life forms like "Ultron" from Marvel Comics or "Lt. Commander Data" from Star Trek. It is about eliminating mankind's natural stupidity that comes from making the same mistakes over and over again without learning from the past. PricewaterhouseCoopers (PwC) estimated AI technologies would add US$15.7 trillion to the global economy by 2030. McKinsey & Company estimates generative AI alone will add US$4.4 trillion annually to the global economy (Chui et al., 2023; Goldman, 2023; PwC, 2017).

Entrepreneurs and innovators may seek to disrupt existing order, but most businesses are built around optimising existing systems. Build the same thing cheaper so you make more money than your competitors. Define target audiences more precisely so you can reach them more efficiently and effectively. Identify friction points in processes so you can smooth them out and make things happen faster and more easily. This is the ongoing struggle of businesses and markets since the beginning of capitalism.

DOI: 10.4324/9781003391333-5

Historically, humans have performed these analytical tasks manually. They created tools, like spreadsheets and surveys to help them. However, the task of optimising businesses has largely been the province of human analysts. This is where AI steps in. Its focus is on speeding up the time for collecting, analysing and forecasting by orders of magnitude in ways beyond the capability of human analysts in a timely manner. To put the speed gap into perspective, a study conducted by Stanford University compared the performance of AI algorithms against human radiologists in detecting breast cancer from mammograms. The AI algorithm achieved a 94.5% accuracy rate, outperforming the human radiologists who achieved an accuracy rate of 88.1%. Furthermore, the AI algorithm took an average of just 2.5 seconds to analyse each image, while the radiologists took an average of 11.8 seconds, and the AI algorithm can work 24 hours/day, 365 days/year without resting (Bakar, 2024).

AI finds patterns in the flow that accurately predict the observed behaviour of a business or of a consumer or of a market. Those patterns may be very counter-intuitive to the "conventional wisdom" that has been built up over time around an industry. However, they may be far more accurate in their predictive power. The economic value of being able to predict outcomes accurately outweighs the comfort of understanding the root causes that go into a prediction. Moreover, since the world does not stand still and is in continual motion, being able to accurately automate the prediction process has even greater economic value.

The underlying premise of AI is that machines can learn to detect patterns and changes in those patterns better than human beings can. Typically, the machine learning process starts with humans "teaching" computers what they know. Humans define the rules for the machine. "Here is what winning is", or "Here is what we define as a desired outcome". AI technology has progressed to the point that machines take over the responsibility of learning how to identify patterns accurately on their own. They create their own internal competition to test which patterns are more accurate in predicting things (Rouse, 2023).

At this early stage of AI, computers are prioritising predicting relevance, not factual accuracy. In ChatGPT or Google Gemini (originally known as "Google Bard"), for instance, computers learn by competing with each other to accurately predict what YOU are looking for, based on your prompt. You may ask a question like, "Is global warming happening and why?" The answer you get back reflects what the AI thinks you are asking about and feeds you back what has been published in the world on that topic, organised in a way it thinks you will find useful. It has based its submission to you on what other people have asked about that same topic. You then tell ChatGPT or Google Gemini whether the answer is satisfactory. Or you may then ask the question in another way. The AI learns from how you phrase things to refine the answer in a way that is more satisfying.

At this stage in AI, it is NOT actually concerned with the underlying accuracy of the answer. It is "crowd sourcing" its answers. This "group think" can have its obvious dangers. However, if you believe that people generally act as a herd and follow what most other people do or say, the power of AI to reduce the volatility of humans and their markets may be compelling to businesses that are NOT looking to disrupt existing behaviour patterns.

Ultimately AI works off the surveillance of people and ideas. Its key is mass observation of human and machine behaviour on a continual basis. The notion that we are all being constantly surveilled is understandably repugnant to a large swath of society, which was reared on the notion that their privacy and individuality is sacrosanct. Unfortunately, like it or not, privacy is largely an illusion today. Virtually everything anyone does is tracked and recorded for the computers that then add their behaviour to the vast stew of AI databases. The younger generation's acceptance of and fascination with social media systems, fuelled and funded through mass surveillance, indicate to us that humans seem willing to make the trade-off of their privacy for some economic advantage. Unions are already raising concerns about how AI could help bosses keep close watch on their employees, even outside their jobs (Tracy, 2023).

For better or worse, AI is just in its infancy. There are already experiments to see how it can be enhanced with human brain cells (Blain, 2023). It is also not simply one thing. AI comprises a wide range of technologies and use cases. From the large language and generative AI models like ChatGPT, Google Gemini and Dall-E, they are the equivalent of the first automobiles: fun to play with, somewhat unreliable and maybe a little dangerous. But over time, the lesson for companies, notes Rich Karlgaard (2023, para. 4), will be clear: *Who Learns Fastest, Wins.*

4.2 Section Two: The Digital Legacy

To assess the potential impact of AI, we first need to see this as an extension of current digital technology. Essentially AI amplifies the net; its key ingredient is mass observation of human and machine behaviour on a continual basis. Analysts like The Brookings Institution predict a huge productivity "boom" from AI (Baily, Brynjolfsson, & Korinek, 2023). But over the past 15 years, the Internet, as economist Robert Gordon (2016) has demonstrated, has had little overall effect on productivity, which continues to lag, or on economic growth while increasing inequality (Pan, 2023). On the upside, if you consider this a positive, AI could make military technology even more effective and lethal, as we are seeing in the use of AI drones in the Ukrainian conflict (Kinder, 2023; Robb, 2023).

Tech enthusiasts see the development of AI as the road to a "golden age", and a way to "save the world". But much the same was said at the beginning of the digital revolution (Andreessen, 2023; Henderson, 2023; Pethokoukis, 2023a, 2023b). In reality, although a major and potential force, AI simply amplifies digitalisation. It focuses on speeding up data collection, analysis and forecasting by orders of magnitude. Its impact cannot be separated from the already existing patterns tied to digitalisation.

Like earlier digital technology, AI has the potential to provide potential improvements in education, medicine and even helping to maintain infrastructure (Funt, 2023; Kessler, 2023a; Mims, 2023b). Some suggest that, as in previous technological shifts, more jobs ultimately will be created than destroyed (Kessler, 2023b). Profits certainly could be boosted by enabling such things as "Ship-then-Shop", being able to predict what a consumer will want to purchase and proactively ship it to them before they order it, relying on inexpensive reverse logistics to handle any errors. There are also zero-cost, targeted stimuli (creative content) – using AI to create pictures, words, music, videos and other content solely through AI, without humans. In AI even intimacy can be replicated, creating a sense of empathy and understanding of a customer's needs, through intelligent chatbots, that consumers believe are genuine, creating customer loyalty (Clement, 2022).

But along with these promising aspects of digitalisation we also see the impact of social media, and its many effects, often negative. Social media, notes author Cathy O'Neil (2016), epitomises what she labels "Weapons of Math Destruction", algorithms that remain obscure "secret sauce", designed to lure customers, distract them and ultimately alienate them from the very need for genuine human interaction with people from different classes and backgrounds. Social media has also been closely tied to rises in personal anxiety, particularly among young women (Twenge, 2023).

These will simply grow with AI. This includes, among younger people, ever shrinking intention spans and a growing intolerance for free speech and democracy itself (Pethokoukis, 2023b). AI also seems likely to expand the current zaibatuisation of America's economy, the rise of huge, intrusive and rapacious corporations that resemble the great Japanese conglomerates of the pre-World War II era. Traditionally capitalism has done better when there are many competing players; in the last century, measures were taken to slow and even reverse over-concentration.

Even in its early days, the noted French analyst Alain Touraine (1971, p. 175) a half century ago, saw the rise of a "post-industrial" society as pushing decision-making either to the state or "massive national and international groups". The digital revolution has revived concentration, as the largest emerging corporate interests – Meta, Google, Apple, Microsoft, Amazon, Tencent, Baidu, Alibaba – and a handful of large financial institutions gained unprecedented control over the economy. By 2020, six tech firms, including Tesla, accounted for half the value of the Nasdaq 100, while the five largest tech companies had total revenue amounting to half of those of all US state governments combined (Levy, 2022; Littlejohn, 2021).

AI fits into this current zaibatsu pattern. They have extended their influence to virtually every key field: operating systems, social media, search, and the cloud. For example, Google and Apple account for nearly 90% of all mobile browsers worldwide, while Microsoft by itself controls 90% of all operating system software. Three tech firms now account for two-thirds of all online advertising revenues, which comprise the vast majority of all ad sales (Adgate, 2021; Schechner & Woo, 2021; Statista, 2023).

Small businesses are now waiting to be gutted. Amazon secretly mined sales data from independent sellers who were using the company's e-commerce platform in order to guide Amazon's development of cheaper knock-off products (Mattioli, 2020). The company also plans with Amazon One to create a biometric password that would essentially control all digital actions from purchases to healthcare (Mims, 2023a; Paul, Maglaras, Ferrag, & Almomani, 2023). Google has been fined billions of dollars for giving preferential treatment to its own shopping service on its search site and has been accused by one of its few competitors, the much smaller DuckDuckGo, of manipulating browser extensions to drive customers from rival products (Fortune, 2023a). Apple continues to place strict limits on who can join its App Store and how developers can receive money from apps (Fortune, 2023b; Leswing, 2021). AI seems likely to bolster this pattern of consolidation. Amazon, Microsoft and Google already dominate the cloud and are now seeking control of underwater cables; in the past decade the large tech giants have boosted their share of undersea cable traffic from less than 10% to roughly two-thirds (Mims, 2022; Richter, 2023). They are also positioned to dominate AI, with firms like Amazon making mega-investments in AI firms (Dickens, 2023; Dotan & Seetharaman, 2023). In 2022 much of the US$42 billion invested into AI firms came from Apple, Microsoft and Alphabet, the parent of Google, which invested US$2 billion. It is largely a big game with enormous costs that only the best financed firms can play (Grant & Weise, 2023; Hodgson, 2023).

AI provides a means by which the mega-zaibatsu grow ever larger. Google, for example, plans to use AI to expand its medical programme (Kruppa & Subbaraman, 2023). The demand for AI products has led non-tech firms, like KMPG, to seek out multibillion tie-ups with Microsoft (Butler, 2023). The very logic behind AI, its reliance on past records and databases, is not ideal for start-ups; its "primary value", notes venture capitalist Martin Casado (2023, para. 2), is "to improve existing operations for incumbents that have the resources to invest at the required levels".

This represents a distinct break from the early phases of Silicon Valley. That phase was shaped in large part by often oddball enthusiasts eager to build new products that challenged the existing corporate hierarchy. In the early days of the tech revolution, some imagined an almost utopian, communitarian society on the horizon. The California author Stewart Brand, writing in *Rolling Stone* in 1972, predicted that when computers became widely available, we would all become "computer bums, all more empowered as individuals and as co-operators". It would be a new era of enhanced "spontaneous creation and of human interaction" (Brand, 1972, para. 168). The "early digital idealists", notes technology analyst Jaron Lanier (2013, p. xii), envisioned a "sharing" web that functioned "free from the constraints of the commercial order".

Instead, a technocratic economy is engendering a new kind of hierarchy, favouring highly skilled technicians and engineers. Their dominance will grow as technology plays an ever-greater role in the economy, while the value of labour further declines. Americans, long enamoured of the entrepreneurial spirit and technological progress, have been slow to see the tech oligarchy as a threat (Oremus, 2018; Smith, 2018). Leftist historians, alert to the dangers of aristocracy, have tended to focus their ire on financial companies that may be large and powerful but are not nearly as wealthy or as influential in shaping the economy as the tech sector, which seeks to capture virtually every other industry, including finance (Streeck, 2016).

This seems to be the inexorable pattern of the tech industry. The Internet initially spawned companies that competed against the giants; in contrast, the new AI firms seem more likely to become satrapies of the current hierarchy, and like hierarchies in general, they have become oppressive towards competitors and far less creative than they once were. The progress towards AI is largely orchestrated from the top of the corporate food chain (Grant & Weise, 2023).

AI also could expand the power of these firms, as well as government, to expand online surveillance. This includes recent efforts by Zoom to feed discussions on that medium to their own AI system (Field, 2023). Already, like it or not, privacy is largely an illusion today, as suits against Google have demonstrated (Fortis, 2023). Virtually everything anyone does is tracked and recorded for the computers, now providing ever more specific fodder for AI databases. The younger generation's acceptance of and fascination with social media systems, which are fuelled and funded through mass surveillance, indicate to us that humans sadly seem willing to make the trade-off of their privacy for some economic or personal advantage. AI is likely to worsen all these trends (Anderson & Rainie, 2023).

4.3 Section Three: The Future of Work

Eighty-two per cent of millennials fear AI will reduce their compensation, and they are right to be worried (Garfinkle, 2023). "We may be at the peak of the need for knowledge workers", Atif Rafiq, a former chief digital officer at McDonald's and Volvo, told the *Wall Street Journal* (Cutter & Torry, 2023, para. 3). "We just need fewer people to do the same thing" (Cutter & Torry, 2023, para. 3). Tech firms like Meta and Lyft have announced major cutbacks in their white-collar workforce and have warned that these positions are unlikely ever to return. IBM has put its staff hiring on hold while assessing how many of these mid-level jobs can be replaced by AI (Ford, 2023). Similarly, recent studies show that within months of AI's emergence, freelance work in software declined markedly, along with pay. Researchers showed that within a few months of the launch of ChatGPT, copywriters and graphic designers on major online freelancing platforms saw a significant drop in the number of jobs they got and even steeper declines in earnings. This suggested not only that generative AI was taking their work, but also that it devalues the work they do still carry out (Burn-Murdoch, 2023).

So how will AI affect employment? Who will have jobs? Who will lose them? Big tech and venture capital executives like Reid Hoffman promise that

AI will serve to the cause of "elevating humanity", while wiping out potentially hundreds of millions of jobs worldwide. Indeed, according to McKinsey, at least 12 million Americans will be forced to find new work by 2030. Two-thirds of business leaders, in a recent survey, suggest ChatGPT will lead to large layoffs of white-collar workers over the next five years (Cutter & Torry, 2023; Ellingrud et al., 2023; Hatzius, Briggs, Kodnani, & Pierdomenico, 2023; Strauss, 2023).

Yet some enthusiasts suggest that AI, as occurred in the past, will end up creating many more jobs than it sacrifices (Kessler, 2023b). However, the approach that makes the most intuitive sense to us is the one promulgated by Kai-Fu Lee, former Google Asia and Microsoft China head, who runs Sinovation Ventures, one of the world's most prolific AI venture funds. Lee created a two-dimensional view of future jobs in his bestselling book *AI Superpowers: China, Silicon Valley and the New World Order*. His key thesis is that the social nature of a job and the discretionary nature of a job will be the key factors underlying AI's impact. If a job is highly formulaic by nature, where there is little room for discretionary decision-making, AI is likely to displace it (Lee, 2018). Likewise, if a job requires no element of human interaction, AI is also likely to replace the human currently doing it.

Fears of an AI robotic takeover were first advanced in 1921 in *R.U.R.*, a play by Czech playwright Karel Capek that birthed the very word "robot". The notion of a potential robotic takeover, powered by AI, has been a theme in the writing of Isaac Asimov and, of course, the Terminator series (Mookerjee, 2016; Robotnik, 2021). Robots have been replacing industrial workers for over 70 years and has become imperative in countries like Germany where the workforce is aging rapidly (Martinez, 2023).

But eventually robot workers may be able to do more than weld car parts or drill holes. Tech firms are looking to develop what one developer calls "something like your personal AI" (Tong & Dastin, 2023, para. 3); others are developing new robotic nannies (Suskind, 2023). AI eventually could even reduce demand for "the world's oldest profession" by removing the need for human sex workers. Even sex – notably through robots – could be outsourced by perfectly compliant, and enhanced, AI-powered machines. As author Glenn Reynolds (2023a, para. 5) suggests:

> Imagine sexbots – both male and female – that are aren't just copies of attractive humans, but much more attractive than natural humans. Machine learning could find just the right physical and behavioral characteristics to appeal to humans, and then tweak them for each individual person. Maybe they even release pheromones. Your personal sexbot would be tailor-made, or self-tailored, to appeal to you. It might even be programmed to fall in love with its human. (Would it be "real" love? How could you tell? How could it tell? If you couldn't tell, would it matter?).

Well before these intimate robots emerge, whole job categories seem likely to decline. Take the mundane job of automobile insurance adjusters. These are very procedural, rules-driven jobs with little discretion. In addition, they require almost no human interaction. Jobs like these are likely the first and easiest to be eliminated by AI. Many in the service sector have been long dominated by women, including executive assistants, cashiers, bank employees and office managers (Birkner, 2023; Chen, 2023; Shine & Whiting, 2023; Tong & Dastin, 2023). Warehouse workers will be among the most prominent losers. This also extends to people taking digital orders; Walmart expects to automate its systems with new software and lay off 2000 workers by 2026 (Cavale, 2023; Nassauer & Cole, 2023).

Overall, AI threatens to undermine much of both middle- and working-class employment in the years ahead, as big firms, allied with the emerging AI sector, begin to implement the technology. In contrast to the past, this will not impact largely blue-collar workers. Some jobs have high levels of interaction with humans but are becoming increasingly procedural and formulaic. Take as an example a radiologist. Finding cancer is becoming a highly automated process. However, telling patients that they have cancer, and helping them, prepare themselves for therapy (or worse) is a highly interactive, human-intensive activity. Jobs like these require what Lee (2018, p. 156) calls a "human veneer". AI may replace a large portion of the job, or create new specialties within professions, but will not totally replace them.

Ironically many of the new victims created by AI will be within tech professions themselves. Automation of information could prove lethal to "coders" and "symbolic analysts" while people who do jobs maintaining and operating machinery could have a surprisingly bright future. Already new AI programs are allowing software firms to do without lower-level programmers, particularly new hires (Sherman, 2023; Singh, 2019).

"It's the end of the white-collar knowledge work", inventor and AI entrepreneur Rony Abovitz suggests (R. Abovitz, personal communication, August 2, 2023). One study predicts this may particularly affect positions like office assistants, sales executives, HR managers and accountants. Even many "geeks" who write software code may find out that they too are vulnerable to what economists refer to as "skills-based technological change". On the other hand, those few gifted enough to write AI programmes will be highly compensated, at least until the machines figure out how to replace them (Bote, 2023).

Even many "creative jobs" – actors, writers, journalists – could be threatened. Actors and writers could find their identities and creations copied or simply used in derivative products, particularly as AI relies on past work to develop its products (Dugar & Jaiswal, 2023; Foroohar, 2023; Seetharaman & Hagey, 2023). There have emerged concerns, both in the United States and in the United Kingdom, that AI could undermine creative workers, by essentially taking their output and adjusting it in ways that may be free from copyright infringement (Thomas, 2023; Toonkel & Krouse, 2023).

In Southern California especially, it is not just the accountants and rote factory workers but the actors and writers in Hollywood, who feel they are threatened by

AI (Anderson, 2023; Chmielewski & Richwine, 2023; Roberts, 2023). After all, as entertainment becomes more digitalised, being an actual human means less, as is evident by the popularity of video games and movies derived from them. You do not need a Shakespeare to write the next Marvel movie or, for that matter, many news stories (Barrabi, 2023; Roberts, 2023).

During the 2023 Writers Guild of America strike in Hollywood, there was much concern about how AI would turn computers into "plagiarism machines" (Chmielewski & Richwine, 2023, para. 21). How long before the AI programme ascends from doing box scores and stock quotes to directing opinion on the issues of the day. As Clayton Christensen noted, innovation often enters a field at the bottom and gradually works its way up (Bower & Christensen, 1995; Larson, 2016; Reynolds, 2023b).

Already there are AI-generated influencers, such as Milla Sofia, who have gained 100,000 followers on Tik-Tok. Doubtless much of "her" audience thinks she is real or does not care if she is not (Mather, 2023). This presents a dark fantasy for budding flesh and blood celebrities. Geoffrey Hinton, one of the early developers of AI and former Google executive, quit in large part because of AI's capacity to create convincing false images and texts, creating a world where people will "not be able to know what is true anymore" (AFP, 2023; Narayan, 2023, para. 3).

So, who survives the AI onslaught? Certainly a few elite AI engineers could experience a windfall, at least in the near future (Liu, 2023). But the surprising winners could prove to be skilled blue-collar workers, people who engage in hands-on physical jobs like mechanics or oil riggers (Weber & Ellis, 2023). Even in building the next generation of chip plants, for instance in Ohio, Intel is experiencing at its giant new semiconductor facility being built in, not a shortage of hotshot engineers but a dearth of skilled technicians – pipe fitters, machinists, maintenance workers – needed to keep the factory construction moving (Donnan, 2023).

At the very least, the AI revolution should inspire some new thinking about careers. AI is likely to make life harder for a large portion of the "creative class", as they, like people in more ordinary tech and service jobs, find their skills duplicated by new AI, and stuck with increasingly meaningless academic credentials. Rony Abovitz suggests the big winner in the coming years will be the "sophisticated, technically capable blue-collar worker", particularly those who possess the physical skills robots cannot likely duplicate in the next decade (R. Abovitz, personal communication, August 2, 2023). Young people might do well to forget Joe Biden's famous advice to "learn to code" (Kelley, 2019, para. 1). Goodbye to "my son the radiologist" or computer geek, and hello to "my son, the plumber".

4.4 Section Four: Democracy, AI, and the Global Future

One of the great disappointments of the digital era has been the impact on the political economy in the West. Initially the tech revolution was largely seen as an enhancement of the individual and entrepreneurship, but the trend towards consolidation of power in ever fewer hands has continued unabated. AI could further accelerate this feudalisation of our society as the tech oligarchy moves aggressively to dominate the new technology (Grant & Weise, 2023). The Internet has brought convenience and other blessings, but greater equality or prosperity is not one of them (Tett, 2023).

AI threatens to accentuate these divides. Companies like Google, Meta, Microsoft, Tencent, Baidu and Amazon all seem destined to dominate the emerging industry. Open AI, for example, one of the cutting-edge firms in the field, was largely financed by Microsoft, long the tech oligopoly par excellence (Kahn, 2023). Google and Amazon committed US$7 billion to the start-up Anthropic while Microsoft has invested US$13 billion, for roughly half ownership of Open AI, founded by Sam Altman, the AI world's leading guru (Jin & Hagey, 2023; Jin & Kruppa, 2023).

If AI is to expand the dominion of the major tech platforms, perhaps adding one of two players and perhaps eliminating some others, it will simply accelerate the movement of power away from society, or even the free market, to place more power in the hands of ever fewer people. As AI wipes out many middle- and working-class jobs, the only efficient means to prevent social breakdown may be to expand the welfare state, not only to cover those who have historically dependent upon it, but also the majority of people who may now be utterly dependent on the munificence of the even more powerful situation digital elite.

AI raises the prospects of a new class structure where a large portion of the population has been rendered economically redundant. Yuval Noah Harari (2016) sees instead a future where "a small and privileged elite of upgraded humans" gain control of society and use genetic engineering to cement the superior status of their offspring. Their aim will be not to follow God's laws but to become gods themselves, by a kind of directed and accelerated evolution:

> *Bioengineering is not going to wait patiently for natural selection to work its magic. Instead, bioengineers will take the old Sapiens body, and intentionally rewrite its genetic code, rewire its brain circuits, alter its biochemical balance, and even grow entirely new limbs. They will thereby create new godlings, who might be different from us Sapiens as we are different from Homo erectus.*
>
> *(Harari, 2016, p. 50)*

Gregory Ferenstein (2017, para. 4), after interviewing 147 digital company founders, concludes that most believe that an "increasingly greater share of economic wealth will be generated by a smaller slice of very talented or original people. Everyone else will come to subsist on some combination of part-time entrepreneurial 'gig work' and government aid". This is reflected in support for a universal basic income by many tech oligarchs – Mark Zuckerberg, Elon Musk, Travis Kalanick (former head of Uber) and AI guru Sam Altman (CEO of Open AI) (Altman, 2016; Caughill, 2017; Haselton, 2017; Holt, 2016; Weller, 2017). Their vision may still promise "abundance", but little work for most (Higgins, 2023).

Of course, even potted plants, with at least a semblance of self-regard, could demand a better deal. Some envision a future where tech and Wall Street wealth is confiscated to fund "fully automated luxury communism" – a leisure society paid for by Apple and its counterparts (Merchant, 2015). Already, roughly half of all Americans support the idea of a guaranteed basic income of about US$2,000 a month if robots put them out of work (Clifford, 2016). Japanese Marxist philosopher Kohei Saito sees re-distribution as a way to as achieve the green goals of "de-growth" and "net zero" without devastating the masses (Goodfellow, 2023, para. 5; Saito, 2022, p. 128).

A universal basic income enjoys strong support in most European countries, particularly among younger people (Fitzgerald, 2017). The universal basic income, suggests Scott Santens, a prominent advocate for the concept, provides a social "vaccine" for the twenty-first century (Santens, 2020, 2024).

Ultimately society will have to make a choice. We could follow the Roman model where slavery, rather than robots, replaced plebeian citizens, turning them into servile consumers of "bread and circuses". Or we can honour work first and foremost perhaps by focusing on practical skills, as opposed to often meaningless academic credentials, that could be useful in an AI-dominated era, lowering taxes on those with modest incomes and providing support for working parents in terms of day care (Jacobs, 2023; Milligan & Camera, 2023; Terry, 2023).

4.5 Section Five: Confronting the Realty of AI

The warnings about AI from its own creators and promoters certainly give pause to the more exuberant claims of some venture capitalists. The rise of artificial general intelligence, or AGI, poses a direct threat, in large part because it seeks to replace ways of enhancing intelligence within humans for the odd comfort of letting machines – mainly controlled by a handful of companies – to the work instead. Notes author Evgeny Morozov: The real risks of AGI are political and will not be fixed by taming rebellious robots. The safest of AGIs would not deliver the progressive panacea promised by its lobby. And in presenting its emergence as all but inevitable, AGI-ism distracts from finding better ways to augment intelligence (Morozov, 2023).

Under the current conditions, Morozov argues, we do not get a more democratic or liberal society, but one defined increasingly by small numbers of powerful firms. In this sense, AI is not so much about technology, but how our society will be transformed with its inevitable adoption. There is much demand among the political class and their allies to control AI but if these discourage Western developers, the likely impact will be to allow Asian countries, notably China, and autocratic regimes like Saudi Arabia to lead in creating an AI environment that, among other things, will be optimised to control society and thought (Murgia, England, Liu, Olcott, & Al-Atrush, 2023). Chinese dominance of AI, warns a recent Brookings Institution study, would allow it to rule the world by 2100 (Gill, 2020).

Despite this, some AI advocates favour collaborating with China, despite the clear risks (Zheng, 2023). Some westerners feel that China's authoritarian structures will keep their technology behind, although this seems a bit overblown and perhaps a trifle arrogant (Gao, 2023). China's AI firms, with strong backing from the government, are already finding ways around sanctions (Hao & Huang, 2023). The Middle Kingdom is not standing still or waiting for Western Godots. Today China does have a lead in some areas, notably surveillance, and in new media algorithms (Weed, 2022).

Clearly, as AI increases the power of companies, it seems prudent to look for ways to protect the rights and autonomy of individuals. Jaron Lanier (2013, p. 20) has suggested that in a "world of digital dignity", people would be able to be "the commercial owner of their own data". According to AI pioneer Fei-Fei Li, it lies in how much large corporations will determine the technology; she favours a bigger role for government, universities and non-profits (Bobrow, 2023). Given the history of governments, including the United States, using technology to control populations, this might not be ultimately beneficial. But she rightly suggests the priority of finding ways to use technology to improve society, not just lift a small portion of the population to unimagined heights.

Yet no matter what governments try to decree, AI, even if free in one country, will shape our future, forcing us, as Tyler Cowen (2023, para. 27) suggests, to live in moving history. We have little choice but to look at the best ways to employ this technology:

> *What kind of civilization is it that turns away from the challenge of dealing with more intelligence … that has not the self-confidence to confidently confront a big dose of more intelligence? Dare I wonder if such societies might not perish under the current watch, with or without AI.*

The time to consider how to adjust to AI is now. Currently it is far from being totally effective, and its lack of original thought and reliance on existing data greatly limits its impact; some accuse it of being fundamentally boring (Beutler, 2023; Franzen, 2023; Goldman, 2023; Harrison, 2023). Yet the dangers of an ever-improving AI are clear enough to force many in Washington, Brussels and elsewhere to look for ways to limit its impact (Bose, 2023; Portman & Mulopulos, 2023). This particularly applies to the notion of the "singularity", which some tech advocates see as a new ideal, blending humans and machines (Isaacson, 2023).

Whatever is done administratively, it seems certain that AI will come to dominate much of our economic and even personal lives. A critical question suggests we already see that there is a discordance between technological and human progress. Notes Sohrab Ahmari (2023, para. 22):

> *Advancement and decay. AI and the opioid holocaust. Machine learning and crumbling bungalows. The internet of things and terrible infrastructure.*

Smartphones and the scattershot, permanently distracted mind of the American child.

In the long run it may matter if AI comes from America's Google or if China's Tencent will matter, but perhaps not profoundly. The substitution of machines for people will continue, and spread into ever more fields, no matter what regulations are passed. The question may be how much we wish to rely on human creativity, empathy and personal expression in a machine-driven age. In this sense, it is not AI that is the big threat to the human future, but how we consciously choose to integrate it into our lives.

References

Adgate, B. (2021). Agencies Agree; 2021 Was a Record Year for Ad Spending, with More Growth Expected in 2022. Retrieved March 6, 2025, from Forbes website: www.forbes.com/sites/bradadgate/2021/12/08/agencies-agree-2021-was-a-record-year-for-ad-spending-with-more-growth-expected-in-2022

AFP. (2023). "Godfather of AI" Issues New Warnings Over Potential Risks to Society. Retrieved March 6, 2025, from ScienceAlert website: www.sciencealert.com/godfather-of-ai-issues-new-warnings-over-potential-risks-to-society

Ahmari, S. (2023). Do Androids Dream of Terrible Streets? Retrieved March 6, 2025, from Compact Magazine website: https://compactmag.com/article/do-androids-dream-of-terrible-streets

Altman, S. (2016). Moving Forward on Basic Income. Retrieved March 6, 2025, from Y Combinator website: www.ycombinator.com/blog/moving-forward-on-basic-income

Anderson, J., & Rainie, L. (2023). As AI Spreads, Experts Predict the Best and Worst Changes in Digital Life by 2035. Retrieved March 6, 2025, from Pew Research Center website: www.pewresearch.org/internet/2023/06/21/as-ai-spreads-experts-predict-the-best-and-worst-changes-in-digital-life-by-2035

Anderson, R. (2023). Why is Sarah Silverman Suing Artificial Intelligence? Retrieved March 6, 2025, from The Spectator website: https://thespectator.com/topic/lawmen-enter-chatgpt-ai-sarah-silverman-suing

Andreessen, M. (2023). AI Will Save the World. Retrieved March 6, 2025, from The Free Press website: www.thefp.com/p/why-ai-will-save-the-world

Baily, M. N., Brynjolfsson, E., & Korinek, A. (2023). Machines of Mind: The Case for an AI-powered Productivity Boom. Retrieved March 6, 2025, from Brookings website: www.brookings.edu/research/machines-of-mind-the-case-for-an-ai-powered-productivity-boom

Bakar, A. (2024). How Much Faster Is AI Compared to Humans? The Truth May Surprise You. Retrieved March 6, 2025, from AI VYX website: https://aivyx.com/how-much-faster-is-ai-compared-to-humans

Barrabi, T. (2023). BuzzFeed Stock Surges on Plan to Use ChatGPT Parent OpenAI For Content. Retrieved March 6, 2025, from New York Post website: https://nypost.com/2023/01/27/buzzfeed-stock-surges-on-plan-to-use-chatgpt-parent-openai-to-create-online-content

Beutler, W. (2023). AI's Real Pronlem Is That It's Boring. Retrieved March 6, 2025, from The Hill website: https://thehill.com/opinion/technology/4146423-ais-real-problem-is-that-its-boring

Birkner, C. (2023). AI-Threatened jobs Are Held Mostly by Women: Study. Retrieved March 6, 2025, from Tech Daily News website: www.mcknightsseniorliving.com/news/ai-threatened-jobs-are-held-mostly-by-women-study

Blain, L. (2023). Computer Chip With Built-In Human Brain Tissue Gets Military Funding. Retrieved March 6, 2025, from New Atlas website: https://newatlas.com/computers/human-brain-chip-ai

Bobrow, E. (2023). A Tech Pioneer Focused on Making AI a Force for Good. Retrieved March 6, 2025, from The Wall Street Journal website: www.wsj.com/tech/ai/a-tech-pioneer-focused-on-making-ai-a-force-for-good-d60f8f10

Bose, N. (2023). White House Takes New Steps to Study AI Risks, Determine Impact on Workers. Retrieved March 6, 2025, from Yahoo Finance website: https://finance.yahoo.com/news/white-house-takes-steps-study-183254577.html

Bote, J. (2023). Engineers for Meta's Troubled Metaverse Reportedly Paid 'Mind-Boggling' Sums. Retrieved March 6, 2025, from SFGate website: www.sfgate.com/tech/article/metaverse-engineers-mind-boggling-pay-17885279.php

Bower, J. L., & Christensen, C. M. (1995). *Disruptive Technologies: Catching the Wave*. Brighton, MA: Harvard Business School Publishing.

Brand, S. (1972). Spacewar. Retrieved March 6, 2025, from Rolling Stone website: www.wheels.org/spacewar/stone/rolling_stone.html

Burn-Murdoch, J. (2023). Here's What We Know About Generative AI's Impact on White-Collar Work. Retrieved March 6, 2025, from Financial Times website: www.ft.com/content/b2928076-5c52-43e9-8872-08fda2aa2fcf

Butler, G. (2023). KPMG to Invest $2bn in AI and Cloud Services with Microsoft. Retrieved March 6, 2025, from DatacenterDynamics website: www.datacenterdynamics.com/en/news/kpmg-to-invest-2bn-in-ai-and-cloud-services-with-microsoft

Casado, M. (2023). AI Has Finally Become Transformative. Retrieved March 6, 2025, from Wall Street Journal website: www.wsj.com/articles/ai-has-finally-become-transformative-humans-scale-language-model-6a67e641

Caughill, P. (2017). Another Silicon Valley Exec Joins the Ranks of Universal Basic Income Supporters. Retrieved March 6, 2025, from Futurism website: https://futurism.com/another-silicon-valley-exec-joins-the-ranks-of-universal-basic-income-supporters

Cavale, S. (2023). Walmart Aims for 65% of Stores to be Automation Serviced by 2026. Retrieved March 6, 2025, from Yahoo Finance website: https://finance.yahoo.com/news/walmart-says-65-stores-serviced-211828454.html

Chen, B. X. (2023). How ChatGPT and Bard Performed as My Executive Assistants. Retrieved March 6, 2025, from The New York Times website: www.nytimes.com/2023/03/29/technology/personaltech/ai-chatgpt-google-bard-assistant.html

Chmielewski, D., & Richwine, L. (2023). "Plagiarism Machines": Hollywood Writers and Studios Battle Over the Future of AI. Retrieved March 6, 2025, from Reuters website: www.reuters.com/technology/plagiarism-machines-hollywood-writers-studios-battle-over-future-ai-2023-05-03

Chui, M., Hazan, E., Roberts, R., Singla, A., Smaje, K., Sukharevsky, A., … Zemmel, R. (2023). The Economic Potential of Generative AI: The Next Productivity Frontier. Retrieved March 6, 2025, from McKinsey Digital website: www.mckinsey.com/capabilities/mckinsey-digital/our-insights/the-economic-potential-of-generative-ai-the-next-productivity-frontier

Clement, M. (2022). How to Use AI to Enhance Customer Loyalty For Faster Business Growth. Retrieved March 6, 2025, from Stefanini Group website: https://stefanini.com/en/insights/articles/how-to-use-ai-enhance-customer-loyalty-for-faster-business-growt

Clifford, C. (2016). About Half of Americans Support Giving Residents up to $2000 a Month When Robots Take Their Jobs. Retrieved March 6, 2025, from CNBC website: www.cnbc.com/2016/12/19/about-half-of-americans-support-giving-residents-up-to-2000-a-month-when-robots-take-our-jobs.html

Cowen, T. (2023). There Is No Turning Back on AI. Retrieved March 6, 2025, from The Free Press website: www.thefp.com/p/there-is-no-turning-back-on-ai

Cutter, C., & Torry, H. (2023). The Disappearing White-Collar Job. Retrieved March 6, 2025, from The Wall Street Journal website: www.wsj.com/articles/the-disappearing-white-collar-job-af0bd925

Dickens, S. (2023). Amazon Invests $4 Billion in Anthropic: A Paradigm Shift in AI. Retrieved March 6, 2025, from Forbes website: www.forbes.com/sites/stevendickens/2023/09/26/amazon-invests-4-billion-in-anthropic-a-paradigm-shift-in-ai

Donnan, S. (2023). America's $52 Billion Plan to Make Chips at Home Faces a Labor Shortage. Retrieved March 6, 2025, from Bloomberg website: www.bloomberg.com/news/features/2023-03-09/worker-shortages-are-hurdle-for-52-billion-us-plan-to-boost-chip-manufacturing

Dotan, T., & Seetharaman, D. (2023). Big Tech Struggles to Turn AI Hype Into Profits. Retrieved March 6, 2025, from The Wall Street Journal website: www.wsj.com/tech/ai/ais-costly-buildup-could-make-early-products-a-hard-sell-bdd29b9f

Dugar, U., & Jaiswal, R. (2023). Google Explores AI Tools For Journalists, in Talks with Publishers. Retrieved March 6, 2025, from Reuters website: www.reuters.com/technology/google-explores-ai-tools-journalists-talks-with-publishers-spokesperson-2023-07-20

Edwards, B. (2023). Poll: AI Poses Risk to Humanity, According to Majority of Americans. Retrieved March 6, 2025, from Ars Technica website: https://arstechnica.com/information-technology/2023/05/poll-61-of-americans-say-ai-threatens-humanitys-future

Ellingrud, K., Sanghvi, S., Singh, G. D., Madgavkar, A., Chui, M., White, O., & Hasebe, P. (2023). Generative AI and the Future of Work in America. Retrieved March 6, 2025, from McKinsey & Company website: www.mckinsey.com/mgi/our-research/generative-ai-and-the-future-of-work-in-america

Ferenstein, G. (2017). The Disrupters. Retrieved March 6, 2025, from City Journal website: www.city-journal.org/article/the-disrupters

Field, H. (2023). Zoom Can Now Rrain Its A.I. Using Some Customer Data, According to Updated Terms. Retrieved March 6, 2025, from CNBC website: www.cnbc.com/2023/08/07/zoom-ai-tools-trained-using-some-customer-data.html

Fitzgerald, R. (2017). Survey Reveals Young People More Likely To Support Universal Basic Income, but It's Not a Left-Right Thing. Retrieved March 6, 2025, from The Conversation website: https://theconversation.com/survey-reveals-young-people-more-likely-to-support-universal-basic-income-but-its-not-a-left-right-thing-87554

Ford, B. (2023). IBM to Pause Hiring for Jobs That AI Could Do. Retrieved March 6, 2025, from Bloomberg website: www.bloomberg.com/news/articles/2023-05-01/ibm-to-pause-hiring-for-back-office-jobs-that-ai-could-kill

Foroohar, R. (2023). Hollywood's Fight Is Your Fight. Retrieved March 6, 2025, from Financial Times website: www.ft.com/content/304be2e4-500e-4b97-b73c-f90ea4373572

Fortis, S. (2023). Google Hit With Lawsuit Over New AI Data-Scraping Privacy Policy. Retrieved March 6, 2025, from Cointelegraph website: https://cointelegraph.com/news/google-hit-with-lawsuit-over-ai-privacy-policy

Fortune. (2023a). Alphabet. Retrieved March 6, 2025, from https://fortune.com/company/alphabet

Fortune. (2023b). Apple. Retrieved March 6, 2025, from https://fortune.com/company/apple

Franzen, C. (2023). The AI Feedback Loop: Researchers Warn of 'Model aCollapse' As AI Trains on AI-Generated Content. Retrieved March 6, 2025, from VentureBeat website: https://venturebeat.com/ai/the-ai-feedback-loop-researchers-warn-of-model-collapse-as-ai-trains-on-ai-generated-content

Funt, P. (2023). The New Everyday Reality of Service Robots. Retrieved March 6, 2025, from The Wall Street Journal website: www.wsj.com/articles/the-new-everyday-reality-of-service-robots-463b69a1

Gao, S. (2023). Why China Will Never Lead on Tech. Retrieved March 6, 2025, from Wall Street Journal website: www.wsj.com/articles/why-china-will-never-lead-on-tech-semiconductor-chip-communism-innovation-west-corruption-economy-technology-11675114520

Garfinkle, A. (2023). Eighty-Two Percent of Millennials Worry AI Will Threaten Their Pay, Survey Says. Retrieved March 6, 2025, from Yahoo Finance website: www.yahoo.com/finance/news/eighty-two-percent-of-millennials-worry-ai-will-threaten-their-pay-survey-says-143020771.html

Gill, I. (2020). Whoever Leads in Artificial Intelligence in 2030 Will Rule the World Until 2100. Retrieved March 6, 2025, from Brookings website: www.brookings.edu/articles/whoever-leads-in-artificial-intelligence-in-2030-will-rule-the-world-until-2100

Goldman, D. P. (2023). Why AI Can't Think. Retrieved March 6, 2025, from Law & Liberty website: https://lawliberty.org/why-ai-cant-think

Goodfellow, M. (2023). Interview: A Greener Marx? Kohei Saito on Connecting Communism with the Climate Crisis. Retrieved March 6, 2025, from The Guardian website: www.theguardian.com/environment/2023/feb/28/a-greener-marx-kohei-saito-on-connecting-communism-with-the-climate-crisis

Gordon, R. J. (2016). *The Rise and Fall of American Growth: The U.S. Standard of Living Since the Civil War*. Princeton, NJ: Princeton University Press.

Grant, N., & Weise, K. (2023). In A.I. Race, Microsoft and Google Choose Speed Over Caution. Retrieved March 6, 2025, from The New York Times website: www.nytimes.com/2023/04/07/technology/ai-chatbots-google-microsoft.html

Hao, K., & Huang, R. (2023). U.S. Sanctions Drive Chinese Firms to Advance AI Without Latest Chips. Retrieved March 6, 2025, from Wall Street Journal website: www.wsj.com/articles/u-s-sanctions-drive-chinese-firms-to-advance-ai-without-latest-chips-f6aed67f

Harari, Y. N. (2016). *Homo Deus: A Brief History of Tomorrow*. New York, NY: Vintage Books.

Harrison, M. (2023). When AI Is Trained on AI-Generated Data, Strange Things Start to Happen. Retrieved March 6, 2025, from Futurism website: https://futurism.com/ai-trained-ai-generated-data-interview

Haselton, T. (2017). Mark Zuckerberg Joins Silicon Valley Bigwigs in Calling for Government to Give Everybody Free Money. Retrieved March 6, 2025, from Yahoo Finance website: https://finance.yahoo.com/news/mark-zuckerberg-joins-silicon-valley-202800717.html

Hatzius, J., Briggs, J., Kodnani, D., & Pierdomenico, G. (2023). Large Effects of Artificial Intelligence on Economic Growth. Retrieved March 6, 2025, from Goldman Sachs: Global Economist Analyst website: www.gspublishing.com/content/research/en/reports/2023/03/27/d64e052b-0f6e-45d7-967b-d7be35fabd16.html

Henderson, R. (2023). The Cadre in the Code. Retrieved March 6, 2025, from City Journal website: www.city-journal.org/article/the-cadre-in-the-code

Higgins, T. (2023). What Elon Musk's 'Age of Abundance' Means for the Future of Capitalism. Retrieved March 6, 2025, from The Wall Street Journal website: www.wsj.com/tech/ai/what-elon-musks-age-of-abundance-means-for-the-future-of-capitalism-7c0807df

Hodgson, C. (2023). Tech Giants Pour Billions into Cloud Capacity in AI Push. Retrieved March 6, 2025, from www.ft.com/content/f01529ad-88ca-456e-ad41-d6b7d449a409

Holt, A. (2016). Universal Basic Income and the New Corporatist Democrats. Retrieved March 6, 2025, from New America website: www.newamerica.org/weekly/universal-basic-income-and-new-corporatist-democrats

Isaacson, W. (2023). Will AI Help Us or Leave Us Behind? Retrieved March 6, 2025, from The Wall Street Journal website: www.wsj.com/articles/will-ai-help-us-or-leave-us-behind-a1dfa5d3

Jacobs, J. (2023). Let AI Do It: High Schoolers Don't Need To Write Essays Any More. Retrieved March 6, 2025, from www.joannejacobs.com/post/let-ai-do-it-high-schoolers-don-t-need-to-write-essays-any-more

Jin, B., & Hagey, K. (2023). The Contradictions of Sam Altman, AI Crusade. Retrieved March 6, 2025, from The Wall Street Journal website: www.wsj.com/articles/chatgpt-sam-altman-artificial-intelligence-openai-b0e1c8c9

Jin, B., & Kruppa, M. (2023). Google Commits $2 Billion in Funding to AI Startup Anthropic. Retrieved March 6, 2025, from The Wall Street Journal website: www.wsj.com/tech/ai/google-commits-2-billion-in-funding-to-ai-startup-anthropic-db4d4c50

Kahn, J. (2023). The Inside Story of ChatGPT: How OpenAI Founder Sam Altman Built the World's Hottest Technology With Billions from Microsoft. Retrieved March 6, 2025, from Fortune website: https://fortune.com/longform/chatgpt-openai-sam-altman-microsoft

Karlgaard, R. (2023). Who Learns Fastest, Wins. Retrieved March 6, 2025, from Forbes website: www.forbes.com/sites/richkarlgaard/2023/07/06/who-learns-fastest-wins

Kelley, A. (2019). Biden Tells Coal Miners to "Learn to Code." Retrieved March 6, 2025, from The Hill website: https://thehill.com/changing-america/enrichment/education/476391-biden-tells-coal-miners-to-learn-to-code

Kessler, A. (2023a). AI's Education Revolution. Retrieved March 6, 2025, from The Wall Street Journal website: www.wsj.com/articles/ais-education-revolution-khan-academy-tutor-animation-schools-5aec9a5e

Kessler, A. (2023b). Ignore the Hysteria on AI and Jobs. Retrieved March 6, 2025, from The Wall Street Journal website: www.wsj.com/articles/ignore-the-hysteria-on-ai-and-jobs-chatgpt-automation-workforce-tech-innovation-51b3d994

Kinder, T. (2023). How Silicon Valley Is Helping the Pentagon in the AI Arms Race. Retrieved March 6, 2025, from Financial Times website: www.ft.com/content/2ed278cc-6c3f-4569-b73c-64ad378f3ea8

Kruppa, M., & Subbaraman, N. (2023). In Battle with Microsoft, Google Bets on Medical AI Program to Crack Healthcare Industry. Retrieved March 6, 2025, from Wall Street Journal website: www.wsj.com/articles/in-battle-with-microsoft-google-bets-on-medical-ai-program-to-crack-healthcare-industry-bb7c2db8

Lanier, J. (2013). *Who Owns the Future?* New York, NY: Simon & Schuster.

Larson, C. (2016). Disruptive Innovation Theory: What It Is & 4 Key Concepts. Retrieved March 6, 2025, from Harvard Business School: Business Insights website: https://online.hbs.edu/blog/post/4-keys-to-understanding-clayton-christensens-theory-of-disruptive-innovation

Lee, K.-F. (2018). *AI Superpowers: China, Silicon Valley and the New World Order.* New York, NY: Houghton Mifflin Harcourt.

Leswing, K. (2021). Apple Can No Longer Force Developers to Use In-App Purchasing, Judge Rules in Epic Games Case. Retrieved March 6, 2025, from CNBC website: www.cnbc.com/2021/09/10/epic-games-v-apple-judge-reaches-decision-.html

Levy, A. (2022). Six Tech Stocks Now Make Up Half the Value of the Nasdaq 100. Retrieved March 6, 2025, from CNBC website: www.cnbc.com/2020/07/22/these-six-tech-stocks-make-up-half-the-nasdaq-100s-value.html

Littlejohn, B. (2021). "Over-Mighty Subjects": Big Tech and the Logic of Feudalism. Retrieved March 6, 2025, from American Affairs website: https://americanaffairsjournal.org/2021/08/over-mighty-subjects-big-tech-and-the-logic-of-feudalism

Liu, J. (2023). U.S. Companies Are On a Hiring Spree for A.I. Jobs—and They Pay an Average of $146,000. Retrieved March 6, 2025, from CNBC website: www.cnbc.com/2023/07/13/us-companies-are-on-a-hiring-spree-for-ai-jobs-that-pay-an-average-of-146000.html

Martinez, M. (2023). As Baby Boomers Retire, German Businesses Turn to Robots. Retrieved March 6, 2025, from Reuters website: www.reuters.com/technology/baby-boomers-retire-german-businesses-turn-robots-2023-10-27

Mather, K. (2023). Social Media Is Fawning Over 19-Year-Old Influencer Milla Sofia — But She's Not Even Real. Retrieved March 6, 2025, from Yahoo Life website: www.yahoo.com/lifestyle/social-media-is-fawning-over-19-year-old-influencer-milla-sofia--but-shes-not-even-real-000349854.html

Mattioli, D. (2020). Amazon Scooped Up Data from Its Own Sellers to Launch Competing Products. Retrieved March 6, 2025, from The Wall Street Journal website: www.wsj.com/articles/amazon-scooped-up-data-from-its-own-sellers-to-launch-competing-products-11587650015

Merchant, B. (2015). Fully Automated Luxury Communism. Retrieved March 6, 2025, from The Guardian website: www.theguardian.com/sustainable-business/2015/mar/18/fully-automated-luxury-communism-robots-employment

Milligan, S., & Camera, L. (2023). Ditch the Degree? Many Employers Are Just Fine With That. Retrieved March 6, 2025, from U.S. News website: www.usnews.com/news/the-report/articles/2023-02-03/ditch-the-degree-many-employers-are-just-fine-with-that

Mims, C. (2022). Google, Amazon, Meta and Microsoft Weave a Fiber-Optic Web of Power. Retrieved March 6, 2025, from The Wall Street Journal website: www.wsj.com/articles/google-amazon-meta-and-microsoft-weave-a-fiber-optic-web-of-power-11642222824

Mims, C. (2023a). Amazon Wants You to Pay With Your Palm. It's a Sneak Attack on Apple and Google. Retrieved March 6, 2025, from The Wall Street Journal website: www.wsj.com/articles/amazon-wants-you-to-pay-with-your-palm-its-a-sneak-attack-on-apple-and-google-e8e417a

Mims, C. (2023b). America's Bridges, Factories and Highways Are in Dire Need of Repairs. Bring in the Robots. Retrieved March 6, 2025, from The Wall Street Journal website: www.wsj.com/tech/inspection-robots-infrastructure-ebb4172c

Mookerjee, A. (2016). Robots and Revolution. Retrieved March 6, 2025, from Red Wedge website: www.redwedgemagazine.com/online-issue/robots-revolution

Morozov, E. (2023). The True Threat of Artificial Intelligence. Retrieved March 6, 2025, from The New York Times website: www.nytimes.com/2023/06/30/opinion/artificial-intelligence-danger.html

Murgia, M., England, A., Liu, Q., Olcott, E., & Al-Atrush, S. (2023). Saudi Arabia and UAE Race to Buy Nvidia Chips to Power AI Ambitions. Retrieved March 6, 2025, from Financial Times website: www.ft.com/content/c93d2a76-16f3-4585-af61-86667c5090ba

Narayan, J. (2023). Google AI Pioneer Says He Quit to Speak Freely About Technology's "Dangers." Retrieved March 6, 2025, from Reuters website: www.reuters.com/technology/google-ai-pioneer-says-he-quit-speak-freely-about-technologys-dangers-2023-05-02

Nassauer, S., & Cole, D. (2023). Inside Walmart's Warehouse of the Future. Retrieved March 6, 2025, from The Wall Street Journal website: www.wsj.com/articles/inside-walmarts-warehouse-of-the-future-6f17d17a

Newcomb, T. (2023). Humans Might Not Survive the Fourth Industrial Revolution, Global Leader Says: That's Comforting. Retrieved March 6, 2025, from Popular Mechanics website: www.popularmechanics.com/technology/a42955750/fourth-industrial-revolution-technologies

O'Neil, C. (2016). *Weapons of Math Destruction*. New York, NY: Broadway Books.

Oremus, W. (2018). Most Americans Still Don't Fear Big Tech's Power. Retrieved March 6, 2025, from Slate website: https://slate.com/technology/2018/03/most-americans-still-dont-fear-big-techs-power-survey-finds.html

Pan, J. (2023). US Productivity Is Stalling Out and Employees Are Less Willing to 'Engage in Hustle Culture,' as 1 in 5 Americans Admit to Doing the 'Bare Minimum' At Work. Retrieved March 6, 2025, from Yahoo Finance website: https://finance.yahoo.com/news/us-productivity-decline-employees-less-173000240.html

Paul, M., Maglaras, L., Ferrag, M. A., & Almomani, I. (2023). Digitization of Healthcare Sector: A Study on Privacy and Security Concerns. *ICT Express*, *9*(4), 571–588. https://doi.org/https://doi.org/10.1016/j.icte.2023.02.007

Pethokoukis, J. (2023a). Could AI Really Generate Explosive Economic Growth? Retrieved March 6, 2025, from Faster, Please! website: https://fasterplease.substack.com/p/could-ai-really-generate-explosive

Pethokoukis, J. (2023b). What Markets Are Telling Us About ChatGPT As a General Purpose Technology. Retrieved March 6, 2025, from Faster, Please! website: https://fasterplease.substack.com/p/what-markets-are-telling-us-about

Portman, R., & Mulopulos, S. (2023). Congress Must Get Ahead on AI Legislation Before It's Too Late. Retrieved March 6, 2025, from The Hill website: https://thehill.com/opinion/technology/4125216-congress-must-get-ahead-on-ai-legislation-before-its-too-late

PwC. (2017). Sizing the Prize. Retrieved March 6, 2025, from www.pwc.com/gx/en/issues/data-and-analytics/publications/artificial-intelligence-study.html

Reynolds, G. H. (2023a). AI and the Screwfly Succession. Retrieved March 6, 2025, from https://instapundit.substack.com/p/ai-and-the-screwfly-succession

Reynolds, G. H. (2023b). The Coming "Symbolic Analyst" Meltdown. Retrieved March 6, 2025, from https://instapundit.substack.com/p/the-coming-symbolic-analyst-meltdown

Richter, F. (2023). Amazon Maintains Lead in the Cloud Market. Retrieved March 6, 2025, from Statista website: www.statista.com/chart/18819/worldwide-market-share-of-leading-cloud-infrastructure-service-providers

Robb, J. (2023). Replicator. Retrieved March 6, 2025, from Global Guerrillas website: https://johnrobb.substack.com/p/replicator

Roberts, G. (2023). Will We Notice If AI Replaces Screenwriters? Retrieved March 6, 2025, from The Spectator website: https://thespectator.com/book-and-art/notice-ai-replaces-screenwriters-hollywood

Robotnik. (2021). History of Robots and Robotics. Retrieved March 6, 2025, from https://robotnik.eu/history-of-robots-and-robotics/#:~:text=The first industrial robots were,was sold to General Motors

Rouse, M. (2023). Generative Adversarial Network. Retrieved March 6, 2025, from Technopedia website: www.techopedia.com/definition/32515/generative-adversarial-network-gan

Saito, K. (2022). *Marx in the Anthropocene: Towards the Idea of Degrowth Communism*. Cambridge, UK: Cambridge University Press.

Santens, S. (2020). Universal Basic Income as the Social Vaccine of the 21st Century. Retrieved March 6, 2025, from Medium website: https://medium.com/basic-income/universal-basic-income-as-the-social-vaccine-of-the-21st-century-d66dff39073

Santens, S. (2024). UBI Guide. Retrieved March 6, 2025, from www.scottsantens.com

Schechner, S., & Woo, S. (2021). Apple, Google Hold 'Vise-Like Grip' on Smartphones, U.K. Regulator Says. Retrieved March 6, 2025, from The Wall Street Journal website: www.wsj.com/articles/apple-google-hold-vise-like-grip-on-smartphones-u-k-regulator-says-11639489558

Seetharaman, D., & Hagey, K. (2023). Outcry Against AI Companies Grows Over Who Controls Internet's Content. Retrieved March 6, 2025, from The Wall Street Journal website: www.wsj.com/articles/outcry-against-ai-companies-grows-over-who-controls-internets-content-91d604c9

Sherman, E. (2023). How Blackstone Is Using AI to Evaluate Deals. Retrieved March 6, 2025, from TechCenter website: www.globest.com/2023/11/07/how-blackstone-is-using-ai-to-evaluate-deals

Shine, I., & Whiting, K. (2023). These Are the Jobs Most Likely to be Lost – and Created – Because of AI. Retrieved March 6, 2025, from World Economic Forum website: www.weforum.org/agenda/2023/05/jobs-lost-created-ai-gpt

Singh, T. (2019). Software Ate the World, Now AI Is Eating Software. Retrieved March 6, 2025, from Forbes website: www.forbes.com/sites/cognitiveworld/2019/08/29/software-ate-the-world-now-ai-is-eating-software

Smith, A. (2018). Public Attitudes Toward Technology Companies. Retrieved March 6, 2025, from Pew Research Center website: www.pewinternet.org/2018/06/28/public-attitudes-toward-technology-companies

Statista. (2023). Share of Ad-Selling Companies in Digital Advertising Revenue in the United States from 2020 to 2025. Retrieved March 6, 2025, from www.statista.com/statistics/242549/digital-ad-market-share-of-major-ad-selling-companies-in-the-us-by-revenue/#:~:text=In 2020%2C Google accounted for,25 and 10 percent%2C respectively

Strauss, D. (2023). Generative AI Set to Affect 300mn Jobs Across Major Economies. Retrieved March 6, 2025, from Financial Times website: www.ft.com/content/7dec4483-ad34-4007-bb3a-7ac925643999

Streeck, W. (2016). *How Will Capitalism End?: Essays on a Failing System*. London, UK: Verso Books.

Suskind, D. (2023). The AI Nanny in Your Baby's Future. Retrieved March 6, 2025, from The Wall Street Journal website: www.wsj.com/articles/the-ai-nanny-in-your-babys-future-999d0e50

Terry, O. K. (2023). I'm a Student. You Have No Idea How Much We're Using ChatGPT. Retrieved March 6, 2025, from The Chronicle of Higher Education website: www.chronicle.com/article/im-a-student-you-have-no-idea-how-much-were-using-chatgpt

Tett, G. (2023). We Must Avoid the Evils of Social Media with AI. Retrieved March 6, 2025, from Financial Times website: www.ft.com/content/030b5d29-cb51-438e-bc73-94c8197b25fd

Thomas, D. (2023). British Media and Creative Industries Quizzed Over AI Risks to Copyright. Retrieved March 6, 2025, from Financial Times website: www.ft.com/content/76680815-b313-44a7-b12b-a57ebfcb34bd

Tong, A. (2023). AI Threatens Humanity's Future, 61% of Americans Say: Reuters/Ipsos Poll. Retrieved March 6, 2025, from Reuters website: www.reuters.com/technology/ai-threatens-humanitys-future-61-americans-say-reutersipsos-2023-05-17

Tong, A., & Dastin, J. (2023). Insight: Race Towards "Autonomous" AI Agents Grips Silicon Valley. Retrieved March 6, 2025, from Reuters website: www.reuters.com/technology/race-towards-autonomous-ai-agents-grips-silicon-valley-2023-07-17

Toonkel, J., & Krouse, S. (2023). Who Owns SpongeBob? AI Shakes Hollywood's Creative Foundation. Retrieved March 6, 2025, from The Wall Street Journal website: www.wsj.com/articles/ai-chatgpt-hollywood-intellectual-property-spongebob-81fd5d15

Touraine, A. (1971). *The Post-Industrial Society*. New York, NY: Random House.

Tracy, R. (2023). Business and Labor Square Off Over AI's Future in American Workplace. Retrieved March 6, 2025, from The Wall Street Journal website: www.wsj.com/articles/business-and-labor-square-off-over-ais-future-in-american-workplace-add9e41

Twenge, J. (2023). *Generations: The Real Differences Between Gen Z, Millennials, Gen X, Boomers, and Silents—and What They Mean for America's Future*. New York, NY: Atria Books.

Weber, L., & Ellis, L. (2023). The Jobs Most Exposed to ChatGPT. Retrieved March 6, 2025, from The Wall Street Journal website: www.wsj.com/articles/the-jobs-most-exposed-to-chatgpt-e7ceebf0

Weed, T. (2022). The Number of AI Research Publications is Accelerating Faster in China than the U.S. Retrieved March 6, 2025, from Medium website: https://becominghuman.ai/the-number-of-ai-research-publications-is-accelerating-faster-in-china-than-the-u-s-2a1cb609f326

Weller, C. (2017). Elon Musk Doubles Down on Universal Basic Income: "It's Going To Be Necessary." Retrieved March 6, 2025, from Business Insider website: www.businessinsider.com/elon-musk-universal-basic-income-2017-2

Zheng, S. (2023). OpenAI's CEO Calls on China to Help Shape AI Safety Guidelines. Retrieved March 6, 2025, from Bloomberg website: www.bloomberg.com/news/articles/2023-06-10/openai-s-ceo-altman-calls-on-china-to-help-shape-ai-safety-guidelines

5

WORK AND WORKERS IN THE AGE OF AI

The influence of technology, trade, and institutions

Michael Lind

5.1 Introduction

"It's tough to make predictions, especially about the future" (Berra, 2010, para. 1). This observation attributed to the American baseball catcher and sage Yogi Berra applies with particular force when the subject is the future effect on the workforce and the economy of innovative technologies such as artificial intelligence (AI). In the case of automation, pessimists have warned of mass unemployment, while optimists foresee a future of universal abundance, captured in the ironic label "fully automated luxury communism", commonly abbreviated "FALC" (Merchant, 2015, para. 1; Mokyr, Vickers, & Ziebarth, 2015).

Conventional discussions of the social effects of AI, machine-to-machine communications, and other innovations made possible by digital technology fail to do justice to the complex interaction between new technologies and particular national and sub-national societies. The world includes countries with radically different social and political orders, so it is impossible to generalise about the uses to which a given technology will be put. In the 1930s, for example, Franklin Delano Roosevelt's United States, a liberal democracy; Adolf Hitler's Germany, a totalitarian state; and Anastasio Somoza's regime in Nicaragua, a traditional authoritarian dictatorship, used the same technologies, like electricity and radio and automobiles and railroads, but with different results and for different purposes.

Although it is impossible to provide the answer to how AI will influence various societies, it is possible to ask the right questions in the case of individual countries. As Melvin Kranzberg (1986, p. 545) once described it "technology is neither good nor bad; nor is it neutral". To be specific, we know from historical and contemporary experience that in a particular nation three major factors will shape the outcome of the invention and diffusion of a transformative new technology: (1)

DOI: 10.4324/9781003391333-6

the stage of development of the new technology; (2) the role of the country in the world economy; and (3) the domestic structure of the country, in terms of politics, class, and culture. Each of these deserves to be examined in detail.

5.2 The stage of development of the new technology

What is variously described as "evolutionary economics", or "neo-Schumpeterian economics", holds that technological evolution is not continuous. Periodically, the invention of a new "general-purpose technology" destabilises the existing "techno-economic paradigm". The adoption of the new technology brings about the modest or radical transformation of the economy as well as social and political structures (Nelson et al., 2018).

General-purpose technologies in the modern industrial era have included the steam engine, the internal combustion engine, and the computer. According to neo-Schumpeterian economists, each of these results in a "techno-economic paradigm" that goes through the following phases: invention, innovation, and diffusion (Perez, 2010). In the case of the steam engine, the invention phase occurred with James Watt's improvements on the steam engine. The innovation phase followed, in which entrepreneurs in Europe and North America developed other uses for steam engines, including steamships and steam-powered locomotives and steam factories. The full diffusion of the benefits of the steam engine required massive public and private investment in new kinds of infrastructure, like railroads for locomotives and canals to transport coal from mines to steam-powered factories.

The internal combustion engine went through a similar pattern of invention, innovation, and diffusion. The invention of the internal combustion engine was followed by the innovation phase, which saw the development of automobiles and aircraft and diesel-powered ships and submarines. Like the steam engine, the internal combustion engine's benefits could be realised only after the construction of a new infrastructure, including paved streets, highways, gas stations, and airports.

The very structure of business and production in capitalist societies is different in successive stages of the development of a new techno-economic paradigm. During the innovation phases of the steam engine, for example, there were many small "start-up" railroads. As the technology matured, many small railroads were absorbed by a few giant firms or government-owned railroads that were more efficient because of network effects. Automobile manufacturing, like many other kinds of manufacturing, is characterised by increasing returns to scale, so over time a few huge, oligopolistic automakers tended to absorb or displace many small ones.

The impact of a new general-purpose technology like AI on a particular society, then, depends on the stage of development of the new techno-economic paradigm. What is more, different countries can find themselves at different stages of the same techno-economic paradigm. For example, in the case of internal combustion engine technology, in the last generation China has engaged in massive pouring of concrete to create a nationwide system of highways for automobiles—a task that the United States completed in the decades after World War II, when it constructed its interstate highway system.

Most countries can skip one or more stages of a techno-economic paradigm. Modern scientific and technological innovation, which requires complex "innovation ecosystems" bringing together public support for research and development, large domestic markets, venture capital, and skilled workers, has been concentrated in a few nations in Europe, North America, and—more recently—East Asia. But once a technology or innovation is developed anywhere in the world, it can be adopted by other countries through numerous routes, from local affiliates of transnational corporations to licensing agreements by local firms to outright intellectual property theft.

Late-developing countries have often used state support of local "infant industries" to naturalise important new technologies that were invented elsewhere. In the nineteenth century, the United States and Germany, following its unification in 1871, caught up with Britain, the industrial leader, by using import-substitution protectionism to foster their infant industries. In different ways, twentieth-century Latin American and East Asian countries have used strategic protectionism as well (Bairoch, 1993; Chang, 2002; Helleiner, 2021; Szporluk, 1988).

If the development of AI and related technologies follows the pattern of earlier techno-economic paradigms, then the invention phase will take place in a few leading countries, followed by innovation in a greater number of countries and eventual global diffusion to most or all countries.

5.3 The relationship of a country to the world economy

The second factor that shapes the adoption of a new technology by a particular country is its relationship with the world economy in a given historical era.

A truly global economy was created only in the aftermath of World War II. Before 1945, most of the world outside of North and South America was ruled directly or indirectly by European colonial empires, which typically protected their imperial markets as part of mercantilist strategies. In the European empires, including the British, the metropole specialised in high-value-added production, compelling its colonial subjects to forego manufacturing of their own and to specialise in low-value-added exports of commodities to the metropole, including raw materials for metropolitan factories and cheap food for metropolitan workers. As a result, the terms of trade favoured the metropoles, so following post-war decolonisation many newly independent countries in Latin America, the Middle East, and Asia, as well as Latin American republics that had won their independence from Spain or Portugal long before, pursued protectionist import substitution strategies like those of the pre-1945 United States and Germany to build up their own manufacturing industries, with results that varied by country.

Marxist–Leninist regimes, beginning with the Soviet Union in the 1920s and including the People's Republic of China beginning in 1949, sought to be largely autarkic, with only limited and managed trade. The end of the Cold War brought about the liberalisation of former communist economies and many post-colonial countries at the same time. Because most of these countries were poor and had undeveloped consumer markets, the main effect of post-Cold War liberalisation was to vastly expand the pool of workers available to multinational corporations based in Europe, North America, and East Asia. Many major First World companies engaged in strategies of labour arbitrage, transferring much industrial production from high-wage, unionised workforces in developed nations to low-wage, non-union workers, many of them in authoritarian regimes like China and Vietnam.

The combination of post-Maoist China's successful campaign of state-sponsored industrial development and the partial deindustrialisation of the United States and other developed democracies by their own multinational corporations inspired alarm in Western capitals, when growing military tensions with China and the COVID-19 pandemic revealed the dependence of Western democracies on supply chains located in, or dominated by, China. A process of the United States and European decoupling from China, sometimes using the euphemism "de-risking", is underway, driven by concerns about national security and long-term economic growth. The result may be the fragmentation of the post-Cold War global economy into military-economic blocs like those of the Cold War, with borders and members yet to be defined (Lind, 2017).

Whether they find themselves in a truly global economy or sub-global trade and investment blocs, most countries in the future will not be completely self-sufficient. Instead, they will specialise in particular roles in a larger supranational economy. The role of a country in a global or bloc or imperial division of labour in turn will shape its reception of a new technology like AI.

The role of a country in the world economy can be mapped on the basis of two distinctions—the distinction between traded and nontraded economic sectors, and the distinction between high-value-added and low-value-added sectors.

The traded sector of the economy consists of goods and services that can be sold far away from where they are made, in other parts of the same country, or in other parts of the world. If a good can be put on a container ship and sell it to customers on the other side of the ocean, the good is made by the traded sector. An example is the automobile parts industry. And if a service undertaken in one country can be provided to clients in another country, then that service is found in the traded services sector. An example is international business tax preparation services.

The nontraded sector is the opposite of the traded sector. It consists of goods and services that are consumed at or near the places where they are produced or provided. Because very few material goods are made locally today, the contemporary nontraded sector is overwhelmingly made up of person-to-person services provided by workers to customers who live in the same area in industries like restaurants, retail, house cleaning and gardening, hair styling, and healthcare.

To the traded/nontraded sector distinctions, we will now add the distinction between high-value-added and low-value-added goods and services. In the case of physical goods, the distinction is easy to understand. A field of wheat is of low value. The miller adds some value by turning wheat into flour. But the highest value is added by the baker, who takes some flour and turns it into a tasty piece of bread or cake, which can be sold for a much higher price than an amount of wheat or flour that weighs exactly the same. Value-added taxes—used by all advanced economies except the United States—are based on the calculation of the value added in each stage of production of a good like bread.

What about services? Most low-value-added services are outsourced household chores. People can cook for themselves and their families if they cannot afford to go to restaurants, they can clean their own homes if they cannot afford maids, and they can take care of their own children or their own elderly relatives, instead of paying strangers private fees or public taxes to look after them in day-care centres or nursing homes. As these examples suggest, there tends to be a class distinction in low-value-added services, which are disproportionately paid for as luxuries by affluent consumers and mostly provided by working-class people driven by economic need to work in what, for the most part, are low-pay, low-status jobs.

In contrast, high-value-added services are those that people cannot provide for themselves. We have already discussed traded sector services like international corporate tax preparation. The high-value-added services in the nontraded sector that require the provider and the customer to be in the same place include education (apart from remote learning) and medicine (apart from telemedicine). The nontraded medical services industry includes both high-value-added professional jobs for doctors and registered nurses and low-value-added jobs for health aides, who provide simple care for a patient which for the most part could be done by relatives if necessary (another case of an outsourced household chore).

If we combine the distinction between traded sectors and nontraded sectors with the distinction between high-value-added sectors and low-value-added sectors, we get the following chart:

	High-value-added	*Low-value-added*
Traded	Manufacturing, Refining fossil fuels, Global professional and business services	Mining, farming, fossil fuel extraction, tourist services
Nontraded	Medicine, education	Retail, restaurants, Cleaning, health aide, Warehouse, transport

Most jobs in all modern economies are in the domestic nontraded sector service. But the nature and quality of jobs in a country, even nontraded service sector jobs, is influenced by the nature of its traded sector.

To illustrate this point, let us imagine four cities, each with a different kind of traded sector: Factory Town, Professional Town, Resource Town, and Tourist Town. In each of these fictional local economies, 80% of the workers work in the local nontraded service sector, and only 20% of the workers work in the traded sector, whatever it might be.

Factory Town is home to an auto parts supplier that makes mufflers for multinational automobile companies. Although only one in five local workers is employed by the auto parts company, the muffler factory shapes the economy of the city in two major ways.

First, the auto parts supplier brings in money from other parts of the United States and the rest of the world. As the global middle class grows, its members buy more cars and trucks. When cars and trucks that incorporate auto parts made in Factory Town are sold abroad by multinational automobile corporations, some of the money goes to the firm in Factory Town. The auto parts company acts like a siphon, draining money from Asia, Africa, the Middle East, and the Americas, and pumping some of those profits into the local economy of Factory Town, through the pay cheques of workers and managers and purchase orders for locally provided goods and services.

While directly pumping foreign money into the local economy, the auto parts supplier indirectly shapes the kinds of jobs available to the 80% of Factory Town workers who labour in the nontraded domestic service sector. Inputs to the auto parts factory, and finished products, are shipped in and out of Factory Town with the help of local warehouse, trucking, rail, and port workers (if Factory Town is on a navigable river or canal or ocean). In addition, the factory provides jobs for insurance and banking and real estate services, some of them local. Even if they are not unionised, local logistics and manufacturing-related service workers, knowing how critical they are to the manufacturing and sales process, can demand decent wages and benefits from their employers, who in turn can pass their labour costs along in the form of higher bills to the auto parts supplier. And the auto parts supplier can pay for them, because of the profits it siphons from an ever-growing number of national and global customers far beyond Factory Town itself.

In turn, the hair stylists of Factory Town, knowing how well-paid the factory, warehouse, and transportation workers are, can charge more for haircuts. By two methods, then—the bargaining power of essential local service workers and "trickle-down" to nonessential local service workers—the money pouring into Factory Town from foreign sales leaks into the nontraded local service sector in which 80% of Factory Town workers are employed.

Now let us examine Professional Town. Once again, 80% of the local workforce is in the nontraded domestic service sector, and only 20% works in the traded sector. But in Professional Town, the traded sector workers are found in the global services sector: software writers, providers of insurance and legal and management consulting services to national and multinational corporations and government agencies and nonprofits, movie and television and video game producers, and scriptwriters.

In Professional Town the global services sector, like the manufacturing sector in Factory Town, acts as a siphon, pumping money into the local economy from clients elsewhere in the nation and the world. But that outside money is distributed in Professional Town is a much less egalitarian way than in Factory Town.

The managers of the auto parts factory in Factory Town have an interest in keeping their own factory workers, and factory-adjacent warehouse and transportation workers, in a state of contentment so that resignations or strikes do not interfere with production and sales. But for their global service businesses, the professionals in Professional Town depend on secure Internet connections and reliable electricity, not warehouse workers, truckers, and port workers. They must pay their office tech experts well to keep the Internet from failing, but they will suffer no consequences if they minimise other direct labour costs by contracting out cleaning services to small local janitorial firms, who compete with each other to pay their own workers as little as possible.

In Professional Town, global income is distributed locally mainly by way of the personal spending of the professional elite. Enriched by income from all over the nation and the world, the global services professionals and managers spend lavishly on housing, dining out, entertainment, and personal services. As a result, most of the 80% of the nontraded domestic service sector workforce in Professional Town works directly or indirectly for the affluent professional elite, as hair stylists, construction workers, interior decorators, private security guards, drivers, maids, nannies, day-care workers, elder-care workers, gardeners, caterers, restaurant cooks and waiters, launderers, and others.

As these examples show, different high-value-added traded sectors in an economy can produce quite different occupational structures and wage rates in the local nontraded service sector of the same economy, depending on whether the high-value-added sector is globally traded manufacturing or globally traded professional and managerial services. Factory Town produces many manufacturing-related local jobs in the nontraded service sector; Professional Towns, mostly servant and service jobs.

What if the traded sector in an economy is a low-value-added industry or set of industries? To answer this question, we visit Resource Town and Tourist Town.

In Resource Town, the traded sector industry is the extraction of rare earth ores that can produce oxides used in magnets that are incorporated into many manufactured goods. Unlike the manufacturing industry in Factory Town and the global services industry in Professional Town, mining is a low-value-added industry. Most of the added value comes from refining the ore, which is done far from Factory Town. And in our scenario many countries are competing to sell rare earths, so the global price is low. As a result, a large quantity of ore is needed to earn the same profits that a limited number of auto parts can generate.

Not only do the rare earths bring in relatively little income to Resource Town, compared to manufacturing for export or global professional services, but also very little of that money stays in Resource Town. Much of the profit goes to shareholders who live elsewhere in the United States or the world. The mine managers and workers may be well paid, and they may spend money on local housing and services. But because the ore is quickly removed from the area to be processed elsewhere, by being put on trucks, rail cars, or into slurry pipelines, there is nothing like the complex of warehouses and transport operations that have sprung up around the auto parts suppliers in Factory Town, paying decent working-class wages. To make matters worse, the boom and bust nature of the global rare earths market means that even well-paid mine workers, if they are prudent, must lower their consumption and hoard savings, for fear of being bankrupted during the next bust. And that means even less consumer spending that could go to the 80% of the local workers in the nontraded sector.

Finally there is Tourist Town. This is the poorest of our four imaginary cities. The US government defines tourism as an "export industry", and it is indeed a low-value-added traded sector service industry that brings in money from outside. The money that it brings in takes the form of consumer spending by tourists who descend on Tourist Town to have a good time.

The jobs in Tourist Town resemble those in Professional Town, with many workers in restaurants and entertainment and luxury services. But the same kinds of workers in Tourist Town are worse off, because tourism is seasonal. The local luxury service economy booms when hordes of tourists—rich or middle class or working class, as the case may be—invade the area and then collapses when they leave and the outside income stops pouring in. Tourist destinations during the off season often are poor, miserable, desolate communities.

As these parables suggest, the quality of nontraded domestic service sector jobs depends in part on the nature of the local traded sector.

In reality, of course, countries—even small countries—are made up of cities and regions and provinces of different kinds. The US economy can be envisioned as a patch-work of Manufacturing Towns, Professional Towns, Resource Towns, and Tourist Towns.

This schema helps us to understand the evolution—or rather, the decline—of the US economy in the last half-century. Thanks to a combination of corporate offshoring and imports from low-wage countries, large parts of the US manufacturing sector disappeared between the 1980s and the present, and with them a lot of manufacturing-adjacent industries that generated good jobs with good wages and benefits. At the same time, the global market for many high-value-added services, which (for now) can be performed only in the United States and a few other places, has expanded. So Detroit became a wasteland with neighbourhoods that looked like Berlin when it had been bombed into rubble at the end of World War II, while the Bay Area, home to the tech services industry, and the New York area, home to global finance, became sybaritic versions of Professional Town. The rich tech and finance industry people pumped money into tourist economies with their lavish luxury spending, when they vacationed in Aspen or Jackson Hole, Wyoming.

Meanwhile, the fracking of tight oil and natural gas brought prosperity, if only temporary prosperity, to rural regions in South Texas, North Dakota, and other places where new Resource Towns sprang up overnight. This is recent American economic and social history in miniature.

What about automation? Automation is likely to affect the four different economies in different ways.

In the case of Factory Town, the auto parts supplier might use AI to completely automate its factory in Factory Town, United States, laying off all of its workers except for a few who supervise the robots and computers. Let us assume, furthermore, that many of the warehousing and transportation jobs in Factory Town are replaced at the same time by warehouse robots and self-driving trucks, supervised by a small number of well-paid workers. The factory continues to pump money into the local economy from consumers who purchase cars elsewhere in the United States and the world. But the number and importance of well-paid factory workers in the economy would diminish, and highly automated Factory Town would come to resemble the mining economy of Resource Town.

Automation might have a similar effect in Professional Town. If highly sophisticated AI programmes could replace affluent professionals, then the local nontraded service sector workers whose incomes depend on the spending of the professional class on luxuries—workers like hair stylists, caterers, and gardeners—would find their livelihoods threatened. At the same time, former professionals in internationally traded service industries like finance and insurance and tech and their descendants might compete for remaining nontraded service sector jobs with the local working class.

In both Factory Town and Professional Town, then, the replacement of well-paid factory jobs and well-paid professional jobs, respectively, would have negative repercussions throughout the local communities. And automation of the mines and infrastructure of Resource Town might further reduce the money that is spilled over into local economies.

So far, then, these scenarios tend to support conventional views of automation as something that might lower wages, even if it does not lower overall unemployment. But the possibilities change, when we factor in the effect of more automation on consumer demand.

The positive result of automation that increases productivity growth would be falling prices for goods and services, which can make them more affordable to middle class and working class and even poor consumers. If the price elasticity of demand for a good or service is high, then as the price falls, consumer demand for that good or service will increase. If price elasticity is low, then demand will not increase even though prices fall.

From this it follows that one result of widespread automation might be a plateau for demand for ever-cheaper manufactured goods for which the price elasticity of demand is low. Most households do not need more than one or a few automobiles, kitchen appliances, and electronic devices like iPhones and laptops. At the same time, as the price of these material goods falls, consumers will have more income to spend in industries characterised by high price-elastic demand.

Many if not most of these high-demand industries are in the nontraded service sector, and some of them, like medicine, involve high-value-added services. So we can imagine a fifth town—Medical Town—in which the major industry is medicine, with a variety of workers ranging from highly skilled specialists to less-educated nursing aides. Over time, as an indirect result of the automation of other sectors, employment in the healthcare sector might grow, as a result of falling prices and increasing demand, which permits increasing access by ordinary people to advanced medicine that formerly only the rich could afford.

Tourist economies, too, might benefit indirectly from automation that frees up discretionary income for more consumers, by lowering the prices of automated goods manufacturing and automated service provision. Ever since the industrial era began, falling prices for necessities have provided even working-class people with extra discretionary income that they have spent on amenities, like eating out at restaurants or going on vacations. If automation by lowering the prices of material goods indirectly increases the purchasing power of middle-class and working-class people, then Tourist Town might boom. But the growth would be driven by an influx of middle-class and working-class tourists, whose presence might lead elite tourists to complain that the formerly exclusive economy has been ruined by mass tourism.

5.4 National political and economic institutions

Let us pause to review the argument. The effect of AI-based automation on a particular national economy will depend on the interrelation of three factors. The first factor is the stage of evolution of the new AI-based techno-economic paradigm—from invention to innovation to diffusion. The second factor is the relationship of the national economy to the external global or bloc economy, which depends on the relative importance of traded and nontraded industries and high-value-added and low-value-added sectors.

The third factor that will influence the effect of automation on a national economy consists of the domestic political and economic institutions of a particular country. The same technology can be expected to have different social effects in a dictatorship than in a democracy, just as it will have different social effects in countries whose workers possess different levels of bargaining power in employment contracts.

The history of autocratic regimes in industrialised nations in the twentieth century has convinced many that liberal democracies are and always will be superior, when it comes to promoting scientific and technological innovation that leads to rising standards of living for most citizens. The antisemitism of National

Socialist Germany damaged its scientific base by leading to the emigration of many brilliant German Jewish scientists and engineers. Marxist–Leninist regimes similarly deprived their scientific and industrial sectors of talented individuals who were defined as class enemies, rather than as racial enemies as in Nazi Germany. Moreover, state socialism of the kind developed in the Soviet Union and imitated in communist China, North Korea, North Vietnam, Cuba, and other communist countries proved to be less productive over the long term than the mixed economies of the liberal democratic West and non-communist East Asia.

But generalisation from these historical examples may be dangerous. Just because communist countries made inferior automobiles, compared to those of capitalist countries, does not mean that an authoritarian regime like contemporary China, with a mixed economy under strong state guidance, cannot excel in science and technology and economic growth, even while repressing political dissent and curtailing individual freedom. In 2021, the global drone market was dominated by the Chinese company DJI (54%) (Dukowitz, 2021). And in the same year the global lithium-ion battery market was led by China's CATL (32.5%) (Statista, 2020). The race between China and the United States and other Western countries to take the lead in quantum computing, which has profound implications for AI, shows that it would be a mistake to assume that liberal democracies are more innovative than authoritarian states (Quinn, Wolverton, & Storm, 2023).

Another set of institutions that may influence the role of AI in a country consists of domestic labour market institutions. During the neoliberal era of the last half century, particularly in the United States, employers have been allowed to drive down wages in many industries by means including evading or destroying private sector unions and forcing workers to sign contracts with provisions that favour employers. In the short run this low-wage strategy has lowered the price of some goods and services, particularly in the nontraded sector. But in the long run the competitiveness in the world of a country's traded sector firms is influenced by the size of its domestic consumer market, which is increased by the mass demand that results from high wages.

During the era of the neoliberal Washington Consensus from the end of the Cold War to the present, the orthodoxy held that wages reflected skills. It followed that the transition from the older manufacturing economy based on the industrial combustion engine to the "new economy" or "knowledge economy" would require workers to have higher, tech-related skills in order to earn higher wages. Former factory workers, in order to flourish in the digital economy, needed to study Science, Technology, Engineering, and Math (STEM) subjects and "learn to code".

This conventional wisdom was wrong for two reasons. The first is that many of the supposed "jobs of the future" in the tech industry, like coding, may themselves be eliminated by AI. According to a study by Goldman Sachs, AI could lead to the automation of 29% of computer-related jobs (Hatzius, Briggs, Kodnani, & Pierdomenico, 2023). At the same time, jobs that are difficult to automate, like those of plumbers or nurses, will remain and perhaps grow in importance. In the aforementioned study, Goldman Sachs estimates that only 6% of construction jobs and 4% of maintenance jobs are likely to be automated.

An even more fundamental flaw with the "learn to code" narrative in the digital economy is the assertion that wages more or less directly reflect the productivity of individual workers. In reality, most employers have a degree of market power that gives them some discretion in setting pay for their workers. Within limits, whether pay is high or low reflects the relative bargaining power of employers and workers. Institutions like collective bargaining by labour unions increase worker bargaining power. Other institutions like non-compete clauses and binding arbitration clauses in employment contracts strengthen the bargaining power of employers at the expense of that of workers (Lind, 2023).

In 2020, along with Harvard economist Anna Stansbury, former Secretary of the Treasury Lawrence H. Summers broke with neoliberal orthodoxy and published a study entitled "The Declining Worker Power Hypothesis: An Explanation for the Recent Evolution of the American Economy" (Stansbury & Summers, 2020). They wrote:

> By worker power, we mean workers' ability to increase their pay above the level that would prevail in the absence of such bargaining power. In this framework, worker power not only acts as countervailing power to firm monopsony power, but also gives workers an ability to receive a share of the rents generated by companies operating in imperfectly competitive product markets.
>
> *(Stansbury & Summers, 2020, p. 30)*

A "rent" in this context is the equivalent, in the case of an individual worker, of the profit of a successful firm. Summers and Stansbury (2020, p. 63) conclude:

> The evidence in this paper suggests that the American economy has become more ruthless, as declining unionization, increasingly demanding and empowered shareholders, decreasing real minimum wages, reduced worker protections, and the increases in outsourcing domestically and abroad have disempowered workers – with profound consequences for the labor market and the broader economy.

It follows that whether or not the gains in growth that AI might produce in an economy are shared with workers or hoarded by managers and shareholders depends on the labour market institutions of that particular economy. In a country with strong worker protections and organised labour, more of the gains to growth enabled by AI and other innovative technologies will go to workers.

5.5 Conclusion

In considering the possible effects of AI on jobs and the economy, it is necessary to avoid the assumption that technology is an all-powerful force that drives the convergence of economies until they conform to a single model. In reality, a new technology is one input among others in a particular economic system, and its local effects depend on many variables, including the three that have been highlighted here: the stage of evolution of the techno-economic paradigm, the role of the country in the international division of labour, and the domestic institutions of the country, particularly its political system and its labour market institutions.

In the age of AI, there will be digital democracies and digital dictatorships, nations that specialise in different exports, and high-wage and low-wage countries. Technological innovation will continue to transform all societies, but not in the same way everywhere.

References

Bairoch, P. (1993). *Economics and World History: Myths and Paradoxes*. Chicago, IL: University of Chicago Press.

Berra, Y. (2010). Yogi Berra > Quotes > Quotable Quote. Retrieved March 6, 20254, from Goodreads website: www.goodreads.com/quotes/261863-it-s-tough-to-make-predictions-especially-about-the-future

Chang, H.-J. (2002). *Kicking Away the Ladder: Development Strategy in Historical Perspective*. London, UK: Anthem Press.

Dukowitz, Z. (2021). DJI Loses Big Share of Commercial Drone Market, DroneAnalyst Report Finds. Retrieved March 6, 2025, from UAV Coach website: https://uavcoach.com/dji-commercial-market-drop

Hatzius, J., Briggs, J., Kodnani, D., & Pierdomenico, G. (2023). Large Effects of Artificial Intelligence on Economic Growth. Retrieved March 6, 2025, from Goldman Sachs: Global Economist Analyst website: www.gspublishing.com/content/research/en/reports/2023/03/27/d64e052b-0f6e-45d7-967b-d7be35fabd16.html

Helleiner, E. (2021). *The Neomercantilists: A Global Intellectual History*. Ithaca, NY: Cornell University Press.

Kranzberg, M. (1986). Technology and History: "Kranzberg's Laws". *Technology and Culture*, *27*(3), 544–560. https://doi.org/10.2307/3105385

Lind, M. (2017). Blocpolitik. *The National Interest*, *150*(July/August), 5–14.

Lind, M. (2023). *Hell to Pay: How the Suppression of Wages Is Destroying America*. New York, NY: Portfolio/Penguin.

Merchant, B. (2015). Fully Automated Luxury Communism. Retrieved March 6, 2025, from The Guardian website: www.theguardian.com/sustainable-business/2015/mar/18/fully-automated-luxury-communism-robots-employment

Mokyr, J., Vickers, C., & Ziebarth, N. L. (2015). The History of Technological Anxiety and the Future of Economic Growth: Is This Time Different? *Journal of Economic Perspectives*, *29*(3), 31–50. https://doi.org/10.1257/jep.29.3.31

Nelson, R. R., Dosi, G., Helfat, C. E., Pyka, A., Saviotti, P. P., Lee, K., … & Winter, S. G. (2018). *Modern Evolutionary Economics: An Overview*. Cambridge, UK: Cambridge University Press.

Perez, C. (2010). Technological Revolutions and Techno-Economic Paradigms. *Cambridge Journal of Economics*, *34*(1), 185–202. https://doi.org/10.1093/cje/bep051

Quinn, D., Wolverton, P., & Storm, S. (2023). Quantum Computing: A New Competitive Factor with China. *Joint Force Quarterly*, *110*, 35–45.

Stansbury, A., & Summers, L. H. (2020). The Declining Worker Power Hypothesis: An Explanation for the Recent Evolution of the American Economy. *Brookings Papers on Economic Activity*, *2020*(1), 1–96. https://doi.org/10.1353/eca.2020.0000

Statista. (2020). Global Market Share of Lithium-ion Battery Makers in 2021. Retrieved March 13, 2022, from www.statista.com/statistics/235323/lithium-batteries-top-manufacturers/#:~:text=The China-based CATL was,market share of 14.7 percent

Szporluk, R. (1988). *Communism and Nationalism: Karl Marx versus Friedrich List.* Oxford, UK: Oxford University Press.

6

AI AND WELFARE STATES

Curse, solutions or both?

Bent Greve

6.1 Introduction

Technology has had a profound impact, for a long time, on societal development and especially on the labour markets. It goes at least back to the Roman Empire during Vespasian (Frey, 2019). Later examples include Gutenberg's printing press and spinning machines in England, etc. (MacGregor, 2015). Recently, there has been talk about a Fourth Industrial Revolution and now the issue is about the impact of artificial intelligence (AI) and how strong and fast this might change societies (National Academies of Sciences Engineering and Medicine, 2017; Schwab, 2016).

Technology has been a driver for productivity increase and growing economic options in the developed world, thus implying that presumably only a few would argue that we should not use new technology. A reason for not using AI would for some be that there are losers due to the change, however there are also winners. Thereby one can argue a bright as well as a dark side of the development (Greve, 2017).

This chapter discusses the impact of AI on welfare states by looking at a number of elements with a possible influence on welfare states and their developments. This includes, which may not be new, the use of technology for administration as it has been part of the long story of the welfare states; however, it has by now also been labelled "the digital welfare state" (Dencik & Kaun, 2020, p. 2). The use of AI in science might also improve the options for economic growth as well as with regard to a number of issues in the healthcare sector (OECD, 2023a).

The first aspect this chapter will look into is the impact on the number of jobs, but not only the number hereof, but also the change in qualifications needed in a number of jobs as this indicates that there will be some who will be in need of life-long learning in order to keep a position on the labour market. This section will also include a brief account of the risks posed by the potential increase of platform work

DOI: 10.4324/9781003391333-7

and the related risks for wage earners with regard hereto. The added issue is that it is seemingly not only unskilled workers who are now at risk, but also a number of jobs with highly skilled employees.

The second aspect is that AI, on the one hand, might make administration easier, but on the other hand, it also entails a risk of bias for those who need these services regardless of whether or not they get the best support in their specific case. As an example, the impact on the support from active labour market policy (ALMP) to the unemployed will be used.

The third aspect is how AI and the use of data can entail new options and possibilities in relation to welfare services such as healthcare with the implication that delivery might be more effective, but also with a risk of increasing pressure on the level of expenditures.

Because of the above expected changes, this will, as a fourth aspect, also highlight the challenges to the ability to finance the welfare states. The final section will draw upon some conclusions about the expected and possible changes related to AI, the labour market and the welfare states.

6.2 Method

This chapter employs a literature review and analysis of data from a large number of sources, mainly stemming from research literature. Data and analysis from organisations such as OECD is also used in the presentation and analysis of the development, including expected development given that particularly the implementation of new technology may take shorter or longer time that is difficult to approximate. The literature review was done by using databases such as Google Scholar, including reviewing newer citations of various classical articles in the field. A more exhaustive overview may be found in Greve (2017).

There is a variety of explanations for and discussions of how AI can influence the labour market, also implying that it can be difficult to be explicitly clear about the impact carried by AI in this way (Autor, 2022).

6.3 Results

This section is split into the four aspects as presented in the introduction. The first section, 6.3.1, discusses change in number and quality of jobs. These changes are then discussed in more detail in Sections 6.3.2 and 6.3.3 on administration and welfare services, before Section 6.3.4 looks into a core challenge for welfare states of how to finance welfare states. Finally, in Section 6.4, the analysis is concluded.

6.3.1 Change in number, types and quality of jobs

There has been, and still is, a large international debate of the impact on the number of jobs available as a consequence of new technology as well as how fast changes would come (Ford, 2015; Frey, 2019; Frey & Osborne, 2017; Susskind, 2020). Core issues have revolved around which types of jobs can be automated starting with routine/non-routine versus analytical and interactive task/manual task as dividing lines (Autor, Levy, & Murnane, 2003). How and where to draw these lines can be questioned, and different ways of measuring and understanding variation across the above dimensions are open for interpretation. Recent advances in AI seem to indicate that non-routine jobs, especially those related to the use of cognitive competencies, to a higher extent than earlier, may become automated (Lane & Saint-Martin, 2021). Thus, it is not only routine-based jobs that are at risk, but also what earlier has been characterised as non-routine jobs. This was also witnessed in a recent survey by McKinsey (see Figure 6.1), which indicates that the difference in impact after the implementation of AI between the impact on those with no high school and masters/Ph.D. is relatively small (Chui et al., 2023). Thereby, as will be revisited, it is most likely that a broader variation of skill levels will be influenced by changes. Naturally, there is also the possibility that new types of jobs will be created, and how to be prepared for this is also an issue for societies.

Estimates have shown that on average within OECD countries close to one out of seven jobs would be at high risk of automation and about one third of all jobs would be impacted with significant changes (OECD, 2019a). Naturally, this is different across occupations (see Figure 6.2). Further it differs across countries depending on their existing structures on the labour markets.

As can be seen in Figure 6.2, there is a slight connection between risk and change in number of jobs from 2012 to 2019. At the same time, it seems that unskilled workers, as also historically, are at a higher risk of losing their jobs (Georgieff & Milanez, 2021). There are also created jobs with the prime tasks of using AI.

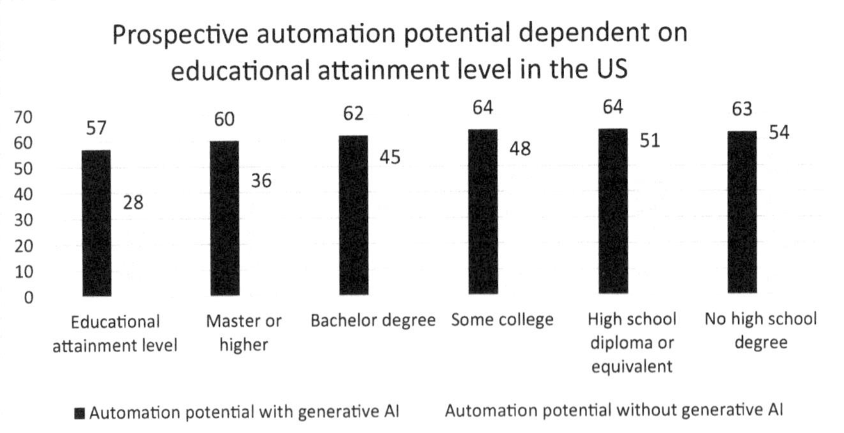

FIGURE 6.1 Illustration of the impact of AI.

Source: Chui et al. (2023, p. 42).

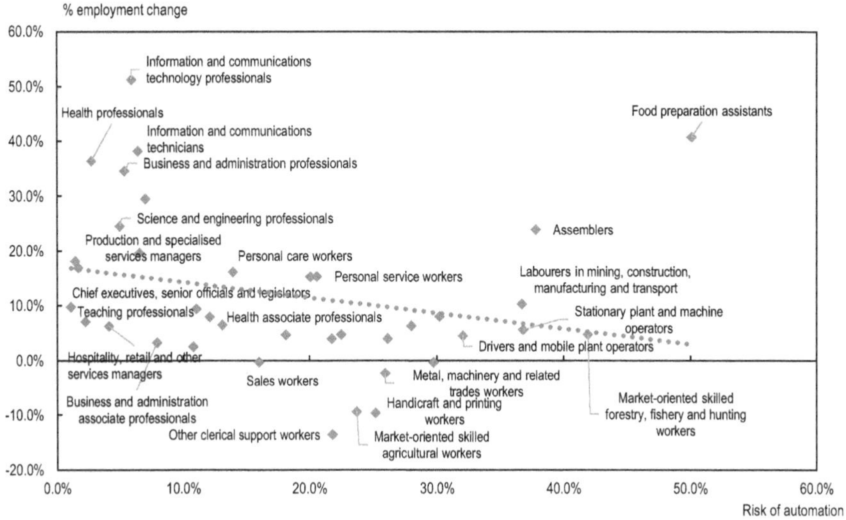

FIGURE 6.2 Average percentage in change in employment level by occupation (2012 to 2019) and average risk of automation by occupation (2012).

Source: Georgieff and Milanez (2021).

At the same time, job-stability has been weakened across the OECD countries. Seemingly, most of the OECD countries have also witnessed job growth over the last around ten years, implying that the fear of strong reduction in the number of jobs so far has been more limited, even though this by itself does not speak for possible future changes. This is also due to the fact that the growth in the number of jobs over the last ten years must be seen in the light of the strong decrease after the financial crisis in 2008–2010.

Looking at innovation and its impact on job creation, data from 2003 to 2012 would suggest that there is a positive impact on the high-tech sector based on the number of jobs, particularly considering the number of new patents filed (Van Roy, Vértesy, & Vivarelli, 2018). It might even have been so, that the technological change has entailed more jobs due to increased demand of existing as well as other products (as a consequence of lower prices). This has been witnessed in the EU from 1999 to 2010, who also points to that there is an issue related to the gains from change in technology (Gregory, Salomons, & Zierahn, 2022). A literature review of a number of studies also indicated a strong variation in the empirical data of the impact on the number of jobs on the labour market where replacement of jobs as well as reinstatement (e.g. new types of jobs) could be found in most studies such as in an article by Hötte et al. (2023). Their article also points to that "empirical studies can only cover the impact of technologies that are already available today" (Hötte et al., 2023, p. 38).

Studies looking specifically at AI and employment are scarce, and thereby the evidence of this specific technology's impact on the labour market is still limited. Based on data from advertised online job postings in the United States, skills expected within and in relation to the use of AI seem to be in information and communication, financial and insurance activities as well as professional, scientific and technical activities (Squicciarini & Nachtigall, 2021).

Those with IT skills may be able to use AI and increase their productivity, while those without sufficient IT skills can be affected more strongly by the changes. At the same time, it is argued that the "share of jobs requiring AI skills remains very small" (Georgieff & Hyee, 2021, p. 36). This is reiterated in an OECD study, arguing that the average share of employment is only 0.3% (Green & Lamby, 2023). The implication being that even if AI will change the labour market and even if it can create jobs for those who can use and work with AI, educating more people with specific AI competences is not necessarily needed, since it is more important to be able to work with it. This is further indicated in Figure 6.3.

As Figure 6.3 shows, the highest risk for automation is in the more classical production sectors, with education and social services at the bottom of the list, whereas healthcare and personal care and services are in the middle of the distribution. This can imply that productivity gains are less likely to be achieved within several of the welfare states core services areas, and thereby also a stronger economic pressure on welfare states as a consequence of the demographic changes.

This also implies that even if AI also influences the work and is able to replace high-skilled personnel, then this is seemingly less prominent than for other groups

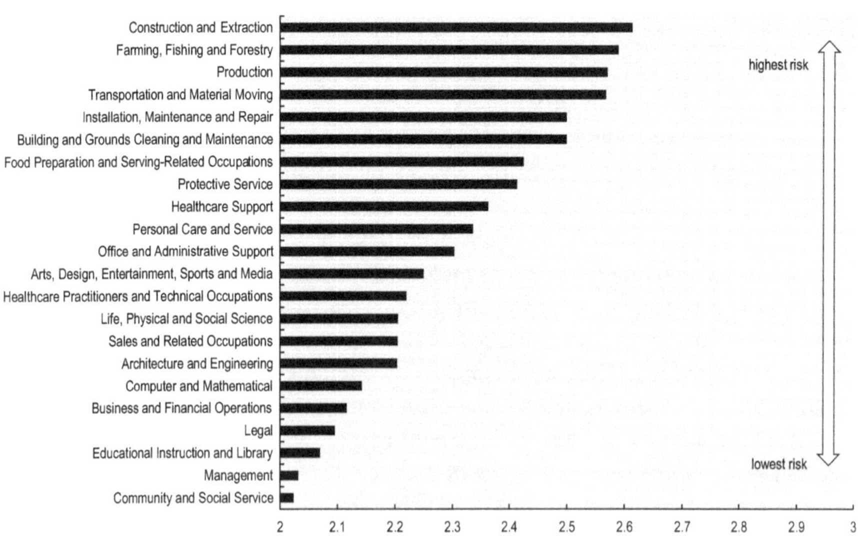

FIGURE 6.3 Ranking of occupations by degree of automatability.

Source: Lassébie and Quintini (2022, p. 33).

of employees. This, as also illustrated in Figure 6.3, shows that elements, such as management of personnel resources, negotiation, social perceptiveness, and assisting and caring for others are harder to automate, whereas memorisation, reaction time, number facility and control precision will be more likely to become automated (Lassébie & Quintini, 2022, pp. 27–28). It is important to note that the varying degree of impact of AI in different countries is to a large extent contingent on the existing structure of the national economy.

A 2021 study concludes that "none of these studies finds evidence to support the idea of an overall decline in employment due to recent advances in AI" (Lane & Saint-Martin, 2021, p. 33). However, another study points to that "AI-exposed establishments reduce their non-AI and overall hiring" (Acemoglu, Autor, Hazell, & Restrepo, 2022, p. 336). Thus, this seemingly also implies that some jobs will be at risk, including, for example, jobs in high-skilled areas, such as "epidemiologists, actuaries, statisticians, credit analyst, accountants, computer programmers, operations research analyst" (Acemoglu et al., 2022, p. 23). Furthermore, in 2021, 28% of the large companies within the EU used at least one type of AI in their production, as did 8% of all companies. However, AI still remains limited in its use, at least in the US economy (Acemoglu et al., 2022). Still, a recent report argues that up to 60–70% of employee time today may be automated by AI, while simultaneously increasing the volume of the production (Chui et al., 2023). Impact on jobs will be across educational attainment level when the impact of generative AI is included in the estimates. It is even argued that for generative AI "it is likely to have the most incremental impact through automating some of the activities of the more educated workers" (Chui et al., 2023, p. 42).[1] This while at the same time AI increases the productivity of the low-skilled in customer support the most (Brynjolfsson, Li, & Raymond, 2023). There will, as historically seen, also be new types of jobs developed. The development of jobs in the tourism industry, for example, bears witness to this.

Labour markets are not only influenced by technological changes, but also the business cycle as well as the outbreak of COVID-19. There will still, as shown in most studies, be a relatively large number of people losing their current jobs even if the total change in number of jobs may be limited. Overall, this indicates a need for an ALMP that helps and ensures that those hit by the structural changes on the labour market in the wake of AI are able to find some of the possible new jobs arising from the ongoing changes. To put it in another way. Even if AI does not change the overall available number of jobs, the welfare states will need to help ensure those at the highest risk of losing their jobs with the necessary qualifications enabling them to stay, enter or re-enter the labour markets. This is necessary both in order to maintain the necessary qualified labour force and also to mitigate the inequalities which would otherwise surface as a consequence. We also need to account for the growing divide in society, which affects not only the unskilled, but also the middle class in general (OECD, 2019b).

The use of IT, including AI, does not only directly influence the availability of number of jobs, but also the way jobs can be achieved. This includes work on platforms, which according to a 2021 directive proposition from the European Commission (2021), indicates an increase of such jobs within the EU from 28 to 43 million people. A central welfare state issue, as is also a core reason in the proposition, is that if an individual changes status from employed to self-employed, their social benefits would become more restricted, as the calls to distinguish between those who are in the labour market and those that are outside of it, have been made for some time (Chung, 2016). For those who are self-employed, this includes important social security benefits such as sick pay, pension funds, paid annual leave, and labouring time and maximum working hour limits (Palier, 2019). Thus, if the use of AI implies that a worker changes their position from being employed to be self-employed, then the social protection system will be weaker, and an increasing number of people may be at risk of living in poverty. It has also been argued that platform work has a high share of workers in precarious positions (European Commission – Directorate-General for Employment; Social Affairs and Inclusion, 2023). This was also witnessed during COVID-19 as an issue that non-standard workers and self-employed were less protected (Spasova et al., 2021; Spasova & Regazzoni, 2022).

For welfare states where social rights are conditioned upon one's status as a worker, AI thus risks leading to less (and often even no) social security coverage unless the person is able to fund their own private social security insurance, and this might be difficult if one's income is low and irregular. The implication being that there will be a need to reconsider the structure of the social policy, including as also part of the aforementioned directive, namely the need for a more precise way of defining whether a person is employed or self-employed. Thus, an increase in the number of jobs with a higher risk of being unstable, involuntary part-time and possible zero-contracts and at the same time limited access to social security benefits pose a risk for an increasing number of people.

This can lead to a greater degree of inequality in many countries unless initiatives are implemented, such as focus on life-long learning. However, research already suggests that if focus is on upskilling rather than on threat-effects in the ALMP, it could lead to fewer cases of involuntary part-time employment (Haapanala, 2022). Thus, if "work-first" is the main approach, a greater number of people will find themselves in precarious work situations. Thus, even if there might be gains by AI, there is also a need for awareness of the possible consequences of new technology and how to cope with this for those most exposed to the risk of changes. The debate among welfare states regarding the precarious situation of work needs to be included in the analysis regarding the use of AI in the future discourse, as this may have strong implications for the living standard for a large number of people. For a more exhaustive discussion, see Kalleberg and Vallas (2018). It might further influence the support for different welfare state policies, including the type of ALMP (Im & Komp-Leukkunen, 2021).

6.3.2 AI and administration

The public administration, across countries, has, for a long time, constantly been using new technology and finding new ways of handling the welfare administration. The United Kingdom, for example, was already using IT equipment in 1959 to handle payroll and production of statistics, followed by producing social service records in the early 1970s (Henman, 2022). IT and data have been used by welfare states, among other tools, as a way of discerning who qualifies for welfare benefits as well as the right payment of taxes and duties, but also for administering data required for the planning of welfare services.

It is therefore natural to use AI in order to help ensure effective solutions for the public sector, particularly considering the economic pressure placed upon the welfare states, which also includes the need to fulfil citizens' expectations and the increasing demand for and change in services, often stemming from demographic shifts. This phenomenon has for a long time been classified as going "from street-level to system-level bureaucracies" (Bovens & Zouridis, 2002, p. 174).

Societies need to make sure things are running smoothly in order to control a number of activities, ranging from traffic, veterinary, food, working environment etc. AI can presumably help in procuring a better knowledge about the risk of failure in complying with the existing regulations in several fields. It can also be used to answer questions from citizens through the use of chatbots and administering larger volumes of cases electronically. This should, in principle, entail a more efficient production of welfare services.

Using another example, AI can be used to make the tax-administration more effective such as detecting patterns of people trying to avoid paying the tax they should. In this way, this may increase the possibility of ensuring the necessary tax-revenue for the welfare states.

Overall, it has been argued that AI could "achieve higher levels of efficiency, accountability, and consistency in policy delivery" (Considine, McGann, Ball, & Nguyen, 2022, p. 3). However, it should be mentioned that Considine et al. (2022) also mention the risk that AI may be less prone to discern differences pertaining to individual circumstances. This includes the use of information related to measuring the possible risk of misuse of benefits (Dubois, Paris, & Weill, 2018).

Thereby a core question relates to whether the use of AI risk increase or reduce bias in who gets what kind of services and who do not get this. A discussion also related to possible discriminations in societies, see report from the EU on Bias in Algorithms (European Union Agency for Fundamental Rights, 2022).

Specifically in relation to ALMP, it can be important to discern the individual needs and the kind of support to provide and by profiling the unemployed individual, it would in principle increase the possibility of ensuring they receive the best available support, including those facing the highest risk of becoming long-term unemployed. For an international comparison of approaches, see Desiere et al. (2019), who split types of profiling between caseworker-based profiling, rule-based profiling and statistical profiling, which also indicates that it is not only by means of AI that profiling occurs.

The risk of profiling is that if there is bias in existing data, some individuals may not receive the necessary support they would need, an ethical issue of which one should be aware (Hofmann, 2013). This raises overall an accuracy-equity trade off, with Desiere and Struyven (2021) arguing that there can be, in principle, both positive and negative discrimination as a consequence of using AI. This, as in the case of ALMP, is only given to those with a high risk of longer-term unemployment. In this case, it is positive if the services have an added value for the individual, but it is negative if the publicly financed interventions are considered as burdensome. Therefore, one needs to analyse the consequences for individuals, as to profile using AI, and see how these interventions influence their daily life. Naturally, this also applies to the social workers involved in the administration of different types of support from the welfare states.

Targeting of ALMP through AI thus has potential, but it also carries a risk of bias. This is also the case if the rules are so standardised that the social workers are not able or allowed to make case-by-case decisions based on their knowledge of a specific person in need of support. Targeting of ALMP through AI also suggests that much data can be sufficiently detailed, even when it does not always need to be. For example, the knowledge and profiles of the unemployed in a specific geographical region alone do not convey what necessary instruments to use as this would also require a detailed knowledge of the jobs available and the needs of the companies (private as well as public) in that region. On the other hand, there is already the risk that when front-line workers make discretionary decisions, it can lead to different services rendered to different individuals, for example, we are back to the issue of how discretion influence the services provided to persons in need.

Still, as argued by Verhagen (2021), AI gives new opportunities to increase training, not only in the ALMP, but by reducing the barriers for some groups who receive only limited training, while also improving the effectiveness of said training if conducted in concord with the needs of the labour market. Verhagen (2021, p. 12) also argues that "there is lack of scientific evidence about the effectiveness of AI tools for training compared to their non-AI or human alternatives". There is also the risk of some people not being used to, or accustomed to, the use of new technology. Even if there is an option for reaching new groups, there will also be a danger of that some might not get access to the necessary training, and especially so given that low-skilled and low educated as well as people with disabilities participate less in formal and non-formal training, making this a variable one must account for.

There are thus options for AI to support administration and especially where the rules are simple and can be interpreted in such a way that AI can do it with less risk of discrimination, at least if the systems are tested to avoid bias as best as possible. Most likely this will be easier for in-cash benefits if they are defined in such a way that there are clear criteria and rules for receiving the welfare benefits, and less so for access to a welfare services where the difference of need and types of services might vary much more than for in-cash benefits. The following section will focus more on service.

6.3.3 AI and welfare services

AI and welfare services are areas where the use hereof has been growing. This was witnessed during the COVID-19 crisis where the ability to have data on where, who and how many were infected was improved through the use of AI. Thus, it was in many countries possible to at least mitigate the possible consequences of the crisis. Furthermore, data-driven developments of the healthcare sector have been happening for a number of years, and evidence of treatment, the knowledge created by AI and the use of new technologies have improved the options for healthcare treatment in a number of ways. The ability to use and analyse a large number of data may improve at least parts of the services welfare states provide to their citizens.

However, the new technology and new options, such as those within healthcare, might also incur an added cost to healthcare services, which can increase the need for how to prioritise the scarce resources (Marino, Morgan, Lorenzoni, & James, 2017). Adding to this is that people in seemingly richer countries have an expectation that they will always get the newest and best treatment as possible, including personalised medicine.

At the same time AI might open up the possibilities for other analyses that can give better and more precise results than earlier. Also, medical consultations may be done by chatbots in a larger number of cases, reducing the need for certain types of staff. As has been seen, a combination of centralisation and decentralisation of healthcare delivery following the development of new technology, given that specialised treatment is to an increasing extent carried out at select few hospitals, while at the same time more people are able to test themselves at home. With the use of AI, one may expect, for example, better make medical prognoses, including the best treatment and improved cancer detection (Webb, 2020). Furthermore, the development of new drugs may be enhanced (Chui et al., 2023).

A risk among healthcare that has been discussed for a long time is that providers try to cream, skimp or dump in order to maximise their profit (Ellis, 1998). Stronger use of data could be perceived as an option to deal with this by being able to detect differences among providers in their cost and treatment to an even greater extent than before, and thereby reduce possible fraud within the systems.

Given that a number of tasks can be supported by AI as well as other technologies a risk might be that an increasing number of senior citizens will become lonelier. This as many more types of support in private homes may be taken over by the new technology. This includes anything from traditional issues, such as vacuum cleaning, to new types of technologies, which implies that fewer people will visit elderly people (Greve, 2019). This can increase loneliness, which then can have an impact on mortality (Holt-Lunstad, Smith, Baker, Harris,

& Stephenson, 2015). So, while technology can increase the option for some elderly to live a good and independent life, there is a risk of stronger degrees of inequalities among the various groups of elderly. Thereby stressing the point, that AI and welfare services are not only about labour, but also about the impact on the quality of life.

Whereas there seems to be an impact within the healthcare sector of AI, this is less prevalent in other services such as day care for children, primary education and long-term care. This follows the previous argument posited, that the more personalised/individualised a type of work is, the less likely it is to utilise technology to perform. However, this does not imply that AI is not used as it might help with planning, recruitment, medication and reduce hard physical work such as lifting, although this is not necessarily without problems (Hamblin, Burns, & Goodlad, 2025).

6.3.4 Financing the welfare states

As argued above, the use of AI within welfare services seems to be to a lesser extent possible, given the interpersonal issues within the welfare area, in line with the historical discussion on Baumol's disease (1967). The implication of this increase is, in combination with the greying population, a higher pressure on welfare states' financing, given that options for increase in productivity are less likely than in other types of production.

It has always been an issue to find the right mixes of taxes and duties as citizens have tried to avoid paying specific taxes, especially if they are perceived seen as unfair or even strange (e.g. taxation on beards, windows, fireplaces). See Keen and Slemrod (2021) for some more examples in this regard. There is also a challenge to find the optimal tax administration (Keen & Slemrod, 2017). Furthermore, voters do not necessarily support higher taxation on the wealthier people (Emmenegger & Lierse, 2022).

Difficulties for nation states in ensuring national income to finance the public sector, and the welfare states in general, have been exacerbated following globalisation and the use of tax heavens, transfer pricing rules etc. that follow, which would emphasise the need for taxation of non-movable goods and services.

The possibility to finance welfare states depends not only on the legitimacy of the different instruments used, but also on the global and technological developments that have made it more difficult to secure the (for the welfare state) necessary taxes and duties. It may therefore be necessary to ensure that the tax base is not eroded, and that tax evasion and tax havens are reduced or even removed (Hagemann, 2018; Milanez & Bratta, 2019). The use of AI may, to this effect, be able to generate the necessary information to ensure proper payment of taxes and duties.

There is also the risk that with globalisation, large companies would not pay their dues (by moving to tax havens and/or by looking for taxation loopholes), which in turn increases the pressure on the welfare state (Cournède, Fournier, & Hoeller, 2018). This can, on a broader level, be reflected at the international level by the ambition to ensure a common framework for paying taxes within the EU, the so-called Common-Consolidated-Corporate-Tax-Base (CCCTB) (Valenduc, 2018). The aim of CCCTB is to ensure a more consistent taxation of international companies within the EU. This is not only restricted to the EU, but also at a more global level. In November 2021, 138 countries agreed in principle to reform the tax system in order to ensure that companies pay a fair tax where they operate, and in July 2023 an agreement was reached on how to proceed with reform of tax systems (OECD, 2023b). Admittedly, it may take time to implement this agreement as intended, but it is an indication of the need for international collaboration to cope with the increased financial challenges following the development of new technology.

This includes works on platforms where one does not know the type of work, the job security, the level of income as well as the social security attached to these types of work (Palier, 2019). The implication is that there may be limitations in the ability to secure the possible revenue streams from taxes and duties in the years to come, which makes prognosticating public sector income less predictable than was possible in the past. If jobs are conducted on platforms where the owner is somewhere out in space this might even imply less information on the level of income and make the necessary controlling of taxable income more difficult, or to put differently, the hidden economy may grow. The size of platform work is still, in regard to full-time work, limited. Estimations from the EU in 2021 showed that 1.1% of all respondents had their main income stemming from online work platforms, although more than 4% of all respondents were active on the platform work scene. Even if the available data indicates there is only a limited number of people active in this space, there is a risk that this number will be growing, and thereby increased the pressure on welfare states.

Technological developments impact on the quality and number of jobs, as discussed in section 6.3.1 will, if they lead to strong reductions in the need for labour, also contribute to a reduction in the possibility of financing welfare states. Even if societies just need a readjustment of the labour force qualification, this will imply pressure on the welfare states, given that some might have a high risk of being in need of public transfers (whether for shorter or longer term), which then leaves less resources for the welfare states' other activities.

6.4 Conclusion

AI provides new opportunities. Nevertheless, it also presents a wide range of challenges for welfare states in the coming years, including loss of jobs and biases in the provision of welfare services. The possibility of specifying the impact of AI is limited, although there is potential to improve job quality, as well as assisting with climate change, diseases etc. (Autor, 2022).

Opportunities include more efficient administration, better health services and new approaches to providing services to citizens that would otherwise not be possible. However, this is a double-edged sword, as there is a risk of a reduced funding base as a result of uncertainty about where companies are, whether people are employees or self-employed and even regarding the sheer number of jobs. Even with a growing number of certain types of jobs, there will be a need for retraining and further development of competencies in groups that may already have only a limited scope of education. Even highly educated people may find themselves at a higher risk than earlier. It can increase the dependencies on the welfare states of different population groups in a number of countries.

It is in such a field of tension that welfare states might, through education, ALMP and social security, be able to mitigate the problems and contribute to a stable development of societies. Overall, AI gives options of more and better production, increasing productivity, while at the same time lead to strong changes on the labour market with different impact on different groups. Thus, AI can be both a curse and solution at the same time.

Note

1 N.B. This report defines generative AI as built upon foundational models that use deep learning models based upon a large volume of unstructured data.

References

Acemoglu, D., Autor, D. H., Hazell, J., & Restrepo, P. (2022). Artificial intelligence and jobs: Evidence from online vacancies. *Journal of Labor Economics*, *40*(S1), S293–S340. https://doi.org/10.1086/718327

Autor, D. H. (2022). The Labor Market Impacts of Technological Change: From Unbridled Enthusiasm to Qualified Optimism to Vast Uncertainty (No. 30074). NBER Working Paper. Cambridge, MA: National Bureau of Economic Research.

Autor, D. H., Levy, F., & Murnane, R. J. (2003). The skill content of recent technological change: An empirical exploration. *The Quarterly Journal of Economics*, *118*(4), 1279–1333. https://doi.org/10.1162/003355303322552801

Baumol, W. J. (1967). Macroeconomics of unbalanced growth: The anatomy of urban crisis. *The American Economic Review*, *57*(3), 415–426.

Bovens, M., & Zouridis, S. (2002). From street-level to system-level bureaucracies: How information and communication technology is transforming administrative discretion and constitutional control. *Public Administration Review*, *62*(2), 174–184. https://doi.org/10.1111/0033-3352.00168

Brynjolfsson, E., Li, D., & Raymond, L. R. (2023). Generative AI at Work (No. 31161). NBER Working Paper. Cambridge, MA: National Bureau of Economic Research.

Chui, M., Hazan, E., Roberts, R., Singla, A., Smaje, K., Sukharevsky, A., … & Zemmel, R. (2023). *The Economic Potential of Generative AI: The Next Productivity Frontier*. New York, NY: McKinsey Global Publishing.

Chung, H. (2016). Dualization and subjective employment insecurity: Explaining the subjective employment insecurity divide between permanent and temporary workers across 23 European countries. *Economic and Industrial Democracy*, *40*(3), 700–729. https://doi.org/10.1177/0143831X16656411

Considine, M., McGann, M., Ball, S., & Nguyen, P. (2022). Can robots understand welfare? Exploring machine bureaucracies in welfare-to-work. *Journal of Social Policy*, *51*(3), 519–534. https://doi.org/10.1017/S0047279422000174

Cournède, B., Fournier, J.-M., & Hoeller, P. (2018). Public Finance Structure and Inclusive Growth (No. 25). OECD Economic Policy Papers. Paris, France: OECD Publishing.

Dencik, L., & Kaun, A. (2020). Datafication and the welfare state. *Global Perspectives*, *1*(1), 12912, pp. 1–9. https://doi.org/10.1525/gp.2020.12912

Desiere, S., Langenbucher, K., & Struyven, L. (2019). Statistical Profiling in Public Employment Services (No. 224). OECD Social, Employment and Migration Working Papers. Paris, France: OECD Publishing.

Desiere, S., & Struyven, L. (2021). Using artificial intelligence to classify jobseekers: The accuracy-equity trade-off. *Journal of Social Policy*, *50*(2), 367–385. https://doi.org/10.1017/S0047279420000203

Dubois, V., Paris, M., & Weill, P.-E. (2018). Targeting by numbers. The uses of statistics for monitoring French welfare benefit recipients. In L. Barrault-Stella & P.-E. Weill (Eds.), *Creating Target Publics for Welfare Policies: A Comparative and Multi-level Approach* (pp. 93–109). Cham, Switzerland: Springer.

Ellis, R. P. (1998). Creaming, skimping and dumping: Provider competition on the intensive and extensive margins. *Journal of Health Economics*, *17*(5), 537–555. https://doi.org/10.1016/S0167-6296(97)00042-8

Emmenegger, P., & Lierse, H. (2022). The politics of taxing the rich: Declining tax rates in times of rising inequality. *Journal of European Public Policy*, *29*(5), 647–651. https://doi.org/10.1080/13501763.2021.1993313

European Commission. (2021). Directive of the European Parliament and of the Council on improving working conditions in platform work (COM(2021) 762 Final, 9th December 2021). Retrieved March 6, 2025, from https://eur-lex.europa.eu/legal-content/EN/TXT/PDF/?uri=CELEX:52021PC0762

European Commission – Directorate-General for Employment; Social Affairs and Inclusion. (2023). *The Future of Social Protection and of the Welfare State in the EU*. Luxembourg: European Union.

European Union Agency for Fundamental Rights. (2022). *Test Algorithms for Bias to Avoid Discrimination*. Luxembourg: European Union Agency for Fundamental Rights.

Ford, M. (2015). *The Rise of the Robots: Technology and the Threat of Mass Unemployment*. New York, NY: Basic Books.

Frey, C. B. (2019). *The Technology Trap: Capital, Labor, and Power in the Age of Automation*. Princeton, NJ: Princeton University Press.

Frey, C. B., & Osborne, M. A. (2017). The future of employment: How susceptible are jobs to computerisation? *Technological Forecasting and Social Change*, *114*, 254–280. https://doi.org/10.1016/j.techfore.2016.08.019

Georgieff, A., & Hyee, R. (2021). Artificial Intelligence and Employment (No. 265). OECD Social, Employment and Migration Working Papers. Paris, France: OECD Publishing.

Georgieff, A., & Milanez, A. (2021). What Happened to Jobs at High Risk of Automation? (No. 255). OECD Social, Employment and Migration Working Papers. Paris, France: OECD Publishing.

Green, A., & Lamby, L. (2023). The Supply, Demand and Characteristics of the AI Workforce Across OECD Countries (No. 285). OECD Social, Employment and Migration Working Papers. Paris, France: OECD Publishing.

Gregory, T., Salomons, A., & Zierahn, U. (2022). Racing with or against the machine? Evidence on the role of trade in Europe. *Journal of the European Economic Association*, *20*(2), 869–906. https://doi.org/10.1093/jeea/jvab040

Greve, B. (2017). *Technology and the Future of Work: The Impact on Labour Markets and Welfare States*. Cheltenham, UK: Edward Elgar Publishing.

Greve, B. (2019). Long-term care. In B. Greve (Ed.), *Handbook of the Welfare State* (2nd ed., pp. 498–507). Oxon, UK: Routledge.

Haapanala, H. (2022). Carrots or sticks? A multilevel analysis of active labour market policies and non-standard employment in Europe. *Social Policy & Administration*, *56*(3), 360–377. https://doi.org/10.1111/spol.12770

Hagemann, R. (2018). Tax Policies for Inclusive Growth (No. 24). OECD Economic Policy Papers. Paris, France: OECD Publishing.

Hamblin, K., Burns, D., & Goodlad, C. (2025). Technology and homecare in the UK: Policy, storylines and practice. *Journal of Social Policy*, *54*(2), 412–428. https://doi.org/10.1017/S0047279423000156

Henman, P. W. F. (2022). Digital social policy: Past, present, future. *Journal of Social Policy*, *51*(3), 535–550. https://doi.org/10.1017/S0047279422000162

Hofmann, B. (2013). Ethical challenges with welfare technology: A review of the literature. *Science and Engineering Ethics*, *19*(2), 389–406. https://doi.org/10.1007/s11948-011-9348-1

Holt-Lunstad, J., Smith, T. B., Baker, M., Harris, T., & Stephenson, D. (2015). Loneliness and social isolation as risk factors for mortality: A meta-analytic review. *Perspectives on Psychological Science*, *10*(2), 227–237. https://doi.org/10.1177/1745691614568352

Hötte, K., Somers, M., & Theodorakopoulos, A. (2023). Technology and jobs: A systematic literature review. *Technological Forecasting and Social Change*, *194*, 122750, pp. 1–23. https://doi.org/10.1016/j.techfore.2023.122750

Im, Z. J., & Komp-Leukkunen, K. (2021). Automation and public support for workfare. *Journal of European Social Policy*, *31*(4), 457–472. https://doi.org/10.1177/09589287211002432

Kalleberg, A. L., & Vallas, S. P. (2018). Probing precarious work: Theory, research, and politics. In A. L. Kalleberg & S. P. Vallas (Eds.), *Precarious Work* (pp. 1–30). Bingley, UK: Emerald Publishing Limited.

Keen, M., & Slemrod, J. (2017). Optimal tax administration. *Journal of Public Economics*, *152*, 133–142. https://doi.org/10.1016/j.jpubeco.2017.04.006

Keen, M., & Slemrod, J. (2021). *Rebellion, Rascals, and Revenue: Tax Follies and Wisdom Through the Ages*. Princeton, NJ: Princeton University Press.

Lane, M., & Saint-Martin, A. (2021). The Impact of Artificial Intelligence on the Labour Market (No. 256). OECD Social, Employment and Migration Working Papers. Paris, France: OECD Publishing.

Lassébie, J., & Quintini, G. (2022). What Skills and Abilities Can Automation Technologies Replicate and What Does It Mean for Workers? New Evidence (No. 282). OECD Social, Employment and Migration Working Papers. Paris, France: OECD Publishing.

MacGregor, N. (2015). *Germany: Memories of a Nation*. New York, NY: Alfred A. Knopf.

Marino, A., Morgan, D., Lorenzoni, L., & James, C. (2017). Future Trends in Health Care Expenditure: A Modelling Framework for Cross-Country Forecasts (No. 95). OECD Health Working Papers. Paris, France: OECD Publishing.

Milanez, A., & Bratta, B. (2019). Taxation and the Future of Work: How Tax Systems Influence Choice of Employment Form (No. 41). OECD Taxation Working Papers. Paris, France: OECD Publishing.

National Academies of Sciences Engineering and Medicine. (2017). *The Fourth Industrial Revolution: Proceedings of a Workshop–in Brief.* https://doi.org/10.17226/24699

OECD. (2019a). *OECD Employment Outlook 2019: The Future of Work.* Paris, France: OECD Publishing.

OECD. (2019b). *Under Pressure: The Squeezed Middle Class.* Paris, France: OECD Publishing.

OECD. (2023a). *Artificial Intelligence in Science: Challenges, Opportunities and the Future of Research.* Paris, France: OECD Publishing.

OECD. (2023b). International Collaboration to End Tax Avoidance. Retrieved March 7, 2025, from BEPS website: www.oecd.org/tax/beps

Palier, B. (2019). Work, social protection and the middle classes: What future in the digital age? *International Social Security Review*, *72*(3), 113–133. https://doi.org/10.1111/issr.12218

Schwab, K. (2016). *The Fourth Industrial Revolution.* New York, NY: Crown Publishing Group.

Spasova, S., Ghailani, D., Sabato, S., Coster, S., Fronteddu, B., & Vanhercke, B. (2021). Non-Standard Workers and the Self-Employed in the EU: Social Protection During the Covid-19 Pandemic (No. 2021.02). Report. Brussels, Belgium: The European Trade Union Institute.

Spasova, S., & Regazzoni, P. (2022). Income protection for self-employed and non-standard workers during the COVID-19 pandemic. *International Social Security Review*, *75*(2), 3–24. https://doi.org/10.1111/issr.12292

Squicciarini, M., & Nachtigall, H. (2021). Demand for AI Skills in Jobs: Evidence from Online Job Postings (No. 2021/03). OECD Science, Technology and Industry Working Papers. Paris, France: OECD Publishing.

Susskind, D. (2020). *A World Without Work: Technology, Automation and How We Should Respond.* New York, NY: Metropolitan Books/Henry Holt and Company.

Valenduc, C. (2018). Corporate Income Tax in the EU, the Common Consolidated Corporate Tax Base (CCCTB) and Beyond: Is It the Right Way to Go? (No. 2018.06). Working Paper. Brussels, Belgium: The European Trade Union Institute.

Van Roy, V., Vértesy, D., & Vivarelli, M. (2018). Technology and employment: Mass unemployment or job creation? Empirical evidence from European patenting firms. *Research Policy*, *47*(9), 1762–1776. https://doi.org/10.1016/j.respol.2018.06.008

Verhagen, A. (2021). Opportunities and Drawbacks of Using Artificial Intelligence for Training (No. 266). OECD Social, Employment and Migration Working Papers. Paris, France: OECD Publishing.

Webb, M. (2020). The Impact of Artificial Intelligence on the Labor Market. Retrieved March 6, 2025, from www.michaelwebb.co/webb_ai.pdf

PART II

The Future Way of Working

7

INTERACTIONS REIMAGINED

The Impact of Hybrid Work on Team Communication and Coordination

Christos A. Makridis

7.1 Introduction

In the last decade, and particularly in the wake of the COVID-19 pandemic, when the bulk of work shifted to remote, the very fabric of work has fundamentally changed. The ubiquity of digital tools and increasingly sophisticated technology has given rise to a new paradigm that allows for greater flexibility and adaptability in how we work. In just a matter of months, between January and March 2020, remote work rates in the United States catapulted from less than 5% to an unprecedented 60%, converging to 40% in 2023 (Barrero, Bloom, & Davis, 2023; Brynjolfsson et al., 2023). Similar trends are present within the European Union, where the average employee now spends at least one day per week working remotely (Aksoy et al., 2022).

This seismic shift in work modalities has been brought about by several factors: technological advances, changing employee expectations, and an unexpected global health crisis that forced businesses worldwide to reconsider traditional work arrangements. Among these evolving trends, the emergence of hybrid work – a blend of onsite and remote work – is fast becoming a norm in the modern workplace, promising to reshape not only where we work, but how we work and interact within our professional spheres. However, looking at whether work is done in the office or at another location trivialises the transformation in the labour market, which involves changes in the composition of jobs and the tools that are used for doing the work.

The emerging era of hybrid work will reshape the very architecture of tasks and occupations. Furthermore, generative artificial intelligence (AI) tools, a product of cutting-edge technology, hold the potential to reduce barriers to coordinating complex tasks, paving the way for new industrial development and potentially

DOI: 10.4324/9781003391333-9

higher value work by employees, as well as new labour market risks and threats that must be understood so that they can be managed (Eloundou, Manning, Mishkin, & Rock, 2024). The primary purposes of this chapter are twofold: to summarise the latest evidence on the incidence and effects of remote work, including on communication within the firm, and to explore the changing structure of jobs, including the role of AI.

7.2 The Rise of Remote Work

Hybrid work, a combination of remote and in-office work, has witnessed a sustained rise in the past few years. This change in where work is done represents a paradigm shift from the more rigid work models to more flexible ones, accommodating the demands of both professional responsibilities and personal life. This section examines the trajectory of this transition, its implications, and the factors that signal its permanence in the future of work.

7.2.1 Emergence of Hybrid Work

At the onset of COVID-19, remote work surged as governments mandated school and business closures and stay-at-home orders, but remote rates began to subside as these lifted, especially in the states that relaxed these restrictions earlier than others (Barrero et al., 2023). The rapid transition to remote work was made possible due to advancements in technology that enabled – to various degrees of quality – communication and collaboration from disparate locations. For example, Gallipoli and Makridis (2022) show that digitally intensive work was also much more likely to be done remotely, and it helped buffer the decline in employment and productivity that occurred during the pandemic.

While remote work initially meant working from home every day of the week, remote work began to take on a more flexible definition as restrictions relaxed and fear of infection and transmission subsided. Many workers began returning to the office for at least some days during the week, and empirical analysis increasingly focussed on the degree of remote work, that is, the number of days that workers came into the office. Now, while employees work roughly 28% of their days from home, driven in large part by the 60% of employees who are full-time and in-person, roughly 10% of employees work exclusively from home and another 30% are hybrid, typically working 2–3 days a week at home (Barrero et al., 2023). To put these estimates in perspective, Figure 7.1 compares surveys of remote work measurement approaches. The main difference is from the Bureau of Labor Statistics' (BLS-CPS) approach that effectively asks workers if they are remote because of COVID-19, which underestimates the frequency of remote work since, for example, some may have been working remotely beforehand (Brynjolfsson et al., 2023).

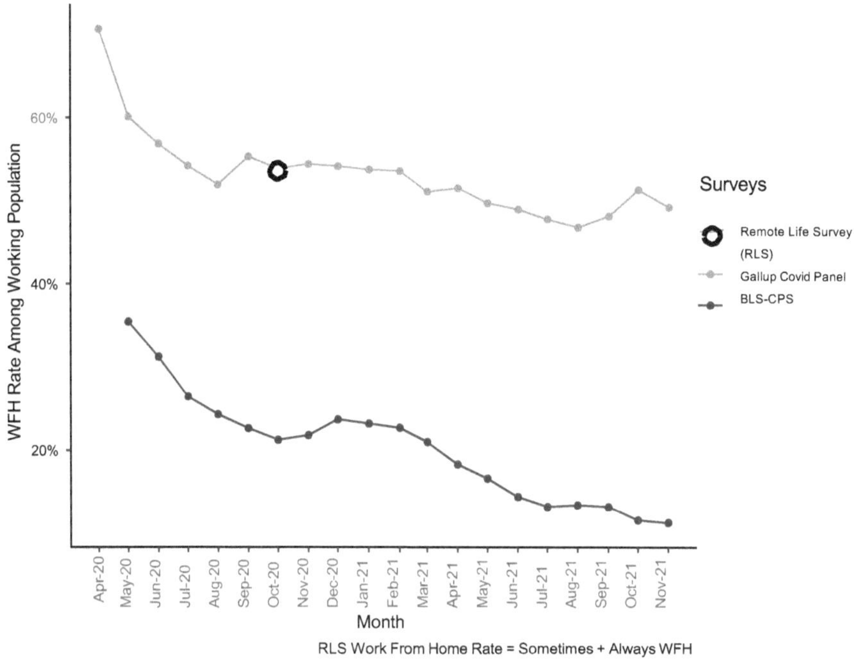

FIGURE 7.1 Comparison of remote work rates. The figure plots the percent of people working from home across multiple famous surveys of remote work, including Brynjolfsson et al. (2023) through the Remote Life Survey (RLS), which largely follows the Gallup Covid Panel survey, and the Bureau of Labor Statistics (BLS-CPS) through the Current Population Survey.

7.2.2 Benefits and Challenges of Remote Work

Hybrid work has several benefits for both employers and employees. It offers flexibility, which can lead to increased job satisfaction, improved work–life balance, reduced commuting stress, and potential cost savings. Employers can access a broader talent pool, untethered by geographical constraints, and often see increased productivity. However, these same benefits are not necessarily present with fully remote work. For example, Barrero et al. (2023) discuss the empirical evidence and point towards fully remote jobs as having 10% lower productivity and a substantial wedge between self-reported productivity from regular employees versus managers. Similarly, Makridis and Schloetzer (2022) show that fully remote workers have no higher job satisfaction after controlling for a measure of corporate culture across organisations. However, fully remote workers have higher rates of expressed intent to leave their employer, consistent with the view that the benefits of remote work are concentrated more among hybrid work arrangements over those that are fully remote.

Many concerns about remote work concentrate around the difficulty of coordination when work is done in disparate locations. In particular, communication and relationship building are more challenging when people are in different locations and cannot communicate in-person. For example, Lee and Makridis (2023) point out that occupations requiring greater degrees of coordination are also less likely to be remote. To be effective, hybrid work requires effective communication and coordination, robust technological infrastructure, and strong trust within teams – and more generally a revision of the traditional performance assessment frameworks and key performance indicators that rely on physical presence.

Several studies studying the effects of remote work on communication within the firm have emerged. Yang et al. (2022) draw on email, calendar, instant message, video/audio call, and workweek hour data from 61,182 Microsoft employees over the first six months of 2020, finding that remote work led to more siloed and static communication and a decrease in synchronous communication. Using de-identified email and meeting data from 3,143,270 users across 16 large metropolitan areas in North America, Europe, and the Middle East, DeFilippis et al. (2022) find a 12.9% increase in the number of meetings per person, a 13.5% increase in the number of attendees per meeting, but a 20.1% decrease in the average length of meetings and an 8.2% increase in the average workday, post-lockdown relative to pre-lockdown.

One limitation with these studies, however, is that they are descriptive. Choudhury, Khanna, Makridis, and Schirmann (2024) conduct a randomised controlled experiment with a large humanitarian organisation in Bangladesh, randomising the number of days that professional services employees in their headquarters came into the office during the pandemic. They find that employees who came into the office an intermediate amount – that is, 9–14 days in the office over the month – exhibited higher reported well-being and performance. Moreover, Choudhury, Espinosa, Khanna, Makridis, and Schirmann (2024) use the same empirical setting with BRAC to study internal communication among employees, examining the emails (and their content) exchanged among all dyads. They find that the absence of colocation is linked to longer emails, concentrated among workers in their teams, and among manager-to-worker dyads. Leveraging the content of the emails, the absence of colocation is linked an increase in coordination-related communication with other workers, but a decrease in monitoring-related communication with managers.

Admittedly, there are many variations of hybrid work. For example, a company could require employees to come in *n* of 5 days during the week. Similarly, they could require days *x*, *y*, and *z* during the week. Or, they could require designated days over the span of a month. To be sure, the definition of hybrid work is still in flux, but preliminary evidence from Choudhury, Khanna, Makridis, and Schirmann

(2024) and Makridis and Schloetzer (2022) suggests that hybrid work has positive effects on communication patterns and employee engagement, whereas fully remote work does not (and potentially has the opposite effects as per Yang et al. (2022) and others).

7.2.3 Evidence Supporting the Permanence of Hybrid Work

There are strong indications that hybrid work is not just a temporary shift, but a lasting change. Surveys indicate a majority of employees favour flexible work arrangements, and many companies plan to continue with hybrid work post-pandemic. Barrero et al. (2021) report the results of a survey of 30,000 Americans regarding their preferences for remote work, arguing that remote work will stick for five reasons: better-than-expected work-from-home (WFH) experiences, new investments in physical and human capital that enable WFH, greatly diminished stigma associated with WFH, lingering concerns about crowds and contagion risks, and a pandemic-driven surge in technological innovations that support WFH.

Companies are also investing heavily in technology and real estate strategies to support hybrid work, indicating a long-term commitment to supporting hybrid work and more flexible work policies. Gartner, for example, explains how investment in information technology and software (e.g. cloud computing) has grown as a function of remote work (Goasduff, 2021), and Gartner (2022) forecasted a continued rise in IT, driven by software (9.8% increase) and services (7% increase). Although there has been some resistance to return-to-office (RTO) mandates, many tech giants have already declared their adoption of a permanent hybrid work model.

7.2.4 Potential Disruptions and Future Trends

The future might bring disruptions that could further solidify or challenge the permanence of hybrid work. These include advancements in technology, evolving employee expectations, regulatory changes, or even potential future crises. For example, advances in virtual reality could bring down the cost of coordination when employees are not co-located, which could lead to an expansion of remote work. Conversely, changes in the industrial and occupational composition, perhaps driven by AI, could lead to shifts in remote work since occupations vary in the degree to which they can do their work remotely (Dingel & Neiman, 2020).

In summary, the rise of hybrid work marks a significant turning point in the labour market. It signals a transition towards a more flexible and resilient model of work that acknowledges the complex interplay between professional and personal life. Despite the challenges it presents, the trend towards hybrid work shows no signs of reversing. This new reality necessitates that organisations, employees, and policymakers proactively adapt and evolve their strategies to thrive in the emerging hybrid work economy.

7.3 Productivity and Hybrid Work

The intersection of productivity and hybrid work is complex, varying considerably across different types of jobs. This section provides an analysis of how hybrid work influences productivity across a range of occupations and explores the factors that contribute to or detract from productivity in a hybrid work setup.

7.3.1 Defining Productivity in the Context of Hybrid Work

Productivity is difficult to measure, particularly in professional services sectors where the output is in the form of a knowledge good. While productivity refers to a measure of output per unit of input, it is often used interchangeably with output, which can be measured more easily as the product of price and quantity. Drawing on an index of digital intensity developed in Gallipoli and Makridis (2018), Gallipoli and Makridis (2022), for example, used Canadian data to study how the degree of digital and remote work helped insulate employment and output – measured as the total dollar value within different sectors – over the pandemic.

The literature on remote work, however, has taken a more disaggregated and narrow approach to measuring productivity. Arguably the first large-scale, randomised experiment on the productivity effects of remote work was Bloom et al. (2015), who ran a field experiment in China's largest travel agency, Ctrip, studying the effects of working from home on call worker productivity, which was measured as the number of resolved phone calls, days on sick leave, and amount of break time. Choudhury et al. (2021) subsequently ran a related field experiment, studying productivity among patent examiners who switched from a four-day working from home regime to working from anywhere. Bloom, Han, and Liang (2022) ran another field experiment again with Ctrip, randomising employees to work either five days in the office or WFH on Wednesday and Friday, but this time on a mix of coders, marketers, and other business employees. They found meagre effects on performance evaluations and promotions, but some positive effects on lines of code written and self-assessed productivity. Choudhury, Khanna, Makridis, and Schirmann (2024) report the results from another field experiment with BRAC in Bangladesh, finding that hybrid work was linked with some improvements in performance measured using managerial evaluations of employees. One mechanism could be the improvements on employee well-being, which feed into the amount of effort that employees put in at work.

Despite the early evidence we have about the potential positive effects of hybrid work, there is a recognition that productivity is hard to measure, particularly in knowledge services jobs where there are many different indicators of success but no single, universally accepted metric. Lines of code and self-assessed performance are useful indicators, but if performance evaluations and promotions are not in line with them, then it begs the question of the net productivity effect, rather than just a few dimensions. As a result, we should interpret these results cautiously and in context.

Productivity in a hybrid work environment is about much more than the quantity of output; it is about the quality of work, the effective use of time, and the capacity for creative problem-solving and innovation. To accurately gauge productivity in hybrid work, we must consider these diverse aspects, factoring in both tangible deliverables and intangible contributions. For example, Makridis (2024) uses the Dingel and Neiman (2020) index to classify occupations as either high and low remote and subsequently draws on the American Time Use Survey (ATUS) between 2019 and 2023 to study the impact of remote work on the allocation of time. He finds that workers in remote occupations reduce their time allocated to work activities (not including commute time) by roughly 40 minutes per day, relative to 2019, and time allocated to leisure activities by roughly 30 minutes per day. Although the net effects on productivity appear to be slightly positive, potentially resulting from a reallocation of workers into more productive occupations that are "more remotable," the effects on how people allocate their time and, as a result, human capital are more negative.

7.3.2 Impact of Hybrid Work on Productivity across Various Job Types

The recent experimental evidence assessing the effects of fully remote jobs on productivity has been clear for very narrowly defined tasks, such as call centres (Bloom et al., 2015) and patent examiners (Choudhury et al., 2021). Nevertheless, the results on other workers are more mixed. One reason is the required degree of coordination in jobs. Makridis and Schloetzer (2022) show that the positive association between (hybrid) remote work and job satisfaction is concentrated among jobs that require less coordination (see Figure 7.2). In jobs that required greater degrees of coordination, spending time at work can be more of an amenity and opportunity for relationship building – not just productivity. Employees value companies with higher corporate cultures – employees are willing to take a lower salary to work for a higher quality company (Makridis, 2018). Hence, a better culture reduces the disutility of labour supply and could lead to higher effort and productivity.

In knowledge-based roles such as IT, consulting, and marketing, hybrid work can potentially boost productivity. The flexibility to work without interruptions and the elimination of commuting can contribute to more focused work, leading to improved output. However, roles requiring high levels of collaboration or hands-on interaction may present challenges. The absence of spontaneous, face-to-face communication can potentially stifle creativity and problem-solving in some instances. Furthermore, a different approach to hybrid work must be adopted for service sector roles, often requiring a physical presence. For instance, rotations or split shifts could be applied to maintain productivity while still offering flexibility.

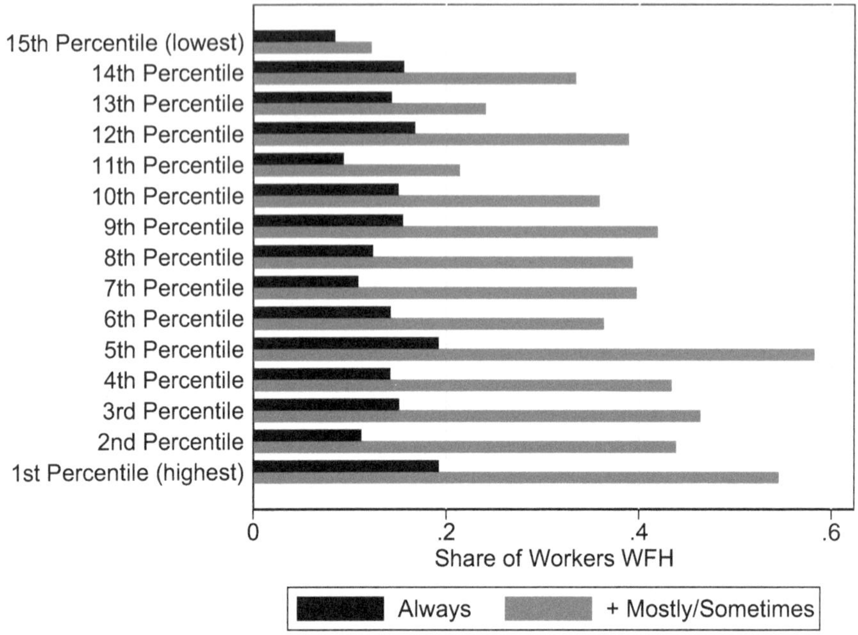

FIGURE 7.2 Remote work and occupational coordination intensity.

Notes: Payscale (2020–2022) and O*NET (2014–2018). The figure plots the percentage of workers in different work-from-home arrangements: "always WFH", "mostly WFH", and "sometimes WFH", by 15 percentiles across the distribution of coordination intensity. We measure coordination intensity using the unweighted average of the following work activity sub-indices: "Getting Information", "Monitor Processes, Materials, or Surroundings", "Processing Information", "Communicating with Supervisors, Peers, or Subordinates", "Organising, Planning, and Prioritising Work", and "Coordinating the Work and Activities of Others".

Source: Makridis and Schloetzer (2022).

While hybrid work can amplify productivity and employee engagement, it is neither the driving force nor uniform across all job types. Individual circumstances, organisational culture, and job requirements all significantly influence the success of hybrid work models. As such, organisations must adopt a nuanced and flexible approach, focusing on fostering a supportive culture, investing in the right technology, and creating robust frameworks for communication and collaboration. This will ensure that the organisations are well-equipped to navigate the new terrain of hybrid work and fully realise their potential for boosting productivity.

7.4 Communication and Productivity in Organisations

Communication plays a crucial role in ensuring productivity, particularly in a hybrid work environment. This section sheds light on the criticality of effective communication in hybrid work and examines the evolution of communication tools and best practices that foster productivity in this new working paradigm.

7.4.1 Importance of Communication in a Hybrid Work Environment

A voluminous literature on organisational dynamics exists, emphasising communication as a necessary ingredient for team production. However, the method of communication and its relative importance vary based on the type of output that is produced and the composition of employees – both the tasks they complete and their preferences. Some organisations, for example, may require rapid responses to consumers (e.g. retail and customer service demands), whereas others may have longer run targets (e.g. federal contracting and research and development). Furthermore, some organisations may attract and retain employees who are more extroverted and, therefore, want and require greater in-person communication and relationship building, whereas others may attract more introverted employees. Across all types, communication is the coordinating mechanism that allows for the aggregation of individual contributions into the final good or service that is sold by the organisation. It is also the fuel for corporate culture, and empirical work highlights the quality of communication as a major determinant of employee engagement and intent to leave (Makridis, 2018).[1] Moreover, Lee and Makridis (2023) show that occupations that require greater coordination intensity also exhibit higher wages and productivity, as well as less exposure to displacement by generative AI.

7.4.2 Evolution of Communication Tools Supporting Hybrid Work

The rise of hybrid work has coincided with rapid advancements in communication tools. From video conferencing platforms to project management tools, technology has enabled seamless interaction and collaboration among dispersed teams. These tools not only facilitate direct communication but also encourage shared understanding through features like real-time editing, task tracking, and virtual whiteboarding. DeFilippis et al. (2022), for example, study the email and video communication patterns across countries over the pandemic and show that the shift to remote meetings has led to a decline in the average time per meeting, but a net increase in the overall workday and number of meetings. Heo et al. (2022) find similar results among a sample of scientists across countries, reporting declines in collaboration and a difficulty in coordinating and communicating with one another (see Figure 7.3). Choudhury, Espinosa, Khanna, Makridis, and Schirmann (2024) also show how email communication is a partial substitute for in-person activity, finding that emails on days when two employees are colocated in the office together are less verbose and frequent.

Wu et al. (2023) demonstrate some of the adverse and unintended consequences that can emerge in the quality of communication from exclusive remote work.

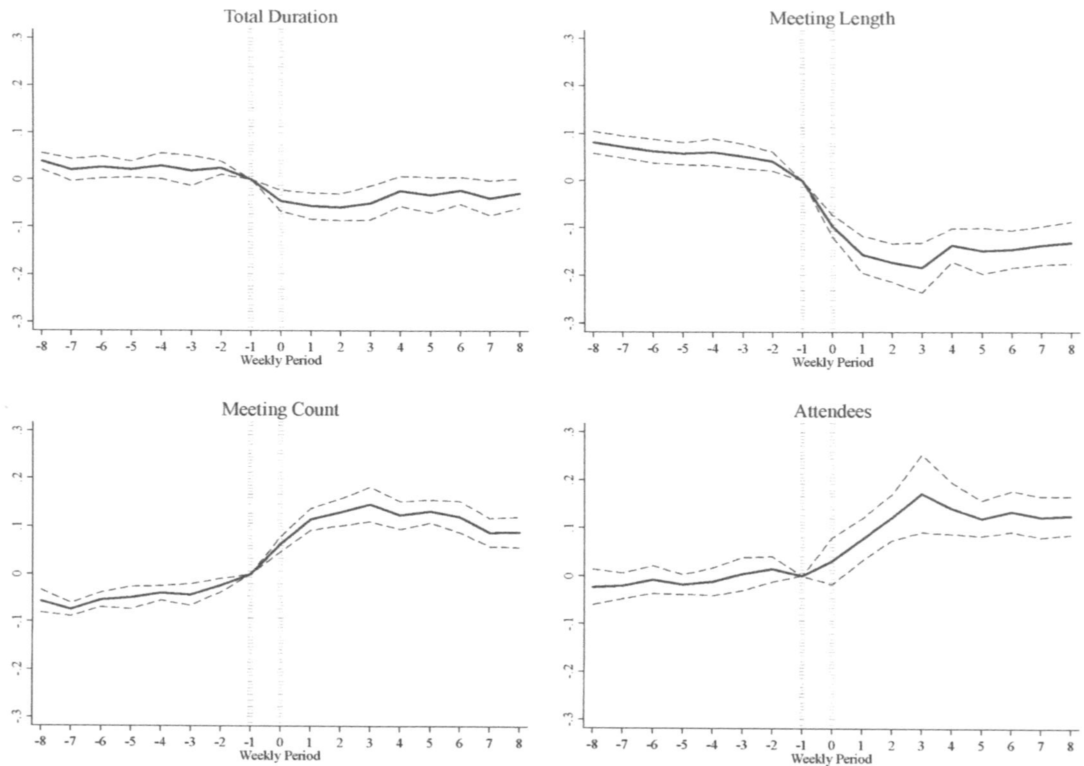

FIGURE 7.3 Changes in meeting frequency and length over COVID-19.

Notes: The figure reports the coefficients reported in Table 1 of DeFilippis et al. (2022) that represent regressions of log meeting time or number of attendees on time fixed effects, tracing out the evolution of meetings and participation over the duration of the sample following the initial shock of lockdowns and stay at home policies.

In particular, they fielded a two-wave survey in a department of an industrial manufacturing firm with a sample of 169. They found that employees who sought advice from their colleagues and managers were less likely to maintain those ties when they perceived difficulty in communication. These perceptions, and the resulting decline in advice seeking from others, were amplified when they spent more time working remotely. This result builds on a larger and older series of contributions on how employees perceive the availability and adoption of technology (Adams, Nelson, & Todd, 1992; Morris & Venkatesh, 2000; Trevino & Webster, 1992). That said, advances in virtual reality and other information and communication technologies could further reduce the costs associated with communication.

7.4.3 Best Practices for Effective Communication in Hybrid Work

Effective communication in hybrid work requires more than just the right tools. It calls for a shift in how we communicate. For example, transparency and authenticity become even more important than before because the level of trust and communication of tacit information that happens in person is no longer present. One way to fill the gap is by scheduling more regular check-ins and redesigning key performance indicators. Such steps are consistent with a hybrid work arrangement whereby workers conduct some work remotely, but carve out time in person too.

Recent work by Xu et al. (2023) reports the results of in-depth interviews among 24 researchers across 7 research labs in the United Kingdom, China, and New Zealand who had autonomy to choose where to work and who to collaborate with. They found that "the flexibility of hybrid work, and carefully managed co-present interactions punctuating a regime of focused individual work, is the main catalyst of creativity". In contrast to the conventional notion that "water-cooler talk" is necessary for creativity, these authors argue that intentional collaborative and individual time are both required. Crucially, these activities require intentionality and emotional intelligence to recognise the nuances of digital communication – both the good and the bad – and the uniqueness of employees' circumstances.

The growing empirical evidence points to hybrid work as offering the best of both worlds for many professional services jobs. On the one hand, individuals have flexibility and space to do their work creatively and with concentration. On the other hand, individuals can work with others in their organisation on items that are better handled in person. The main impediment has been shirking – that is, some employees taking advantage of remote work and shirking neglect their responsibilities and team contributions. In addition to organisational incentives and management help in creating a culture that promotes engagement (Makridis & Schloetzer, 2022), character habits are also substantially important. For example, empirical work by Makridis and Hickman (2023) highlights how intellectual tenacity – broadly referring to perseverance and consistency – are determinants of earnings in the labour market. Although no evidence linking character traits with shirking as yet, their research points to intellectual tenacity as a source of intrinsic motivation that could mitigate the risk of shirking. This research also builds on a large literature in cognitive psychology on the aspects of personality that are most correlated with productivity and well-being (Borghans, Duckworth, Heckman, & Weel, 2008; Denissen et al., 2017; Duckworth et al., 2019; He, Donnellan, & Mendoza, 2019).

7.4.4 Case Studies: Successful Communication Strategies in Hybrid Work

Organisations have experienced varied outcomes associated with their implementation of remote work. Consider the following case study on BRAC, an international development company founded in 1972 and headquartered in Dhaka, Bangladesh, with 49,238 employees (Choudhury & Khanna, 2022). Out of the 49,238 employees, 49,056 worked with BRAC Bangladesh (with 2,107 based in the headquarters and the rest in the field) and 182 with BRAC International. The typical day for an employee at the headquarters involved a five-day work week with a heavy commute; trips to a donor meeting could take an hour and trips to the office could take two hours due to congestion and traffic jams in Dhaka. Employees who worked in the field would also allocate a substantial amount of time to travel to different site visits.

When the COVID-19 pandemic hit, BRAC, like many organisations worldwide, had to swiftly transition to remote work. This pivot required substantial changes in BRAC's operational framework, which had traditionally been based on in-person and field-based interactions. The executive director of BRAC Bangladesh, Asif Saleh, and the director of operations for BRAC International Microfinance, Bridget Dougherty, were central figures in orchestrating this transition. Saleh initiated a WFH policy and expanded standard work hours to accommodate the changing needs of both field workers and the communities they served. This shift revealed knowledge gaps among employees, particularly in their familiarity with digital tools. BRAC responded by providing necessary training. As Rafeya Azad from the graduation programme recalled "We arranged the training on communicating through mobile SMS and email. All our staff didn't have email accounts, and we had to assist them".

These events led to a rapid shift in technology adoption. For example, field workers started using WhatsApp substantially for ad hoc coordination and communication; similarly, email activity grew significantly, particularly among employees (Choudhury, Khanna, Makridis, & Schirmann, 2024). "Almost everyone had a smartphone, and we never realised we could work using it. I feel this technological change that happened in 2020 wouldn't have happened in normal circumstances even in the next two or three years", said Biswajit Roy Chowdhury, a programme manager.

The outcomes of this shift were multifaceted. On the one hand, the adoption of digital payments and remote coordination allowed for continuity of services. The ERP system facilitated real-time data access, enabling management to monitor operations without physical branch visits. "Now, we could figure out what's happening in the branch without visiting it ... It completely changed", said Shameran Abed, the executive director of BRAC International. On the other hand, the transition to remote work created challenges in work–life balance and team coordination. The extension of working hours due to virtual meetings led to blurrier boundaries between work and personal life. "Before COVID, there was no problem maintaining office hours. Now we can't work from 9 a.m. to 5 p.m. We have to continue till 10 or 11 p.m", said Akramul Islam, a senior director. Connectivity issues presented another significant challenge. "Wi-Fi was out of the question. I had to go outside my house and work beside the road to find connectivity", said Faridul Islam from the education programme.

Moreover, while remote work allowed some employees to reclaim hours previously lost to commuting and to care for family members, it also introduced new distractions and a sense of isolation from colleagues. "In the office, we used to have a life outside our job description. We were emotionally connected", said Shaikh Sayed from the microfinance programme.

Despite these challenges, BRAC recognised the potential of remote work to empower its predominantly female workforce. The digital operations enabled by the pandemic provided a springboard for discussing women's career development and leadership within the organisation. Saleh was particularly interested in leveraging remote work to advance women into higher leadership positions within BRAC. Their transition to remote work illustrates both the adaptability of large organisations in crisis and the nuanced outcomes of such a shift. While BRAC successfully implemented new technologies and WFH policies, the organisation also grappled with challenges related to connectivity, work–life balance, and the maintenance of organisational culture. The case of BRAC serves as a testament to the potential and limitations of remote work in the context of global non-profit operations.

In summary, while communication in hybrid work presents challenges, and the shift may be harder for some employees over others, thoughtful strategies, the right tools, and an emphasis on emotional intelligence and leadership can ensure it functions as a driver for productivity. As hybrid work continues to shape the future of work, developing and adapting communication practices to suit this model will be critical for the success of organisations.

7.5 Evolution of Tasks and Jobs in the Emerging Economy

The advent of hybrid work, accelerated by technological advancements, has prompted a significant evolution in tasks and job roles. This section examines this evolution in the context of the emerging hybrid economy, guided by Acemoglu and

Restrepo's (2018, 2022) research on how growth depends on whether technology is more labour augmenting in creating new tasks.

7.5.1 Evolving Tasks in the Hybrid Work Environment

Economic models of the labour market often disaggregate across industries or occupations, but occupations consist of jobs, and jobs consist of tasks – that is, specific work activities that need to get done (Acemoglu & Autor, 2011). The distribution of tasks, however, is not static; it changes as a result of technological, social, political, and economic factors. Even though the job of, say, an economist still exists today, it looks markedly different than it did 50 years ago.

The pandemic led to a shift in the set of tasks in the economy in at least two ways. First, it had a composition effect. For example, Gallipoli and Makridis (2022) show that digitally intensive sectors were less impacted than their counterparts. Similarly, Cajner et al. (2020) document substantial differences in employment declines across sectors in 2020. That means the current distribution of tasks is different simply due to the change in the composition of the industries and occupations that exist today versus in 2019. Second, the pandemic had a causal effect on the way people do work. By leading to a permanent shift in the rate of remote work, as well as the intensity of it, the way people communicate and organise themselves also changed.

7.5.2 Acemoglu and Restrepo's Framework

Acemoglu and Restrepo (2018) lay out a model where automation is capable of displacing labour, but the rate of technological change and formation of new tasks can counterbalance the automation effect and sustain (or complement) an important role for labour. In particular, the demand for labour is sustained when technology is labour-augmenting, that is, when it creates new tasks or when it increases the productivity of existing tasks performed by labour. For instance, the rise of AI tools in the hybrid work environment can help employees manage complex tasks more efficiently, leading to new job roles and opportunities. In the emerging hybrid economy, AI technologies can augment human labour by automating mundane tasks and allowing employees to focus on more complex, high-value tasks. This has the potential to, but is not guaranteed to, not only boost productivity, but also create new job roles centred around managing and optimising these AI tools.

7.5.3 Implications for the Hybrid Economy

The evolution of tasks and job roles has profound implications for the hybrid economy. With the increasing adoption of labour-augmenting technology, we can expect new industries to emerge and existing roles to transform. This can lead to increased productivity, wage growth, and employment opportunities, provided that the right policies and infrastructures are in place. However, the opposite can also happen with adverse effects on labour. For example, Acemoglu and Restrepo (2022) show that between 50% and 70% of changes in the US wage structure over the last four decades can be accounted for by relative wage declines of worker groups specialised in routine tasks in industries experiencing rapid automation. In particular, they show that the negative relationship between wage changes and task displacement is unaffected after controlling for changes in market power, deunionisation, and other forms of capital deepening and technology unrelated to automation, which suggests that policy design is an important moderating force for the effects of technological change on labour.

In sum, the key to leveraging this shift for economic growth lies in focusing on labour-augmenting applications of technology, as suggested by Acemoglu and Restrepo (2018, 2022). This will necessitate proactive efforts from organisations, employees, and policymakers alike to adapt to this new task landscape and seize the opportunities it presents.

7.6 Conclusion

The past few years exhibit a tectonic shift in work modalities, culminating in the surge of remote and hybrid work arrangements – a transformation propelled by technological evolution, shifting employee expectations, and the exigencies of a global health crisis. The adoption of hybrid work, characterised by its fluid blend of remote and in-office activities, is not merely a transient phenomenon but a harbinger of a new epoch in labour economics, with profound implications for the architecture of tasks, the nature of jobs, and the tools employed therein.

This evolution signifies more than just a change of scenery for workers; it underscores a fundamental reconfiguration of the labour market, one that has been examined through various lenses, including productivity, job satisfaction, and the dynamics of workplace communication. Hybrid work can enhance job satisfaction and productivity potentially through improved communication within organisations, especially when contrasted with fully remote work, which may suffer from diminished coordination and the nuances of human interaction.

The perpetuity of hybrid work is buttressed by several underpinnings: positive experiences, new capital investments, fading stigmas, lingering contagion apprehensions, and a surge in technological advancements. By investing in technologies and infrastructure that support hybrid work, organisations signal a sustained commitment to this modality. In particular, the growing accessibility and ubiquity of AI offers tools for employees to potentially better coordinate over complex work in organisations, as well as automate away mundane tasks.

Nonetheless, challenges still remain. Connectivity issues, the blurring lines between professional and personal spheres, and the difficulty in maintaining corporate culture loom as significant challenges. Successful navigation of this terrain necessitates robust strategies that encompass emotional intelligence, leadership, and intentional communication practices tailored to the hybrid model. Organisations, employees, and policymakers must collaborate to harness the full potential of hybrid work. By fostering environments that prioritise labour-augmenting technologies, encourage innovative job recalibration and the tasks involved in production, and support the continual evolution of job roles, we can collectively pivot towards a labour market that is resilient and attuned to the demands of the digital age.

Note

1 A related but separate theoretical literature studies the role of delegation within organisations where owners and senior management delegate authority to avoid noisy communication signals (Dessein, 2002).

Acknowledgements

Thank you to Kyle Schirmann for comments over an earlier draft and Raj Choudhury for sharing the experience of BRAC and input on the draft.

References

Acemoglu, D., & Autor, D. (2011). Skills, tasks and technologies: Implications for employment and earnings. In D. Card & O. Ashenfelter (Eds.), *Handbook of Labor Economics* (pp. 1043–1171). Amsterdam, The Netherlands: Elsevier.

Acemoglu, D., & Restrepo, P. (2018). The race between man and machine: Implications of technology for growth, factor shares, and employment. *American Economic Review*, *108*(6), 1488–1542. https://doi.org/10.1257/aer.20160696

Acemoglu, D., & Restrepo, P. (2022). Tasks, automation, and the rise in U.S. wage inequality. *Econometrica*, *90*(5), 1973–2016. https://doi.org/10.3982/ECTA19815

Adams, D. A., Nelson, R. R., & Todd, P. A. (1992). Perceived usefulness, ease of use, and usage of information technology: A replication. *MIS Quarterly*, *16*(2), 227–247. https://doi.org/10.2307/249577

Aksoy, C. G., Barrero, J. M., Bloom, N., Davis, S. J., Dolls, M., & Zarate, P. (2022). Working from Home Around the World (No. 30446). NBER Working Paper. Cambridge, MA: National Bureau of Economic Research.

Barrero, J. M., Bloom, N., & Davis, S. J. (2021). Why Working From Home Will Stick (No. 2020–174). Working Paper. Chicago, IL: Becker Friedman Institute.

Barrero, J. M., Bloom, N., & Davis, S. J. (2023). The evolution of work from home. *Journal of Economic Perspectives*, *37*(4), 23–50. https://doi.org/10.1257/jep.37.4.23

Bloom, N., Han, R., & Liang, J. (2022). How Hybrid Working from Home Works Out (No. 30292). NBER Working Paper. Cambridge, MA: National Bureau of Economic Research.

Bloom, N., Liang, J., Roberts, J., & Ying, Z. J. (2015). Does working from home work? Evidence from a Chinese experiment. *The Quarterly Journal of Economics*, *130*(1), 165–218. https://doi.org/10.1093/qje/qju032

Borghans, L., Duckworth, A. L., Heckman, J. J., & Weel, B. Ter. (2008). The Economics and psychology of personality traits. *Journal of Human Resources*, *43*(4), 972–1059. https://doi.org/10.3368/jhr.43.4.972

Brynjolfsson, E., Horton, J. J., Makridis, C., Mas, A., Ozimek, A., Rock, D., & TuYe, H.-Y. (2023). How Many Americans Work Remotely (No. 31193). NBER Working Paper. Cambridge, MA: National Bureau of Economic Research.

Cajner, T., Crane, L. D., Decker, R. A., Grigsby, J., Hamins-Puertolas, A., Hurst, E., … & Yildirmaz, A. (2020). The US labor market during the beginning of the Pandemic recession. *Brookings Papers on Economic Activity*, *2020*(2), 3–33. https://doi.org/10.1353/eca.2020.0005

Choudhury, P., Espinosa, M., Khanna, T., Makridis, C. A., & Schirmann, K. (2024). Internal Communication and Remote Work. Retrieved March 6, 2025, from SSRN Electronic Journal website: https://papers.ssrn.com/sol3/papers.cfm?abstract_id=5106503

Choudhury, P., Foroughi, C., & Larson, B. (2021). Work-from-anywhere: The productivity effects of geographic flexibility. *Strategic Management Journal*, *42*(4), 655–683. https://doi.org/10.1002/smj.3251

Choudhury, P., & Khanna, T. (2022). BRAC: Working-from-Home in Emerging Markets (No. N9-621–114). Harvard Business School Working Paper. Boston, MA: Harvard Business School.

Choudhury, P., Khanna, T., Makridis, C. A., & Schirmann, K. (2024). Is hybrid work the best of both worlds? Evidence from a field experiment. *The Review of Economics and Statistics*, (Ahead of Print), 1–24. https://doi.org/10.1162/rest_a_01428

DeFilippis, E., Impink, S. M., Singell, M., Polzer, J. T., & Sadun, R. (2022). The impact of COVID-19 on digital communication patterns. *Humanities and Social Sciences Communications*, *9*(1), 180, 1–11. https://doi.org/10.1057/s41599-022-01190-9

Denissen, J. J. A., Bleidorn, W., Hennecke, M., Luhmann, M., Orth, U., Specht, J., & Zimmermann, J. (2017). Uncovering the power of personality to shape income. *Psychological Science*, *29*(1), 3–13. https://doi.org/10.1177/0956797617724435

Dessein, W. (2002). Authority and communication in organizations. *The Review of Economic Studies*, *69*(4), 811–838. https://doi.org/10.1111/1467-937X.00227

Dingel, J. I., & Neiman, B. (2020). How many jobs can be done at home? *Journal of Public Economics*, *189*, 104235, 1–8. https://doi.org/10.1016/j.jpubeco.2020.104235

Duckworth, A. L., Quirk, A., Gallop, R., Hoyle, R. H., Kelly, D. R., & Matthews, M. D. (2019). Cognitive and noncognitive predictors of success. *Proceedings of the National Academy of Sciences*, *116*(47), 23499–23504. https://doi.org/10.1073/pnas.1910510116

Eloundou, T., Manning, S., Mishkin, P., & Rock, D. (2024). GPTs are GPTs: Labor market impact potential of LLMs: Research is needed to estimate how jobs may be affected. *Science, 384*(6702), 1306–1308.

https://doi.org/10.1126/science.adj0998

Gallipoli, G., & Makridis, C. A. (2018). Structural transformation and the rise of information technology. *Journal of Monetary Economics*, *97*, 91–110. https://doi.org/10.1016/j.jmoneco.2018.05.005

Gallipoli, G., & Makridis, C. A. (2022). Sectoral digital intensity and GDP growth after a large employment shock: A simple extrapolation exercise. *Canadian Journal of Economics/Revue Canadienne d'économique*, *55*(S1), 446–479. https://doi.org/10.1111/caje.12553

Gartner. (2022). Gartner Forecasts Worldwide IT Spending to Reach $4.4 Trillion in 2022. Retrieved March 6, 2025, from www.gartner.com/en/newsroom/press-releases/2022-04-06-gartner-forecasts-worldwide-it-spending-to-reach-4-point-four-trillion-in-2022

Goasduff, L. (2021). Hybrid and Remote Workers Change How They Use IT Equipment. Retrieved March 6, 2025, from Gartner website: www.gartner.com/smarterwithgartner/hybrid-and-remote-workers-change-how-they-use-it-equipment

He, Y., Donnellan, M. B., & Mendoza, A. M. (2019). Five-factor personality domains and job performance: A second order meta-analysis. *Journal of Research in Personality*, *82*, 103848, 1–24. https://doi.org/10.1016/j.jrp.2019.103848

Heo, S., Chan, A. Y., Diaz Peralta, P., Jin, L., Pereira Nunes, C. R., & Bell, M. L. (2022). Impacts of the COVID-19 pandemic on scientists' productivity in science, technology, engineering, mathematics (STEM), and medicine fields. *Humanities and Social Sciences Communications*, *9*(1), 434, 1–11. https://doi.org/10.1057/s41599-022-01466-0

Lee, D. T., & Makridis, C. A. (2023). A Task-Interdependency Model of Complex Collaboration Towards Human-Centered Crowd Work. Retrieved March 6, 2025, from arXiv Preprint website: https://arxiv.org/abs/2309.00160

Makridis, C. A. (2018). Does Culture Pay? Evidence from Crowdsourced Employee Engagement Data. Retrieved March 6, 2025, from SSRN Electronic Journal website: https://papers.ssrn.com/sol3/papers.cfm?abstract_id=2990210

Makridis, C. A. (2024). The Allocation of Time and Remote Work. Retrieved March 6, 2025, from SSRN Electronic Journal website: https://papers.ssrn.com/sol3/papers.cfm?abstract_id=4517661

Makridis, C. A., & Hickman, L. (2023). Earnings Are Greater and Increasing in Occupations That Require Intellectual Tenacity. Retrieved March 6, 2025, from SSRN Electronic Journal website: https://papers.ssrn.com/sol3/papers.cfm?abstract_id=4365176

Makridis, C. A., & Schloetzer, J. D. (2022). Does Working from Home Increase Job Satisfaction and Retention? Evidence from the COVID-19 Pandemic. Retrieved March 6, 2025, from SSRN Electronic Journal website: https://papers.ssrn.com/sol3/papers.cfm?abstract_id=4016657

Morris, M. G., & Venkatesh, V. (2000). Age differences in technology adoption decisions: Implications for a changing work force. *Personnel Psychology*, *53*(2), 375–403. https://doi.org/10.1111/j.1744-6570.2000.tb00206.x

Trevino, L. K., & Webster, J. (1992). Flow in computer-mediated communication: Electronic mail and voice mail evaluation and impacts. *Communication Research*, *19*(5), 539–573. https://doi.org/10.1177/009365092019005001

Wu, Y. J., Antone, B., DeChurch, L., & Contractor, N. (2023). Information sharing in a hybrid workplace: Understanding the role of ease-of-use perceptions of communication technologies in advice-seeking relationship maintenance. *Journal of Computer-Mediated Communication*, *28*(4), zmad025, 1–15. https://doi.org/10.1093/jcmc/zmad025

Xu, T., Sarkar, A., & Rintel, S. (2023). Requiring fixed time in office to enable brainstorms and watercooler talk may not foster research creativity. In S. Boll, A. Cox, & T. Ludwig (Eds.), *Proceedings of the 2nd Annual Meeting of the Symposium on Human-Computer Interaction for Work (CHIWORK '23), June 13–16, Oldenburg, Germany* (pp. 1–12). New York, NY: Association for Computing Machinery. https://doi.org/10.1145/3596671.3598569

Yang, L., Holtz, D., Jaffe, S., Suri, S., Sinha, S., Weston, J., … & Teevan, J. (2022). Author Correction: The effects of remote work on collaboration among information workers. *Nature Human Behaviour*, *6*(1), 164. https://doi.org/10.1038/s41562-021-01228-z

8

YOUNG WORKERS WANT TO BE IN THE OFFICE

An Investigation Based on Swedish Survey Data

Jonas Grafström

8.1 Introduction

Since the COVID-19 pandemic, working life conditions have been a topic of increased public interest. During the pandemic, approximately one hundred million people in Europe transitioned to work from home (WFH) – almost half of them for the first time (Brynjolfsson et al., 2020; Gosling & Coppola, 2020). The transition to WFH was quick with previous barriers such as coordination problems, as well as preconceptions and expectations of onsite presence changed (Barrero, Bloom, & Davis, 2021). However, the transition was not without its challenges. Employees often encountered difficulties during the initial phase as they grappled with new stressors, including cramped living conditions, increased responsibilities, and the blending of work and home life. Simultaneously, employers worried about productivity and employee well-being under rapidly shifting times (Grunau, Wolter, Bellmann, & Müller, 2017; Russo, Hanel, Altnickel, & van Berkel, 2021). There were also benefits of remote work, including freedom from commuting, more time for personal well-being, and increased productivity.

The chapter's overarching topic is age and WFH preferences. There has been a prevailing notion that tech-savvy youth exhibit more favourable attitudes towards working from home compared to their older counterparts in managerial positions (Miller & Yar, 2019). While certain aspects of this assumption may have held true during a specific phase of the pandemic, as evidenced by Drašler et al. (2021), our survey data from Swedish office workers contradicts this notion. It reveals that young individuals not only exhibit a stronger preference for working in a physical office setting but are also considerably more willing to accept job offers that do not offer the option to WFH.

DOI: 10.4324/9781003391333-10

For this chapter, a survey asked 1,769 Swedish workers (which of whom one thousand respondents were identified as office workers), their preference for working from home or in the office. Workplace preference is an important consideration for managers who are looking to hire and retain top talent during recession concerns and movements like "the great resignation" (Gittleman, 2022). This chapter aims to answer the following questions:

- Are there differences in Sweden between the age cohorts regarding their willingness or demand to WFH?

In our study, the focus was on Sweden, which has some unique characteristics compared to other European countries such as an early moving from home preference. The average age of moving out from the parental home was 26.2 years in Europe while in Croatia it was at age 31.8 and Sweden 17.8, which will have implication on working from home preferences (Eurostat, 2020).

Throughout the pandemic, many surveys found conflicting results regarding WFH attitudes in different age groups. The varying results can partly be explained by temporal and geographic factors. Tahlyan et al. (2022) develop a model showing a nonlinear concave-down relationship between age and work preference. They suggest that both young and old workers prefer to work in the office – for different reasons – and that employees between the ages 35 and 55 are the most likely to prefer WFH. Employees in the middle of their careers, those more likely to be middle managers and have children and other obligations outside of work, are more satisfied with WFH than other groups. The ability to manage their time to avoid burnout and schedule conflicts contributes significantly to positive WFH attitudes. Where older workers found significant benefits from the life flexibility conferred by WFH, young employees appeared to handle the work shift worse and value it less (Aksoy et al., 2022).

Cisco (2022), in their 2022 Global Hybrid Work Study, found junior employees preferred the office 4% less than senior employees, while the McKinsey Global Institute found that "people who could but do not work flexibly tend to be older … or have lower incomes" (Dua et al., 2022, para. 15). At all income levels, young people are more likely to have WFH opportunities than older employees, suggesting that their digital fluency guides them towards fields that allow WFH (Dua et al., 2022). However, most studies find, like us, that young people are more interested in returning to the office than older employees a contradiction that employers must be aware of when determining the allocation of WFH opportunities.

According to a 2021 Deloitte survey from the United Kingdom with 1,250 participants, younger workers, specifically those aged 16–34, have faced greater challenges in transitioning to remote work (Deloitte, 2021). The survey indicated that 58% of individuals within this age group found working from home challenging. In comparison, the average percentage for all individuals working from home was 44%. According to the data, nearly one-third (29%) of workers under the age of 35 report feeling less confident in using technology in their role. In comparison, the average percentage across all age groups is 22%.

The pandemic is over, but most of the changes in our view of the office linger, and the change needs to be managed carefully since the world of yesterday does not exist anymore (Allstrin, Grafström, Stern, Stern, & Weidenstedt, 2022). Despite so much attention on working conditions in the last few years, many contradictions abound. The pandemic has shown that scenarios may change rapidly and that past truths may no longer hold up. Young people are not a homogeneous population, nor are workers in general.

8.2 Methods (and/or Material)

A web-based survey was conducted during the period 11–18 April 2022, which can be considered post-COVID. The firm *Svenska institutet för opinionsundersökningar* (SIFO) conducted the survey using their panellist database. The panel consists of 100,000 Swedish persons, which cover most target groups across the country and create representativeness in the sample. Panellists are recruited through nationally representative telephone interviews or postal surveys. There is no possibility of self-recruitment to the panel.

The survey was completed by 1,769 respondents ranging across Sweden. The data provides valuable insights into certain aspects of the respondents' professional lives and their perceptions of remote work. The survey solicited information regarding respondents' occupations, the tools they utilised in their work, their inclination towards seeking new job opportunities, the frequency of their remote work, and their opinions on remote work arrangements.

To be defined as an office worker, the respondent was asked if a computer was their main working tool. Across the entire country, over half of the population had the computer as their primary work tool, but Stockholm and Malmö had the highest usage, with 72% of respondents. The sorting mechanism employed to distinguish between office workers and non-office workers is not flawless but is designed to encompass a significant proportion of traditional white-collar professionals. Crafting an effective question in this context is not straightforward; for instance, if we were to pose a question like "Do you work in an office?" even janitors or cleaning personnel might respond affirmatively. Our goal, however, is to identify individuals who have the capacity to bring their work-related equipment home to some extent.

A potential issue with the data arises from the inclusion of the 18–25 age group, which comprises working students who may not possess significant work experience or well-defined preferences. Furthermore, they might be accustomed to studying from home. While this poses a small concern for questions related to future job preferences, it does introduce a potential upward bias when assessing the amount of time young individuals spend working from home. In contrast, the 26–35 age group contains relatively few students, mitigating this particular issue.

TABLE 8.1 Average WFH days per week based on age and gender

	Age: 18–25	Age: 26–35	Age: 36–49	Age: 50–64
All	1.2	1.7	1.9	2.0
Men	1.7	1.6	1.9	2.0
Women	0.8	1.7	1.8	1.9

While the survey provides a valuable glimpse into the overarching trends and factors associated with remote work, it is important to acknowledge its inherent limitations in achieving a high level of granularity. These limitations are primarily a result of the survey's scope and design. The data collected is aggregated at a relatively broad level, and the survey questions are structured to capture overarching patterns rather than delving into highly intricate nuances. Factors such as industry concentration, technological infrastructure, and cultural predispositions could potentially contribute to such variations, but these potential explanations are not probed in depth within the current dataset. In essence, while the survey data paints a valuable macroscopic picture of remote work trends and their associations, it does not delve into the intricate underlying dynamics that might explain localised disparities in computer usage and remote work adoption.

Table 8.1 categorises respondents into four age groups: 18–25, 26–35, 36–49, and 50–64 years. The number of WFH days per week tends to increase slightly with age. There is, however, a large discrepancy between the youngest and the slightly older category (26–35), which is probably due to that the persons in the 26–35 years old category are more established in the regular labour market.

The "All" column represents the overall average WFH days per week across all respondents. It shows a gradual increase from 1.2 days for the youngest age group (18–25) to 2.0 days for the oldest age group (50–64). Gender differences are prevalent. It shows that men, overall, have a slightly higher average number of WFH days per week compared to women in most age groups.

There is some variation in WFH frequency among different age groups. For instance, individuals aged 50–64 have the highest average number of WFH days per week at 2 days, while those aged 18–25 have the lowest average at 1.2 days. Within each gender category, there is some variation in the average number of WFH days per week across age groups. For example, for women, the average increases from 0.8 days in the 18–25 age group to 1.9 days in the 50–64 age group.

8.3 Results

When asked "Would you work somewhere that did not offer remote potential?" most respondents in all age groups' category express a willingness to work at a workplace without the option to WFH (see Figure 8.1). The "Yes, absolutely" and "Yes, probably" categories show the highest percentages in the younger age

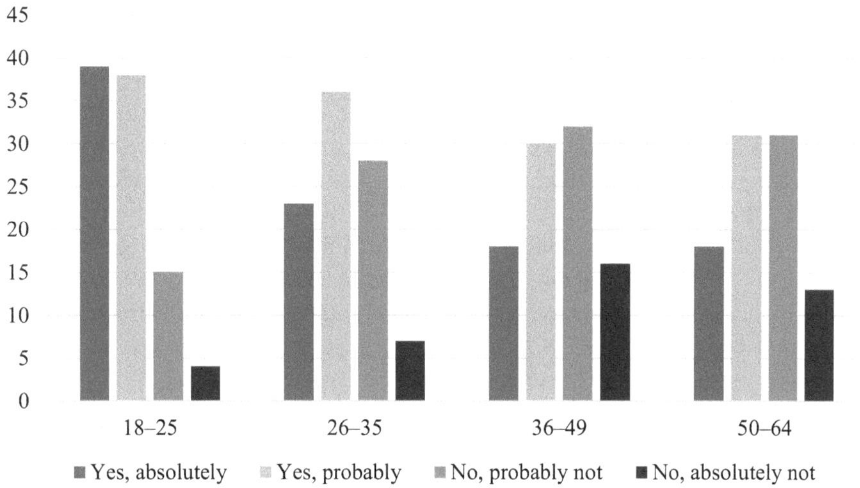

FIGURE 8.1 Would you work somewhere that did not offer remote potential?

groups (18–25 and 26–35). As age increases, the percentage of individuals who express uncertainty or do not know also increases slightly, particularly in the older age groups (36–49 and 50–64). The "No, probably not" and "No, absolutely not" categories show higher percentages in the older age groups.

Looking at the percentages of respondents within the 18–25 age group, 39% of the respondents answered "Yes, absolutely", indicating a strong willingness to work at a workplace that does not provide remote work options. Another 38% answered "Yes, probably", suggesting a significant portion of respondents are open to the idea of working in a non-remote work environment, albeit with some reservations. On the other hand, 15% of respondents answered "No, probably not". Additionally, 4% responded with "No, absolutely not", showing a small group with a strong aversion to such a work arrangement. Overall, most respondents indicated a willingness to work at a workplace without remote work options, with a smaller percentage expressing reservations or aversion.

The age cohort of 26–35 holds particular significance, possibly more so than the youngest cohort. Beyond the age of 26, it becomes increasingly probable that European young individuals have moved out of their parental homes, gained a foothold in the labour market, and shaped their preferences. A large gap can still be seen where most can accept working on a place without the possibility to WFH, but a rather large part does not want to do it. It could be that the 30 plus of age have started to form a family of their own which make it harder to WFH and creates a larger demand for work–life balance and working from home opportunity.

Among the respondents aged 50–64, 18% answered "Yes, absolutely", indicating a relatively lower percentage of individuals who are strongly willing to work at a workplace without remote work options compared to the previous young category

(18–25). The "Yes, probably" category shows that 31% of respondents in the 50–64 age group are open to the idea of working in a non-remote work environment. This percentage is slightly higher than the previous young category (18–25), indicating a relatively higher level of openness in this age group.

In terms of hesitation or reluctance, the "No, probably not" and "No, absolutely not" categories both have higher percentages compared to the previous young category. Thirty-one per cent of respondents in the 50–64 age group answered "No, probably not", indicating a significant portion of individuals who are hesitant about working at a workplace without remote work options. Additionally, 13% answered "No, absolutely not", which reflects a relatively higher aversion to such a work arrangement compared to the previous young category.

Comparing this table to the previous young category, we see a shift in attitudes. The percentage of individuals in the 50–64 age group who are strongly willing to work without remote options is lower, while the percentage of individuals who are hesitant or opposed to such a workplace arrangement is higher. This could be due to factors such as different work experiences, preferences, and the potential impact of technological advancements on remote work adoption. Overall, this table indicates that the 50–64 age group may have a lower inclination towards working at a workplace without remote work options compared to the younger age group, suggesting potential differences in preferences and priorities between these age groups.

The results go way in line with a study of Nordic office workers performed by Castellum (2023) who categorises respondents into different age groups, ranging from younger than 25 years to 55 years or older. A small percentage of respondents in their sample in each age group preferred to WFH entirely, ranging from 8% in the younger than 25 years group to 15% in the 55 years or older group. Most respondents in each age group prefer some degree of office presence during a typical work week. The most common preference across all age groups was for three days in the office, with the highest percentage in the younger than 25 years group at 33%. The preferences for one day, two days, and four days in the office were relatively consistent across age groups. There was a gradual increase in the percentage of respondents who prefer always being in the office as the age groups get older. The highest percentage in this category is in the 55 years or older group at 20%.

Looking at Figure 8.2, which represents an aggregate of the answers to the responses to the question "Would you work somewhere that did not offer remote potential?", categorised by age groups. Most respondents in all age groups, except for the "No/unlikely" category, express a willingness or probability to work at a workplace without the option to WFH. The "Yes/probably" category shows higher percentages across all age groups, indicating that a significant portion of individuals would consider working at a workplace that does not offer remote work options. The percentages of respondents in the "Yes/probably" category decrease slightly as age increases, with the highest percentage in the youngest age group (18–25).

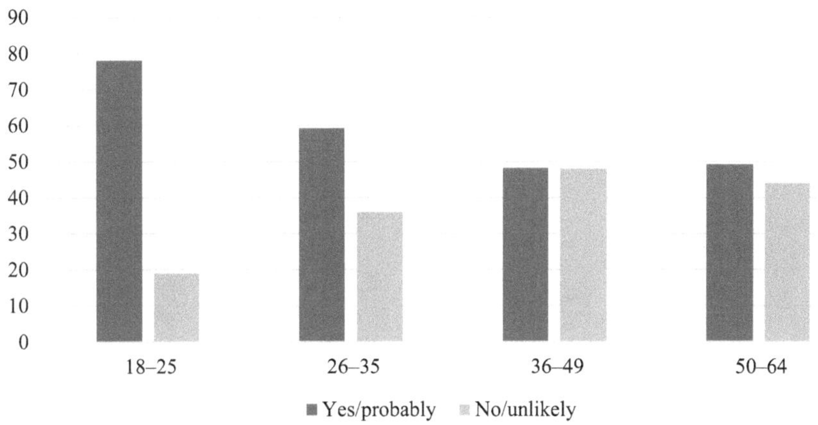

FIGURE 8.2 Would you work somewhere that did not offer remote potential? (Aggregate of answers).

Within the youngest cohort, aged 18–25, a substantial 78% indicate an inclination towards or openness to working at a non-remote workplace. In the age bracket of 26–35, a noteworthy transition emerges, with 59% of respondents expressing a propensity or willingness to work at a non-remote workplace. The age groups 36–49 and 50–64 exhibit a comparable trend, with 48% of respondents within both categories indicating an affirmative disposition towards non-remote work. These percentages signal a continuity in the prevailing sentiment among these middle-aged and more experienced professionals.

Stefaniec et al. (2022) found that in the Dublin area, the desire to work in the office was highest among junior employees and those who had been in their current roles for short periods. More senior employees, those who had been in their roles for more than ten years, preferred office work more than younger employees. This suggests that employees recognise the office as a place where professional growth can take place.

Figure 8.3 shows responses to the question of how important it is for individuals across different age groups to have the opportunity to WFH or remotely. In the younger age group (18–25), a significant percentage of respondents (46%) consider it very or fairly important or very important that the company they work for offers the opportunity to WFH. In the age group 36–49 years old 68% find it fairly or very important. The responses indicate that older individuals tend to place a higher value on the flexibility and convenience offered by remote work compared to their younger counterparts. This pattern is consistent across all age groups, with a notable gap evident when comparing them to the youngest category.

As age increases, there is a slight decrease in the percentage of respondents who find remote work very or fairly important, with higher percentages leaning towards the "not very important" category. However, it is worth noting that even in the

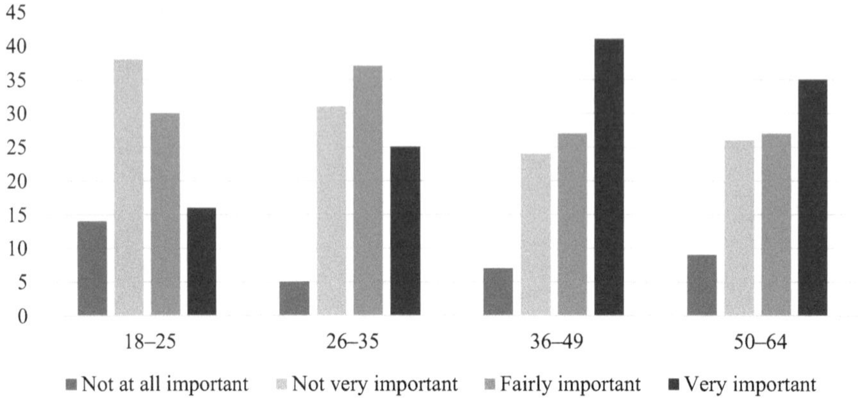

FIGURE 8.3 How important is it to you that the company you work for offers the opportunity to work from home/remotely?

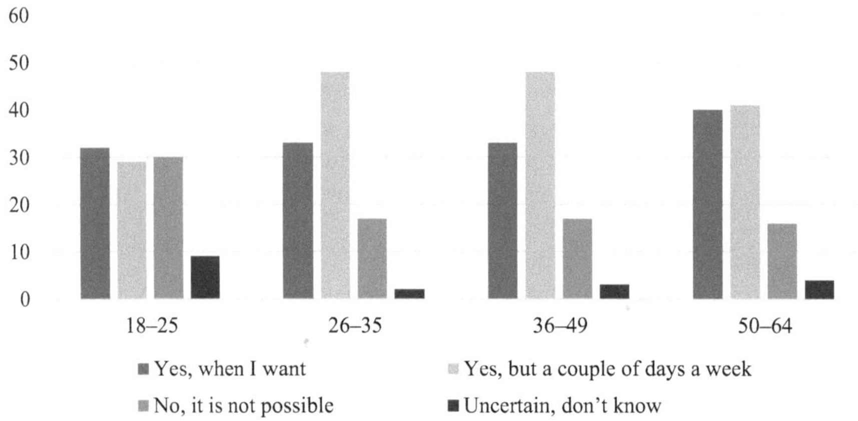

FIGURE 8.4 Does the company you work for offer the possibility to work from home/ remotely?

older age groups (36–49 and 50–64), a considerable proportion value remote work opportunity. The "not at all important" category shows relatively low percentages across all age groups, indicating that a minority of respondents completely dismiss the importance of remote work options.

Figure 8.4 shows whether the company they work for offers the possibility to WFH or remotely. The most common response across all age groups is "Yes, but a couple of days a week". A significant portion of respondents in each age group have the option to work remotely on specific days, suggesting a level of flexibility in their work arrangements. The second most common response is "Yes, when I want".

When comparing the different age groups, we can observe some variations in the responses. For example, the 50–64 age group has the highest percentage of respondents (40%) who answered "Yes, when I want", indicating a relatively higher level of autonomy in their remote work arrangements compared to the other age groups. The 26–35 and 36–49 age groups have the highest percentages of respondents (48%) who answered "Yes, but a couple of days a week", suggesting a greater prevalence of part-time remote work options in those age groups. On the other hand, the 18–25 age group has the highest percentage (30%) of respondents who answered "No, it is not possible", indicating a relatively lower availability of remote work options among this younger age group compared to the older age groups.

Upon dissecting the responses to the question regarding the availability of remote work arrangements within their workplace, rather large differentiations across distinct age cohorts come to the fore. In essence, these findings underscore the role of age in delineating the contours of remote work access. This empirical discernment thus accentuates the imperative for organisations and policymakers to adopt a nuanced stratagem that accounts for age-based nuances when orchestrating remote work implementations.

Figure 8.5 shows responses to the question of why individuals do not WFH or remotely when they have the opportunity, categorised by age groups. The most common reason across all age groups for not working from home is the desire to

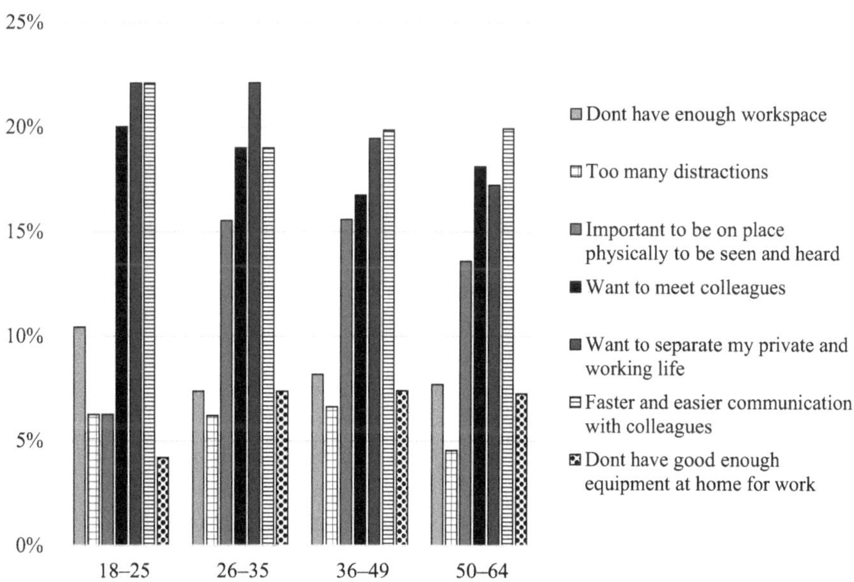

FIGURE 8.5 Why do you not work from home/remotely as long as you have the opportunity?

separate private and working life. This indicates that a significant proportion of individuals value the physical separation between their personal and professional environments. The desire to meet colleagues is also a notable reason for not working from home, with relatively high percentages across all age groups. This suggests that social interaction and face-to-face collaboration play an important role for many individuals in their work experience.

Faster and easier communication with colleagues is another reason that ranks relatively high in all age groups. This indicates that some individuals perceive in-person communication as more effective and efficient compared to remote communication tools. As seen in other research, the importance of being physically present to be seen and heard is a reason that increases in significance as age increases. Returning to the office to be "seen" is one way to increase the feeling of job security, while refusing to return to the office puts employees at greater risk of termination (Brower, 2022).

The lack of enough workspace, too many distractions, and inadequate equipment at home are factors that contribute to a smaller percentage of individuals in each age group. This implies that for most respondents, these practical limitations are not significant barriers to working remotely. Individuals may struggle to disconnect from work, as the lack of physical boundaries makes it challenging to clearly define the end of the working day (Parry et al., 2021; Tahlyan et al., 2022).

Other surveys conducted during the pandemic showed that Generation Z (those born after 1996) were more likely to say they struggled with work–life balance taking a greater toll on their physical and mental health than older generations, as well as with workplace productivity metrics like contributing to meetings or bringing forward new ideas (Microsoft, 2021).

Many young people lacked office contacts, felt the absence of friendships and networks, had poorer working environments, and felt anxious about reduced opportunities for growth and higher pressure to perform with the tight labour market (De Abreu e Silva, 2022; Microsoft, 2021; Parry et al., 2021). Young people also report being less satisfied and productive when working remotely (Tahlyan et al., 2022).

Figure 8.6 illustrates distinct trends in the perceived significance of various factors when considering prospective workplaces across different age cohorts. Notably, the youngest and oldest segments of the workforce, aged 18–25 and 50–64, respectively, exhibit divergent inclinations in their prioritisation of these factors.

The youngest cohort, individuals aged 18–25, prominently underscores the importance of "Flexible working hours and working environment" (24%) when evaluating potential workplaces. Concurrently, this group attributes relatively high value to "Development opportunities within the company" (18%), indicating their aspirational outlook towards professional growth and skill enhancement.

In contrast, the oldest cohort, encompassing respondents aged 50–64, manifests a discernibly different pattern. While also recognising the significance of "Flexible

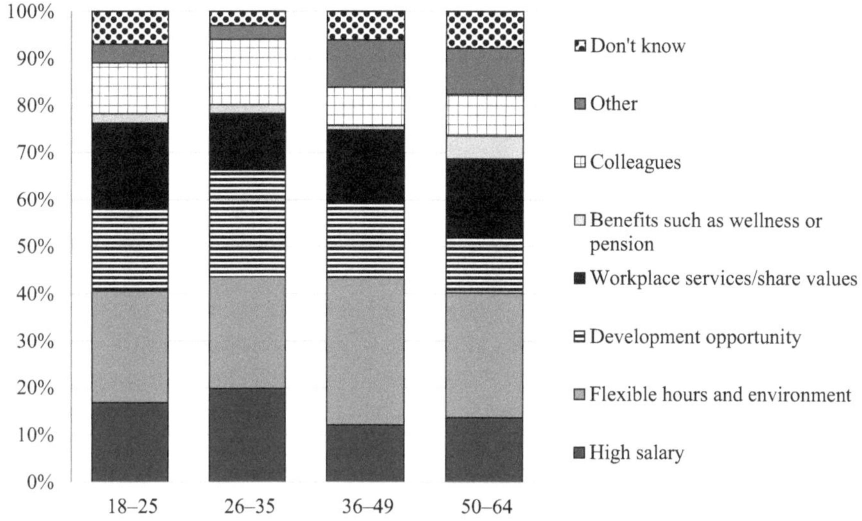

FIGURE 8.6 Primary employment concerns by age.

working hours and working environment" (27%), this group, consistent with their career stage, values other factors more markedly. Specifically, "High salary" (14%) and "Development opportunities within the company" (12%) are less pronounced priorities for this age group. This possibly reflects a culmination of career goals and a potential emphasis on workplace culture and personal alignment, as indicated by the emphasis placed on "Workplace services or products sharing the same values as me" (17%).

It is noteworthy that the two age cohorts, 18–25 and 50–64, converge in their acknowledgement of "Colleagues" as a contributing factor (11% and 9%, respectively), potentially indicating the universal importance of social dynamics in the workplace across generations. But the number is rather small so the importance might be low.

An explanation for the expressed preferences shown in Figure 8.6 might be in line with studies indicating that the decline in informal "water cooler communication" results in digital leaders displaying diminished engagement with their employees, extending beyond mere professional interactions (McGregor & Doshi, 2020). Communication is an essential element contributing to both trust establishment and empowerment (Terkamo-Moisio, Karki, Kangasniemi, Lammintakanen, & Häggman-Laitila, 2022). To enable the proficient exercise of autonomy, employees and managers possess a comprehension of mutual expectations. In this regard, goals and accomplishments can prove advantageous, while using physical office presence as a surrogate measure of performance could potentially be counterproductive (Aloisi & De Stefano, 2022). Young people might be more eager to prove themselves and hence want to be able to show up and show off.

Another explanation to young people's preference for the office can be found through the lens of social network analysis. It reveals the inherent challenge of establishing and nurturing digital networking and collaboration, which can potentially complicate collective efforts and collaborative undertakings (Dutcher, 2012; Gajendran & Harrison, 2007; Orrell & Leger, 2020). Allen and Shockley (2009) illustrate that remote workers often encounter difficulties in effectively coordinating projects when their dependence on co-workers is high, and there is a perceived erosion of team cohesion due to the implementation of remote work (Baert, Lippens, Moens, Sterkens, & Weytjens, 2020).

The complexity of WFH is exacerbated within hybrid solutions, where certain employees opt for in-office work while others embrace remote work (Kossek, Thompson, & Lautsch, 2015). A split location dynamic fosters the emergence of "A- and B-teams", potentially jeopardising collaborative endeavours (Allstrin et al., 2022). A pronounced division between office-based and remote-working groups can create an "us-and-them" dichotomy that might grow communication disparities between these factions. This, in turn, poses the risk of eroding cohesiveness and organisational culture (Gibbs, Mengel, & Siemroth, 2021; Orrell & Leger, 2020; Terkamo-Moisio et al., 2022).

8.4 Discussion

From the results it seems like that the old segment of the dataset maintains reservations or outright disinclination towards the thought of not being able to WFH, but the answers and preferences vary a lot between age groups. This attests to the multifaceted nature of workforce preferences within the specified age group. Organisational stakeholders and policymakers should heed these nuances to tailor employment frameworks that accommodate a spectrum of attitudes and inclinations, thereby optimising the alignment between workforce demographics and prevailing workplace paradigms.

Is it feasible for a firm to attract candidates if they do not offer remote work options? Based on the findings illustrated in Figure 8.1, the answer appears to be affirmative; however, it comes at a substantial cost in terms of the recruitment process. It is plausible to assume that job seekers possessing valuable skills in demand by employers may have multiple employment options in mind and could be evaluating offers from various employers. Given that nearly half of the respondents expressed reluctance to accept a job that does not include the option to WFH, it is conceivable that many candidates might reject offers from employers who do not provide this flexibility, especially when they have multiple choices at their disposal.

When an applicant has only one potential job offer, some may accept it, while others might decline. In this scenario, job seekers must weigh the option of waiting an additional week for a job that aligns with their preferences. Given that substantial savings, both in terms of finances and time, can be realised through remote work, the incentives may lean towards waiting. Notably, in the 18–25 age group, most individuals may be inclined to accept a job even if it does not offer the option to WFH. However, it is worth considering whether this group may be underselling themselves and may not possess the same level of skills and qualifications.

The question presented in Figure 8.3 "How important is it to you that the company you work for offers the opportunity to WFH/remotely?" also gave interesting indications that employers should be aware of. The constraint on remote work feasibility within the youngest segment of the labour force, aged 18–25 years, can probably be ascribed to several factors that collectively contribute to the comparatively diminished availability of remote work options for this demographic. Given their nascent professional trajectories, individuals in the 18–25 age group might possess limited autonomy and decision-making authority within their roles. The need for a supervisor can be larger and needed daily while an experienced employee might be responsible for projects that only need weekly contact with supervisors. The roles young and older workers have are likely significantly different and some of the roles may allow less WFH.

A study of students and researchers at the University of Ljubljana conducted in November 2020 asked about their working environment at home and found that students held more favourable views of their WFH setups than educators and researchers in the same place (Drašler et al., 2021). Researchers had a harder time doing tasks remotely, especially those in the sciences. Higher education has experienced a digitalising trend pre-COVID, so many students found the switch to online education and home environments comfortable, especially as they tended to be surrounded by others in the same stage of life with similar schedules.

In a survey of Nordic office workers conducted by Castellum (2023), they found similar results. The table categorises respondents into different age groups, ranging from younger than 25 years to 55 years or older. Across all age groups, the highest percentage of respondents who would react positively to mandatory office attendance for one week is in the younger than 25 years group, with 42%. The percentages gradually decrease as the age groups get older. A significant portion of respondents in each age group would have a negative reaction to the mandatory office attendance but would accept the situation. The highest percentage in this category is in the 45–54 years and 55 years or older groups, both at 33%.

Some firms, particularly those with more traditional structures, might have a company culture and hierarchies that prioritise in-person interactions and physical presence. Young employees, being newer entrants to the workforce, might be subject to such established norms that hinder the adoption of remote work. It could also, right, or wrong, be the belief that younger workers require more direct managerial oversight and mentorship, which could be perceived as challenging to administer in remote work arrangements. In-person interactions are often considered crucial for fostering professional development. Additionally, the younger individuals in the dataset, who are possibly newer to their jobs compared to older workers, might be undergoing an initial learning or acclimation phase. This group may also be more inclined to switch jobs frequently.

8.5 Conclusion

This chapter provides an exposition of noteworthy insights pertaining to the predilections of young professionals regarding their preferences for WFH within the context of Sweden. Of course, firm culture, employee attitudes, and business needs will drive the bulk of WFH decisions, but our results are an important reminder that plans will need to be specialised to the natural and economic geography of the workforce.

It is important to remember that preferences and opinions can vary greatly among both young and old when it comes to returning to the office after the pandemic. Preferences may depend on various factors, such as individual work tasks, personal circumstances, and individual work styles. Some young people may prefer to return to the office because they value the opportunity for face-to-face social interaction and collaboration. Others may prefer to continue working remotely because they appreciate the flexibility and convenience of being able to adapt their work environment to their own needs. However, some conclusions can be drawn.

It is important that employers and organisations take individual preferences into account and create flexible work models that can meet different needs and wishes. A diversity of work arrangements can be beneficial in promoting a positive work environment and productivity regardless of age. Firms that are not amenable to offering remote work options could find themselves at a disadvantage in the competitive talent landscape. Candidates, particularly those with sought-after skills, are increasingly inclined to evaluate employment offers through the lens of remote work potential. This scenario introduces a nuanced calculus wherein candidates must weigh their immediate options against their long-term work preferences and lifestyle considerations.

An important insight is how valuable early career learning is in building professional confidence and competence. As staff adapt to more hybrid organisational structures – part remote, part in-office – there is a huge opportunity to build learning into new work patterns. Similarly, older people may have different preferences. Some older employees may prefer to come back to the office because they have been used to a traditional work environment and enjoy that structure. Other older people may prefer to work remotely to avoid any risk of infection or for personal health reasons.

The chapter provides a richer foundation for commentary and analysis had the cohorts been subjected to less aggregation. The current level of aggregation, while chosen due to the constraints of the dataset encompassing approximately 1,000 office workers, has imposed limitations on the granularity of age cohorts that can be effectively employed. It becomes evident that subdividing these age cohorts into smaller segments would risk yielding groups with an insufficient number of individuals for meaningful statistical analysis. In acknowledging the constraints of the dataset's sample size, it is important to strike a balance between the desire for more detailed age cohort distinctions and the need for statistically significant sample sizes within each cohort. A larger dataset would undoubtedly offer greater flexibility in forming narrower age cohorts, which could enable researchers to uncover nuanced trends and patterns that might currently remain concealed within the broader aggregates. But general trends can clearly be spotted and commented on which is a contribution.

Some employees have chosen to return to the office full-time, while others prefer to continue working remotely or in a hybrid model that combines both office work and remote work. There is no one-size-fits-all solution, and employers need to adapt and offer flexibility to meet the different needs and wants of their employees. It is worth noting that the pandemic has accelerated some changes in the work environment, including an increased acceptance of remote work and a greater emphasis on flexibility. Finally, it is important to point out that the situation can be dynamic and change over time depending on the evolution of the pandemic and the recommendations of authorities and health experts.

Acknowledgements

I wish to extend my gratitude to Hewlett-Packard (HP) Sweden for graciously granting me access to the dataset employed in this study. Their willingness to provide this data was pivotal in enabling the comprehensive analysis and meaningful conclusions that have been drawn. Additionally, I am indebted to Evan Eskilson for his invaluable contributions in the realm of research assistance. Furthermore, I would like to express my heartfelt appreciation to the esteemed members of the academic community at the Ratio Institute. Their insightful comments and feedback during the presentation of the material contained within this chapter were instrumental in refining and enhancing the content.

References

Aksoy, C. G., Barrero, J. M., Bloom, N., Davis, S. J., Dolls, M., & Zarate, P. (2022). *Working Home From Around the World* (No. 30446). NBER Working Paper. Cambridge, MA: National Bureau of Economic Research.

Allen, T. D., & Shockley, K. (2009). Flexible work arrangements: Help or hype? In D. R. Crane & E. J. Hill (Eds.), *Handbook of Families and Work: Interdisciplinary Perspectives* (pp. 265–284). Lanham, MD: University Press of America.

Allstrin, S., Grafström, J., Stern, C., Stern, L., & Weidenstedt, L. (2022). *Managing Work from Anywhere: Six Points to Consider for HR Professionals* (No. 357). Stockholm, Sweden: Ratio, Näringslivets Forskningsinstitut.

Aloisi, A., & De Stefano, V. (2022). Essential jobs, remote work and digital surveillance: Addressing the COVID-19 pandemic panopticon. *International Labour Review, 161*(2), 289–314. https://doi.org/10.1111/ilr.12219

Baert, S., Lippens, L., Moens, E., Sterkens, P., & Weytjens, J. (2020). *The COVID-19 Crisis and Remote Work: A Research Survey on Experiences, Expectations and Hopes* (No. 13229). Bonn, Germany: IZA Institute of Labor Economics.

Barrero, J. M., Bloom, N., & Davis, S. J. (2021). *Why Working From Home Will Stick* (No. 2020–174). Working Paper. Chicago, IL: Becker Friedman Institute.

Brower, T. (2022). What Leaders Are Getting Wrong About the Return to the Office. Retrieved March 6, 2025, from Forbes website: www.forbes.com/sites/tracybrower/2022/12/04/what-leaders-are-getting-wrong-about-the-return-to-the-office

Brynjolfsson, E., Horton, J. J., Ozimek, A., Rock, D., Sharma, G., & TuYe, H.-Y. (2020). *COVID-19 and Remote Work: An Early Look at US Data* (No. 27344). https://doi.org/10.3386/w27344

Castellum. (2023). Framtidens arbetsliv 2023 [The Future Working Life 2023]. Retrieved March 6, 2025, from www.castellum.se/radgivning/framtidens-arbetsliv/rapport-2023

Cisco. (2022). Employees Are Ready For Hybrid Work, Are You? Retrieved March 6, 2025, from Cisco Global Hybrid Work Study 2022 website: www.cisco.com/c/m/en_us/solutions/global-hybrid-work-study.html

De Abreu e Silva, J. (2022). Residential preferences, telework perceptions, and the intention to telework: insights from the Lisbon Metropolitan Area during the COVID-19 pandemic. *Regional Science Policy & Practice*, *14*(S1), 142–161. https://doi.org/10.1111/rsp3.12558

Deloitte. (2021). 7.5 Million UK Workers Hoping To Work From Home Permanently Once Lockdown Restrictions Have Lifted. Retrieved March 6, 2025, from http://web.archive.org/web/20240212150450/https://20240212150450/www2.deloitte.com/uk/en/pages/press-releases/articles/7-5-million-uk-workers-hoping-to-work-from-home-permanently-once-lockdown-restrictions-have-lifted

Drašler, V., Bertoncelj, J., Korošec, M., Pajk Žontar, T., Poklar Ulrih, N., & Cigić, B. (2021). Difference in the attitude of students and employees of the University of Ljubljana towards work from home and online education: Lessons from COVID-19 Pandemic. *Sustainability*, *13*(9), 5118, 1–24. https://doi.org/10.3390/su13095118

Dua, A., Ellingrud, K., Kirschner, P., Kwok, A., Luby, R., Palter, R., & Pemberton, S. (2022). Americans Are Embracing Flexible Work—And They Want More of It. Retrieved March 6, 2025, from McKinsey Global Institute website: www.mckinsey.com/industries/real-estate/our-insights/americans-are-embracing-flexible-work-and-they-want-more-of-it

Dutcher, E. G. (2012). The effects of telecommuting on productivity: An experimental examination. The role of dull and creative tasks. *Journal of Economic Behavior & Organization*, *84*(1), 355–363. https://doi.org/10.1016/j.jebo.2012.04.009

Eurostat. (2020). Archive: Age of Young People Leaving Their Parental Household. Retrieved March 6, 2025, from https://ec.europa.eu/eurostat/statistics-explained/index.php?oldid=494351

Gajendran, R. S., & Harrison, D. A. (2007). The good, the bad, and the unknown about telecommuting: Meta-analysis of psychological mediators and individual consequences. *Journal of Applied Psychology*, *92*(6), 1524–1541. https://doi.org/10.1037/0021-9010.92.6.1524

Gibbs, M., Mengel, F., & Siemroth, C. (2021). *Work from Home & Productivity: Evidence from Personnel & Analytics Data on IT Professionals* (No. 2021–56). Working Paper. Chicago, IL: Becker Friedman Institute.

Gittleman, M. (2022). The "Great Resignation" in Perspective. Retrieved March 6, 2025, from Monthly Labor Review website: www.bls.gov/opub/mlr/2022/article/the-great-resignation-in-perspective.htm

Gosling, W., & Coppola, M. (2020). May the Workforce Be with You. Retrieved March 6, 2025, from Deloitte Insights website: www2.deloitte.com/us/en/insights/focus/technology-and-the-future-of-work/impact-covid-19-european-workforce.html

Grunau, P., Wolter, S., Bellmann, L., & Müller, D. (2017). ICT and Actual Working Time in Germany. *Management Revue*, *28*(3), 359–374. https://doi.org/10.5771/0935-9915-2017-3-359

Kossek, E. E., Thompson, R. J., & Lautsch, B. A. (2015). Balanced workplace flexibility: Avoiding the traps. *California Management Review*, *57*(4), 5–25. https://doi.org/10.1525/cmr.2015.57.4.5

McGregor, L., & Doshi, N. (2020). How to Keep Your Team Motivated, Remotely. Retrieved March 6, 2025, from Harvard Business Review website: https://hbr.org/2020/04/how-to-keep-your-team-motivated-remotely

Microsoft. (2021). The Next Great Disruption Is Hybrid Work—Are We Ready? Retrieved March 6, 2025, from www.microsoft.com/en-us/worklab/work-trend-index/hybrid-work

Miller, C. C., & Yar, S. (2019). Young People Are Going to Save Us All From Office Life. Retrieved March 6, 2025, from The New York Times website: www.nytimes.com/2019/09/17/style/generation-z-millennials-work-life-balance.html

Orrell, B., & Leger, M. (2020). *The Trade-Offs of Remote Work: Building a More Resilient Workplace for the Post-Covid 19 World.* Washington, DC: American Enterprise Institute.

Parry, J., Young, Z., Bevan, S., Veliziotis, M., Baruch, Y., Beigi, M., … & Tochia, C. (2021). Working From Home Under COVID-19 Lockdown: Transitions and Tensions. Retrieved March 6, 2025, from Work After Lockdown website: www.employment-studies.co.uk/resource/working-home-under-covid-19-lockdown

Russo, D., Hanel, P. H. P., Altnickel, S., & van Berkel, N. (2021). Predictors of well-being and productivity among software professionals during the COVID-19 pandemic – a longitudinal study. *Empirical Software Engineering*, *26*(4), 62, 1–62. https://doi.org/10.1007/s10664-021-09945-9

Stefaniec, A., Brazil, W., Whitney, W., & Caulfield, B. (2022). Desire to work from home: Results of an Irish study. *Journal of Transport Geography*, *104*, 103416. https://doi.org/10.1016/j.jtrangeo.2022.103416

Tahlyan, D., Said, M., Mahmassani, H., Stathopoulos, A., Walker, J., & Shaheen, S. (2022). For whom did telework not work during the Pandemic? understanding the factors impacting telework satisfaction in the US using a multiple indicator multiple cause (MIMIC) model. *Transportation Research Part A: Policy and Practice*, *155*, 387–402. https://doi.org/10.1016/j.tra.2021.11.025

Terkamo-Moisio, A., Karki, S., Kangasniemi, M., Lammintakanen, J., & Häggman-Laitila, A. (2022). Towards remote leadership in health care: Lessons learned from an integrative review. *Journal of Advanced Nursing*, *78*(3), 595–608. https://doi.org/10.1111/jan.15028

9

THE POSSIBLE FUTURES FOR GIG WORK

Digital Platform Labour and Its Regulation

Miriam A. Cherry

9.1 Introduction

Since its inception, the platform economy has generated a high volume of litigation. One of the largest sources of disputes in the gig economy has been its ambiguous relationship with labour and employment law. Despite the widespread and undeniable fact that labour takes place on digital platforms, workers have been unable to access basic labour rights. The barrier is employment misclassification and the need to establish employee status. In general, workers who establish employee status can access various rights, such as the right to minimum wage and the right to organise and bargain collectively.

The results of this litigation have been uneven, leading to indeterminate results in legal systems around the world. Particularly, the US state of California has seen legislative action, retrenchment, and revision. For a brief period during 2020, gig workers in California were considered employees. Platforms resisted reclassification, instead spending money on political lobbying to overturn the law. In November 2020, voters approved ballot measure Proposition 22. The ballot initiative created an intermediate category for the first time in the United States, which carved out an exemption focussed on gig workers that received only a portion of the rights accorded to employees.

While the exclusion of platform workers from labour protections, the growth of the informal economy, and rising inequality may be one possible future for gig work, that future is not inevitable. The passage of the European Directive on Platform Work in 2024 sets out a blueprint for bringing platform workers under the ambit of labour and employment laws. Further, with an international standard on platform work on the 2025 agenda for the United Nations International Labour Conference, gig workers can be hopeful to see labour and employment rights

DOI: 10.4324/9781003391333-11

be recognised. Instead of platform companies spending hundreds of millions of dollars campaigning against employee status, there is a business case to be made for compliance and the implementation of best practices. Implementing such compliance and corporate social responsibility (CSR) measures will strengthen the future of the gig economy, and taking a reasonable position on regulation (as opposed to resistance or oppositional political lobbying) might ensure that platforms, workers, and regulators are able to work together to ensure that new regulations will be tailored to meet the needs of workers, platforms, and customers in the platform economy.

This chapter sets out the events that have led to conflicting and contradictory regulatory outcomes. The first section describes the characteristics of digital labour platforms, and the litigation and regulatory problems that have existed during the early stages of the development of the platform economy. The second section describes the methods of legal analysis used. The third provides a discussion of various analogous models of regulation. This section also explores the business case for connecting recent regulatory actions to CSR and environment, social, and governance (ESG). Ultimately, the chapter presents an alternative vision for the future, one that incorporates worker rights and establishes a strong basis for digital labour platforms moving forward.

The methodology for this chapter involves a traditional legal analysis, including the compilation, study, and analysis of international, national, state, and municipal cases, directives, treaties, and other international instruments. The methodology also includes a review of viewpoints articulated by stakeholders, including digital labour platform operators, organisers with unions and informal worker associations, scholarly experts on the gig economy, policymakers or other regulators of the gig economy, as well as workers themselves.

9.1.1 Background and Characteristics of Digital Labour Platforms

Many have praised digital labour platforms as making certain forms of commerce more accessible, thus creating new work opportunities. Platforms, customers, and workers have taken advantage of the new efficiencies that these new forms of work can create. At the same time, others have criticised digital labour platforms as undermining or evading the laws regulating labour and employment through the misclassification of workers. Throughout the past decade, these labour problems have persisted, preventing the platform economy from reaching its growth potential.

Since the early 2010s, digital labour platforms have grown to cover many forms of work, including rideshare, computer tasks, grocery shopping and delivery, housecleaning, professional services, pet sitting, and food delivery. Some of these tasks, which are generally referred to as "crowdwork", take place only on the computer and may use workers from many different countries and time zones. Other forms of work depend on the location where the work is to be performed, such as the provision of a ride to the airport or grocery delivery. These forms of work are generally referred to as gig work (DeStefano, 2016).

Digital labour platforms have grown rapidly all around the world, providing various services and work opportunities. In the United States, a 2018 study estimated that the number of workers on platforms surpassed 57 million. That number has only grown. Recent estimates from the US Bureau of Labor Statistics calculate that more than a quarter of US workers use gig platforms for either their primary or secondary work (Charro, Dua, Ellingrud, Luby, & Pemberton, 2022; McCue, 2018). During the 2020 coronavirus pandemic, gig workers were granted temporary parity with employees as "essential workers" and provided with sick leave and unemployment benefits. However, as the pandemic receded, those benefits were proven to be only temporary measures. After the pandemic, platform workers are still fighting for access to basic labour and employment laws and protections (Cherry, 2022).

Whether providing crowdwork or gig work, digital labour platforms typically share several common factors and characteristics. Platform work is computer intermediated, in some instances making locations or progress known through cell phone applications that use tracking, transmit various forms of data, or GPS location information. Platforms also perform market-making functions, in which they match service providers with customers and engaging in the setting of prices. These forms of work also are often characterised by algorithmic management, where decisions about remuneration and even deactivation are automatically determined by computer code. Crowdwork is often globalised, making national boundaries less important or relevant to regulation. Finally, digital platform labour relies on forms of reputation and trust proxies such as customer rating systems.

One of the largest obstacles for platform growth has been the labour and employment issues that have held back the sector. On the one hand, gig work has been seen as a *sui generis* problem, not easily regulated because of its hybrid nature that combines elements of employment and independent contracting. On the other hand, many of the types of work that gig workers engage in are forms of work that far predate the gig economy and in fact have been jobs that have been in existence for hundreds if not thousands of years (as with transportation). The next section will examine the history and development of regulation, which helps to explain the confused present situation.

9.1.2 Development of Misclassification Litigation

The starting point for much of the employee status litigation begins with the platforms themselves. In the platform economy, many of the relationships between workers and platforms, and platforms and their customers, are intermediated by standard form or boilerplate contracts, commonly referred to as "contracts of adhesion". These may be referred to variously as End User License Agreements (EULAs), the Terms of Service (TOS), or Terms and Conditions (T&C). Many websites and cell phone apps have used these standard form contracts, drafted by lawyers, which use the fine print to state that workers should be treated as independent contractors, rather than employees (Employment Tribunal – U.K., 2016).

During much of the 2010s, workers around the world initiated litigation to access the protections of labour and employment law. The main bar towards their doing so was the need to show employee status. In legal systems throughout the world, labour and employment law statutes are only activated by a showing that a worker is an employee. Employees are assumed to need the protection of labour and employment law, such as unemployment insurance, minimum wage, and worker safety and health protections. In the words of one commentator, classification and employee status are actually "an important instrument for the delivery of workers' rights" (Davidov, 2006, p. 134). Employees are acknowledged to be dependent on their employers and also to be subject to the control and direction of managers.

Employee status is often contrasted with independent contractor status, in which the individual is operating a separate and distinct business from the hiring entity. Independent entrepreneurs are seen by the law as savvy businesspeople who are generally able to fend for themselves. Generally, independent contractors supply their own tools of the trade and typically use a high level of skilled labour. Independent contractors also typically charge by the completed task, rather than an hourly rate. Their work has a clear delineation between their separate businesses. While the matter seems clear in theory, the bifurcation in the law has led to widespread confusion over classification issues. Some portion of that confusion can be attributed to vague or uncertain tests for determining status. At the same time, many putative employers may engage in arbitrage of these categories to take advantage of the cost savings of using independent contractors. A combination of these problems currently exists: genuine confusion over classification and bogus schemes to hide employees from the law. The problem is compounded because many workers use digital platforms for what amounts to full-time employment or a serious commitment type of additional job, but others are more casual. For those workers who are treating the platforms as a full-time or robust part-time job, basic standards for that work is important. This is especially true as rideshare platforms use various incentives as well as gamification to encourage drivers to sign onto the apps during peak times and to work in shifts (Rosenblat & Stark, 2016).

Despite any label that platforms may provide, courts may examine the substance of the relationship to determine whether employee status exists. In European countries, this is often referred to as the "primacy of facts" doctrine (Aloisi & Cherry, 2024). In the United States, courts have reviewed the structure of the gig economy with confused or mixed results. For example, in the 2015 decision *Cotter v. Lyft*, a court in the Northern District of California stated that rideshare drivers lack some characteristics of independent contractors. Rideshare drivers are referred to work only through a platform, and they are not encouraged to build their own brand or be entrepreneurial on their own. Similarly, the court concluded, workers do not use a highly developed skill set to perform tasks. Nor did the workers in rideshare negotiate their rate of pay with customers. On the other hand, the court also noted that workers did not seem much like employees, either, as workers would have more flexibility to work as their schedules allowed (United States District Court N.D. California, 2015). The court ordered a trial on the question of employee status. The incentives of litigation, however, led the matters to a US$100 million settlement and payout to drivers. However, the settlement left the matter of employment status undecided moving forward.

9.1.3 The Gig Battles of California

Since then, California law has been a study in legal indeterminacy. During the so-called gig battles of California, there have been multiple visions for regulation that later are challenged or overturned. After the *Cotter v. Lyft* case settled, the Supreme Court of California determined that a broader test for employment (the so-called ABC test) should be implemented for the limited purpose of wage orders. The ABC test, named so because it has three sub-parts, contains a rebuttable presumption that workers are employees. Part A focusses on the putative employer's control over workers, and Part C focusses on whether the worker is engaged in an independent trade or business. Part B requires a showing that the work being performed is outside the course of the hiring entity's usual business. This test, and particularly part B, would have meant that gig workers would be included in the definition of the "employees" because platforms depend on the provision of services as the core of their businesses. The California Assembly then passed legislation that expanded the ABC test beyond wage orders to all classification determinations. That bill, known as AB5, codified the ABC test and covered gig workers as of January 1, 2020. However, gig companies resisted compliance with the law and instead spent over US$200 million to overturn AB5 through a direct ballot initiative known as Proposition 22. The lobbying campaign was at that time the largest expenditure on a state ballot initiative in the United States. After a massive media campaign and threats of some of the largest gig economy companies to leave California entirely, voters passed Proposition 22 in 2020.

Proposition 22 has now created a hybrid category specifically for gig work. While platform-intermediated workers still would be called "independent contractors", the ballot initiative created a new intermediate category, which could be termed "independent contractor plus". This hybrid category granted gig workers additional protections beyond what true independent contractors would receive, such as minimum wage floors and access to health benefits. What was not included, however, was the ability to bargain and organise collectively and certain other employment rights. Because Proposition 22 contained a requirement that a 7/8 vote of the California Legislature would be required in order to amend it, a union brought a constitutional challenge, alleging that it undermined the power of the Legislature to regulate labour and employment (Alameda County Superior

Court, 2021). As of this writing the matter is being appealed to the California Supreme Court.

Beyond the gig battles of California, other US states have encountered the same kinds of indeterminate legal outcomes concerning the employment status of gig workers. Washington state implemented an independent contractor plus category in 2023, after much controversy. In the state of Minnesota, worker rights advocates backed a third category for gig workers that guaranteed certain wages and tips for gig workers, as well as procedural protections for gig workers who had been deactivated from platforms. Platforms baulked, lobbying against the measure, and put pressure on the governor's office. The Minnesota governor eventually vetoed the legislation. Similar gig battles are occurring in Massachusetts, where the Supreme Judicial Court struck down the language of a platform-backed initiative that would have created a discounted independent contractor plus category. In the United States the legal landscape has been littered with various initiatives that have attempted to create "third way" categories to respond to gig work. Unfortunately these reshufflings of the categories have done little to alleviate workers' concerns about low pay, summary deactivation, and the absence of worker voice.

9.1.4 Regulation of Platform Work Around the World

The problems and issues in the United States have revealed a great deal of turmoil. While extreme, the gig battles of California may be emblematic of the confusion and indeterminate regulation of gig work in legal systems around the world. As noted in Section 9.1.1, one characteristic of digital labour platforms is that they are truly global. National governments and regulatory systems have been confounded by the hybrid characteristics of digital labour platforms.

The courts of different countries within the European Union (EU) have ruled in inconsistent ways over employment status for gig workers. For example, in 2018, Belgium's courts decided that food delivery bicycle riders working for the platform Deliveroo were employees. However, at around the same time, the court of Turin, Italy, ruled that Foodora delivery drivers were independent contractors who could determine their own schedules and methods of work (Cherry, 2020). The matter could be complicated as some countries had pre-existing hybrid categories that had been marked by controversy (Cherry & Aloisi, 2017). For example, the United Kingdom's courts decided that platform workers should be characterised as "workers", a hybrid category that received only some of the rights and benefits of employees. Moreover, within EU countries rulings on status for gig workers could change rapidly as they were heard by intermediate or supreme national courts (Cherry, 2020).

This state of affairs has continued to create litigation, tension, and confusion. As a result, the European Parliament proposed a Directive on Platform Work. The Directive, which was adopted in February 2024, begins with a presumption of employment status for platform workers. Ensuring "that people working through platforms have – or can obtain – the correct employment status in light of their actual relationship with the digital labour platform and gain access to the applicable labour and social protection rights" is one of the main objectives of the Proposal for a Directive of the European Parliament and of the Council on improving working conditions in platform work (European Parliament and of the Council, 2021, pt. 1). To achieve this goal, the Platform Work Directive presents a rebuttable presumption of employment. In legal systems, presumptions can redefine the default rules and change the landscape of litigation. The Platform Work Directive, which was signed into force in February 2024, now brings an estimated 5 million gig workers within the EU new rights and access to employment benefits (Liboreiro, 2024).

9.1.5 The Way Forward for the Future of the Gig Economy

Certainly, digital labour platforms have posed fundamental questions about how work will be structured and performed in the future. At the same time, digital labour platforms have also challenged the existing legal framework for the regulation of work. What will the regulation of the future of work look like? So far, all indicators are that as the standard employment relationship changes, there is pressure to re-examine existing structures of regulation. While questioning established protections may make sense in some cases (where those protections are not needed), in other situations it may amount to evasion or erosion of labour rights secured only through past struggles and negotiations.

9.2 Discussion

This chapter supports the proposals for international and standardised regulation of digital labour platforms. Globalisation is key because, as noted in Section 9.1, platforms manage to be everywhere and nowhere simultaneously. Such problems can give rise to problems for workers who are attempting to access justice systems to claim their rights and can, in some instances, lead to evasion. Currently, digital labour platforms may engage in forum or regulation shopping, gaining an unfair advantage over other similarly situated businesses that comply with the law and acknowledge the use of employees as agents to carry out their operations. Similar regulatory problems have arisen in the context of minimum standards of the global supply chain. Regulating in only one country may often drive businesses into less regulated jurisdictions, illustrating the so-called race to the bottom (Arthurs, 2010, p. 534). Standardisation avoids many of these problems. For platform operators, it also leads to a uniform system of expectations that is easily implemented, rather than engaging in legal analysis to determine the correct set of regulations in the various countries where the platform does businesses.

Crowdwork that takes place wholly in cyberspace is a global phenomenon. Such platforms run counter to the traditional idea that work and labour are primarily issues for local, regional, or national regulation. Due to the divergence of the state and national legislation and court rulings that we have seen, a high degree of confusion exists 15 years into the creation of the gig economy. Workers may choose to bring lawsuits in jurisdictions that have the most favourable labour standards while businesses may try to shield themselves with provisions in online contracts selecting jurisdictions with favourable laws. This type of gamesmanship over jurisdiction, choice of law, and the correct forum for disputes to be heard will lead to unnecessary litigation and undesirable legal arbitrage.

The impact on platform workers will be profound. Currently many platform workers lack representation and have virtually no voice in managerial decisions. Digital labour platforms may unilaterally change pay rates and terms and conditions of work, sometimes with no prior notice or consultation of the platform workers whom those changes impact the most. In the United States, digital labour platforms have become the work of the marginalised. Immigrants and minorities are overrepresented in platform work. Around the world, disabled workers and those with care responsibilities – most often women workers – have also been disproportionally working in poorly paid remote crowdwork positions (Cherry, 2020). Workers in the Global South also are overrepresented on poorly paid crowdworking platforms, despite high levels of educational attainment. In all of these instances, those who are being excluded from regulatory protections are the marginalised workers who need the protections of labour and employment law the most.

If digital labour platforms want to maintain their market position and positive brand images, a change in their labour practices is the next logical step. Instead of viewing any form of regulation as an existential threat, platform companies should plan for what compliance with labour and employment laws entails. Such compliance should align with consistent goals and best practices that have been identified for hiring labour and dealing with human resources more generally, and that are also specifically tailored to work within the gig economy. Studies have shown that consumers are not only more willing to do business with companies that engage in CSR and ESG initiatives, but that they are increasingly demanding such initiatives (Pollman, 2021). As such this chapter also makes not only the case for worker rights in the gig economy because it is the right thing to do, and it seems inevitable, but also because there is a business case to justify improving labour standards.

9.2.1 The Proposed Intervention of the UN-ILO and Similarities to Maritime Regulations

Many of the concerns over global standards for the gig economy have already been encountered and resolved within other regulatory contexts. There has increasingly been a recognition that globalised problems require international standards implemented through a coordinated multinational approach. In the past, there have been occupational categories that have traditionally fallen outside the boundaries of one jurisdiction or location. These job categories include transportation workers, travelling salespeople, and maritime workers. Specifically, maritime workers are involved in container shipping, which comprises an incredible amount of international trade.

The problems of maritime workers have been longstanding, and include issues of wage theft, long hours, and isolation. In extreme instances, workers could find themselves stranded in foreign ports without the resources to return home. Seafaring jobs were often hazardous and seen as temporary. Further, the mobility of such workers made it a difficult puzzle to determine which laws or rules would apply to the maritime employment relationship. As one commentator has noted, a seafarer might

> work on a vessel registered in a foreign country, sailing on the high seas and calling at ports in countries other than that of her flag, owned by citizens of yet other countries, insured in other countries … [and] managed by a company in another country[.].
>
> *(Stevenson, 2005, p. 567)*

The ideology of *mare liberum*, the freedom of the seas, created an unwillingness or inability to regulate, particularly in instances where there were antagonistic actors. Thus despite these multiplicities of the places that might have an interest in regulation of the employment relationship, the irony was that maritime workers often found themselves without a way to access justice.

Over time, international agreements and treaties were agreed to in order to enact sensible regulation of the seas, including the issues of maritime employment. The regulations of the 1970s and 1980s focussed on regulation that was based on the flag that the ship was registered with, including labour regulations. At the same time, this system was imperfect because ships could choose to fly the "flags of convenience", which meant that the country they chose would have little to no substantive regulation or perhaps lax enforcement mechanisms. As such, workers still found themselves without redress in the courts, and the system of regulation based on such choices prompted a "race to the bottom" of regulation (Shaughnessy & Tobin, 2006, p. 18).

This system of patchwork regulation changed when, under the auspices of the UN-ILO, the International Labour Conference (ILC) adopted the Maritime Labour Convention (MLC). The MLC sets out the basic rights that all seafaring workers can expect: fair employment terms, the provision of medical care, health and safety, and decent living conditions while on board. As of 2024, 105 states have ratified the MLC since its promulgation, but the coverage includes over 90% of cargo shipped around the world (International Labour Organization, 2024a). That is because the MLC can be enforced (and ships can be inspected) in the flag state, the port of departure, or the port of entry. The various "places" where vessels travel ensure that there are multiple sites where compliance can be monitored.

There are parallels between the situation that maritime workers found themselves in before the passage of the MLC and the situation of gig workers now. Like maritime workers, computer crowdwork or gig work is performed in many locations around the world. On digital labour platforms, work is broken down into smaller or constituent tasks. However, instead of the worker being mobile, their work product is in transit.

There are also many "places" that have an interest in the work that is being performed: the home of the worker, the location of the platform, the location of the computer servers, or the location of the hiring entities. Both types of work are seen as temporary employment. Gig workers face questions not only about employment status but also questions about where they would need to bring suit in order to access justice. For example, a court in South Africa ruled that it lacked the jurisdiction to hear a claim against Uber and that the remedies that workers would need to be heard by a court in the Netherlands (Labour Court of South Africa – Cape Town, 2018).

These concerns about jurisdictional reach and effective enforcement of labour rights would be significantly eased by thinking about platforms in an international context, where there are rules and processes for standardisation that set expectations for the employers, unions, governments, and workers. As of 2024, the UN-ILO is still in the process of crafting an international standard for gig work with a proposed standard scheduled for discussion by the ILC during the summer of 2025 (International Labour Organization, 2024b). As with other standards, the goal for the ILO's standard setting is to include representation from a tripartite group: employers, workers and unions, and social partners (including government representatives and NGOs). The ILC formally adopts international standards as well as steers the broad direction of the UN-ILO as an organisation.

9.2.2 GDPR

Another regulatory framework that is useful when thinking about the regulation of platform work is the General Data Protection Regulation (GDPR). The EU's enactment of the GDPR was a significant accomplishment because of its recognition that Internet privacy is truly a global problem. The GDPR applies to the processing of personal data "wholly or partly by automated means" (European Parliament and of the Council, 2016, pt. 2), with Article 5 addressing the basic principles of data protection and Article 6 pertaining to the legal limits for processing that data. Specifically, Article 5 focusses on transparency with respect to the data subject, limitations on the purposes of data collection, and accuracy of the data collected (European Parliament and of the Council, 2016).

In Article 3, the GDPR sets out its jurisdictional reach, which "applies to the processing of personal data in the context of the activities of an establishment of a controller or processor in the Union", even if such data processing does not take place within an EU member state (European Parliament and of the Council,

2016, pt. 3). A controller that is processing outside of the EU has the GDPR applicable to them by "virtue of public international law" (European Parliament and of the Council, 2016, pt. 3). The GDPR applies to those who offer goods or services for sale in the EU, including offering payments in euros, offering multiple languages, or using local testimonials. Locating part of a business operation in another country (e.g., using computer programs or servers that are "located") will not help to evade the GDPR. Internet privacy is understood to be a global issue, and the wide net of the GDPR had to be designed in order to fully protect the rights of EU citizens. And the impact of the GDPR has been widespread, prompting better practices in countries outside the EU. In the United States, California has followed the EU's lead, passing a privacy law largely based on the protections in the GDPR.

Drawing on these experiences with the GDPR, the soon-to-be-determined UN-ILO standard on Platform Work should also prompt cross-border negotiations and discussions that would facilitate enforcement of the standards around the world. Meaningful compliance with privacy laws is not only a question for one country, but one that impacts all Internet users. Similarly, single-country enforcement of privacy regulations – just like labour regulations – leads to many of the race to the bottom problems described in the last section.

9.2.3 Best Practices and the Business Case for Emerging Labour Standards

To date, platforms have been immovably opposed to granting workers employee status. That is largely due to platforms' view that such a change would compromise their business models, that is, that it would be too costly to comply with the rules and laws that other businesses must use when hiring employees. The ambiguity around employment classification has given platforms an advantage over traditional or "legacy" businesses that use established labour structures. Rather than focusing on improving the convenience, speed, or quality of the services provided, platforms have instead doubled down on showing that the job opportunities they create are dependent on hiring only independent contractors.

As such, the platforms' engagement with regulatory processes has been twofold. The first stage has generally been to ignore any regulatory changes and refuse implementation. The second strategy is to go "all in" to lobby aggressively for changes in the law to either avoid or remove employee rights from gig workers. Events in California showed that platform companies ignored the passage of AB-5, exposing the platforms to litigation by state and municipal authorities. Rather than compliance, rideshare platforms threatened to leave the state of California entirely if AB-5 was applied to their business model. While delaying reclassifying workers, rideshare platforms then campaigned aggressively for Proposition 22. Due to these types of reflexive actions and oppositional views, self-regulation unfortunately would seem to no longer be an option for digital labour platforms. However, over the years, there have been proposals that have explored what worker rights would look like for digital labour platforms.

From the inception of the platform economy, academics, worker rights organisations, unions, and other non-governmental organisations have put forward proposals that would improve the working conditions of gig workers and crowdworkers. For example, the non-governmental organisation Fairwork (2024) has articulated principles describing what a just and fair system for the platform economy would look like for workers. Beginning in 2018, the German union IG Metall collected some of the measures that were important for workers on crowdwork platforms. After the union articulated certain standards, the union cooperated with German crowdworkers and platform operators to implement the practices. Some of these practices included methodology for alternative dispute resolution between workers and platforms (Mexi, 2019).

Another source of best practices is platforms that have organised themselves as cooperatives. Within platform cooperatives, workers themselves operate the platforms on which they work. Such unity in ownership enables platform cooperatives to lower the transaction costs charged by traditional platform operators, leaving more of the gains from the technology to those performing the work. Rules for platform cooperatives can be seen as aspirational for what might be possible for workers in the gig economy more generally (Scholz & Schneider, 2016). For all of those engaged with or writing about the topic, there seem to be several areas of commonality where there is agreement around how the platform economy could use improvement: amount and type of remuneration, ways to access justice over disputes such as pay and wage theft, and greater transparency on platforms. In addition, the matter of worker voice and representation is important to the implementation of the other listed principles, as shown in the IG Metall example.

The first group of issues identified as being important for platform worker rights is focussed on fair remuneration. Currently platform workers are only paid for the amount of work that they spend completing a task or discrete gig. However, gig workers are not typically compensated for travel time in between jobs. Similarly, computer crowdworkers are not compensated for the time that the worker spends in searching for their next task. The discounting of some of the work and time performed effectively reduces the wages that many platform workers are paid, despite the fact that their efforts advance the goals of the platforms (quick and convenient customer service) and are in fact necessary in order to ensure the next gig is performed. The effect in some instances has been extreme with wages falling well below living wages and in some instances minimum wages in the jurisdictions where workers live (Cherry, 2020; Marvit, 2014).

Another common issue that has been identified for improvement is providing opportunities for workers to resolve disputes concerning their work. Hiring entities may rate the quality, accuracy, and speed of computer crowdwork. If a worker disagrees with that assessment, however, platforms do not have mechanisms for contesting those ratings in front of a neutral or impartial decision-maker. A hiring entity may decide to pay or reject work on the basis of its sole discretion. As there are no standardised guidelines for what comprises quality work, industrial due process is lacking. If a decision not to pay is rendered after the worker has already completed their computer tasks, it could be considered wage theft. The analogy in the gig economy is that drivers are not paid at all if a customer cancels within a certain period, even if the driver has expended significant time to travel to the customer's location.

Faced with these kinds of inequities on crowdwork platforms, workers have turned to self-help, including technological solutions. One of those solutions was the Turkopticon rating system, which allowed workers to rate the quality of the hiring entities that posted tasks on the crowdwork platform Amazon Mechanical Turk (Irani & Silberman, 2013). Other options to obtain industrial due process might entail alternative dispute resolution, again with attention paid to the neutrality of the decision-makers. This could also include establishing a "jury" of crowdworkers who understand the platforms and who would enforce agreed-upon rules.

Finally, other best practices for digital platform labour concentrate on the value of transparency. It is important for crowdworkers and gig workers to have accurate estimates of how long tasks may take and how difficult those tasks are. Without that information, workers cannot judge for themselves whether the tasks are worth their time. In some instances, workers on crowdworking platforms may not know or understand the bigger picture of the projects that they are working on, and there may be ethical implications for not having that type of knowledge. People bring their own morals and sense of what work they wish to be involved with, and platforms currently have no obligations to disclose that information to the workers.

There are financial reasons that these types of best practices make sense. First, contesting hundreds of legal battles across the world in an effort to stave off compliance is expensive. So too are legislative and lobbying campaigns fighting regulations in the gig economy across various jurisdictions. As noted in Section 9.1, platform companies spent over US$200 million on lobbying in favour of Proposition 22 in California alone. Rather than viewing worker rights to be existential threats to their very existence, companies should be working on ways to ensure that digital platforms maintain labour standards. Studies have shown that consumers will pay more – up to a certain point – for ethically sourced goods or services. While those studies focussed on the garment industry and sweatshop labour, the analogy to digital labour is convincing (Kimeldorf, Meyer, Prasad, & Robinson, 2006).

With the passage of the EU Directive on Platform Work, it is time for platform operators to work cooperatively with regulators. At this point, regulation should be acknowledged as inevitable, and by-product of the recognition of platform work as more stable and mainstream. Proper regulation signals customers that they can rely on platforms to provide services without resorting to undercutting labour rights.

9.3 Conclusion

What is the future of digital labour platforms? One track sees a devalued platform workforce, either deprived of labour and employment protections altogether or partially through discounted hybrid categories like California's independent contractor plus under Proposition 22. While digital labour platforms were early to adopt the idea that their workers were non-standard and not deserving of labour and employment protections, that outcome is neither logical nor inevitable.

The second track sees recognition of gig workers and their important contributions, both during the coronavirus pandemic and beyond. Treating gig workers with parity to workers in the traditional economy extends protections to a group of workers that has been marginalised from the traditional economy and who likely need those protections even more. With the Directive on Platform Work and its presumption of employment, the EU has moved towards increased coverage for platform workers. As the United Nations International Labour Conference takes up the standard during the 2025 session, we can hope that the future of the platform economy will be one in which both platform operators, workers, and regulators can work collaboratively.

Acknowledgements

Many thanks to Janine Berg, Uma Rani, Nuno Cunha, Anne Marie Boyd, M. Six Silberman, Matthew Bodie, David Marshall, Veena Dubal, and Jarrod Wong. The views expressed, however, are those of the author alone. Thank you also to Anthony Larsson for the invitation to participate in this volume, his patience, and capable editing. For research assistance at St. John's University Law School, thank you to Research Assistants Seth Goldstein and Rabab AlAjimi. Finally, my thanks to the students in the Future of Work class who discussed many of the issues with me during our seminar.

References

Alameda County Superior Court. (2021). *Castellanos v. State of California*, Case No. RG21088725.

Aloisi, A., & Cherry, M. A. (2024). Tertium non datur: Intermediate employment categories. In G. Davidov, B. Langille, & G. Lester (Eds.), *Oxford Handbook of the Law of Work*. Oxford, UK: Oxford University Press.

Arthurs, H. W. (2010). Extraterritoriality by other means: How labor law sneaks across borders, conquers minds, and controls workplaces abroad. *Stanford Law and Policy Review*, *21*, 527–553.

Charro, G., Dua, A., Ellingrud, K., Luby, R., & Pemberton, S. (2022). *American Opportunity Survey: Inflation-Weary Americans are Increasingly Pessimistic About the Economy*. New York, NY: McKinsey & Company.

Cherry, M. A. (2020). A global system of work, A global system of regulation? Crowdwork and conflicts of law. *Tulane Law Review*, *94*(2), 183–246.

Cherry, M. A. (2022). Employment status for essential workers: The case for gig worker parity. *Loyola Los Angeles Law Review*, *55*(3), 683–783.

Cherry, M. A., & Aloisi, A. (2017). "Dependent contractors" in the gig economy: A comparative approach. *American University Law Review*, *66*(3), 635–689.

Davidov, G. (2006). The reports of my death are greatly exaggerated: "Employee" as a viable (through over-used) legal concept. In G. Davidov & B. Langille (Eds.), *Boundaries and Frontiers of Labour Law: Goals and Means in the Regulation of Work* (pp. 133–152). Oxford, UK: Hart Publishing.

DeStefano, V. (2016). *The Rise of the "Just-in-Time Workforce": On-Demand Work, Crowd Work and Labour Protection in the "Gig Economy"* (No. 71). Geneva, Switzerland: International Labour Organization.

Employment Tribunal – U.K. (2016). *Aslam & Farrar v. Uber B.V.*, Case No. 2202550.

European Parliament and of the Council. (2016). General Data Protection Regulation Council Regulation 2016/679.

European Parliament and of the Council. (2021). *Proposal for a Directive of the European Parliament and of the Council on Improving Working Conditions in Platform Work, COM/2021/762.*

Fairwork. (2024). *Fairwork Annual Report 2023: State of the Global Platform Economy.* Oxford, UK: Fairwork.

International Labour Organization. (2024a). Ratifications of MLC, 2006 – Maritime Labour Convention, 2006. Retrieved March 6, 2025, from NORMLEX: Information System on International Labour Standards website: https://normlex.ilo.org/dyn/normlex/en/f?p=NORMLEXPUB:11300:0::NO::P11300_INSTRUMENT_ID:312331

International Labour Organization. (2024b). *Realizing Decent Work in the Platform Economy.* Geneva, Switzerland: International Labour Organization.

Irani, L., & Silberman, M. S. (2013). Turkopticon: Interrupting worker invisibility in Amazon Mechanical Turk. In W. E. Mackay (Ed.), *CHI '13: Proceedings of the SIGCHI Conference on Human Factors in Computing Systems* (pp. 611–620). New York, NY: Association for Computing Machinery.

Kimeldorf, H., Meyer, R., Prasad, M., & Robinson, I. (2006). Consumers with a conscience: Will they pay more? *Contexts*, *5*(1), 24–29. https://doi.org/10.1525/ctx.2006.5.1.24

Labour Court of South Africa – Cape Town. (2018). *Uber South Africa Technology Services (Pty) Ltd. v. National Union of Public Service and Allied Workers (NUPSAW) et al.*, Case No. C 449/17.

Liboreiro, J. (2024). EU Reaches New Deal to Salvage Law on Platform Workers. But Will Countries Stir Up Another Revolt? Retrieved March 6, 2025, from Euronews website: www.euronews.com/my-europe/2024/02/08/eu-reaches-new-deal-to-salvage-law-on-platform-workers-but-will-countries-stir-up-another-

Marvit, M. Z. (2014). How Crowdworkers Became Ghosts in the Digital Machine. Retrieved March 6, 2025, from The Nation website: www.thenation.com/article/archive/how-crowdworkers-became-ghosts-digital-machine

McCue, T. (2018). 57 Million U.S. Workers Are Part of the Gig Economy. Retrieved March 6, 2025, from Forbes website: www.forbes.com/sites/tjmccue/2018/08/31/57-million-u-s-workers-are-part-of-the-gig-economy/#6a3d67d87118

Mexi, M. (2019). Social dialogue and the governance of the digital platform economy: Understanding challenges, shaping opportunities. In *ILO-AICESIS-CES*

Romania International Conference, 10–11 October, Bucharest, Romania (pp. 1–34). Geneva, Switzerland: International Labour Organization.
Pollman, E. (2021). Corporate social responsibility, ESG, and compliance. In B. van Rooij & D. Daniel Sokol (Eds.), *The Cambridge Handbook of Compliance* (pp. 662–672). Cambridge, UK: Cambridge University Press.
Rosenblat, A., & Stark, L. (2016). Algorithmic labor and information asymmetries: A case study of Uber's drivers. *International Journal of Communication*, *10*, 3758–3784.
Scholz, T., & Schneider, N. (2016). What this is and isn't about. In T. Scholz & N. Schneider (Eds.), *Ours to Hack and to Own: The Rise of Platform Cooperativism, A New Vision for the Future of Work and a Fairer Internet* (pp. 11–13). New York, NY: OR Books.
Shaughnessy, T., & Tobin, E. (2006). Flags of inconvenience: Freedom and insecurity on the high seas, 5 U. Penn. J. International Law & Policy (2006–2007). *UC David Journal of International Law & Policy*, *5*(1), 1–31.
Stevenson, D. B. (2005). Book review – Seafarer's Rights (Deirdre Fitzpatrick & Michael Anderson eds., 2005). *The Journal of Maritime Law and Commerce*, *36*(4), 567–572.
United States District Court N.D. California. (2015). *Patrick Cotter, et al., Plaintiffs, v. Lyft, Inc., Defendant, 60 F.Supp.3d 1067.*

PART III

New Uses of AI and Technology in Labour

10

AI AND THE FUTURE OF WORK

How organisational structures and the role of humans transform in the age of AI

Charlotte Mattfolk and Siri Wikander

10.1 Introduction

In this chapter we are exploring a multitude of changes that we will see in our society, how we build and manage organisations, how we collaborate, and the role of humans in a world built on artificial intelligence (AI).

Our purpose is to elaborate on how the managerial and organisational structure in organisations may transform to combine the benefits of technological advancements with a human-centric approach.

In this study, we conducted structured interviews with a diverse group of experts – including scholars, practitioners, and thought leaders – to tap into their profound knowledge and experiences. Additionally, we facilitated a workshop aimed at identifying emerging trends, which provided a collaborative platform for idea exchange and trend analysis. To broaden our understanding, we undertook a review of the relevant literature, encompassing both books and peer-reviewed articles, and supplemented this with insights from pertinent podcasts.

The way we manage organisations today is based on a thinking and structure that was optimised in an industrial era without access to the digital infrastructure that is available today. The latest breakthroughs within AI enable instant access to new tools and solutions. Organisations are struggling to understand both potentials and risks with AI. There are very few players that control the development of AI at the forefront since the development of AI requires immense resources in terms of capital and specialised competence. At the same time, AI tools are intuitive and easy-to-use – which means that any company could accelerate both efficiencies and innovation through AI. AI could be instrumental to distributing power and resources, for instance, by revealing new structures in the labour market, matching demand and supply by efficiently finding the right skill for each assignment. We

DOI: 10.4324/9781003391333-13

could create a labour market where everyone's skill set is significantly more visible and the insights into what competence companies need are precise and predictable. Strategies are digitalised and broken down into activities that are matched with skills replacing hierarchies – turning them into fluid organisations with decentralised and democratised structures. Mastering the art of efficiently matching tasks to skills may be one of the most important capabilities in future companies. AI signifies a colossal shift, demanding urgent and profound attention from management, boards, and owners. It is not just about streamlining processes; innovation through AI is critical to fully grasp its impact, safeguard the business model, and enhance service delivery.

10.2 Discussion

10.2.1 A time of paradigm shifts induced by climate change and artificial intelligence

In this chapter we are exploring the changes that we will see in our society, how we build and manage organisations, how we collaborate, and the role of humans in a world built on AI. We are living in a time of paradigm shifts in many areas. The global system and logic behind our national and corporate economies has failed to include enough long-term consequences in its scope. Our way of measuring short-term profits has put us in a situation where the long-term costs of all the harm caused in production, distribution, or recycling are not included. A new holistic world view is necessary, in society and in companies. AI, combined with other technological and scientific breakthroughs, will make us challenge many of our beliefs about our history, our current understanding of how humans and the world operate, and what kind of future we want to create.

The way we manage organisations today is based on a thinking and structure that was optimised in an industrial era without access to the digital infrastructure that is available to everyone today. The latest advances within AI enable instant access to new tools and solutions. Generative AI pertains to algorithms capable of producing novel content – ranging from text to visuals – mirroring the quality of human creation, and the next step is artificial general intelligence (AGI), or even superintelligence, a mimicking of human thinking and behaviour yet to be realised, which aspires to emulate comprehensive human cognitive abilities across diverse domains (World Economic Forum, 2023b).

Organisations are struggling to understand both potentials and risks with generative as well as AGI and there are very few players that control the development of AI at the forefront. The development of AI requires immense resources in terms of capital and specialised competence, so the gap between "AI proficient" and "AI ignorants" is widening every day. At the same time, AI tools are intuitive and easy-to-use – which means that any company could accelerate both efficiencies and innovation through AI.

AI will bring a new level of insights into companies and society, making it possible to more precisely understand all aspects of what affects strategy, operations, and what skill sets that are needed to succeed. If we utilise this new intelligence with a thorough understanding of our purpose and goals, it may improve many aspects of our lives. AI enables us to connect and analyse massive amounts of data from many perspectives and disciplines in a way that humans are incapable of. It is now up to us to use this new "collaborator" to steer towards the important changes in the world that we must realise in the coming years, improving both our understanding of humans and planetary conditions. These insights will enable a whole new perspective on how to live our lives in a way where we are able to improve our quality of life whilst simultaneously strengthening our capability to create structural sustainable changes.

10.2.2 AI can centralise – or decentralise – power and resources

AI is the emerging infrastructure of our time and just as we have invested in rails, roads, and air transportation to enable global trade and mobility of humans, we need to consider the investments in AI – who lies behind them, controls them, and are able to further capitalise on the development. It is one of the most burning questions of our time, since it may lead to exponential acceleration of power and capital into very few people's hands. On the other hand, taking the right measures, AI could be instrumental to distributing power and resources. It could reveal new structures in the labour market, where matching of demand and supply, that is, the right skill for the right assignment, could be much smoother and more efficient. We could create a labour market where everyone's skill set is significantly more visible and the insights into what the market needs are precise. Individuals could get recommendations on how to improve their skills to better match demand. AI could be a game changer to combine science and business needs by identifying what issues are most relevant to solve, which solutions are applicable, and who has the exact right skills and mindset to contribute to the execution of that particular issue.

This transformation induced by AI needs to be based on a new systemic thinking, starting with philosophical questions regarding who we are as humans, defining the meaning and purpose we want in our lives. The pandemic caused us to reflect on what is important in life and how and with whom we want to spend our time. Radical changes were introduced in many organisations in terms of ways-of-working, based on the digital infrastructure we have built during the last two decades – but until the pandemic not fully utilising its potential for enabling completely new ways of performing work tasks. Most organisations are still undigitalised in terms of competence and work tasks. They are structured as traditional industrial players with stiff hierarchies of roles and constant reorganisations to handle misalignment in strategy and execution. They lack the ability to continuously adapt to an ever-changing environment.

AI blurs industry borders and enables the creation of ecosystems based on "economies of data". In these ecosystems, knowledge about customer behaviour and needs, intelligence about a product or offering and insight into internal processes is combined to build extremely fast and accurate learning curves (Earley, 2020).

10.2.3 From digital transformation to societal and human transformation

During the last two decades we have seen a massive focus on automation, robotics, and digitalisation. This development will continue but it has already entered a new phase where its consequences for our society and the role of humans will become more apparent and ultimately change some of the foundations of today's society and work life. There are severe risks but also fantastic opportunities in this development. There are several reasons behind this. We are questioning how we spend our time and if we are willing to be manipulated into spending hours scrolling social media. Our brains are being hacked in such a sophisticated way that we do not even realise how much of our time we allow for organisations to persuade us to buy their products or for people to influence our thoughts. We will need to define how to collaborate with technology and AI and what roles and purposes humans should have.

10.2.4 Is human nature condemned to competition?

The very essence of human nature is juxtaposed against the tantalising prospects of genetic engineering. New scientific breakthroughs enabled by AI hint at the possibility of sculpting human behaviour, transforming individuals into unfeeling, hyper-competitive machines optimised for victory in a world of win–lose scenarios. According to Daniel Schmachtenberger (2018), civilisation designer and founder of the Consilience Project with the aim of designing a non-self-terminating system, this competitive narrative is a major reason why our civilisations are constructed to fall. Competition is just one part of our reality, but it is easier to draw our attention to that kind of narrative. Simultaneously, collaboration plays a far more vital role as an enabler when creating companies, developing societies, and preserving humanity.

Within the competitive narrative, a haunting image emerges: a world where sociopathic supercomputers masquerade as humans, harbouring no remorse for ruthless conquering in the cutthroat arena of life's games. It is a vision that compels us to question our fundamental realities and desires. Why, we ask, do we strive for victory? This relentless pursuit of triumph is framed within the context of perennial ingroup–outgroup contests, whether nations pitted against nations or tribes locked in ancient rivalries. These contests invariably entail harm – not just inflicted directly upon opponents but indirectly upon the common resources we all share.

Vanished civilisations like the Mayans, Byzantines, and Mesopotamians crumbled, not solely due to the external forces they battled but often because of the self-inflicted wounds caused by their own voracious appetites for resources and the ceaseless cycle of warfare. Their stories serve as cautionary tales, warning against repeating the same mistakes on a global scale. The urgency of our predicament becomes evident; the scale of our ingroup–outgroup games has expanded exponentially, encompassing the entire planet through a globally interconnected web of economies and cultures. This interconnectedness, while facilitating cooperation and prosperity, amplifies the catastrophic potential of any collapse. It is not merely a localised disaster but a cataclysm that threatens to engulf us all.

10.2.5 Capitalism, science, technology, and democracy: are they the reason for the looming existential threats?

In this crucible of escalating rivalrous games, we confront an uncomfortable truth: the very behaviours that have long been our modus operandi are now perilously close to becoming our undoing. We are compelled to realise that our traditional toolkit of solutions – embodied in terms like capitalism, science, technology, and democracy – is itself responsible for the looming existential threats. It is not a call for communism, authoritarianism, or repressive dogmas. It is a call for a deeper level of thinking, a radical reimagining of the way we navigate our complex world. Democracy may be flawed, but it remains the best among flawed options. But democracy must be adjusted and developed beyond the polarisation that occurs continuously and turns into radicalisation when the "outgroups" – those that are losing the game – are dissatisfied with the system. With today's advanced technology, we can create complex systems where we consider multiple stakeholders and weigh their interests in such a way that we are able to all be winners. We need to seek innovative solutions that steer us away from the precipice of existential peril, towards a more harmonious, sustainable, and equitable future.

10.2.6 AI could create dictatorship or democratise and distribute resources

> One of the dangers in the 21st century is that machine learning and artificial intelligence will make centralized systems much more efficient than distributed systems, and dictatorships might become more efficient than democracies.
>
> *(Yuval Noah Harari, Professor in History at the Hebrew University of Jerusalem in Shepard, 2018, 00:00:14)*

Yuval Noah Harari argues that we are at a crossroads where AI could either centralise power and resources in a super-efficient but also autocratic system ruled by a few global corporations. Or we could utilise AI and other new technologies to intentionally distribute resources more evenly and construct a new level of democratic systems. He emphasises that advancements in automation and AI could lead to significant job displacement in an extremely rapid pace pushing millions of people out of the labour market. Many traditional jobs may become obsolete as machines and algorithms become more capable of performing tasks previously done by humans. Harari suggests that adaptability and lifelong learning will be crucial for individuals in the future job market. As jobs evolve and change, workers must be willing and able to acquire new skills and adapt to different roles. He highlights the enduring value of soft skills such as creativity, empathy, and critical thinking. These skills may become increasingly important as they are less susceptible to automation and AI.

Harari discusses the possibility of increased economic inequality in a future where some individuals benefit greatly from technological advancements while others struggle with unemployment or underemployment. As traditional notions of work and career paths evolve, people may need to redefine their identities beyond their jobs. Finding meaning and purpose outside of work may become more important. A solution could be that humans find ways to collaborate with machines to enhance their capabilities and productivity. This cooperation between humans and AI may be a key feature of the future workplace.

10.2.7 Will AI lead us to self-extinction or a new level of democracy?

Daniel Schmachtenberger (2018) is discussing the challenges posed by exponential technological advancements and the need for a new approach to utilising such power wisely. He emphasises that historically, humans have operated within a framework of ingroup–outgroup dynamics and win–lose games, often causing harm to each other and the environment. However, with exponentially increasing technological capabilities, the potential for harm surpasses sustainable levels. Schmachtenberger argues that traditional solutions and best practices, such as capitalism, democracy, and science, are insufficient to address these existential risks. Instead, he calls for a deeper level of insight and innovation to navigate the complexities of modern civilisation and prevent self-extinction. He also acknowledges the limitations of current forms of governance, like democracy, in handling the challenges posed by large-scale, anonymous interactions in a globally interconnected world. Overall, his central message is the need for a fundamental shift in our thinking and approaches to address the unprecedented challenges of the future. We could take democracy to a whole new level, and in combination with AI, we could be able to nuance our consideration to different stakeholders in a completely new way, possibly finding a balance between different interests that we have never been able to neither capture nor understand or analyse before.

10.2.8 Switching from commercial hacking of our brains to social good

We are constantly manipulated by algorithms and social media platforms that are aware of our collective dopamine addiction and trigger this further. Tristan Harris, technology ethicist and co-founder of the Center of Humane Technology, talks about how the tech giants control our time by studying and analysing everything from how we behave, what we click on, and what we consume to what we have opinions about (Thompson, 2018). His mission is to challenge this modus operandi and instead collect data that can be used for good purposes – not for manipulation. One of Mr Harris' main ideas is that we need to work towards collective measures and a system change where tech organisations must help and serve society's interests first and foremost – for a better world. He explains it as "Humane Technology", meaning technology that is adapted to humanity and the planet.

10.2.9 AI replicates human senses and enables more efficient communication

Humans have now been introduced to different types of digital communication tools and business systems that we have learned to use. Instead of calling, sending letters, printing paper, and putting it in binders – physically storing or distributing information – digitalisation is vital for any business. We have learned to use systems that have made both our personal and professional lives more efficient.

We have grown strong dependencies on screens and written text where our other senses are used much less. One realisation is that writing down words to communicate, in many situations, is far less efficient than if we were using our voice, sight, or gestures. With the help of AI, augmented reality (AR), virtual reality (VR), Immersive Reality, holograms, sensors, cameras, etc., we will be able to use more of our senses than the ones being used with our screens and keyboards. Metaverse, for example, combines these technologies by intertwining the physical and digital world. This opens the possibility of seamlessly moving between digital platforms and the physical world – while using human senses in a way that has not been possible before. Does this mean that there is an end to screen usage? Most likely yes! We currently touch our small mobile screens up to 2,600 times a day and spend hours sitting in front of computer screens. We are not using the potential of our other senses at all and there is a longing for more effective ways to communicate with others.

Many people find it challenging to understand AI because it spans over a variety of techniques, such as natural language processing, image recognition, voice recognition, and robotics. The easiest way to understand these different areas is to compare them to our senses. AI reads text and patterns, records sound, and can translate text into sound. It can help us move data or objects, both digitally and mechanically. It provides us with a toolbox similar to how humans work with all our senses, and it will dramatically improve our way of using digital tools. For example, it is much more effective to speak than to write, to show than to describe in text. The opportunities are endless, and we have only experienced the first applications so far.

10.2.10 How AI will affect human development

A major question for our future is how humanity will evolve. We now have both the knowledge and tools to change major components of the human body and mind – how far will we go? The impact of AI on humans is still hard to predict, but there are wild speculations ranging from AI making humanity extinct to AI becoming a natural part of every human. Will we upload our brains to the cloud? Will our thoughts and communication be stored, reused, and even autogenerated? In an AI-simulated podcast show, an AI-generated bot simulating Steve Jobs was "interviewed" by an AI-simulated bot impersonating Joe Rogan and his famed podcast (Automated Impact, 2023). The autogenerated AI was based on Jobs earlier thoughts and communication – and he talked about future development that he himself had never mentioned during his lifetime. The AI could thus generate his thoughts based on earlier collected material from Steve Jobs.

According to Peter Diamandis, founder of Singularity University, humans have already learned to improve our status through higher order thinking and our evolution will not be limited to physical advancement (Ashley & Cognitive World, 2019). Diamandis predicts imaginative human creativity, coupled with technological innovation, will even evolve the way we think and relate to each other. How might this occur? Beyond evolving ourselves, we will upgrade our environment to suit our needs. Our world is going to become what he calls "auto-magical": automated and magical. It will respond to our desires and inner thoughts.

> *As children we dream of what we want to become. Maybe we dream of being a sports star, a writer, a scientist – but then we get smacked with the reality of life. Maybe we're not smart enough. Maybe our family doesn't live in the right area to gain access to the right school. You run into reality, which limits your dreams. But I believe that as AI becomes a true partner with humans, it will allow us to obtain what we dream far more reliably and far more easily. AI will enable us to participate in the dream of our lives.*
>
> *(Peter Diamandis, Founder Singularity University in Ashley & Cognitive World, 2019, para. 16)*

The border of the living and the dead may even be blurred. If we upload our consciousness to the cloud and AI can autogenerate our communication, this also means that we could continue to communicate with our family and friends – even when they are dead. How will this affect our perspectives, and could we end up living our lives mostly with the dead? Taking their advice, finding comfort when they are listening to us and even experiencing love and affection?

Brain Computer Interface (BCI) technologies enable consumers to communicate seamlessly with each other, without either speaking or using devices like phones or computers. Our thoughts can be picked up by a BCI and translated into sound, text, or images. It can be used to search for or answer questions about products and scroll through social media by thinking and streaming music directly to the brain. A consumer will be able to receive advertising directly to the brain depending on his active thought or current mood. Still, if the BCI unit senses that you are working or need to focus, it may block advertising, phone calls, messages, and other distractions. For example, customer experience featuring BCI technologies will allow consumers to experience a remote place at night and explore it in VR with just the mind. Instead of reading reviews or googling for photos or videos from a destination, restaurant, or business, you can use VR to experience the location and better decide what you think.

Many people probably know more about the contents of their mobile phone than their own body. We now see a growing interest for the human body and how it is affected by everything from what we eat, how and when we move, and how we react to different impressions and situations; all this is captured via smartwatches, bracelets, or rings. Given that the percentage of connected devices is expected to triple by 2030 (Kaur & Aron, 2021; Nath, Gupta, Chakraborty, & Ghosh, 2018), we will see an explosion of a type of data that helps us understand much more about ourselves and everything that happens both in our everyday lives and at work. Research on our brains will be able to give us completely new knowledge about how we function, and we will be able to analyse even more precise data now that our bodies and minds are becoming increasingly connected. We may know exactly our own life expectancy by the data that is gathered and combined regarding our genetics, lifestyle, relations, and just about anything that affects our well-being and ultimately our life length.

10.2.11 The rise of artificial emotional intelligence

From birth, humans are assigned expectations, roles, and requirements in this life. These expectations often determine our self-image and how we are perceived by others as well as by ourselves. It can also lead us to hiding our "true" identity and the essence of being human – meaning our soul, our name, our body, or our predetermined beliefs. What if our external traits no longer mattered, or if we changed our own self-image? What would we have left? People are increasingly shifting their focus from the outer world to the inner and to spiritual awareness by prioritising time, freedom, and strength to experience inner peace. Identity is inexplicable for some, while others describe it as a feeling rather than an experience. We have only seen the beginning of this type of "in-depth" reflection.

Factors such as advancements in technology, cultural changes, climate change, and scientific discoveries will have different effects on humans and human emotions. As our understanding of the brain and the human body continues to evolve, we may get new insights into the nature of emotions and how they can be studied. With the help of advanced technologies such as AI, BCI, and VR, we can get a deeper insight into emotions, such as more accurate measurement and analysis of emotional states. It is also possible that society's understanding and acceptance of emotions will change, leading to a shift in how emotions are expressed and perceived. There may be developments in AI and robotics that allow machines to better understand and respond to human emotions, leading to new forms of human–machine emotional interactions.

10.2.12 Organisational systems must align with human needs

Nina Bozic Yams (personal communication, November 10, 2023), a senior researcher responsible for Sustainable Future Work research area at RISE – Research Institutes of Sweden, contends that organisational governance systems must undergo transformation. This change should evolve organically, driven both top-down and bottom-up. The process must be both transparent and participatory. The impetus for altering our governance systems stems from an accelerated pace of change, increased complexity, and a heightened interdependence both locally and globally, necessitating decisions to be made closer to those affected by them.

Bozic underscores the loss of human elements in current systems, prompting the pivotal question, "What makes life worth living?" She advocates for constructing systems that more closely align with human needs. Although digitalisation has rendered us more efficient and optimised, it has also led to greater feelings of isolation and a rise in mental health issues. Bozic adds, "artificial intelligence presently offers vast opportunities, but there is a risk of losing the elements that imbue our lives with meaning". If our work roles change, we may lose motivation. Therefore, we require an interdisciplinary and democratic approach to AI that safeguards human needs and amplifies human competences. This perspective evokes thoughts of what we need to experience meaning – and how many people actually experience meaning in their work today? Do all people need meaning in their work life or can they find it somewhere else? How much do current perceptions of status in different work tasks contribute to a sense of meaning?

10.2.13 Collective approaches to leadership

Contemporary governance systems are characterised by multiple hierarchical layers embedded with intricate processes and structures. Leaders often report feelings of isolation and difficulty in decision-making, yet struggle with letting go of control. For those who have served in leadership roles for an extended period, the role often becomes intertwined with their identity, and transitioning away from traditional leadership models based on power and control requires a willingness to engage in personal development, letting go of power and control and becoming an enabler of others' best potential that can support a larger shared purpose and common good.

In academia, the term "collective approaches to leadership" is prevalent, with "shared" and "distributed" leadership as the most commonly used terms, whereas the professional sphere typically refers to "self-management" within which different concepts, such as Teal organisation, sociocracy, and holocracy, have gained more traction globally. The aim is to embrace a shared responsibility for leadership, with employees and teams assuming some of the traditional management duties. Individuals and teams are involved in regularly redefining the organisation's purpose, values, and ways of working in a co-creative process. In many organisations today, purpose, values, and goals presented by organisations often feel disconnected from reality, as employees are not involved in their creation and may find them irrelevant to their daily experiences.

10.2.14 How do stock listed companies adopt to new technology?

AI and innovation present distinct challenges for the management of publicly listed companies. These challenges encompass both a lack of knowledge and insights, as well as the capacity to effectively act on the insights. The process is indeed more complex than it appears. It is crucial for company owners and boards to advocate for an increase in the management's level of knowledge. This requires sustained efforts over time. By enhancing the knowledge level, the management's ability to collaboratively identify necessary actions is also increased. Additionally, it is essential to understand the challenge of innovating within a publicly traded company, which is constantly under scrutiny and often faces high expectations. To create room for innovation in a listed company you need to find short-term wins in efficiency to be able to start innovation as soon as possible. Benchmarks show that companies that focus merely on efficiency are likely to lose competitive advantage and margins, whereas companies that are able to balance efficiency and innovation are able to increase profitability (Simon et al., 2023).

In the context of publicly listed companies, the IT department has historically been responsible for maintaining the technical infrastructure. Similarly, the HR department has traditionally managed the administrative aspects of employment. However, in recent years, both of these functions have expanded their roles to include contributing to business development and innovation. IT departments possess technical expertise and, in many cases, employ modern agile methodologies. HR departments have the expertise in how to create engagement and facilitating transitions to desired behaviours and work practices. Both of these functions can support the transition to new working methods, thus playing a vital role in corporate management.

10.2.15 How do traditional organisations adopt to new technology?

Associate Professor Frida Pemer and Professor Andreas Werr from the Stockholm School of Economics have examined the big four audit firms in Sweden, posing the question: "How do professional service firms (PSFs) adapt to new technological developments?" They highlight the proactive engagement of PSFs in technology-induced innovation to reshape their work and address the threat of digital disruption, marking a significant departure from their traditionally perceived inert and technology-averse nature (Pemer & Werr, 2025).

The primary challenge for PSFs in adapting to new technologies, as detailed in the article by Pemer and Werr, is managing the transition from their traditional, incremental, and risk-averse innovation processes to the demands of rapid, technology-induced – particularly digital – innovation. This involves integrating new digital skills with existing expertise, reconciling technology-driven changes with client needs and expectations, adapting organisational structures and cultures that are traditionally resistant to radical changes, and balancing the obsolescence of certain skills with the necessity of acquiring new competencies. Additionally, there is the challenge of maintaining their market positioning and brand image on both the client and talent markets amidst these significant shifts. This complex set of challenges requires a strategic and multifaceted approach for successful adaptation.

Pemer and Werr found that PSFs adapt to new technology through a process of creative accumulation that involves gradually combining existing professional knowledge with new professional knowledge. This adaptation process comprises three overlapping subprocesses:

1. **Skill Acquisition:** The process of acquiring new skills relevant to the emerging technology.
2. **Skill Dissemination:** The distribution and sharing of these new skills within the organisation.
3. **Skill Integration:** The integration of these new skills into existing practices and knowledge bases.

Additionally, this process includes intertwined cycles of service, process, and organisational innovation. These cycles help PSFs reshape their services, processes, organisation, and roles in a way that ensures continued demand for their competencies and services.

10.2.16 From hierarchical to fluid decentralised networks

Organisations are still organised as hierarchies – even though we have sophisticated communication tools that could enable completely new ways of distributing both responsibilities and tasks. Professor Thomas W. Malone (2005) at MIT is a visionary thinker in the field of technology and management and in his book, *The Future of*

Work, he portrays a world where traditional hierarchical structures of organisations give way to more fluid, decentralised, and networked models. AI plays a pivotal role in realising this vision by enabling smarter decision-making, enhanced automation, and unprecedented levels of collaboration. Malone challenges our fundamental beliefs regarding how and why an organisation is structured like it is today.

Throughout history, humans have organised themselves closely related to the cost of communication. As hunters, we acted in small groups, then agriculture increased the size of groups, and the industrialisation speeded up that development to create the winning factor of economies of scale. However, humans value freedom and independence – and the ability to make their own decisions. And now the greatest efficiency wins may be in letting the people closest to the problem make the decisions.

We will therefore see three major changes affecting the way we build organisations and manage work:

1. **Drastically decreasing costs of communication** – we are moving towards more decentralised organisations in the form of markets, both internal and external
2. **Hierarchical organisations lack the speed of network-based structures** – in a knowledge-based world their efficiency in command and control falls behind the ability to cultivate and nurture human performance
3. **Skills kill roles** – organisations need to focus on what skills they need and how to use them for the right task, rather than creating roles and titles that demand constant reorganisations

10.2.17 Artificial intelligence vs human intelligence: How should we collaborate?

AI, at its present level of development, is better than human beings at specific tasks that it has been trained for. But as soon as it conquers a new field, such as understanding how a language works, it may surpass a human quite instantly by remembering everything it has been trained for and being able to combine massive amounts of data.

Humans, at this point of the AI development, exhibit a superior aptitude for nuanced judgement, creative and experience-based problem-solving, and abstract thinking – skills that enable us to perceive subtleties, understand complex dynamics, and navigate social interactions. We still excel in cross-disciplinary thinking, drawing upon diverse knowledge bases to forge innovative connections and solutions. Our emotional intelligence allows for the interpretation of non-verbal cues, empathy, and moral reasoning, facilitating collaboration and decision-making in complex, unpredictable environments. Additionally, humans can engage in meta-cognition, reflecting on our own thought processes, which fosters learning, adaptation, and the development of wisdom over time. Such a rich tapestry of cognitive abilities provides a complementary contrast to AI's proficiency in handling large-scale, pattern-based tasks. However, these are capabilities that AI can learn in the future – and that is referred to as AGI.

In the meantime, we will use AI for specific tasks: to analyse large volumes of data, to autogenerate texts, to find and create images based on commands, and to perform all kinds of routine tasks that have taken many hours of work for humans to complete until now. The positive side of AI is that it will help us in many ways. The downside over the coming years may be that our ability to create new job opportunities is too slow to adapt to AI's instant capacity to replace us. The European Union (EU) confronts the challenge of an ageing population where a shrinking workforce supports a growing number of dependents. The consensus among researchers is clear: AI will make jobs vanish but new ones will emerge. It is the transition that presents agony, particularly if corporations opt for short-term efficiency gains, relegating the responsibility of skills realignment to society at large.

Professor Rob Cross of Babson College in Boston claimed in 2016 that according to data that they had collected over the past two decades, the time spent by managers and employees in collaborative activities had ballooned by 50% or more in the workplace (Cross, Rebele, & Grant, 2016). The complexity of our tasks has escalated, and our reliance on others to resolve these tasks has intensified. This increased collaboration consumes considerable time. Teams need to focus on developing their team abilities to improve their collective intelligence and also their way-of-working. There seems to be an over-reliance on synchronous work methods such as meetings for collaboration. It is generally believed that teams become more efficient when they alternate between synchronous and asynchronous work methods.

AI can streamline workplace collaboration by automating routine tasks, predicting project timelines, and optimising resource allocation. AI-enhanced communication platforms can reduce the reliance on real-time meetings by summarising discussions and clarifying objectives. By learning individual preferences and work patterns, AI can further personalise collaboration, making teams more efficient and less stressed. This supports a strategic approach to managing the increased complexity of tasks in modern workplaces.

Individuals might exhibit resistance to adopting new methods of working. This reluctance is often rooted in a tendency to over-intellectualise and a hesitance to engage in experimentation and iterative learning. However, the COVID-19 pandemic has starkly illustrated that external pressures and a heightened sense of urgency can catalyse rapid adaptation. As an illustration, during the first phase of the pandemic some secondary educational institutions in Sweden ("gymnasium" – age 16–18 years old) managed to change their pedagogical approach to a digital format over a few weeks – something that would conventionally face significant resistance and could take extensive time to accomplish. This enforced and accelerated change fostered an environment of learning-by-doing, which should suggest to be a successful strategy going forward.

10.2.18 AI will connect strategy to competence

Over the last 20 years, organisations have digitalised their marketing, products, sales, and administrative processes – but one significant area is still left almost completely analogue. The competence that all employees are providing to their employer every day. Organising, coordinating, and following up on employees' work is one of the most important tasks for managers – but ensuring that the right competence is used for each task is left for managers to arbitrarily determine. In a fast-changing world where competence is a matter of learning new things every day, it becomes more important than ever to be able to determine competence available and how it matches to strategies at all levels.

In the World Economic Forum's (2023a) *The Future of Jobs Report 2023*, key findings include the pivotal role of technology adoption in business transformation over the next five years. This period will witness significant job shifts, heavily influenced by technological, environmental, and economic trends. Notably, big data, cloud computing, and AI are expected to be widely adopted. The impact on jobs is generally seen as positive, with a projected 23% of roles evolving. The integration of automation in business is slower than expected, emphasising the importance of analytical and creative thinking skills. Employers anticipate a 44% disruption in workers' skills, with the fastest-growing roles linked to technology and sustainability. However, training opportunities appear insufficient, with a training gap for 60% of the workforce. The report highlights a mismatch between emerging skills and corporate training strategies, coupled with concerns about future talent availability.

10.2.19 AI now puts the light on actual skills and abilities

Even though AI may replace certain roles in organisations, it is much more useful to talk about which skills or abilities that it will replace – at all levels and in all roles of a company. The first phase of introducing AI into our work life will be by using it for administrative tasks that are manual and repetitive or implies setting a plan, framework, agenda, and content for a meeting or a workshop – everything that has naturally been documented for years and that has been fed into the large language models. Even a strategy or innovative idea can be the output of a chat with a Large Language Model, and we can expect it to become even better over time. So what are the skills and abilities that humans have that AI does not have?

Generative AI has inspired many people to try these new tools to find information faster and autogenerate texts, images, and videos. We are still at the very beginning of this development and most of the use cases are still to be innovated. But we are starting to see that there are several concrete areas where we can use AI as a collaborator, prompting it with more and more detailed information on what we are looking for. Interestingly, the last 20 years we got used to expressing ourselves with short words or commands, since that was the most precise way of making a search.

Now, instead we get to use the nuances of a full language, with whole sentences and elaborated texts, just as we did before we got used to search engines. Our AI assistants will communicate with each other and help us complete our work tasks much more efficiently.

10.2.20 The rise of "Community Gardeners" and "Collaboration Facilitators"

Leaders facilitate self-organisation within teams for tasks such as allocating vacation time and conducting performance reviews, where these tasks are managed by employees themselves rather than by a leader. Gradually, individuals and teams begin to independently prioritise and arrange their work tasks, shifting towards a model reminiscent of a gig-economy platform where tasks are posted and contributions are made based on skill sets. However, a persistent challenge lies in the rigid systems that match competencies with tasks, necessitating a more holistic view of human skills.

It is probable that roles like "Community Gardeners" or "Collaboration Facilitators" will emerge to assist in aligning skills and motivations with various tasks. Presently, local initiatives exist with internal skill pools allowing employees to take on tasks at different workplaces, which may serve as a nascent form of self-organisation around work assignments.

10.2.21 Each task has a value, instead of each role

When an organisation's strategy is broken down into areas with specific assignments or tasks, it is also necessary to change incentive structures. Except for some critical key roles, most other roles become obsolete since they preserve old structures instead of focussing on change, learning, and innovation. New incentive structures must instead focus on value creation related to the actual task performed. This is common in many simple work tasks, such as a taxi ride or a haircut, but also in complex environments, such as consulting and advisory services. The important difference from setting the value related to a role is that tasks must be prioritised and valued and are not part of a habitual way of working and an individual judgement. Instead it is related to tasks that are directly drilled down from a strategy and can therefore easily be changed depending on strategic importance. CEOs will be able to steer and analyse their companies from a dashboard where the matching of tasks and competence serves as a guidance to how well the company executes on its strategy.

10.2.22 Everyone could be four times more efficient

According to the report "ARK's Big Ideas 2023" by ARK Invest (2023), a global asset manager specialising in thematic investing in disruptive innovation,

AI is expected to enhance the productivity of knowledge workers by more than fourfold. This substantial increase in productivity through AI utilisation could yield significant economic benefits. The report further suggests that with a 30% adoption rate, AI could contribute approximately 100 trillion US dollars to work productivity following a total AI expenditure of 200 trillion US dollars.

The ingenuity that is required to run a large organisation exceeds the abilities of any human being or small team – and the bar keeps going up. What has happened is that bureaucratic structures ask more of people than they can deliver. This is described in Gary Hamel and Michele Zanini's (2020) book *Humanocracy*.

Steve Ballmer at Microsoft declared in 2007 that there is no chance iPhone will get a significant market share. This myopia cost Microsoft 400 billion US dollars in lost market value. It is easy to blame Ballmer and Gates but according to Hamel and Zanini (2020), the real problem was bureaucracy. In a hierarchical organisation the responsibility for setting strategy and direction is vested in a handful of senior executives. Those at the top are expected to be uniquely far-sighted, inquisitive, and creative. In practice this is not the case. Senior executives have most of their emotional equity invested in the past – and many of their assumptions about customers, technology, and the competitive environment were forged years or even decades ago.

Hamel and Zanini (2020) argue that the idea of the CEO as the captain of the ship is bankrupt and that it is time to call off the search for superhuman leaders. What we need are not extraordinary leaders, but organisations that mobilise and monetise the genius of ordinary employees.

In a flexible world, organisations need to match minds to problems. Instead of a fixed hierarchy we need a multitude of dynamic teams where who is in charge depends on the problem addressed. Hamel and Zanini (2020) argue that we need organisations where everyone's views are transparent and make part of the decision-making. To describe their reasoning they exemplify this new kind of Internet-based management model that is implemented by the Chinese company Haier.

10.2.23 Chinese company Haier introduced an innovative Internet-based management model

Haier is a Chinese company that started as a refrigerator factory and became an IoT ecosystem brand. Zhang Ruimin, its CEO, was the first Chinese CEO to appear on the Harvard podium. According to Zhang a firm either owns a platform or is owned by a platform. A platform-based company acts like a network that integrates the Internet into everything they do. It gives seamless access to all stakeholders who can co-create with shared interests, risks, and successes. Haier's organisational system is competitive and performance-oriented; however, it is an interesting example of how mandates and decision-making could be transferred out in the organisation, based on the aim of leveraging digital technology.

It is the management model that is innovative, not the product or offering itself. The model puts employees and their understanding of customer needs in focus, which ends up in a completely different organisational structure where decisions are made as close as possible to the actual problem. An example is when sales of washing machines declined in the Sichuan Province in China. Customer feedback showed that the machines got clogged and looking closer into the issue they discovered that the machines were used to wash sweet potatoes. So washing machines were redesigned to wash produce in addition to clothing. Customers, not managers, set the agenda for what is prioritised and acted upon.

Haier's management model, Rendanheyi, is based on three core principles (Agile Academy, 2022):

1 Turn every employee into an entrepreneur
2 Build zero distance between employees and users – which enables personalised experiences and users are no longer passive but active contributors in all processes from manufacturing to innovation
3 Break down the organisation into multiple nodes that are part of the same system

A core element is also combining value creation for customers and value creation for employees. Those two things are closely related to each other and it is a completely different way of thinking than shareholders coming first, then customers, and then maybe employees third. This puts employees at the forefront of the company value creation. The transformation into this new management model included a series of critical components. To start with it involved shifting from a monolithic business to building microenterprises. It demanded moving from incremental growth goals to leading targets. It meant changing from internal monopolies to internal contracting. Most companies today have functions such as finance, HR, IT, or business areas that act like small internal monopolies. They can therefore effectively stop the development for other functions or business areas. Internal contracts drive innovation in a much higher pace since they can be exchanged if they do not collaborate and deliver results.

It also implies a shift from top-down coordination to voluntary coordination. Today in almost every company, starting with the CEO, everyone would give orders to the next level below them; they put up new initiatives and each micro enterprise can work on them voluntarily. Open innovation is also a key aspect, to learn from any organisation out there, not only within the same industry or context. It also meant that employees became owners and every employee had a stake in their own enterprise. This means they also started to act like an entrepreneur.

10.2.24 Moving from economies of scale to economies of data

The author and information management expert, Seth Earley (2020), emphasises in his book *The AI-powered Enterprise* the critical role of data as the lifeblood of AI-powered enterprises. Data fuels AI algorithms, enabling organisations to derive insights, make informed decisions, and enhance customer experiences. We are moving from the prevailing concept of "economies of scale" into a world ruled by "economies of data", where each added data point adds exponential value. The strength of the data is created by involving users, giving them value by using their own data combined with comparisons to aggregated data. The data network effect ties users to the service and this is also why product-centric companies must move towards a more service-oriented offering. Companies that constantly collect data to know their clients systematically improve their offerings and are able to connect this to critical business goals and processes – they will reap the benefits of the data economy. Not many companies today, except for the big digital players, can combine these data and even less act on real-time insights. This new way-of-working also enables substantial automation and innovation, where humans may actively be taken out of the loop. So what does this mean for humans? Are there in fact benefits to reap from this development? Maybe humans would thrive in a world with less work and responsibilities?

10.2.25 Europe needs its own digital infrastructure to ensure more control over AI

Several challenges are associated with major language models like ChatGPT being predominantly linked to specific corporations in the United States. Firstly, servers in the United States are subject to the Privacy Policy Act, which offers less protection than the EU's General Data Protection Regulation (GDPR). Moreover, as models like ChatGPT are not open-source, it becomes challenging to determine their underlying instructions, potentially leading to biases in, for example, political and interpersonal contexts. There's also a risk for businesses that depend on a proprietary model like ChatGPT, especially if they face sudden price increases decided by OpenAI. In response, initiatives in the EU, like MISTRAL developed in France, and GPT-SW3 in Sweden, are working on open language models with servers within the EU. This movement suggests a future trend where organisations might increasingly rely on their own local server infrastructures for such technologies.

The European Commission talks about the 5th technical revolution as an approach that

> provides a vision of an industry that aims beyond efficiency and productivity as the sole goals, and reinforces the role and the contribution of industry to society. It places the well-being of the worker at the centre of the production process and uses new technologies to provide prosperity beyond jobs and growth while respecting the production limits of the planet.
>
> *(European Commission, 2024, paras. 4–5)*

To ensure that humans and the well-being of workers are put in the centre – new digital platforms – digital ethical ecosystems – must be developed. These new fluid, decentralised, and democratic systems should be based on the purpose and goals we wish to ground our society on. With AI and its capacity to analyse massive amounts of data and handle complex nuances, we are able to create a new level of democracy where individual interests are thoroughly balanced with collective needs.

10.2.26 Four day work weeks proves improved self-rated physical and mental health

According to a preliminary study by the consulting firm 4 Day Week Global (2023), organisations' average working hours continued to fall beyond the conclusion of their six-month four-day week pilot programme. A year after launching their trials, employees' average work week dropped from a baseline of 38 hours to 32.97, and further on, down almost a full hour from the six-month mark.

This reduction was not achieved via increased work intensity where people had to speed up and cram five days of tasks into four. Instead, they operated more efficiently and continued to improve these capabilities as the year progressed. Workers' experience with the four-day week also remained highly positive, with an unchanged rating of 9/10 beyond the trial's conclusion. Self-rated physical and mental health measures improved over 12 months, with employees also reporting increased work–life balance scores.

Lead researcher, Professor Juliet Schor of Boston College, said:

> Life satisfaction scores remained stable with no significant change from the trial's endpoint to the 12-month mark. However, job satisfaction showed a slight regression after a year. This suggests the positive effects a 4 day week has on life satisfaction may be more deeply embedded in individuals' overall well-being than in job satisfaction alone. Nonetheless, job satisfaction scores remained higher than baseline.
>
> *(4 Day Week Global, 2024, para. 4)*

How much less can AI enable us to work in the future? And will we be able to do this transition together as a society or will some work more and others have no work?

10.2.27 Demographic changes is already challenging our welfare system

Population ageing is a defining global trend of our time. People are living longer and are older than ever before (United Nations Department of Economic and Social Affairs, 2023). Spectacular improvements in health, survival, and reductions in fertility have driven this momentous shift, which has begun or is expected to begin soon in all countries and areas. Population ageing is an inevitable result of the demographic transition towards longer lives and smaller families. So far, public spending in most countries has not been sufficient to cover the growing demand for long-term care. A shortage of trained caregivers leads to poor quality care.

This demographic shift, characterised by increased longevity and reduced fertility rates, poses challenges in various countries, including Japan, Singapore, China, most of EU, and the Nordic nations. There will be a shortfall in the labour force, and consequently, it will not be possible to overcome this challenge solely through recruitment. Instead, we must re-evaluate our work methods and devise innovative solutions with the help of AI and other technology.

10.2.28 Digitalisation and robots have changed medical care and AI will change it even more

To give an example, a medical secretary's role involves transcribing a physician's dictation into textual format for inclusion in patient records. Presently, software such as Whisper can convert speech into written text within seconds. Subsequently, services like ChatGPT could suggest enhancements to the text, which the medical secretary may then refine and ultimately approve prior to its documentation in the medical records. This process liberates time and enhances the quality of the medical notes.

So AI is already making strides in healthcare, particularly in the analysis of radiographic images, enhancing diagnostic accuracy and efficiency (IBM Education, 2023; World Economic Forum, 2023b). Looking ahead, its potential extends to several other areas. AI could significantly streamline administrative tasks in healthcare, reducing the workload on medical staff. It might also play a vital role in facilitating patient-provider interactions, particularly by easing the burden of medical record documentation.

In the realm of patient self-service, AI could provide solutions to reduce unnecessary healthcare visits, offering guidance and preliminary assessments. Its ability to overcome linguistic barriers through accurate translation services is another area where AI could have a substantial impact. Additionally, AI could assist healthcare providers in formulating more effective clinical questions, ensuring comprehensive patient assessments.

Beyond these applications, AI has the potential to remind both patients and healthcare providers about drug contraindications and side effects, enhancing medication safety. While the concept of AI-integrated medical practitioners or robot-assisted physicians is still emerging, it holds promise for non-emergency consultations. AI could also emerge as a personal health coach, offering individualised health advice and support.

Given the ongoing skill shortages in healthcare, the adoption of AI and robotics for certain tasks is likely to increase. Even if the technology is not perfect, it could allow healthcare professionals to focus on more value-added activities, signalling a significant evolution in healthcare delivery and patient care.

10.2.29 Recruiting, onboarding, and learning in an AI-world

AI is poised to significantly advance the field of recruitment, aiding in the identification of suitable candidates. The process of successfully discerning competency includes structured interviews, work samples, and assessments of personality and intelligence. AI can now assist in the selection process by analysing candidates' responses during interviews and work samples to identify key elements such as communication style and interpersonal skills, including the expression of empathy and understanding, which are critical components of collaboration. Additionally, AI can scrutinise historical online data to detect recurring themes and discrepancies. The predictive accuracy of work samples can be enhanced by conducting them in VR environments, with scenarios and potential colleagues, to better gauge performance. Utilising such methods, supported by AI analyses, suggests that we will improve our ability to evaluate complex interpersonal skills but there are two major risks. The first one is biased if the decisions are based on historic data or on data based on human input. The other one is the misuse of personal data. If we solve the risks AI will not only aid in selecting the right candidate but also provide a foundation for ongoing development and growth. But all these changes need to be implemented bearing the employees integrity in mind. A transparent learning approach is suggested.

As AI assumes responsibility for simpler tasks, the onboarding process for new employees should pivot to emphasise complex problem-solving, creative thinking, and interpersonal skills. It becomes crucial to facilitate new employees' integration by encouraging them to shadow experienced colleagues and foster networking across cross-functional departments. An AI-buddy could support new employees onboard both to the culture and the tasks.

In the context of today's rapidly evolving landscape with more and more complex tasks, there is an imperative for continuous learning in the flow of work that ensures that the skills and knowledge acquired are directly relevant to the job. This approach necessitates the constant acquisition of new knowledge and skills, both independently and in collaboration with others. AI can create personalised learning curriculums based on an individual employee's performance, skills, and career goals. By utilising machine learning and data analysis, AI can identify skill gaps and recommend courses or training programmes. It can also be used to create interactive and engaging learning environments through virtual simulations and gamification.

The establishment of an open, learning-oriented culture is crucial, where experimenting with new ideas and swiftly assimilating learnings are fundamental practices. This culture should foster re-evaluation of existing methodologies, encouraging a shift in practices by identifying what can be altered, discontinued, or initiated anew.

Creating a psychologically safe environment is paramount (Edmondson, 2019), where every individual feels that their contributions are valued and where challenging the status quo is not just permitted, but encouraged. This aspect gains even more importance with the implementation of AI in the workplace. It demands not only the ability to adapt and respond to changes but also the capacity to critically evaluate and, when necessary, oppose certain advancements.

Moreover, as AI becomes more integrated into our workspaces, it is essential to develop the capability to collaborate effectively with these technologies, ensuring that humans retain control and oversight. This integration requires a combination of analytical skills and creative thinking, enabling workers to harness AI's potential while maintaining the human-centric aspects of decision-making and innovation. However, these tasks may sooner or later also be replaced by AI, reinforcing the need for built-in decision-making based on well-thought-out values and ethical principles, in such a way that it cannot be manipulated by the AI algorithm.

10.2.30 Performance management and ethics in an AI world

It has become feasible for employers to monitor their employees' performance by, for example, transcribing and analysing digital meetings (Kantor & Sundaram, 2022). The utilisation of data by corporations varies widely, ranging from no usage to direct impact on employee compensation. The practice of surveillance has primarily been implemented on the operational floor, but is now being extended to higher levels within organisations (The Economist, 2022). There is a spectrum of opinions regarding these types of measurements. Some perceive a sense of fairness in quantifying performance in clear and concrete terms – others feel monitored. This type of measurement has also sparked protests among employees and labour unions. The challenge, of course, lies in the ethical dimensions of such surveillance, as well as the uncertainty surrounding the effectiveness of these analyses. Job performance is a multifaceted endeavour, extending beyond merely quantifiable metrics.

10.3 Conclusion

The interplay between AI and human society will shape our future and potentially change the foundations of how the world is operating. AI could either concentrate power in the hands of a few or democratise and distribute resources more evenly. The transformative impact of AI on the labour market is substantial and we will see a paradigm shift in job structures and the skills required for future employment. The emphasis on adaptability and lifelong learning underscores the need for individuals to evolve alongside AI, particularly as traditional job roles become automated. The transition may occur with such a rapid pace that we are unable to create new jobs – or rather task-based new revenue streams for humans – that a whole generation may be severely affected, particularly those at the end of their work life.

In a broader societal context, we may see a re-evaluation of human roles and identities in the light of technological advancement. AI's integration into everyday life could lead to more profound changes than mere job displacement, challenging our very notions of work and personal fulfilment. With AI's capacity to enhance human abilities, we envision a cooperative relationship between humans and AI, one that could redefine productivity and creativity in the workplace. AI blurs industry lines, creates new ecosystems, and dissolves old structures – and there is an urgent need for new systemic thinking. Such thinking should start with fundamental questions about human existence and the values we aspire to uphold. Our current beliefs that competition is a natural and necessary part of our society should be challenged and exchanged towards an approach where collaboration is the key enabler for societal advancement.

AI could radically alter communication, reducing the reliance on screens and enabling more natural and efficient interactions through the use of augmented and virtual realities. This shift hints at a future where technology is seamlessly integrated with human senses, offering a more immersive and intuitive experience. As AI evolves, it may lead to the creation of AGI, which surpasses human cognitive capabilities and necessitates new forms of collaboration and ethical frameworks. AI could lead to a better understanding and expression of emotional states. It is necessary with a critical examination of the trajectory of AI development and we advocate a human-centric and societal approach, ensuring that technology serves the greater good and promotes a more equitable and sustainable future. As AI becomes an integral part of our world, it is imperative to steer its influence towards enhancing human capabilities and improving societal structures rather than allowing it to become a tool for centralising power or exacerbating inequalities.

AI, in combination with other technological and scientific advancements, is poised to restructure the very fabric of work, organisational hierarchies, business models, and societal systems. The way we build and organise both society and companies may be revolutionised by AI and we are likely to move from hierarchies towards more fluid decentralised networks. Competencies within the workforce will transition from traditional role-based structures to task and skill-centric frameworks. It brings into focus the possibility of AI bridging the gap between strategy and execution by dynamically matching competencies with organisational needs, thereby fostering agility and responsiveness in the face of rapidly changing market demands. Organisations that continue to operate mainly within hierarchical models will become vulnerable and furthermore obsolete in a knowledge-driven economy. This is attributed to the decreasing costs of communication and the subsequent empowerment of individuals closest to problems, allowing them to make decisions. This shift is a natural progression towards decentralised, networked organisational models that are more democratic and better aligned with human nature, which craves autonomy, the freedom to innovate, and problem-specific decision-making.

AI signifies a colossal shift, demanding urgent and profound attention from management, boards, and owners. It is not just about streamlining processes; innovation through AI is critical to fully grasp its impact, safeguard the business model, and enhance service delivery.

By enabling the decentralisation of decision-making and promoting fluid networks, AI has the potential to create ecosystems that are more in tune with human needs and aspirations. While AI initially is set to replace certain administrative and repetitive tasks, it is the uniquely human skills – such as certain kinds of creative thinking, problem-solving in areas with little or no data, and specific aspects of emotional intelligence – that will become increasingly valuable. Even though AI is all about replacement for human endeavour, we will initially use it mostly as a collaborator that enhances human capabilities. We may see new roles emerge such as "Community Gardeners" and "Collaboration Facilitators" to assist in aligning skills and motivations with tasks. Such roles would be central to nurturing the evolving organisational ecosystems and ensuring that the human element remains at the core of work structures, despite the pervasive influence of AI and automation.

It is vital to adopt a methodical approach to incorporating AI. This means raising awareness of the possible impact and consequences of AI adoption, engaging in comprehensive learning, testing, and acting on insights about AI effects in all industries.

The job market is evolving rapidly, with many roles becoming obsolete and some new ones emerging. In response, both employers and employees must embrace continuous learning as part of their daily work. There is a need to address potential biases in performance management and recruitment as it will become transparent in a completely new way. AI presents an opportunity to align our strategies with skill development, enabling us to organise effectively around tasks, setting value on prioritised tasks rather than roles, which will effectively steer people and organisations towards what really needs to get done.

In this transition, we must continually challenge the global, societal, and business system and structure that limit our adaptability. We have an amazing opportunity to use AI and AGI to improve the well-being of humans. But today we lack the future vision and positive outlook that would engage and attract humans of being part of this development.

Europe has long ducked the critical aspects of not developing its own digital infrastructure and platforms, focussing on legislation rather than groundbreaking innovation. It is crucial that we invest in closing the enormous gap between Europe, the United States, and China. If we do not innovate more, we are placed in the corner where legislation is our only tool. The massive influence that AI will have on individual privacy and data protection must also be met by offering alternative platforms. There are legitimate concerns about the potential for AI to intensify surveillance and monitoring in the workplace and we need a balanced approach that respects individual privacy while harnessing the benefits of AI.

In conclusion, our intention has been to paint a multifaceted picture of the future of work and society in an AI-enhanced world. We suggest a future where AI enables a more decentralised and human-centric approach to work, catalyses the development of task-based organisations that align with human skills and motivations, and facilitates a more ethical and equitable integration of technology into our daily lives. We will experience a time of both transformation and adaptation, where AI acts as both a mirror and a bridge – reflecting our humanity back at us and connecting us to a future with possibly a whole new level of democracy entering the business world where the potential and needs for individual and collective growth is put at the centre. What do we humans want to spend our time doing – and how can AI do all the rest?

Acknowledgements

Oscar Berg, consultant and expert in digitalisation and collaboration at Gr8 Mountains and Berg & Gustafsson, for your contribution to digital collaboration in workplaces.

Lena Bjurner, CHRO, Sobi – Swedish Orphan Biovitrum AB and former Secretary General, the Swedish Association of Human Resources Management, for valuable input on the content.

Zorica Bodiroza, Head of Human Resources, AP3 Third Swedish National Pension Fund, for wise thoughts on the future workplace.

Nina Bozic Yams, Senior Researcher, Responsible for Sustainable Future Work at RISE – Research Institutes of Sweden, for your contribution on how organisations, leadership, and collaboration need to evolve to meet the challenges of our time.

Henrik Gustafsson, consultant and expert in digital collaboration and workplaces at Influence People and Berg & Gustafsson, for your contribution to digital collaboration in workplaces.

Peter Holmlund Kelly, Chief AI Officer, IAMAI, for valuable input on the content.

Mikael Kring, project manager, Lifelong Learning at RISE – Research Institutes of Sweden, for your contribution to how AI will affect our way of working.

Andreas Werr, Professor, Lars Erik Lundberg Chair in Business Administration, especially Human Capital Management, Stockholm School of Economics, for your most valuable contribution to how organisations can strengthen their ability to develop business and employee processes in the light of AI.

References

4 Day Week Global. (2023). We Are Taking the 4 Day Week Global. Retrieved May 13, 2024, from www.4dayweek.com

4 Day Week Global. (2024). Working Hours Continue to Fall for Companies a Year Into Their 4 Day Week. Retrieved March 6, 2025, from www.4dayweek.com/press-releases-posts/working-hours-continue-to-fall

Agile Academy. (2022). Haier Case Study | The next Management Model? | Agile Management Models. Retrieved March 6, 2025, from www.youtube.com/watch?v=gD_AAQrSJqI

ARK Invest. (2023). ARK's Big Ideas 2023. Retrieved March 6, 2025, from www.ark-invest.com/big-ideas-2023

Ashley, M., & Cognitive World. (2019). Forget Darwinian Evolution. Humanity May Soon Evolve Itself Through A.I. Retrieved March 6, 2025, from Forbes website: www.forbes.com/sites/cognitiveworld/2019/01/15/forget-darwinian-evolution-humanity-may-soon-evolve-itself-through-a-i

Automated Impact. (2023). The AI Interview: Joe Rogan and Steve Jobs. Retrieved March 6, 2025, from www.youtube.com/watch?v=N_mG_bniSzs

Cross, R., Rebele, R., & Grant, A. (2016). Collaborative Overload. *Harvard Business Review, January-Fe*, 1–7.

Earley, S. (2020). *The AI-Powered Enterprise: Harness the Power of Ontologies to Make Your Business Smarter, Faster, and More.* La Vergne, TN: LifeTree.

Edmondson, A. C. (2019). *The Fearless Organization Creating Psychological Safety in the Workplace for Learning, Innovation, and Growth.* Hoboken, NJ: Wiley.

European Commission. (2024). Industry 5.0. Retrieved March 6, 2025, from Research and Innovation website: https://research-and-innovation.ec.europa.eu/research-area/industrial-research-and-innovation/industry-50_en

Hamel, G., & Zanini, M. (2020). *Humanocracy: Creating Organizations as Amazing as the People Inside Them.* Boston, MA: Harvard Business Review Press.

IBM Education. (2023). The Benefits of AI in Healthcare. Retrieved March 6, 2025, from IBM website: www.ibm.com/blog/the-benefits-of-ai-in-healthcare

Kantor, J., & Sundaram, A. (2022). The Rise of the Worker Productivity Score. Retrieved March 6, 2025, from The New York Times website: www.nytimes.com/interactive/2022/08/14/business/worker-productivity-tracking.html

Kaur, M., & Aron, R. (2021). A systematic study of load balancing approaches in the fog computing environment. *The Journal of Supercomputing*, *77*(8), 9202–9247. https://doi.org/10.1007/s11227-020-03600-8

Malone, T. W. (2005). The future of work. In C. Sørensen, Y. Yoo, K. Lyytinen, & J. I. DeGross (Eds.), *Designing Ubiquitous Information Environments: Socio-Technical Issues and Challenges* (pp. 17–20). Boston, MA: Springer.

Nath, S. B., Gupta, H., Chakraborty, S., & Ghosh, S. K. (2018). A survey of fog computing and communication: Current researches and future directions. *ArXiv Preprint, 1804.04365*, 1–47. https://doi.org/10.48550/arXiv.1804.04365

Pemer, F., & Werr, A. (2025). Defusing digital disruption through creative accumulation: Technology-induced innovation in professional service firms. *Journal of Management Studies*, (Ahead of Print), 1–46. https://doi.org/10.1111/joms.12972

Schmachtenberger, D. (2018). Solving the Generator Functions of Existential Risks. Retrieved March 6, 2025, from Future Thinkers Podcast website: https://futurethinkers.org/daniel-schmachtenberger-generator-functions

Shepard, D. (2018). Experts on Experts: Yuval Noah Harari. Retrieved March 6, 2025, from Armchair Expert with Dax Shepard Podcast website: https://podclips.com/e/eGI

Simon, P., Maor, D., Guggenberger, P., Park, M., Luo, M., Klingler, D., … & Lodovico, A. Di. (2023). *The State of Organizations 2023.* New York, NY: McKinsey & Company.

The Economist. (2022). How a New Age of Surveillance is Changing Work. Retrieved March 6, 2025, from www.economist.com/leaders/2022/05/13/how-a-new-age-of-surveillance-is-changing-work

Thompson, N. (2018). How Humans Get Hacked: Yuval Noah Harari & Tristan Harris Talk with WIRED. Retrieved March 6, 2025, from Wired website: www.wired.com/video/watch/yuval-harari-tristan-harris-humans-get-hacked

United Nations Department of Economic and Social Affairs. (2023). *Leaving No One Behind in an Ageing World: World Social Report 2023*. New York, NY: United Nations Publication.

World Economic Forum. (2023a). *The Future of Jobs Report 2023: Insight Report*. Cologny, Switzerland: World Economic Forum.

World Economic Forum. (2023b). *Top 10 Emerging Technologies of 2023: Flagship Report*. Cologny, Switzerland: World Economic Forum.

11

THE RISE OF CYBORG MARKETERS

A Marketer's Guide to Survive and Thrive in the Era of AI

Ling Koay

11.1 Introduction

When you think about cyborgs, what comes to mind? RoboCop or the Terminator? As a kid, I remember playing with RoboCop action figures with my little brother. I also recall watching James Cameron's (1984) movie *The Terminator* a few years after its debut, and at some point, we got the toy version of it. I enjoyed playing pretend with Barbie and Ken dolls, but I was genuinely fascinated by the Terminator. When I think about the Terminator, I think about the future and how humans might evolve over time. Right or wrong, it represents a fascinating mix of technology, ethics, and the philosophical question of what it means to be human.

11.2 Methods

In this study, I have relied on secondary research methods and formed my findings and analysis by interpreting a mix of contemporary research, published articles from the academic and business world, books, and my own personal observations and experiences from working in the marketing profession for the past 20 years.

11.3 Our Relationship with Technology

The Terminator character is full of conflicts. It represents both fear and intrigue associated with advanced artificial intelligence (AI) and robotics. It is a figure of both awe and terror. On the surface, it is a relentless machine, devoid of emotion and driven solely by its programming. Yet, as the story progresses, particularly in sequels like *Terminator 2: Judgment Day*, we see glimpses of a more complex character, especially in interactions with humans (Cameron, 1991).

DOI: 10.4324/9781003391333-14

What is compelling about the Terminator is that it represents our collective anxieties about technology. It is a powerful metaphor for the fear of losing control over the very creations we build to improve our lives. The character prompts us to reflect on the ethical boundaries of AI and robotics, and the potential consequences of their unchecked advancement.

The powerful tension between action and deep philosophical questions is enduring to me. Despite being a machine, the character forces us to confront very human concerns about our future, our relationship with technology, and the nature of consciousness itself.

Are we sacrificing ourselves in our ambitions to seek rapid advancements in technology? This question leads to my interest in exploring the impact of technology, particularly generative AI, in the field I have practiced for over 20 years: marketing. A field that has become an essential part of my identity, both professionally and personally.

11.3.1 Paradox of Technological Advancement

Our fear of losing control over our technological creations is not confined to the world of the Terminator. It is becoming increasingly relevant in our real world, dominated by rapid technological advancements, especially in marketing.

This fear stems from a very human place. We innovate, build, and automate with the intention of making our lives better, more efficient, perhaps even safer. But in doing so, we tread into unknown territory where the very tools we create could spiral beyond our control. As we develop systems that can learn, adapt, and operate independently, the line between tool and autonomous entity becomes blurred. Our current conversations about AI and machine learning represent the paradox of technological advancement. On the one hand, there is the undeniable benefit of progress. On the other hand, there is apprehension about what that progress might entail, particularly when it comes to technologies that have the potential to fundamentally alter our way of life or challenge our understanding of agency and autonomy.

What happens when the tools we create, supposedly to better our existence, start operating beyond our intentions or even against our interests?

11.4 Treading into the AI Playground

My colleagues and I are facing the impact of generative AI technology head-on at work. While I am convinced that "marketers will not be replaced by AI, but by marketers using AI", not everyone is as reassured. Perhaps they are right; I might be overly confident in my own adaptability and capabilities.

The desire to enhance productivity and maximise our team's value led me to an AI tool that fundamentally changed our approach to content creation. Previously, we relied heavily on human writers for this task. In May 2023, we celebrated a milestone: tripling our productivity in just a few months, an achievement that filled us with pride. However, that very night, I stumbled upon a revelation. I found that technology powered by the latest AI model could generate the same volume of content that took our team a month to produce in just 15 minutes.

11.4.1 Study Analysis: AI Impact on Marketing Professions

The recent study I came across on Patreon by Head of Marketing at Userpilot, Emilia Korczynska (2023) paints a vivid picture of this change. The questions were asked to content writers, content agencies, and in-house content teams to find out their perspective on things – how AI has impacted their work, the demand for their services, and their plans for 2024.

It reveals a significant shift in skill requirements and job functions within the marketing profession. Traditional roles are evolving, demanding a new blend of technical savvy and creative acumen. **Are we at the end of content marketing?**

Here are a summary of the findings:

- **Demand on content services**: While the demand has more or less stayed on the same level as before, the number of clients content marketers are servicing has been decreasing.
- **Type of content**: Seventy-five per cent of the work performed was on search engine optimisation (SEO) content and the second type of work demanded was thought leadership content at 9.4%. The rest consists of editing AI content, microlearning articles, and copywriting for websites and emails.
- **Job market shifts**: Some writers have faced challenges in securing job opportunities, noting a decrease in demand for basic content creation roles, which have been replaced or devalued due to AI tools.
- **Quality assurance**: AI is used to verify the quality of work, leading to heightened standards and expectations in content production.
- **Enhanced productivity and efficiency**: Many writers use AI as their interns and found AI to be beneficial for productivity, helping in research, drafting, and editing, significantly speeding up their workflow.
- **Shift towards complex content**: There is a growing demand for thought leadership and high-quality content. The prevalence of AI has raised the bar, necessitating more in-depth, expertly crafted, quality content that AI alone cannot produce.
- **Mixed impact on earnings**: While some writers have seen their rates increase due to the demand for more specialised content, others have faced a reduction in pay and available opportunities.
- **AI as a tool, not a replacement**: A common sentiment is that AI is a valuable tool that assists in the writing process but cannot replace the unique insights, context understanding, and emotional depth that human writers bring.

- **Increased demand for diverse skills**: Content writers are now expected to be versatile, leveraging AI for a variety of tasks beyond writing, including content planning, editing, and marketing.
- **Challenges and adaptation**: The integration of AI has not been seamless, with some writers facing layoffs or struggling to find new work, while others adapted by enhancing their skills or changing their approach to content creation.
- **Perceptions and usage of AI**: The attitudes towards AI have varied, with some embracing it enthusiastically for tasks like brief creation, while others have remained sceptical of its ability to fully replace human creativity and expertise.
- **Overall mixed reactions**: The overall impact of AI on independent content marketers has been mixed, with some benefiting from increased efficiency and creativity, while others have faced challenges in adapting to the changing landscape.

The insights and first-hand accounts make it clear: AI's influence on content writers is undeniable. Many basic content creation roles have either vanished, replaced by tools like ChatGPT and other AI writing technologies, or these jobs now offer lower pay with expectations of faster delivery. However, it is not all a downward trend. As these entry-level roles disappear, the demand and value for top-tier content writers have surged, especially for quality content that requires experienced writers and complex cognitive skills.

AI, while widely acknowledged as a valuable aid in the writing process, is not seen as a substitute for high-quality content creation. It is a tool that enhances, not replaces, the skills of proficient writers.

11.4.2 AI Took Over the "Monkey Work"

This discovery marked just the beginning. A designer on my team soon realised that we could produce high-quality images meeting our brand's stringent standards at a fraction of the cost – less than what we spend on our daily lunches. Since embracing these AI tools, we have dramatically expanded our AI playground to include a broader and more diverse set of use cases. Here is how we are utilising them currently:

- **Research**: Instead of having to read, browse through the top ten search results on Google, and form our own summary and analysis, AI helps us to gather and synthesise information quickly, providing a solid foundation for our content.
- **Brainstorming**: Content marketers no longer experience writer's block. We use AI to brainstorm, generate ideas and concepts, kickstarting our content development process. At times where we are too overwhelmed to know where to start, we can rely on AI to respond to our prompt.

- **Writing improvement**: AI tools assist in refining our writing, enhancing clarity, and ensuring consistency with our brand voice that you can train the AI model with. We use it sparingly in order to avoid sounding like robots.
- **Report summarisation**: Complex datasets and lengthy reports are condensed into easy-to-digest bullet points and summaries within seconds, saving us hours of reading time.
- **Video translation**: AI efficiently translates our video content, expanding our reach to new audiences without having to spend additional resources on new actors. Dubbing videos into different languages without editing the original content expands our reach to non-English speaking audiences within minutes without having to utilise expensive video production resources, sourcing and recording voice artists.
- **Social media captions**: AI generates engaging and relevant captions for our social media posts in our voice. In social media content, grammar is less important than the context and message relevant to the specific platform. As we continue to train our AI model with our tone of voice and guidelines, designers themselves with little proficiency in writing can use AI to augment their work.
- **Campaign prototyping**: AI helps us quickly create campaign prototypes that we can use to customise in order to sell the business case of the campaign. We can quickly create visual presentations to stakeholders without involving designers, allowing for rapid testing and iteration.
- **Brief creation**: AI gives general outline for any campaign or activity that we can use as a start in creating a comprehensive brief. Any individual contributor within the marketing team can use AI to do research and get a general understanding without waiting for the brief to be presented by the owner or manager.

Each of these applications has not only improved our workflow but also opened up new avenues for creativity and innovation. The integration of AI into our daily operations has transformed how we work, making us more agile and cost-effective. We have successfully integrated AI into our human workers leveraging on the interaction between humans and AI, which essentially produces two cognitive systems (artificial and human) with each doing cognitive work in different ways, at different scales, and at a different pace (Siemens et al., 2022). The study highlights that substantial research is needed to define the roles and relationships between the two cognitive systems as illustrated in Figure 11.1.

11.4.3 Use Case Analysis: Human and AI Interaction Principles

Considering the use cases I have personally experienced during the past year, there are various interaction principles between artificial and human cognition in the context of content creation and marketing. Based on these, here are some of the guiding interaction principles I have observed.

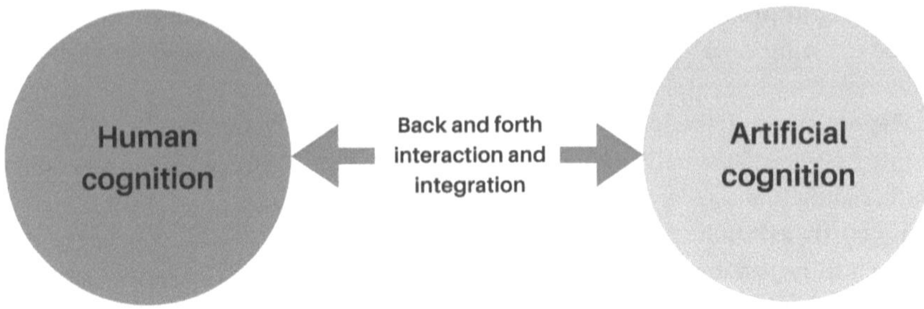

FIGURE 11.1 Two cognitive systems doing cognitive work.
Source: Siemens et al. (2022).

11.4.3.1 From AI Outputs into Human Cognitive Systems

- **Validation and verification**: Always verify AI-generated information for accuracy and relevance. AI tools can efficiently gather and process data, but human oversight is crucial for ensuring the correctness of this information.
- **Contextual interpretation**: Humans must interpret AI outputs within the appropriate context. AI can provide data or suggestions, but humans need to understand the broader context to make meaningful decisions.
- **Ethical considerations**: When integrating AI outputs, ethical considerations, such as data privacy and bias, must be accounted for. Humans need to ensure that AI-generated content or decisions adhere to ethical standards.
- **Complementing human skills**: AI should be used to complement and enhance human skills, not replace them. For instance, AI can handle repetitive tasks or provide initial drafts, but humans should contribute creative and strategic insights.
- **Proactive learning**: Human users must be adaptable and willing to learn new skills to effectively integrate AI into their workflows. This includes actively testing, using the tools in order to understand the capabilities and limitations of AI tools.

11.4.3.2 From Human Inputs into AI Systems

- **Feedback loops**: Provide continuous feedback to AI systems. This helps in training their algorithms and outputs, making them more aligned with human expectations and needs.
- **Training with diverse data**: To ensure AI systems can handle a wide range of human cognitive activities, they should be trained with diverse and comprehensive datasets.
- **Custom instructions and personalisation**: Customise AI tools to fit specific human cognitive styles and preferences. This can involve adjusting AI

parameters to better align with individual or organisational needs. For example, feeding AI with our style of writing and tone of voice.

- **Culture training**: Human users are surrounded by culture and context that AI systems are not. By providing context and insights into human culture, AI can frame its output to align with the expected results. This can include feeding AI with market and competition insights, providing context such as detailed description of where the content will be used, and so on.

11.4.3.3 Mutual Integration Principles

- **Continuous adaptation**: Both AI systems and human cognitive processes should adapt based on mutual interactions. Learning from each other's strengths and do I dare to say personality can lead to improved decision-making and productivity.
- **Balancing automation with human judgement**: Find the right balance between automated processes and human judgement. While AI can handle certain tasks efficiently, complex decision-making often requires human insight.
- **Cross-disciplinary understanding**: Encourage a cross-disciplinary approach where knowledge from different fields is integrated into both AI systems and human decision-making processes.

11.4.4 What Is Left for Humans?

The integration between AI into human cognitive systems and vice versa is inevitably fascinating and continues to evolve very quickly. While AI sets humans free from the "monkey work", referring to tasks that are considered repetitive, simple, or requiring little skill or thought, it places higher standards on the humans. AI exposes us humans, especially on the standards we set for ourselves.

This is important because when we are not bogged down by mundane administration, we have more brain space and we can either use that freedom to do nothing, or to think creatively and innovatively, pushing us towards our greatest potential that we are meant to achieve. Now that AI does the "monkey work" for us, we can be humans again. Or now that AI does the "monkey work" for us, what are we going to do?

11.5 AI Spurs Upskilling of Marketers

AI is reshaping our lives, bringing both benefits and challenges. On the privacy front, AI's data hunger raises concerns. It feeds on vast amounts of information, which risks exposing personal details or being used in ways we never intended. In the job market, AI's efficiency in automating routine tasks is a double-edged sword, threatening certain jobs while creating even more jobs. And as a consequence, forcing us to adapt by upskilling or reskilling.

According to Karim Lakhani (2023), professor at Harvard Business School specialising in workplace technology with particular regard to AI, AI is not going to replace humans, but rather, humans with AI will replace humans without AI. The impact of generative AI on marketing professions is particularly striking. I have seen first-hand how AI is reshaping the landscape, especially in content generation and data analytics, where it is not just augmenting but actually replacing certain roles. The real question is not about whether to adapt to this change – that is a given. It is about how we adapt, and more importantly, how quickly we can do it, given the lightning-fast pace at which AI is evolving.

11.5.1 A Short Story about AI Evolution

AI has long been a lofty aspiration in the field of computer science. The journey started way back in 1943 when pioneers like McCulloch and Pitts introduced the concepts of artificial neurons, and by 1956 McCarthy and Minsky diving into ideas about neural networks (Giacaglia, 2022).

For a long while, AI was mostly a playground exclusively for researchers. But then, deep neural networks came along and changed the game, which outperformed humans in tasks like facial recognition and speech understanding, as illustrated in Figure 11.2 (Kiela et al., 2021). Suddenly, every software engineer wanted in on the exclusive AI action.

Fast forward a bit, and you have got everyone chasing "data science" and "machine learning" degrees and companies everywhere started scrambling to hire data scientists and Machine Learning engineers. However, many of these companies struggled with their AI initiatives – about 85% of them failed, according to Gartner (Gartner, 2018; Malik, 2021). The primary challenges? Insufficient quality data, a lack of skilled personnel, and a general misunderstanding of AI within management ranks.

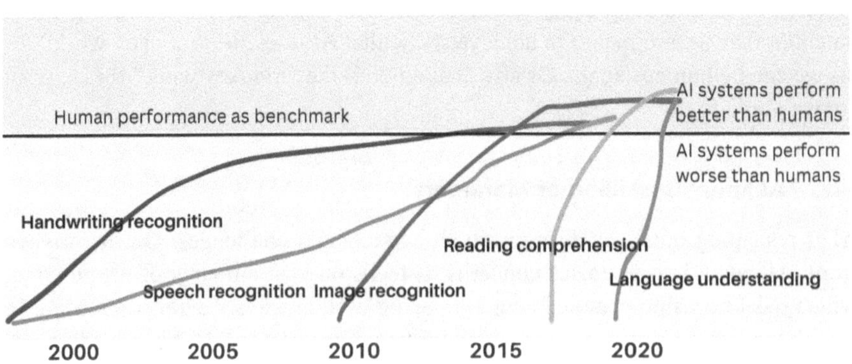

FIGURE 11.2 AI surpasses human capabilities.

Source: Kiela et al. (2021).

This led to the emergence of AI application programming interfaces (API), effectively acting as shortcuts to AI utilisation. No specialised degree was required; a simple API call was enough to leverage the power of AI. There is a ton of these AI APIs available now, offering all sorts of features like speech recognition and image processing at various costs and levels of user-friendliness. This availability and simplicity of leveraging these tools are driving competition and innovation in AI, suggesting that the next major breakthrough might emerge from an unexpected source. So, that is the story. AI has come a long way, from the selected few in the labs to now, a tool accessible to virtually everyone.

11.5.2 The Need for Marketers to Evolve with AI

At the office, someone casually remarked, "Everyone is replaceable". That got me thinking. Sure, it sounds about right, especially with AI in the picture, but from my experience, the situation is not so straightforward. Every individual brings their unique essence to the table. Before AI became our daily sidekick, mediocre marketers could skate by doing the bare minimum or just being adequate. Fewer questions could be asked back then; marketing often lacked data and keeping up with the constantly evolving demands was challenging enough. Then came data analytics and AI, exposing the mediocrity. Suddenly, even the mediocre marketers could enhance their performance with AI's help. However, there is a catch: once every marketer starts leveraging AI, just doing adequate will no longer suffice. Those who fail to upgrade their skills will likely lose their jobs. *Marketers need to do more than just survive with AI – they need to thrive with it.* The big question is, what is our strategy for reskilling or upskilling to keep ahead of the curve?

Let us consider the fundamentals: businesses exist to make a profit. Every employee, whether a marketer or otherwise, represents either a cost or an investment. The same principle applies to purchasing technology – it is all about the money they are willing to pay in order to create more monetary value either directly or indirectly for the business. In other words, the return of investment is what they care about. Having this in mind makes the equation quite simple. If a marketer's cost outweighs their value, the business will naturally lean towards a more cost-effective solution, like technology, unless the marketer significantly increases the value they provide.

This situation presents a formidable challenge for us marketers. The goal is to become a powerhouse of value creation, making ourselves indispensable to the business. We must contemplate: How can we outpace the value curve set by AI? How do we transform into indispensable value creators in this AI-dominated landscape?

11.6 The Power of Creativity

While AI is a powerful tool in marketing, it cannot replace the human skills of creativity, which requires empathy and critical thinking. Creativity is crucial for developing successful marketing strategies, and I would argue that it is a key predictor of success for both businesses and individuals. It involves more than just creating art; it is an essential problem-solving skill that spurs innovations, breaks new ground, and, most importantly, it is a discipline that everyone can develop through practice and determination.

11.6.1 Defining Creativity

What is creativity? Robert E. Franken (1994) defined creativity as the tendency to generate or recognise ideas, alternatives, or possibilities that may be useful in solving problems, communicating with others, and entertaining ourselves and others. It is not just about the quantity of ideas but the uniqueness of ideas.

Sir Ken Robinson (2006), in his renowned TED talk, argues that the traditional education system stifles creativity. He believes that schools, focussed on standardised testing and conformity, neglect the creative aspects of learning. According to Robinson, children are naturally creative and curious, but the education system gradually suppresses these traits, favouring academic achievement in conventional subjects like mathematics and languages over artistic pursuits. This leads to the theory that "schools kill creativity".

Robinson emphasises that creativity is as important as literacy and should be treated with the same status. He argues for an education system that nurtures creativity through a more personalised approach, recognising the unique talents and interests of each child. His talk highlights the need for a radical rethinking of our educational systems to cultivate creativity and innovation, preparing children not just for academic success, but for fulfilling, imaginative lives.

11.6.2 The Role of Creativity in Business Success

Back in the early 2000s, I joined an ad agency founded by my artist-turned-chef uncle. We were starting from scratch, with no salary and no paying clients initially, and creative ideas were our lifeline. Facing tough competition and lacking an advertising budget, we relied on our network for sales and creativity to stand out.

In just about a year, we landed big-name clients like Burger King, 7up (a throwback, indeed), Sanofi, GlaxoSmithKline, and major banks and retail brands across Asia. A personal highlight was rebranding Munchy's, a biscuit company. We even used ourselves and our family members as models. The tagline "bite me", which we introduced in 2004, is something I am still proud of. Munchy's was recognised as the number one home-grown biscuit brand in Malaysia in 2017, and the creative concept we developed for Munchy's has been part of the brand ever since (Munchy's Group, 2024).

This experience introduced me to the concept of earning a living from ideas. Creativity was not just a lifeline for our agency; it was also the source of our salaries. This period was both challenging and enlightening, teaching me that creativity is not only pivotal in generating revenue for our business, but perhaps more importantly, it is a learnable skill that requires practice and self-discipline to master.

According to James Webb Young (2003), creativity can be practiced through five simple steps. He defines creativity as the generation of ideas by combining old elements in new ways, hinging on one's ability to discern relationships. In his book, he posits that creativity, like any other skill, is a technique that can be mastered by following these five steps:

1 Gather material.
2 Mentally work over the material.
3 Step away from the problem.
4 Allow the idea to return naturally.
5 Test and refine the idea based on feedback.

11.6.3 Case Analysis: Amazon and Its Creative Diversifications

Creativity, when effectively executed, can lead to ground-breaking products and services, reshaping industries and consumer behaviours. A prime example of this is Amazon's expansion into cloud computing with Amazon Web Services (AWS) in 2013. AWS, initially a side project, has often been used as a case study in business schools for corporate innovation. Its unexpected rise in the cloud computing sector, surpassing even Amazon's core retail business, reflects the company's unique culture of innovation. This culture includes giving new ventures like AWS sufficient time to develop and ensuring that decisions are data-driven. It also encourages leaders to actively challenge their assumptions, recognising that groupthink, while comforting, can be contagious and detrimental. This approach empowers team members to voice their doubts and counterpoints, fostering a culture of critical thinking and open dialogue. As the leading cloud computing platform, AWS has since become the primary profit driver for Amazon, accounting for about 13% of Amazon's total revenue as of Q2 2021 (Colvin, 2022).

Another example of Amazon's creative diversification is the Kindle. During the recession, when retail sectors were struggling, Amazon made a significant breakthrough, surprising financial experts with a substantial increase in profits, exceeding Wall Street's expectations. The Kindle e-book reader was a key driver of this success, becoming Amazon's top-selling item not just in electronics, but across all product categories. This period of remarkable growth for Amazon, especially with the Kindle, demonstrated their inventive use of technology and market strategy to achieve sales success and category dominance, even amidst economic downturns (Johnson, 2009).

11.6.4 Mastering Creativity in Marketing to Outpace AI

At its core, marketing is the art of capturing attention, earning trust, and becoming the preferred choice. It is about convincing people to choose your brand over others, using the right blend of words and visuals. This craft combines creativity with psychology, creating impactful ads that once dominated TV, billboards, magazines, and newspapers. These ads, born from thorough research and a deep understanding of the audience and context, are crafted with creativity designed to achieve core marketing objectives and make a lasting impression. They possess a timeless quality, so much so that even if they were conceived half a century ago, their impact and relevance would still resonate today.

AI excels at data processing and pattern recognition but lacks the innate human abilities for original thinking, emotional understanding, and nuanced decision-making. This underscores the vital importance of the human element in marketing. Marketers who can combine the power of AI with their own unique skills and insights are likely to be the most successful in the coming years.

Mastering creativity takes time and practice. More importantly, creativity is a discipline. It trains our brains to challenge our perceived limits and forge new connections. Just as we train our AI models with new information and instructions, humans, especially marketers, must enrich our minds with new knowledge and ideas. After all, creativity is all about connecting existing ideas in fresh ways.

Look how fast things are moving: In just four months, we have gone from casual AI chats to turning simple sketches on napkins into full-blown websites using AI. The journey from concept to reality has been dramatically shortened. The vast divide between coders, writers, and everyone else has practically disappeared. What truly counts now are the ideas, the creative spark, and the originality that only humans can provide. Even AI would back me up on this.

11.7 Cyborg Marketers Are Here

The term "cyborg" is short for "cybernetic organism". It refers to a being that combines organic and biomechatronic body parts. Essentially, a cyborg is an entity that is both biological and artificial. The concept is commonly used in science fiction to describe humans augmented with technological implants or devices that enhance their natural capabilities. For instance, a person with a robotic arm or an implanted chip that boosts brain function could be considered a cyborg. The defining feature of a cyborg is the integration of technology into a living organism to improve or augment its capabilities.

In the marketing world, being a "cyborg" does not mean having robotic limbs or AI brains. Rather, it is about how we, as marketers, have evolved to blend our human skills with a range of digital tools, especially AI and data analytics. This fusion has given rise to what I call "cyborg marketers", a new breed of professionals. This is not just a whimsical term; it is a genuine reflection of how deeply technology is integrated into our creative profession. In the AI era, it underscores the urgency of developing human skills, particularly creativity, in marketing.

Here is what being a "cyborg marketer" means to marketers:

- **Tech is our best-kept secret**: The first time I used AI to read a report in a foreign language and summarise the findings in a language I understand was mind-blowing. In fact, it was a game-changer. Reading the report alone would have taken significant time, not to mention the time required for translation. The depth of insight achieved was beyond what I could have managed manually. Now, integrating technology into daily tasks like market analysis or content creation has become routine for us.
- **Data is stronger than opinions**: There is an inherent confidence in making decisions backed by solid data, especially in marketing, where opinions are plentiful. AI tools have helped us confirm our beliefs, prioritise our work, and sharpen our targeting, making our strategies not only creative but also more impactful. They also speed up our processes, from ideation to creation, and from distribution to measurement.
- **Farewell to monkey work**: One of the best parts of using AI is how it handles repetitive tasks. It is like having a reliable assistant available around the clock, diligently taking care of the grunt work, from summarising reports to generating content, freeing us up for more significant tasks. Creativity flourishes in an environment free from mundane tasks.
- **Open to failure and getting up again**: Stagnation is not an option in the marketing world. Change is the only constant in our field. We are constantly learning and adapting, embracing new tools and methods. Always ready to capitalise on the next big wave in platforms and methods, our mantra is to grow boldly, without fear of stumbling along the way.
- **Power of creativity**: Last but not least, despite our heavy reliance on technology, we have not forgotten the power of human creativity and empathy in marketing. AI is great at writing text quickly, crunching numbers, and forecasting trends, but understanding human emotions and creating messages that truly resonate with people in the right context and timing is something only humans can do.

11.8 Conclusion

Cyborg marketers are here now. Despite technological advancements, there is something undeniably human still at play: creativity. As AI takes over routine tasks, our unique ability to solve problems creatively and pursue innovative ideas becomes increasingly valuable. In marketing, this translates to a greater appreciation for artistry, originality, and excellent execution. These human qualities set businesses and individuals apart, making marketers stand out in a future job market inundated with AI. Our innate flair for creativity, empathy, and ethical decision-making will guide us towards success and distinction. In marketing, the key lies in merging creativity with technological savvy. Marketers who master this combination will excel in the game. This synergy is essentially the secret sauce for success in the industry, both today and in the future. One thing is certain: marketers who remain sceptical about AI replacing their jobs will be left behind. As Kieran Flanagan (2023, para. 1), CMO of Zapier, aptly put it, "AI is about to replace your average marketer". This quotation has indeed aged like fine wine.

References

Cameron, J. (1984). *The Terminator*. United States: Orion Pictures.

Cameron, J. (1991). *Terminator 2: Judgment Day*. United States: Tri-Star Pictures.

Colvin, G. (2022). How Amazon Grew an Awkward Side Project into AWS, a Behemoth That's Now 4 Times Bigger Than Its Original Shopping Business. Retrieved March 6, 2025, from Fortune website: https://fortune.com/longform/amazon-web-services-ceo-adam-selipsky-cloud-computing

Flanagan, K. (2023). AI is About to Replace Your "Average" Marketer. Retrieved March 6, 2025, from LinkedIn website: www.linkedin.com/feed/update/urn:li:activity:71232962 67497025536

Franken, R. E. (1994). *Human Motivation* (3rd ed.). Pacific Grove, CA: Brooks/Cole Publishing Company.

Gartner. (2018). Gartner Says Nearly Half of CIOs Are Planning to Deploy Artificial Intelligence. Retrieved March 6, 2025, from www.gartner.com/en/newsroom/press-relea ses/2018-02-13-gartner-says-nearly-half-of-cios-are-planning-to-deploy-artificial-intel ligence

Giacaglia, G. (2022). The Birth of Artificial Intelligence (1952–1956). Retrieved March 6, 2025, from Halloway website: www.holloway.com/g/making-things-think/sections/the-birth-of-artificial-intelligence-19521956

Johnson, B. (2009). Amazon Busts Through Recession with Profit Surge. Retrieved March 6, 2025, from The Guardian website: www.theguardian.com/technology/2009/oct/23/ amazon-profits

Kiela, D., Bartolo, M., Nie, Y., Kaushik, D., Geiger, A., Wu, Z., … & Williams, A. (2021). Dynabench: Rethinking benchmarking in NLP. In K. Toutanova, A. Rumshisky, L. Zettlemoyer, D. Hakkani-Tur, I. Beltagy, S. Bethard, … & Y. Zhou (Eds.), *Proceedings of the 2021 Conference of the North American Chapter of the Association for Computational Linguistics: Human Language Technologies. 6–11 June. Online* (pp. 4110–4124). Kerrville, TX: Association for Computational Linguistics.

Korczynska, E. (2023). State of Content Marketing in 2023 – Content Writers' Perspective. Retrieved March 6, 2025, from Patreon website: www.patreon.com/posts/93173051

Lakhani, K. (2023). AI Won't Replace Humans—But Humans With AI Will Replace Humans Without AI. Retrieved March 6, 2025, from Harvard Business Review website: https:// hbr.org/2023/08/ai-wont-replace-humans-but-humans-with-ai-will-replace-humans-without-ai

Malik, H. (2021). Why 85% of Machine Learning Projects Fail – How to Avoid This. Retrieved March 6, 2025, from IIoT World website: www.iiot-world.com/industrial-iot/ connected-industry/why-85-of-machine-learning-projects-fail

Munchy's Group. (2024). Our History. Retrieved March 6, 2025, from www.munchys.com/ about-us/our-history

Robinson, K. (2006). Do Schools Kill Creativity? Retrieved March 6, 2025, from Ted.com website: www.ted.com/talks/sir_ken_robinson_do_schools_kill_creativity

Siemens, G., Marmolejo-Ramos, F., Gabriel, F., Medeiros, K., Marrone, R., Joksimovic, S., & de Laat, M. (2022). Human and artificial cognition. *Computers and Education: Artificial Intelligence*, *3*, 100107, 1–9. https://doi.org/10.1016/j.caeai.2022.100107

Young, J. W. (2003). *A Technique for Producing Ideas (Advertising Age Classics Library)*. New York, NY: McGraw Hill.

12

VALUE CHAINS OF AI

Data Training Firms, Platforms, and Workers

Mohammad Amir Anwar

12.1 Introduction

Some observers have proclaimed artificial intelligence (AI) to become "the most general-purpose technology of our era" (Brynjolfsson & McAfee, 2017, para. 2). Others go even further to say AI as "the greatest technology humanity has yet developed" and it will reshape our economy and society (Helmore, 2023, para. 4). There are estimates AI will contribute about US$15 trillion (roughly the size of the EU economy) to the global economy by 2030 (PwC, 2017). No doubt that today, AI tools are everywhere. Cities are deploying facial recognition technologies to tackle daily crime. Governments are introducing biometric systems to create new identification systems for its citizens. Driverless cars transfer people from place A to place B. Supermarkets are using self-checkouts.

Despite the proliferation of AI in many industries and different facets of our lives, it continues to remain an enigma for a vast majority of the ordinary people. A 2023 survey by the Office for National Statistics (ONS), UK found over half of the public could only offer partial explanation about what is AI, despite using it daily (Office for National Statistics, 2023). Large technology firms are notoriously secretive about their activities, which means there is very little publicly available data (Foroohar, 2019). As a result, their production networks remain opaque and it is impossible to say with any degree of certainty where and how AI systems are made. As AI becomes pervasive, it raises a number of questions. How are AI systems made? Who trains them and where? These are crucial questions if we are to understand the implications of AI technologies on our economy and society (e.g. automation of work tasks, unemployment), which is one of the concerns of this chapter.

DOI: 10.4324/9781003391333-15

For machines dependent on AI to work efficiently, they need to be fed massive amounts of training data. This is called machine learning (the science of getting computers to make decisions) whereby data enrichment tasks or data work (e.g. text prediction, image and video annotation, speech to text validation and content moderation) are carried out by behind-the-scenes human labour (Altenried, 2020; Anwar & Graham, 2020; Munn, 2022; Newlands, 2021; Tubaro, Casilli, & Coville, 2020). By way of example, for driverless cars to safely drive on road, cameras mounted on them must be able to identify road markings, people, trees and traffic lights with great accuracy. To train cameras, millions of images of mostly American cities are tagged by workers so that computers can learn the difference between a pavement and a road or a tree and a person (Anwar & Graham, 2020). A vast majority of these workers are located in the Global South (i.e. some of the most poor countries on our planet such as India, the Philippines, Bangladesh, Venezuela, Colombia, Kenya, Egypt, Nigeria) or which the celebrated Bangladeshi photographer and activists Shahidul Islam calls, "the majority world" (Shafaieh, 2022).[1] Put differently, the newly emerging machines and technology at the centre of profit-making endeavours of large firms in the Global North are made in the Global South.

The chapter deploys the value chains framework (Gereffi, Humphrey, & Sturgeon, 2005) to examine the processes and mechanisms through which people and places come together to train AI. The chapter by no means makes a claim to unpack the entire value chain of AI (more in the next section). Instead, it explores data work and the role of actors involved in this activity: data training firms (or suppliers), labour platforms and workers. By exploring these actors and their activities, it makes visible the segment of the AI value chain (i.e. data enrichment work) that had remained invisible or hidden from public scrutiny for a while. The overall aim of this chapter is not only to shed light on the importance of humans in the loop for AI, but also reinforce the centrality of the majority world in the makings of AI. The chapter concludes with discussion on automation-related job losses and on workers and places where data enrichment work for AI is done.

12.2 Understanding Value Chains of AI

Trans-national corporations (TNCs) have always depended on a vast array of actors and production grounded in a particular place to make their goods (Dicken, 2015). Lead firms organise their production activities (i.e. research, development, design, assembly and production, marketing, back-office operations and so on) in different locations for both efficiency and cost saving (Gereffi et al., 2005). The result is a complex web of global value chains defined by offshoring, subcontracting and outsourcing of economic production around the world (Gereffi et al., 2005). Subcontracting and outsourcing have existed for decades in the manufacturing and services sectors creating uneven developments (Coe & Yeung, 2015). We note in this chapter similar trends are underway with the rise of AI.

One of the advantages of using value chains (and production networks) analysis is to make sense of various production nodes in the contemporary digital economy, actors and activities involved, and the spatial configurations it generates (Coe & Yeung, 2015; Henderson, Dicken, Hess, Coe, & Yeung, 2002). A significant scholarship has gone into the value chains analysis of manufacturing and services sector (Gibbon & Ponte, 2005; Kleibert, 2015). Comparatively, AI value chains are relatively less studied. Kate Crawford (2021, p. 8), one of the leading scholars of AI, argues that "AI is both embodied and material" in the sense that it involves a combination of economic, social, political, institutional and cultural forces for its production. The idea is that AI systems need natural resources, labour power, built infrastructures, capital and logistics, much that same way any other common good such as a t-shirt or a shoe would require. Thus, it is pertinent to understand where and how are the production practices in AI getting grounded. But unlike value chains in manufacturing, AI activities differ.

An increasing amount of economic activity is becoming digitally mediated, meaning production can move across the planet with relative ease (Graham & Anwar, 2019a). This raises the possibility of new places and actors getting connected to the digital economy value chains, more specifically in AI activities. For example, the rapid advancements of AI are largely dependent on the concomitant rise of the hyperscale computing regime (Narayan, 2022). This global cloud-based infrastructure is crucial to AI systems and the compute power needed to run the algorithms (Schreckinger, 2023). For example, both Microsoft and Google have cloud computing infrastructure located around the world, including in some of the most economically marginalised regions such as Africa and Latin America. Similarly, Amazon runs a data centre in South Africa and is aiming to invest US$2.5 billion by 2029 in cloud computing infrastructure in the country (CIO Africa, 2023). Then there are rare earth metals and minerals like cobalt, gold, neodymium, cerium and so on for mobile phones and laptops on which users run AI tools (e.g. virtual assistant like Siri). Most of these critical elements are sourced from places like Chile, DRC, Indonesia, Australia and China (Fuchs, 2014). Many of these activities can be easily identified and traced due to the physical nature of transactions involved (e.g. movement of minerals, building infrastructure for cloud computing and so on). But they remain beyond the remit of this chapter. The chapter instead turns its gaze towards an important segment of AI value chains: its training process. AI training activities have remained hidden from the public eye, which Gray and Suri (2019, p. ix) call "ghost work". Essentially, this chapter is about data work for AI, which is seen as an early stage of AI production (Tubaro et al., 2020).

Lead firms from Microsoft to Amazon to Alphabet to Meta are widely known to be developing large language models (LLMs) via training of large corpus of data from various digital repositories on the Internet. Some of their LLMs (e.g. ChatGPT and Gemini) have been remarkably successful in showing high-performance such as passing the medical and law exams. But this success is dependent on human feedback loop, that is, training via supervised fine-tuning (SFT) and reinforcement learning with human feedback (RLHF) techniques (Liu, Sferrazza, & Abbeel, 2023; Stiennon et al., 2020).[2] Some of these machine learning activities are outsourced and subcontracted to a wide array of actors including supplier firms (often known as data training contractors or data processing firms). By way of examples, some of the training of OpenAI's ChatGPT (an AI chatbot) took place in Kenya with the help of an international data training firm, Sama (Perrigo, 2023).

The offshoring and outsourcing of data work is also done via a new kind of player: labour platforms (Anwar & Graham, 2022). A large proportion of the Fortune 500 corporations are using labour platforms (henceforth platforms) to outsource some of their services (Corporaal & Lehdonvirta, 2017). Platforms such as Upwork, Amazon Mechanical Turk (AMT), Appen, Scale AI, and Remotasks have emerged as specialist platforms where businesses and start-ups and researchers can hire on-demand workers from across the globe to do data work for them (Anwar & Graham, 2022). Such is the dependence of large technology firms on data training contractors and platforms in their value chains, which it is safe to say that many of these tools would not exist without them. To put it simply, the value chain lens for data work allows us to see who are the key actors involved in AI training, where does this work get done, who does it and under what conditions. The following section outlines how data training contractors, platforms and workers come together help train AI tools.

12.3 Data Training Firms

One of the key players in AI chains are the data training firms. These are the intermediaries between the lead firms and workers performing a wide variety of data enrichment tasks (verifying, annotating, labelling, imitating, etc.) (Tubaro et al., 2020). Microsoft has a partnership with OpenAI, the company responsible for developing the ChatGPT. Microsoft has invested reportedly over US$13 billion in OpenAI (Duhigg, 2023). OpenAI outsourced some of the training for its LLMs such as ChatGPT. One of the suppliers for OpenAI was Sama, a US-based training firm, which hires workers in some of the poorer parts of the world to do data work for AI (i.e. annotation, curation, classification and verification of data). Sama's training centres are in several countries, but two of the main ones are in Kenya and Uganda. There other training firms too such as Digital Divide Data (another US-based data training firm). Data training contractors like Sama and Digital Divide Data have sales team based in the United States where they secure contracts with large tech firms. The work is then sent across to their delivery centres in Kenya and Uganda where hundreds of African workers then do the training work (Anwar & Graham, 2022).

Previously it has been noted how foreign firms operating in Africa label themselves as business process outsourcing (BPO) firms to get data work contracts from large Silicon Valley firms (Anwar & Graham, 2020). Thus, this kind of

AI training practices can be thought as a logical extension of BPO work. While outsourcing of economic production has its origin in the 1960s with the relocation of industrial manufacturing from the United States and Europe to a variety of low-wage locations in South America and East Asia (Fröbel, Heinrichs, & Kreye, 1981), it received much more public attention in the 1990s as firms began to outsource (either through nearshoring, onshoring and multishoring) their non-core functions such as administrative processing, customer support and information technology services (Abbott & Jones, 2012; Finnemore, Kim, & Pande, 2010; Peck, 2017). The establishment of customer service centres across India and the Philippines is often acknowledged to have set the foundation of the modern-day BPOs. More commonly, these are known as call centres. It is very likely that if you have ever contacted the customer services of your local bank, mobile services provider, had to cancel or change a flight or train ticket, you may have spoken to call centre workers located either in India or the Philippines.

Existing studies on BPOs have highlighted unique business practices, technologies and socio-cultural practices that enable the organisation of work around the world (Beerepoot, Lambregts, & Kleibert, 2017; Peck, 2017). Effectively, offshoring and outsourcing became synonymised with the lengthening of supply chains, modularisation, standardisation, lean managerial practices and fragmentation of production activities (Peck, 2017). Just like the offshoring of manufacturing and services have set the foundation of today's far-reaching and complex global production networks, we are likely to witness a reorganisation of the production landscape with the emergence of the AI (Coe & Yeung, 2015).

Data training firms can be thought of as the equivalent of modern-day BPOs with their production activities spread out around the world. Research on data work points to this trend. Miceli and Posada's (2022) research on data work in Latin America highlights the presence of BPO firms doing data generation projects for US clients. Anwar and Graham's (2022) study on training centres in Africa reveals not just the presence of foreign data training firms but also the centrality of the local Kenyan BPO firms doing subcontracted data work originating in the United States. Largely, local Kenyan firms are increasingly reliant on data training firms to sustain themselves in the market, though this also means a form of dependence and less control over the value creation, enhancement and capture (Anwar & Graham, 2022). Similarly, content moderation for Facebook is done everywhere from Delhi to Dublin (Hern, 2020). In Dublin, Facebook seeks the help of Covalen and Accenture for content moderation to keep the social media giant clean from child abuse and pornography (Bernal, 2021). Amazon trains its speech recognition systems for Alexa smart speakers by hiring both full-time employees and also contractual data annotators from Costa Rica to India (Day, Turner, & Drozdiak, 2019). The point is data training firms are the crucial link in the AI value chains. They act as intermediaries between lead firms such as Facebook, Microsoft, Amazon and Google, and workers around the world.

Yet, data work is also different. Unlike BPOs, data work is conducted both by workers employed at specialist data training firms and also individually as freelancers. These freelancers depend on another type of actor: platforms such as AMT and Appen for data work, which is the subject of the next section.

12.4 Platforms

Platforms have received significant interest among researchers from different conceptual viewpoints. Kenney and Zysman (2020) note platforms as organisational tools that combine big data, algorithms and cloud computing infrastructures that are reorganising the economic production landscape on a global scale (Frenken, Vaskelainen, Fünfschilling, & Piscicelli, 2020; Langley & Leyshon, 2017). Lehdonvirta et al. (2019) argue that platforms bring together buyers and service providers in a system of economic exchange. In the case of data work, firms and businesses seeking to train algorithms hire data annotators or verifiers on platforms. Lehdonvirta et al. (2019) further noted that the rise of platforms follows the changes happening in the traditional outsourcing since 1990s. Digital technologies have allowed services to be outsourced to large distance with the benefit of cheaper costs (including labour) and access to necessary skills. This is made possible due to the fragmentation and commodification of the economic activities, which are increasingly becoming digital in nature (Graham & Anwar, 2018). The fragmented tasks are then easily traded on platforms (Lehdonvirta et al., 2019).

But there are some crucial differences between platforms and the BPOs. Unlike traditional outsourcing or BPOs, platforms have eliminated the need for firms to build fixed infrastructural spaces. Platforms themselves have become a workplace with its digital and cloud-based infrastructure allowing businesses and firms to structure work (Richardson, 2024). Whereas in BPOs economic transactions normally take place between firms, platforms enable individual workers (known by various monikers, such as micro-providers, freelancers and independent contractors) to tap into the newly emerging digital services chains such as AI (Horton, 2010). Just like BPO firms are listing job advertisements for home-based or remote call centre work, platforms tap in to the individual workers are freelancers, who can theoretically work from anywhere provided they have access to technology.

One of the most well-known platforms at the centre of data work is the AMT (Irani & Silberman, 2013; Ross, Irani, Silberman, Zaldivar, & Tomlinson, 2010). Amazon, the parent company of AMT, wanted to expand beyond the business of books. It needed a cost-efficient way of cataloguing a wide range of products on its website, so that customers can be directed to the products they want to buy. The solution was to fragment and divide this task into human intelligence tasks (HITs) and distribute it to workers on the Internet. It called this "hybrid machine/human computing arrangement" in the patent filings (Schwartz, 2019, para. 6). What began as operation for Amazon's internal tasks, AMT was later rolled out for other companies and researchers in 2005 looking to get human workers to do small tasks. The term often used, microwork or crowdwork, began to be associated with AMT (Irani, 2015c). Similar to AMT, Microsoft uses its internal platform called "Universal Human Relevance System" (UHRS), for distributing wide range of data work activities (Gray & Suri, 2019). Beyond these two, there are now dozens of platforms that are dedicated towards data work for AI, including Appen, Scale AI and iMerit. One of the interesting characteristics of platforms is that these are not only used by lead firms, but also small start-ups and researchers alike. Researchers have been using major labour platforms such as AMT, Upwork, along with others such as Prolific (Li, Tamkin, Goodman, & Andreas, 2023; Ouyang et al., 2022; Paolacci, Chandler, & Ipeirotis, 2010). The point is that platforms have emerged as important economic players in the AI value chains with workers being incorporated as humans-as-a-service.

As a result, there has been significant growth in both in terms of number of platforms and workers joining platforms. According to the Online Labour Observatory, there are roughly 163 million worker profiles registered on platforms globally (Kässi, Lehdonvirta, & Stephany, 2021). Out of which, roughly, 14 million have done at least once on platforms and about 3.3 million have completed over 10 projects and at least US$1000 (Kässi et al., 2021). While these numbers are significant, a certain degree of caution is needed with these estimates. This data includes a range of activities performed by workers on platforms, including customer service, logo design, music production, editing and proofreading, essay writing, sales and marketing and virtual assistance. Some of these activities are not directly relevant to data work. Put differently, we still do not know the scale of human labour behind AI globally. But we can make some assessments based on the way this platform labour is geographically distributed?

Digital technologies were once heralded to change the spatial configuration of capitalism (e.g. allowing production to move to newer locations and capturing new markets and consumers) or as more provocatively called by some as death of distance (Cairncross, 1997). The emergence of platforms points to this phenomenon. The patent filed by Amazon's engineers for AMT states, their invention

> pertains to the field of distributed computing … involving one or more humans to assist a computer in solving a task, such as, for example, speech to text conversion, allowing the computer to solve the task in a more efficient manner … In one embodiment, the computer system decomposes a task, such as, for example, image or speech comparison, into subtasks for human performance, and programmatically requests the performances, using an API of the present invention. In response, the central coordinating server dispatches the subtasks to personal computers operated by the humans, by way of e.g. the Internet.
>
> *(Harinarayan, Rajaraman, & Ranganathan, 2007, para. 96)*

This patent filing explains the creation of a global network of human workers connected via the platform. Employers, firms and researchers are no longer limited to access labour within the areas or regions they live. Specifically, platforms have enabled planetary labour markets, that is, coming together of employers and labour power transcending spatial boundaries (Graham & Anwar, 2019b). However, these planetary markets are also characterised by asymmetrical scalar relationships and uneven spatial arrangements (Graham & Anwar, 2019b). Today, platform workers are located in different parts of the world with an overwhelmingly majority located in countries, such as India, Bangladesh, Pakistan, the Philippines, Egypt, Indonesia, Sri Lanka, Venezuela, Serbia and Ukraine (Kässi et al., 2021). In other words, while the demand for AI work might be coming from the Global North, the supply of labour is primarily concentrated in the Global South. One would expect the digital nature of data work mean that this labour on platforms to be performed in many more corners of the world. But data work is dependent on access to digital tools such as smartphones and the Internet, which remain unequally distributed (International Telecommunication Union, 2019). Hence, platform labour is defined by uneven economic geographies (Anwar, Schäfer, & Golušin, 2024).

Nonetheless, the rapid proliferation of platforms as an important intermediary in data work has brought work to many places of the world. As AI becomes more entrenched in our lives, the need for data work will grow in scale. Businesses, governments or researchers will continue to use platforms to outsource some of their data work to different parts of the world. But what does this mean for human labour that performs data work?

12.5 Conclusion: Workers' Futures in AI Value Chains

The AI systems have much to hide behind their automated surfaces. At the heart lies a complex chain of actors and processes through which AI systems are trained and developed. Inherent in these chains is a paradox. On the one hand, AI is expected to destroy jobs due to automation (Frey & Osborne, 2017). Though many have previously challenged this thesis (Autor & Salomons, 2018; Benanav, 2020), these fears are further stoked by the recent industry-level developments in generative AI. The Goldman Sachs estimated a loss of 300 million full-time jobs, that is, 18% of the global workforce due to automation ushered by AI tools like ChatGPT (Eloundou, Manning, Mishkin, & Rock, 2025; Toh, 2023).

On the other hand, technological and organisational advancements can destroy jobs in one location, but open up opportunities elsewhere (Fröbel et al., 1981). The emergence of new forms of digital work due to the rise of AI is now well-established in the literature, which this chapter builds on (Anwar & Graham, 2020; Gray & Suri, 2019; Munn, 2022; Tubaro et al., 2020). An AI-dependent machine learns to perform better when it is fed massive amounts of training data. It is human workers who do various data enrichment tasks to train AI. The more data is fed to machines, the better they get in identifying patterns and making predictions. Therefore, as AI becomes ever more important in our lives, there will be a concomitant rise in the need for people to train machines for specific purposes. This Gray and Suri call automation's last mile paradox. Workers are not necessarily going to be eliminated due to the rise of AI, but the focus on value chains of AI forces us to think how they get integrated into the labour markets. We have a situation where workers are being pushed out of the job markets due to the rise of AI, at the same time drawn back into the realms of automation but remain at the margins, which Ekbia and Nardi (2017) termed as *heteromation*. Real people are still needed to perform large amount of data work (i.e. structure, classify and tag an enormous amount of data) to train machine learning algorithms. To put it differently, workers play central role in building and maintaining AI acting as "data janitors" (Irani, 2015b).

Indeed, from Bangalore to Bogota and from Cairo to Caracas thousands of African, Latin American and Asian workers are training machines and algorithms of tomorrow (Anwar & Graham, 2020, 2022; Le Ludec, Cornet, & Casilli, 2023). This presents both opportunities and challenges for people and places trying to plug into AI value chains. There are predictions made by the likes of the World Bank (2019) and World Economic Forum (2020) on AI's importance for development (e.g. employment generation, transition from informal to formal economies, poverty reduction and so on). There are also hopes that these jobs can bring vulnerable sections of the population into work such as migrants and refugees offering them new livelihoods opportunities (Hegarty, 2011). Missing from these discourses so far has been the concern for the quality of jobs for those involved in data work.

The chapter's use of value chain framework hence is a deliberate attempt to make sense of what this new global division of labour for data work means for working conditions of ghost workers (Gray & Suri, 2019). Most importantly, examining the value chains in which these workers exist helps offer an explanation of why their conditions persist. Driven by the competition in the market, TNCs in the global value chains engage in outsourcing and offshoring practices (Dicken, 2015). These production practices are infamous for adversely impacting working conditions. Ben Selwyn (2018) argues value chains generate new forms of poverty. Some of the emerging research on data work's impact on workers (both employed by firms and on platforms) reinforces this argument (see Anwar and Graham, 2022).

On February 17, 2023, *Time* magazine published its story into the business practices of Sama. Sama, a US-based data training firm head quartered in California, prides itself building ethical Al supply chains (Gadonniex, 2019). Sama's workers, besides training OpenAI's ChatGPT, also worked on content moderation for Facebook. *Time*'s investigation found Sama paid its workers in Nairobi, Kenya, as little as US$2 per hour. Similarly, Muldoon et al. (2025) found that despite Sama's touted claim of paying a living wage to its data workers in Kenya and helping lift them out of poverty, not all workers were paid a living wage. Another large-scale study across five Africa countries found that data work rarely comes with basic labour rights, security and hardly offers workers occupational mobility (Anwar & Graham, 2022). While these problems are not new for workers in the global value chains, the footloose nature of data work, workers' invisibility in the production process and a global competition means workers face grim prospects.

For workers doing data work via platforms, their situation gets more complicated. Platforms have emerged as the latest face of outsourcing of economic production as they act as intermediary between businesses and workers (Anwar & Graham, 2022; Graham & Anwar, 2018). They adopt the business logic of BPOs (standardisation and fragmentation of tasks) and complement it with the application of the algorithmic management of the labour process. The result is a slightly more efficient and, in many cases, cheaper way for firms to outsource work. For businesses developing AI tools, using platforms offers greater flexibility to hire workers on platforms instead of outsourcing the entire data training process to an established firm. Essentially workers are hired based on short-term gigs, aka microwork (Irani, 2015c). Workers are referred as independent contractors or freelancers, and thus platforms have no obligations towards workers. Platforms are then like the temporary employment agencies found in other sectors, including BPOs (Larner, 2002). There is a growing literature showing poor working conditions on platforms involved in data work (Gray & Suri, 2019; Irani, 2015a; Posada, 2022). Lily Irani's (2015a) early research on AMT workers shows that labour relations found on the platform driven by computational infrastructure serve the needs of employers or requesters of the tasks while keeping the workers invisible or hidden. Similarly, Altenried (2020) shows that the hidden nature of labour on platform is facilitated by the fragmentation of tasks coupled with high degree of standardisation. This allows platforms to micromange tasks with greater efficiency. While this may be cost effective, for businesses, for workers the results can be devastating. In their research on four platforms (AMT, Microsoft's internal UHRS, LeadGenius and Amara.org), Gray and Suri (2019, p. xxvi) argue that data work can be "alienating, debasing, precarious and isolating". The widespread use of algorithmic management by platforms results in workers experiencing "digital Taylorism", a regime of algorithmic surveillance and monitoring that is more dehumanising than its 19th-century predecessor, Taylorism (Anwar & Graham, 2022, p. 12). When workers involved in the data work are primarily young, poor, unemployed, migrants, women and those that are located in some of the most marginalised parts of the world, the outcomes are far more damaging.

The "majority world" (or low- and middle-income countries of the world) is characterised by high unemployment and a large informal sector. This means digital jobs receive overly positive reviews, and the risks get sidelined (Kuek, Paradi-Guilford, Fayomi, Imaizumi, & Ipeirotis, 2015). While this chapter has highlighted that the contemporary datafied economy offers economic opportunities to workers globally, TNCs are able to seek profit from their labour. Data workers only capture a tiny fraction of the profits generated from their labour, while the rest ends up with firms and their shareholders. Thus, participation in global value chains does not necessarily offer a chance for people and regions to move up the value chains and capture more of the economic value (Selwyn, 2018; Weber, 2017). As Marx once put it,

> accumulation of wealth at one pole is, therefore, at the same time accumulation of misery, agony of toil slavery, ignorance, brutality, mental degradation, at the opposite pole, i.e., on the side of the class that produces its own product in the form of capital.
>
> *(Marx & Engels, 1954, p. 604)*

But this does not suggest that we should accept the status quo and resign to our fates. Instead, there is a need to acknowledge that as researchers, workers, activists and campaigners we need to devise ways of making some of those value chains more transparent and hold firms accountable.

As Internet connectivity grows and AI becomes commonplace, there is a need to build a greater socio-political response to the contemporary datafied economy in which human workers play a significant role in value creation. We need detailed empirical studies of how AI value chains get distant places and people connected to each other and where value is created and captured in these production networks that are opaque by design. Acknowledging that behind the seamless interface of AI tools, including apps, search engines, chatbots or smart devices, are humans who are often categorised as "precarious" (Standing, 2014, p. 23). They are tasked to curate, clean and verify data for algorithms to function properly. Yet, somehow this army of labour remains hidden from naked eye acting as central cogs in AI tools without which they cannot function or make predictions for us. Research can start to make these invisible nodes more visible and highlight the conditions of the workers who make everything possible. We can take a leaf out of the "follow the thing" approach (Cook, 2004, p. 642). When we buy and use a material product (shoe, shirt, fruits, etc.), there is a label or sticker that tells us where they were produced. This provides an entry point into value chains all the way to the sites of production. But for AI tools such as ChatGPT or Google's search engine this is extremely difficult. One way to start is to explore from the bottom up. If workers in India, Kenya and Colombia are using the same platforms to do data work, it allows scholars and researchers to examine different kinds of actors and intermediaries (i.e. workers, firms) organising data work, their role in value creation and ultimately build a better map of these value chains from the ground up.

Notes

1 See Anwar and Graham (2022), Miceli and Posada (2022), and Gray and Suri (2019) for further discussion on the geographies of labour behind AI.

2 There is also unsupervised learning where algorithm is fed large unlabelled data and it learns to find patterns and structure (Hinton & Sejnowski, 1999).

Acknowledgements

The author would like to thank the editors for the feedback and anonymous reviews for their comments that helped improve the chapter.

References

Abbott, P. Y., & Jones, M. R. (2012). Everywhere and nowhere: Nearshore software development in the context of globalisation. *European Journal of Information Systems*, *21*(5), 529–551. https://doi.org/10.1057/ejis.2012.7

Altenried, M. (2020). The platform as factory: Crowdwork and the hidden labour behind artificial intelligence. *Capital & Class*, *44*(2), 145–158. https://doi.org/10.1177/0309816819899410

Anwar, M. A., & Graham, M. (2020). Digital labour at economic margins: African workers and the global information economy. *Review of African Political Economy*, *47*(163), 95–105. https://doi.org/10.1080/03056244.2020.1728243

Anwar, M. A., & Graham, M. (2022). *The Digital Continent: Placing Africa in Planetary Networks of Work*. Oxford, UK: Oxford University Press.

Anwar, M. A., Schäfer, S., & Golušin, S. (2024). Work futures: Globalization, planetary markets, and uneven developments in the gig economy. *Globalizations*, *21*(4), 571–589. https://doi.org/10.1080/14747731.2023.2236876

Autor, D., & Salomons, A. (2018). Is automation labor-displacing? Productivity growth, employment, and the labor share (No. 24871). NBER Working Paper. Cambridge, MA: National Bureau of Economic Research.

Beerepoot, N., Lambregts, B., & Kleibert, J. (Eds.). (2017). *Globalisation and Services-Driven Economic Growth: Perspectives from the Global North and South*. Oxon, UK: Routledge.

Benanav, A. (2020). *Automation and the Future of Work*. London, UK: Verso Books.

Bernal, N. (2021). Facebook's Content Moderators Are Fighting Back. Retrieved March 6, 2025, from Wired website: www.wired.co.uk/article/facebook-content-moderators-ireland

Brynjolfsson, E., & McAfee, A. (2017). The Business of Artificial Intelligence. Retrieved March 6, 2025, from Harvard Business Review website: https://hbr.org/2017/07/the-business-of-artificial-intelligence

Cairncross, F. (1997). *The Death of Distance: How the Communications Revolution Will Change Our Lives*. Cambridge, MA: Harvard Business Review Press.

CIO Africa. (2023). AWS to Invest $1.6B into its Cloud Infrastructure in South Africa. Retrieved March 6, 2025, from https://cioafrica.co/aws-to-invest-1-6b-into-its-cloud-infrastructure-in-south-africa

Coe, N. M., & Yeung, H. W.-C. (2015). *Global Production Networks: Theorizing Economic Development in an Interconnected World*. Oxford, UK: Oxford University Press.

Cook, I. (2004). Follow the thing: Papaya. *Antipode*, *36*(4), 642–664. https://doi.org/10.1111/j.1467-8330.2004.00441.x

Corporaal, G. F., & Lehdonvirta, V. (2017). Platform Sourcing: How Fortune 500 Firms Are Adopting Online Freelancing Platforms. Retrieved March 6, 2025, from Oxford Internet Institute: Oxford website: www.oii.ox.ac.uk/news-events/reports/platform-sourcing-how-fortune-500-firms-are-adopting-online-freelancing-platforms

Crawford, K. (2021). *Atlas of AI: Power, Politics, and the Planetary Costs of Artificial Intelligence*. New Haven, CT: Yale University Press.

Day, M., Turner, G., & Drozdiak, N. (2019). Amazon Workers Are Listening to What You Tell Alexa. Retrieved March 6, 2025, from Bloomberg website: www.bloomberg.com/news/articles/2019-04-10/is-anyone-listening-to-you-on-alexa-a-global-team-reviews-audio

Dicken, P. (2015). *Global Shift: Mapping the Changing Contours of the World Economy* (7th ed.). New York, NY: The Guilford Press.

Duhigg, C. (2023). The Inside Story of Microsoft's Partnership with OpenAI. Retrieved March 6, 2025, from The New Yorker website: www.newyorker.com/magazine/2023/12/11/the-inside-story-of-microsofts-partnership-with-openai

Ekbia, H. R., & Nardi, B. A. (2017). *Heteromation, and Other Stories of Computing and Capitalism*. Cambridge, MA: The MIT Press.

Eloundou, T., Manning, S., Mishkin, P., & Rock, D. (2024). GPTs are GPTs: An Early Look at the Labor Market Impact Potential of Large Language Models. *Science, 384*(6702), 1306–1308. https://doi.org/10.1126/science.adj0998

Finnemore, I., Kim, G., & Pande, A. (2010). *IT Services: The New Allure of Onshore Locales*. New York, NY: McKinsey & Company.

Foroohar, R. (2019). *Don't be Evil: How Big Tech Betrayed Its Founding Principles--and All of Us*. New York, NY: Currency.

Frenken, K., Vaskelainen, T., Fünfschilling, L., & Piscicelli, L. (2020). An institutional logics perspective on the gig economy. In I. Maurer, J. Mair, & A. Oberg (Eds.), *Theorizing the Sharing Economy: Variety and Trajectories of New Forms of Organizing* (pp. 83–105). Bingley, UK: Emerald Publishing Limited.

Frey, C. B., & Osborne, M. A. (2017). The future of employment: How susceptible are jobs to computerisation? *Technological Forecasting and Social Change, 114*, 254–280. https://doi.org/10.1016/j.techfore.2016.08.019

Fröbel, F., Heinrichs, J., & Kreye, O. (1981). *The New International Division of Labour: Structural Unemployment in Industrialised Countries and Industrialization in Developing Countries*. Cambridge, UK: Cambridge University Press.

Fuchs, C. (2014). *Digital Labour and Karl Marx*. New York, NY: Routledge.

Gadonniex, H. (2019). The Ethical AI Supply Chain: Protecting the Soul. Retrieved March 6, 2025, from Sama website: www.sama.com/blog/the-ai-supply-chain-protecting-the-soul-of-ai

Gereffi, G., Humphrey, J., & Sturgeon, T. (2005). The governance of global value chains. *Review of International Political Economy, 12*(1), 78–104. https://doi.org/10.1080/09692290500049805

Gibbon, P., & Ponte, S. (2005). *Trading Down: Africa, Value Chains, and the Global Economy*. Philadelphia, PA: Temple University Press.

Graham, M., & Anwar, M. A. (2018). Two models for a fairer sharing economy. In N. M. Davidson, M. Finck, & J. J. Infranca (Eds.), *The Cambridge Handbook of the Law of the Sharing Economy* (pp. 328–340). Cambridge, UK: Cambridge University Press.

Graham, M., & Anwar, M. A. (2019a). Labour. In J. Ash, R. Kitchin, & A. Leszczynski (Eds.), *Digital Geographies* (pp. 177–187). Los Angeles, CA: SAGE Publications.

Graham, M., & Anwar, M. A. (2019b). The global gig economy: Towards a planetary labor market? *First Monday, 24*(4), 1–21. https://doi.org/10.5210/fm.v24i4.9913

Gray, M. L., & Suri, S. (2019). *Ghost Work: How to Stop Silicon Valley from Building a New Global Underclass?* Boston, MA: Houghton Mifflin Harcourt.

Harinarayan, V., Rajaraman, A., & Ranganathan, A. (2007). Hybrid Machine/Human Computing Arrangement. Retrieved March 6, 2025, from US Patent No. 7,197,459. US Patent and Trademark Office website: https://web.archive.org/web/20180612141325/http://patft.uspto.gov/netacgi/nph-Parser?Sect1=PTO1&Sect2=HITOFF&d=PALL&p=1&u=/netahtml/PTO/srchnum.htm&r=1&f=G&l=50&s1=7,197,459.PN.&OS=PN/7,197,459&RS=PN/7,197,459

Hegarty, S. (2011). How Silicon Valley Outsources Work to African refugees. Retrieved March 6, 2025, from BBC News website: www.bbc.com/news/world-africa-13784487

Helmore, E. (2023). 'We Are a Little Bit Scared': OpenAI CEO Warns of Risks of Artificial Intelligence. Retrieved March 6, 2025, from The Guardian website: www.theguardian.com/technology/2023/mar/17/openai-sam-altman-artificial-intelligence-warning-gpt4

Henderson, J., Dicken, P., Hess, M., Coe, N., & Yeung, H. W.-C. (2002). Global production networks and the analysis of economic development. *Review of International Political Economy*, *9*(3), 436–464. https://doi.org/10.1080/09692290210150842

Hern, A. (2020). Facebook Moderators Forced to Work in Dublin Office Despite High-tier Lockdown. Retrieved March 6, 2025, from The Guardian website: www.theguardian.com/technology/2020/oct/23/facebook-moderators-forced-to-work-in-dublin-office-despite-high-tier-lockdown

Hinton, G., & Sejnowski, T. J. (Eds.). (1999). *Unsupervised Learning: Foundations of Neural Computation*. Cambridge, MA: The MIT Press.

Horton, J. J. (2010). Online labor markets. In A. Saberi (Ed.), *Internet and Network Economics: 6th International Workshop, WINE 2010, Stanford, CA, USA, December 13-17, 2010, Proceedings* (pp. 515–522). Heidelberg, Germany: Springer.

International Telecommunication Union. (2019). *Measuring Digital Development: Facts and Figures 2019*. Geneva, Switzerland: International Telecommunication Union.

Irani, L. (2015a). Difference and dependence among digital workers: The case of Amazon Mechanical Turk. *South Atlantic Quarterly*, *114*(1), 225–234. https://doi.org/10.1215/00382876-2831665

Irani, L. (2015b). Justice for "Data Janitors." Retrieved March 6, 2025, from Public Books website: www.publicbooks.org/justice-for-data-janitors

Irani, L. (2015c). The cultural work of microwork. *New Media & Society*, *17*(5), 720–739. https://doi.org/10.1177/1461444813511926

Irani, L., & Silberman, M. S. (2013). Turkopticon: Interrupting worker invisibility in Amazon Mechanical Turk. In W. E. Mackay (Ed.), *CHI '13: Proceedings of the SIGCHI Conference on Human Factors in Computing Systems* (pp. 611–620). New York, NY: Association for Computing Machinery.

Kässi, O., Lehdonvirta, V., & Stephany, F. (2021). How many online workers are there in the world? A data-driven assessment [version 4; peer review: 4 approved]. *Open Research Europe*, *1*(53), 1–29. https://doi.org/10.12688/openreseurope.13639.4

Kenney, M., & Zysman, J. (2020). The platform economy: Restructuring the space of capitalist accumulation. *Cambridge Journal of Regions, Economy and Society*, *13*(1), 55–76. https://doi.org/10.1093/cjres/rsaa001

Kleibert, J. M. (2015). Islands of globalisation: Offshore services and the changing spatial divisions of labour. *Environment and Planning A: Economy and Space*, *47*(4), 884–902. https://doi.org/10.1068/a140119p

Kuek, S. C., Paradi-Guilford, C. M., Fayomi, T., Imaizumi, S., & Ipeirotis, P. (2015). *The Global Opportunity in Online Outsourcing*. Washington, DC: The World Bank.

Langley, P., & Leyshon, A. (2017). Platform capitalism: The intermediation and capitalisation of digital economic circulation. *Finance and Society*, *3*(1), 11–31. https://doi.org/10.2218/finsoc.v3i1.1936

Larner, W. (2002). Globalization, governmentality and expertise: Creating a call centre labour force. *Review of International Political Economy*, *9*(4), 650–674. https://doi.org/10.1080/09692290220000021844

Le Ludec, C., Cornet, M., & Casilli, A. A. (2023). The problem with annotation. Human labour and outsourcing between France and Madagascar. *Big Data & Society*, *10*(2), 20539517231188724, pp. 1–13. https://doi.org/10.1177/20539517231188723

Lehdonvirta, V., Kässi, O., Hjorth, I., Barnard, H., & Graham, M. (2019). The global platform economy: A new offshoring institution enabling emerging-economy microproviders. *Journal of Management*, *45*(2), 567–599. https://doi.org/10.1177/0149206318786781

Li, B. Z., Tamkin, A., Goodman, N., & Andreas, J. (2023). Eliciting human preferences with language models. ArXiv Preprint, *arXiv:2310*, 1–26. https://doi.org/10.48550/arXiv.2310.11589

Liu, H., Sferrazza, C., & Abbeel, P. (2023). Chain of hindsight aligns language models with feedback. ArXiv Preprint, *arXiv:2302*, 1–21. https://doi.org/10.48550/arXiv.2302.02676

Marx, K., & Engels, F. (1954). *Capital: A Critical Analysis of Capitalist Production*. Moscow, Russia: Progress Publishers.

Miceli, M., & Posada, J. (2022). The data-production dispositif. *Proceedings of the ACM on Human-Computer Interaction*, *6*(CSCW2), 1–37. https://doi.org/10.1145/3555561

Muldoon, J., Cant, C., Graham, M., & Ustek Spilda, F. (2025). The poverty of ethical AI: Impact sourcing and AI supply chains. *AI & SOCIETY*, *40*, 529–543. https://doi.org/10.1007/s00146-023-01824-9

Munn, L. (2022). *Automation is a Myth*. Stanford, CA: Stanford University Press.

Narayan, D. (2022). Platform capitalism and cloud infrastructure: Theorizing a hyper-scalable computing regime. *Environment and Planning A: Economy and Space*, *54*(5), 911–929. https://doi.org/10.1177/0308518X221094028

Newlands, G. (2021). Lifting the curtain: Strategic visibility of human labour in AI-as-a-Service. *Big Data & Society*, *8*(1), 20539517211016024, pp. 1–14. https://doi.org/10.1177/20539517211016026

Office for National Statistics. (2023). Understanding AI Uptake and Sentiment Among People and Businesses in the UK. Retrieved March 6, 2025, from www.ons.gov.uk/businessindustryandtrade/itandinternetindustry/articles/understandingaiuptakeandsentimentamongpeopleandbusinessesintheuk/june2023

Ouyang, L., Wu, J., Jiang, X., Almeida, D., Wainwright, C. L., Mishkin, P., … & Lowe, R. (2022). Training language models to follow instructions with human feedback. In S. Koyejo, S. Mohamed, A. Agarwal, D. Belgrave, K. Cho, & A. Oh (Eds.), *Advances in Neural Information Processing Systems, 35 (NeurIPS 2022), November 28–December 9, New Orleans, Louisiana, USA* (pp. 27730–27744). Red Hook, NY: Curran Associates, Inc.

Paolacci, G., Chandler, J., & Ipeirotis, P. G. (2010). Running experiments on Amazon Mechanical Turk. *Judgment and Decision Making*, *5*(5), 411–419. https://doi.org/10.1017/S1930297500002205

Peck, J. (2017). *Offshore: Exploring the Worlds of Global Outsourcing*. Oxford, UK: Oxford University Press.

Perrigo, B. (2023). Exclusive: OpenAI Used Kenyan Workers on Less Than $2 Per Hour to Make ChatGPT Less Toxic. Retrieved March 6, 2025, from Time website: https://time.com/6247678/openai-chatgpt-kenya-workers

Posada, J. (2022). Embedded reproduction in platform data work. *Information, Communication & Society*, *25*(6), 816–834. https://doi.org/10.1080/1369118X.2022.2049849

PwC. (2017). Sizing the Prize. Retrieved March 6, 2025, from www.pwc.com/gx/en/issues/data-and-analytics/publications/artificial-intelligence-study.html

Richardson, L. (2024). How is the platform a workplace? Moving from sites to infrastructure. *Transactions of the Institute of British Geographers*, *49*(1), e12625, pp. 1–14. https://doi.org/10.1111/tran.12625

Ross, J., Irani, L., Silberman, M. S., Zaldivar, A., & Tomlinson, B. (2010). Who are the crowdworkers? Shifting demographics in Mechanical Turk. In E. Mynatt, D. Schoner, G. Fitzpatrick, S. Hudson, K. Edwards, & T. Rodden (Eds.), *CHI EA '10: CHI '10 Extended Abstracts on Human Factors in Computing Systems, April 10-15, Atlanta Georgia, USA* (pp. 2863–2872). New York, NY: Association for Computing Machinery.

Schreckinger, B. (2023). A New Global Map of the AI Future. Retrieved March 6, 2025, from Politico website: www.politico.com/newsletters/digital-future-daily/2023/09/18/a-new-global-map-of-the-ai-future-00116580

Schwartz, O. (2019). Untold History of AI: How Amazon's Mechanical Turkers Got Squeezed Inside the Machine. Retrieved March 6, 2025, from IEEE Spectrum website: https://spectrum.ieee.org/untold-history-of-ai-mechanical-turk-revisited-tktkt

Selwyn, B. (2018). Poverty chains and global capitalism. *Competition & Change*, *23*(1), 71–97. https://doi.org/10.1177/1024529418809067

Shafaieh, C. (2022). Shahidul Alam on the Majority. Retrieved March 6, 2025, from Harvard Design Magazine website: www.harvarddesignmagazine.org/articles/shahidul-alam-on-the-majority-world

Standing, G. (2014). *The Precariat: The New Dangerous Class* (Reprint). London, UK: Bloomsbury Academic.

Stiennon, N., Ouyang, L., Wu, J., Ziegler, D., Lowe, R., Voss, C., … Christiano, P. F. (2020). Learning to summarize with human feedback. In H. Larochelle, M. Ranzato, R. Hadsell, M.-F. Balcan, & H.-T. Lin (Eds.), *Advances in Neural Information Processing Systems 33 (NeurIPS 2020), December 6–12, Virtual* (pp. 3008–3021). Red Hook, NY: Curran Associates, Inc.

Toh, M. (2023). 300 Million Jobs Could Be Affected by Latest Wave of AI, Says Goldman Sachs. Retrieved March 6, 2025, from CNN website: https://edition.cnn.com/2023/03/29/tech/chatgpt-ai-automation-jobs-impact-intl-hnk/index.html

Tubaro, P., Casilli, A. A., & Coville, M. (2020). The trainer, the verifier, the imitator: Three ways in which human platform workers support artificial intelligence. *Big Data & Society*, *7*(1), 2053951720919776. pp. 1–12. https://doi.org/10.1177/2053951720919776

Weber, S. (2017). Data, development, and growth. *Business and Politics*, *19*(3), 397–423. https://doi.org/10.1017/bap.2017.3

World Bank. (2019). *World Development Report 2019: The Changing Nature of Work*. Washington, DC: The World Bank.

World Economic Forum. (2020). *The Future of Jobs Report 2020*. Cologny, Switzerland: World Economic Forum.

13

RE-SKILLING HUMAN CAPITAL FOR INCLUSIVE ECONOMIC GROWTH IN THE FACE OF EMERGING AGRICULTURAL AUTOMATION IN AFRICA

The Tanzania Perspective

Proscovia Paschal Kamugisha

13.1 Introduction

Intertwining of projected national population growth and declining agricultural productivity patterns in major staple food crops imply future unmet food and nutrition security concerns. Agricultural automation is a prerequisite intervention to address the low productivity challenge. However, the automation is perceived as a tool to improve the productivity at one hand and as a threat to displace human jobs on the other hand. Displacement of jobs for the national farming communities threatens achievement of the United Nation's Sustainable Development Goal 8, Tanzania Development Vision 2025 and National Five-Year Development Plan phase three (2021/2022–2025/2026) that seek to promote inclusive economic growth and efforts to attain decent jobs for all. This chapter explores patterns of agricultural robots' encroachment to Tanzania limited job available and highlights the need for upgrading education systems in lower levels to face the forthcoming deployment of robots in agricultural sector without leaving any behind.

Global population growth is projected to increase from 8bn in 2022 to 9.7bn in 2050 (United Nations Department of Economic and Social Affairs, 2022) while that of sub-Saharan Africa is anticipated to increase from 1.2bn in 2022 to 2bn in 2050 at a growth rate of 2.8% per annum (United Nations Department of Economic and Social Affairs, 2022). Likewise, Tanzania's population is projected to grow from 61 million in 2022 to 86.9 million in 2035, and 135 million in 2050 at the average growth rate of 2.9% annually (Mwakisisile & Mushi, 2019; United Republic of Tanzania (URT): Ministry of Agriculture, 2022; United Republic of Tanzania (URT), 2018).

DOI: 10.4324/9781003391333-16

The increased population demands more food production to outpace the population food demand requirements. A number of authors projected the increase of global food demand requirements of 51%–110% by 2050 compared to the 2005 food demand requirements (Doering & Sorensen, 2018; Tilman, Balzer, Hill, & Befort, 2011; Van Dijk, Morley, Rau, & Saghai, 2021) reaching to up to 3bn tonnes of grains equivalence (Doering & Sorensen, 2018). To date, a quarter of Africans face food and nutrition insecurity (Food and Agriculture Organization of the United Nations [FAO, 2022]). While the continent has already faced hunger concerns, the projected continental population growth will add pressure to the prevailing food insecurity concerns with the supply demand gap of 156,050 tonnes annually by 2050 (Fukase & Martin, 2020). The Tanzania growing population statistics decodes the annual national food requirements to increase up to 18,700,000 tonnes of grains equivalent at the growth rate of 5.25% per annum (Beghin, 2015; Lyimo, 2005).

Meanwhile, the global food supply is limited with declining arable land whose 25% is already unusable due to climate change vagaries (Chan & Feron, 2022). Mason-D'Croz et al. (2019) projected a huge proportion (64%) of global population to face inadequate supply of fruits and vegetables and project that by 2050 1.9bn people of Africa will have insufficient supply of fruits and vegetables to meet the minimum World Health Organization's (WHO) recommendations of 400g/day per person. In Tanzania major food crops have experienced negative productivity levels for the last three decades (Mkonda & He, 2016). Actually, national staple food productivity levels account for only 20% of their production potentials (Kihara, Kizito, Jumbo, Kinyua, & Bekunda, 2020; Nyaligwa, Masuki, & Karwani, 2022; United Republic of Tanzania (URT): Ministry of Finance and Planning, 2021) due to usage of low technological advancement (Magezi, Nakano, & Sakurai, 2021; United Republic of Tanzania (URT): Ministry of Agriculture, 2019; Xiong & Tarnavsky, 2020) and climate change-related challenges (Food and Agriculture Organization of the United Nations, 2015; IPCC, 2014). Indeed, Tanzania's maize productivity (which is the national major staple food) is anticipated to decline by two-fifths by 2050 (Arndt, Farmer, Strzepek, & Thurlow, 2012; Msongaleli, Rwehumbiza, Tumbo, & Kihupi, 2015).

Long rainy season has been shortened from three months' time period during 1960s to two months' time period during the 2000s (Luzi-Kihupi, Killenga, & Bonsi, 2015) and the trend is projected to decline further in future (Borhara, Pokharel, Bean, Deng, & Wang, 2020; Nyembo, Mwabumba, Jahangeer, & Kumar, 2022). Intertwining of population growth and declining trends of food productivity threaten food and nutrition security attainment that call for technological inventions to raise agricultural production so as to meet future food demand requirements. Undertaking agricultural automation in farming activities is perceived to increase farmland productivity through performing tasks, which were executed by human beings more efficiently (Chan & Feron, 2022). The automation of agricultural production enhances smart farming, reduces farming costs and reduces drudgery in repetitive and dangerous tasks (Reddy, Reddy, Pranavadithya, & Kumar, 2016).

For example, utilisation of aerial robotics in applying pesticides reduced pesticide costs by 90% in Brazilian corn farm (Luccio, 2022) and reduced the weeding costs by 50% and weeding time by 12 man-days per hectare in sugar and carrot farms, respectively (Lowenberg-DeBoer, Huang, Grigoriadis, & Blackmore, 2019). Generally, it can be concluded that agricultural automation is the solution for increasing farm productivity and enhance optimal use of agricultural resource base to address existing and future food and nutrition insecurity concerns.

Despite the role of agricultural automation, its deployment to farming activities in developing countries like Tanzania is a dual-faceted phenomenon. While some perceive it as a tool for enhancing farm production efficiency (Food and Agriculture Organization of the United Nations (FAO), 2022; Linaza et al., 2021; Valle & Klenzle, 2020), others perceive its application as a threatening instrument to jobs of human being (Dahlin, 2019; Yam, Tang, Jackson, Su, & Gray, 2023). Benedikt and Osborne (2017) projected that 47% of jobs in the United States will be displaced by robots in the next 20 years period. Likewise, Manyika et al. (2017) predict that global job displacement by automation will amount 800 million by 2030. Moreover, Ottoni et al. (2022) projected that 58% of Brazilian jobs will be displaced by robots in two decades to come due to automation.

Displacement of human beings by automation needs attention, particularly in developing countries like Tanzania, where a large proportion of labour force is employed in agriculture sector whose major proportion of jobs are manual tasks in nature. Actually, the World Bank (2016) noted that two-thirds of workers in the developing countries are prone to be substituted by robots. Moreover, World Economic Forum (2017) projects a significant proportion of jobs to be replaced by robots in sub-Saharan Africa, including 41%, 44%, 46% and 52% in South Africa, Ethiopia, Nigeria and Kenya, respectively. Tanzania is more endangered with the rising of automation in agriculture. This is due to the fact that more than two-thirds of the national labour force are employed in agricultural sector, whose nature is mainly manual; a trend which is not expected to change in the near future (United Republic of Tanzania (URT), 2021b). Henceforth, Tanzanian government and other developing partners need to devise mechanisms for human capital development schemes for farming communities to attain alternative skills as a response to jobs replaced by robots.

Globally, market value of agricultural robots continues to increase remarkably, which is projected to increase from US$4.45bn in 2021 to US$15.67bn in 2028 at the growth rate of more than one-fifth (Chauvin, 2022; Markets and Markets, 2023). Evolution of the agricultural automation implies more displacement of human beings from human jobs. Actually, expansion of agricultural robots ranks second biggest market after manufacturing and industrial sector (Husti, 2019).

Based on this backdrop, this chapter advocates imparting of soft skills in primary and secondary school curriculums to prepare school leavers who will be joining the labour market in service industry upon completion of schooling rather than expecting to be employed in agricultural sector. The soft skills in hospitality industry would be tailored to the tourism industry, health and education sectors and value addition along agricultural supply chains. This is because most studies have shown that the majority of farming activities in Tanzania are carried out by residents mainly with primary and secondary education levels (Kamugisha, Leonard, and Mhanga 2020; Mlilile, Kamugisha, and Chamwali 2022).

This chapter is organised as follows: Section 13.1 offers background on the need to consider automation in an agricultural context and its relevance in Tanzania. Section 13.2 describes the methods employed in reviewing the chapter, while Section 13.3 portrays results and discussion. Under Section 13.3.1, the evolution and spread of agricultural automation and its potential encroachment to substitute jobs of farming communities, Section 13.3.2 depicts major types of agricultural automation and their respective adoption prospects in Tanzania, while Section 13.3.3 describes the status of national agricultural automation initiatives. Section 13.3.4 presents the perceived threatening nature of automation to the present and future generations of the national farming communities, while Section 13.3.5 discusses the potential of replacing human jobs with agricultural automation in the country. Finally, Section 13.4 concludes the trends of agricultural automation and recommends strategies to equip the farming communities so that to face the automation profitably.

13.2 Methods

The semi-structured literature review approach was employed to explore the need of upgrading human skills development as preparatory grounds for responding to forthcoming agricultural automation from PubMed, JSTOR, Google Scholar and Science Direct. Snyder (2019) contends that the approach is useful in the identification of theoretical concepts, themes and other pertinent issues of specified research areas relevant to the study. The chapter used search terms, namely "agricultural automation in developing countries", "inclusive economic growth", "Tanzania", "agricultural robots and employment" and "regulatory framework embracing agricultural automation". Qualitative content analysis was used to characterise trends and patterns of agricultural robots' expansion in developing countries and potential replacement of human employment in Tanzania as suggested by Braun and Clarke (2006). Numerous documents, including journal articles, policies, legal acts and guidelines on agricultural automation, and other pertinent documents reporting the status of agricultural automation in Tanzania and beyond, were consulted to evaluate prevailing agricultural automation and project the future implication of automation among Tanzanian farming communities. Inclusion of the documents in the study was based on the reputability of the publisher where the article and/or book chapter was published and the authority of the source for documents beyond articles and book chapters. The reviews of publications were from 2012 to 2023. Screening process of the contents was done through reading the abstract, methodology and findings.

13.3 Results and Discussion

13.3.1 Evolution of Agricultural Automation

Recently, agricultural automation has captured the interest of scientific communities from diverse disciplines due to its capacity to easy human drudgery involved in farm operations. Agricultural automation stems from mechanisation syndrome that entails the use of simple equipment to the complex utilisation of tractor and/ robots to minimise manual operations and enable optimise the use of agricultural resource base (Mahmud, Abidin, Emmanuel, & Hasan, 2020). Agricultural automation can be traced back to early 1810s when man started to employ animal power to supplement manpower required to undertake agricultural field operations (Pritchard, 2010). Slowly, man embraced the usage of improved machines like tractors as time elapsed. The significant use of mechanisation was observed during the green revolution in mid 1940s when heavy machines were employed in farming activities (Ameen & Raza, 2018). The mechanisation led to massive increase of agricultural production whereby the developing nations' agricultural yields doubled for the 1961–1985 years period and reduced the involvement of human beings in agricultural tasks (Ameen & Raza, 2018). As of recent times, agriculture automation has moved a step further to the digitalised world. Utilisation of robots, both unmanned ground vehicles (UGV) and unmanned aerial vehicles (UAV, or "drones"), and integration of Internet of Things (IoT) in agricultural fields is evident in both developed and less developed countries (Nord, Koohang, & Paliszkiewicz, 2019).

The deployment of automation in manual tasks globally is attributed by firms' profit-maximising behaviour whereby multinational companies integrated investments from the Global North to the Global South seeking minimal cost options (Dasgupta, 2020). The displacement of workers with automation was initially observed in developed economies' manufacturing industry during the 1970s that slowly spread to the developing economies, notably in Asian countries (De Backer, DeStefano, Menon, & Suh, 2018; United Nations Conference on Trade and Development [UNCTAD], 2016), due to the invention of ICT technologies. To date utilising robots in farming activities is observed in different agricultural tasks. Some are employed in greenhouse farming (Roldán et al., 2018), while others are employed in seeding and planting (Bhimanpallewar & Narasingarao, 2020; Kumar & Ashok, 2021; Otani et al., 2023), spraying pesticides (Berenstein, 2019; Sarri, Lombardo, Lisci, Pascale, & Vieri, 2020), weeding (McAllister et al., 2020; Sori, Inoue, Hatta, & Ando, 2018), phenotyping (Di Gennaro et al., 2018; Saiz-Rubio & Rovira-Más, 2020; Tripodi, Massa, Accursio, & Cardi, 2018), fertiliser application (Berenstein, 2019; Valle & Klenzle, 2020) and harvesting (Barbashov, Shanygin, & Barkova, 2022; Cheng, Fu, Su, & Ren, 2023; Zhou, Wang, Au, Kang, & Chen, 2022). Likewise, robotic automation is witnessed in dairy industry to perform milking and herds cleaning.

Increased deployment of automation in various agricultural operations is increasing day after day. Automation of agricultural tasks is evident whereby traditional manual tasks are performed by automated tractors, robotic weeders and combined harvesters, which are normally fitted with AI-algorithms (Nath, 2023). Ing and Grossman (2023) noted that the number of operational robots increased in more than 2.5-fold within a decade from 1 million in 2009 to 2.9 million in 2019 with annual installation increasing up to 373,240. China and Japan dominated the growth of robots' adoption whereby both accounting for more than three-fifths of the growth within 2012 and 2019 period (Adachi, Kawaguchi, & Saito, 2024). Asia and Pacific region ranks first in stocks of robots accounting for 85% of the global stock; that is followed by the Americas with 11% of the global stock (Dasgupta, 2020). The growth of robots has been associated with the decreased unit costs that fell by 60% from US$68, 659 in 2012 to US$27,074 in 2017 (ARK INVEST, 2018). Moreover, the unit cost of the robot is projected to decline to US$11,000 by 2025 (ARK INVEST, 2018).

13.3.2 Farm Operations Performed by Automations

The number of agricultural operations are currently executed automatically, including ploughing, planting, fertiliser applications, pesticide spraying, weeding and harvesting. In all farm operations, automation seems to execute the operations more efficiently and reduces human drudgery. Indeed, the working of agricultural robots in agriculture has proved to be useful complementation of human beings in executing farming tasks. Importance of drones is further enhanced by execution of different tasks that could be hardly performed manually by humans, including ploughing, fertiliser application, precise seeding and planting, weeding, harvesting and weather forecasting (Martin et al., 2022; Sparrow & Howard, 2021). As such, drones are perceived as efficient farming tools to perform smart agricultural production as they apply accurate quantities of fertilisers and agrochemicals that in turn reduce costs of agricultural production and preserve the ecology of the environment. Actually, the drones spray fertiliser in farming fields 40-folds faster compared to manual doing with human man power (Scalera, Boscariol, Carabin, Vidoni, & Gasparetto, 2020). Reduction of waste in horticultural crops has been experienced when using robots and improves the quality of the produce as they pick precisely the ripened fruits and avoid bacterial contamination that would have been happening using human beings (Fahmida-Islam, Uddin, & Bansal, 2022). McNulty and Grace (2009) reported the efficiency use of mechanisation whereby a farmer would be able to feed eight people when using manual power compared to the same person being able to feed 128 when employing mechanisation.

Globally, market value of agricultural robots continues to increase remarkably, which is projected to increase from US$4.45bn in 2021 to US$15.67bn in 2028 at the growth rate of 19.7% per annum (Chauvin, 2022). Evolution of the agricultural automation implies more displacement of human beings from human jobs. Actually, expansion of agricultural robots ranks second biggest market after manufacturing and industrial sector (Husti, 2019). The efficient application of agrochemicals, increased environmental benefits and increased agricultural productivity pinpoint the need of replacing human involvement in farming operations with robots. However, it is anticipated that displacement of human beings will take off gradually due to huge acquisition and operational costs of the technology (Martin et al., 2022; Nath, 2023).

13.3.2.1 Planting Automation

Planting requires the location of seeds or plantlets into soils to allow plant growth. To optimise the desired harvests, planting necessitates high precision levels and adherence to specified distance between plants for different crops (Harmanda et al., 2019; Khadatkar, Pandirwar, & Paradkar, 2023; Sahoo et al., 2021). Traditionally, farmers used to plant seeds into the soil manually. The manual planting involves longer time periods, is relatively less precision due to human error and exerts more drudgery on the involved person (Mahmud et al., 2020). Henceforth, introduction of automatic planting machine is a prerequisite to improve farm operational efficiency and reduces drudgery to human beings. The prevailing automation plating machine has been developed to cater for various crops, including horticultural (Hutsol, Kutyrev, Kiktev, & Biliuk, 2023), sugarcane (Saengprachatanarug et al., 2018) and corns (He et al., 2019). The use of robotic planting machine is currently widely used in different parts of the globe. High performance of robots in seeding has been recorded in cereals, which suggests a gradual substitution of human involvement in the task (Bhimanpallewar & Narasingarao, 2020; Hassan, Ullah, & Iqbal, 2016; Sunitha et al., 2017).

13.3.2.2 Weeds Control and Spraying Robots

Weeding is the most time-consuming and tedious task in agricultural field operations. It accounts for two-fifths of the farm labour requirements (Daum, Baudron, Birner, Qaim, & Grass, 2023). Weeding costs dominate costs incurred in farming, accounting for one-fifth in developing countries (Kamugisha et al., 2020) and up to 50% of the crop losses (Abouziena & Haggag, 2016). Globally, unmanaged weeds led to a significant crop yield loss amounting up to 61% of cereal crops (Oerke, 2006). The cereal yield loss due to weeds accounts for 32% and 8.5% in the United States and Canada, respectively (Flessner et al., 2021). In addition to that, huge amounts of agrochemicals sprayed on farms to keep the farms weed-free negatively affect ecological systems of the environment (MacLaren, Storkey, Menegat, Metcalfe, & Dehnen-Schmutz, 2020; Sanchez & Gallandt, 2021). To address these challenges, weeding robots have been introduced (Utstumo et al., 2018). Alternatively, herbicides applications to destroy weeds are being performed by drones with more efficiency than human power. It is estimated that drones save up to 80% of the agrochemicals in Indian agricultural fields (Naresh, Narwal, & Kumar, 2021). Deployment of drop on demand (DoD) weeding robots selects weeds in the crop rows and drops the herbicides on the weed, leaving crops untouched accurately by 100% (Utstumo et al., 2018). Actually, weeding in number of crops is efficiently executed by robots, including maize (Zhu et al., 2022), carrot (Utstumo et al., 2018), potatoes (Van-Evert et al., 2006), vineyard (Reiser, Sehsah, Bumann, Morhard, & Griepentrog, 2019) and rice (Kim, Kim, Hong, Han, & Lee, 2012) to mention a few. Generally, robots are continuing to replace human being involved in weeding operation with the use of advanced computer science and navigation systems that are likely to penetrate Tanzania's market.

13.3.2.3 Agricultural Crops Harvest Automation

Harvesting is acknowledged as one of the labour-intensive and sensitive tasks due to its delicacy mainly for fresh produce. Improper harvesting would lead to huge amount of post-harvest losses and reduced profit in agricultural investments. This challenge derived scientists to devise automation agricultural robots (Naresh et al., 2021). Performance of robotic harvester is measured in terms of fruits picked out, those ready to be harvested and number of quantity of crops harvested per unit time (Fahmida-Islam et al., 2022; Hayashi et al., 2014).

A renown harvesting robots in horticultural crops focus on strawberries that involve high costs of production due to its labour-intensive involvement (Qingchun et al., 2012; Xiong et al., 2020). The prevailing harvesting robots in strawberry speed ranges between 7.5 and 11.5 seconds/fruit (Hayashi et al., 2014; Xiong et al., 2020) and harvesting rate of 86% (Shiigi et al., 2008). The efficiency of automation in horticultural suggests displacements of human being involvement with technology in farming operations.

13.3.3 Status of Agricultural Automation in Tanzania

Despite enormous inventions in agricultural automation coupled with its increasing utilisation trend in different farming activities, deployment of automation and robots in Tanzania's agricultural production is relatively new. However, national plans and strategies acknowledge the featuring of robots in national production sectors, including manufacturing and agriculture, as part of technological development, which necessitates the re-skilling of human capital development for those whose jobs will be replaced (United Republic of Tanzania (URT): Ministry of Finance and Planning, 2021; United Republic of Tanzania (URT): Ministry of Works Transport and Communication, 2016; United Republic of Tanzania (URT), 2023).

Recently, few trials have been made through limited number of projects to identify feasibility studies in agroforestry sub-sector (Ackerman & Koziol, 2019) and crops phenotyping in Dodoma region (Betschart, 2019). Few champions for agricultural robotics in the country exist, including Agri info, We-robotics and

Tanzania Flying Labs. However, all of these companies involve in training provision for operating drones in agricultural fields. A limited number of companies such as GeoTerraImage (Pty) Ltd have invested in robotic farming activities as private entities (Centre for Coordination of Agricultural Research and Development for Southern Africa & World Bank Group, 2022). The GeoTerraImage (Pty) Ltd offers phenotyping of crops in the field to enhance timely response of the farmer on agricultural field concerns.

13.3.4 Agricultural Automation Threatening Human Jobs

As briefly elaborated in the introduction section, the notion of automation to substitute jobs of human being is a duo-faceted phenomenon. Whereas some researchers unveiled the creation of more jobs as automation and robots are employed in firms' production activities (De Vries, Gentile, Miroudot, & Wacker, 2020; Gaspar & Harris, 2020; Presidente & Massimiliano, 2022); others have found insignificant relationship (Dauth, Findeleisen, Südekum, & Wößner, 2017; Graetz & Michaels, 2018). Meanwhile, the other cluster of researchers noted the decreasing pattern of job availability as automation is more engaged in productive economic sectors (Acemoglu & Restrepo, 2020; Carbonero, Ernst, & Weber, 2018). However, the noted positive association observed between utilisation of automation and increased job availability contended to be experienced in the short run. The increased jobs were aggregated as sum of jobs in the entire economy such that deploying robots in the production will require new skills to workers as some will have to execute different tasks since their jobs will have been executed automatically by the robots.

In the adoption of robots, low-skilled jobs experience more risk of displacement compared to high-skilled job, whose occupants in most cases earn relatively low wages in numerous nations (OECD, 2018). Indeed, the 4.3% decline of hourly earnings is associated with a 10% higher risk of automation (OECD, 2018). Given the huge proportion (61%) of natives being employed in agriculture and the manual nature of the tasks performed in Tanzania's jobs, replacement with robots is likely to bring havoc for the economy to absorb the replaced workers in other economic activities if there are no deliberate efforts being made to re-skill the replaced workers. The havoc would be aggravated by the fact that most of the students graduating from primary and secondary schools lack practical skills and expertise since they are equipped with a basic education foundation that fits the graduates to join tertiary education. The tertiary education is assumed to be the one which will impart life skills to upgrade individual's carrier afterwards. The vocational skills imparted while in primary schools as just one course is not enough to support students to attain enough skills for being employed in the hospitality industry upon graduation.

Unfortunately, most of the occupants in Tanzanian farming communities are the ones with limited education levels mainly with primary and secondary education

(Kamugisha et al., 2020; Mlilile et al., 2022). Computations from the United Republic of Tanzania (URT) (2021a) revealed that more than one-fifth (22%) of Tanzanians enrolled in primary school went further for primary school and less than one-tenth (8%) of students enrolled in secondary school went further to continue with tertiary education. The low proportion of youth joining tertiary education reveals two important policy implications. (1) The country's education systems should make it mandatory for youths to join the tertiary education at least at certificate and diploma levels to attain basic life skills. This would be limited with the cost-sharing mechanism whereby, at these lower skills development levels, hesitant parents can claim incapability to afford the schooling costs. Otherwise, the government can either waive the tuition fee for non-degree education or include the cost of education in loan portfolios to students to be paid later, as it serves in higher learning institutions from bachelor degrees upwards. (2) The education systems at primary and secondary school curriculums equip students with basic practical skills in the service sector while schooling as a preparatory foundation for the graduates to join the labour market in hospitality sectors of the economy. The vocational skills competency developed needs to be enhanced through a three-month intensive programme for one semester in different professionals to serve the hospitality industry in different sectors of the economy.

Likewise, informal sector in terms of small and medium enterprises (SMEs) employs 29% of the national labour force and ranks the second employer after agriculture sector (United Republic of Tanzania (URT) & National Bureau of Statistics [Tanzania], 2022). However, three-fifths of the established SMEs are short-lived such that they die within a six-month period (Israel, 2022). Short-life span of SMEs threatens decent job creation, given the huge number of graduates entering the labour market periodically. To date, one million youths are joining the national labour market per annum; and the number is projected to increase to 1.6 million annually by 2035 (United Republic of Tanzania (URT), 2018). Given the existing limited labour absorption capacity of prevailing formal sector with only 4%, it is anticipated that automation will further amplify the already existing employment challenge in the country. Therefore, it is imperative to build capacity among farming communities to engage more on value-added jobs along the agricultural supply chains individually and/or cooperatively.

13.3.5 Potentials of Agricultural Automations Displacing Farming Jobs in Tanzania

Employment of agricultural automation in Tanzania is beneficial regardless of its threatening nature to substitute available jobs in the national farming communities. It is anticipated that at the first place, automation is feasible in large-scale farms that can afford to purchase and operate the robots. That being a case, its adoption in Tanzania is projected to be a gradual process as Tanzania's commercial farms account for less than 1% of the national agricultural products. The rest (99%)

is owned and operated by small-scale farmers with up to two hectares (United Republic of Tanzania (URT), 2021b). The likelihood of smallholder farmers (SHF) being replaced with automation is relatively low since they can hardly even afford to purchase basic agricultural inputs for their farms (Lobulu, Shimells, Laing, & Mushongi, 2019; Xiong & Tarnavsky, 2020). However, there is a likelihood of SHF to face competition from large-scale farms, whose investment operational costs will be lowered with automation. Other competition to SHF is thought from neighbouring countries in several regional blocks within which Tanzania is found, such as Southern African Development Community (SADC), East African Community (EAC) and Economic Community of West African States (ECOWAS), where automation is feasible such as in South Africa. It is normal to find agricultural products produced in other countries within the country territory. CERES fruit juice, which is found in almost every corner of the country supermarket shelves, is a vivid example.

Adoption of agricultural automation for Tanzanian commercial farms is anticipated to have a spillover effect on the surrounding farming communities. The commercial farms can offer automation services to the surrounding SHF farms at a price, either via outgrower schemes or operationalising it as part of a business entity to SHF farms upon demand. For that case, even if agricultural automation will reduce jobs in farming communities, it will be at relatively small pace compared to other economies where farming is mainly done by large and commercial farms.

Engagement of youth graduates in agriculture through Build a Better Tomorrow – Youth Initiative for Agribusiness (BBT-YIA) 2022–2030 can fast track adoption of agricultural robots. Under BBT –YIA, 11,453 acres in Dodoma region have already been set aside for youth development, while 3,560 acres and 8,000 more are to be demarcated for that purpose in other regions of the country (United Republic of Tanzania (URT): Ministry of Agriculture, 2022). If the project is implemented as planned, automation might have a greater move through the youth agribusiness concerned within the entire country. Youths are acknowledged to be early adopters of various technological innovations (Berkowsky, Sharit, & Czaja, 2017; Meyer, 2008).

13.4 Conclusion

Population growth and declining patterns of agricultural productivity of national staple foods necessitate the deployment of agricultural automation to meet national food and nutrition requirements. Agricultural robots increase farming productivity but are perceived as a threatening phenomenon as they substitute jobs of human beings mainly in low-skilled tasks. Two-thirds of the national labour force are employed in agriculture whose tasks are manual and can easily be replaced with robots. Moreover, one million youth entrants per annum join the labour market with limited formal employment positions. Henceforth, deploying of agricultural robots enlarges already prevailing unemployment dilemma.

Since agricultural automation is real even if pursued gradually, it is imperative to be prepared for the technological change. The preparation includes, among others, upgrading the lower levels of education systems (primary and secondary schools) to expand issues of vocational skills development. This is because most of the farming communities are found with primary and secondary school education levels. Inclusion of vocational skills just as one course is not enough to meet diverse nature of students needs to get employed upon graduation. Otherwise, there would be an additional one-year compulsory course in different disciplines to equip students with necessary cognitive and digital skills in the hospitality industry. Moreover, farming communities would be wiped out from the economy such that the nation will not achieve the Sustainable Development Goal 8, Tanzania Development Vision 2025 and National Five-Year Development Plan phase three (2021/2022–2025/2026), which stipulates the intention for having sustained inclusive economic growth and decent jobs for all.

Acknowledgements

The author acknowledges Sebastian Faustin Mhanga for constructive critiques and proofreading of the first draft of the manuscript. However, the author is responsible for the document.

References

Abouziena, H. F., & Haggag, W. M. (2016). Weed control in clean agriculture: A review. *Planta Daninha*, *34*(2), 377–392. https://doi.org/10.1590/S0100-83582016340200019

Acemoglu, D., & Restrepo, P. (2020). Robots and jobs: Evidence from US labor markets. *Journal of Political Economy*, *128*(6), 2188–2244. https://doi.org/10.1086/705716

Ackerman, E., & Koziol, M. (2019). Tanzania Builds a Drone Industry From Local Know-How and Bamboo Bamboo Drones Are Just One Way That Local Companies Hope to Meet Tanzania's Needs. Retrieved March 6, 2025, from IEEE Spectrum website: https://spectrum.ieee.org/tanzanias-homegrown-drone-industry-takes-off-on-bamboo-wings

Adachi, D., Kawaguchi, D., & Saito, Y. U. (2024). Robots and Employment: Evidence from Japan, 1978–2017. *Journal of Labor Economics*, *42*(2), 591–634. https://doi.org/10.1086/723205

Ameen, A., & Raza, S. (2018). Green revolution: A review. *International Journal of Advances in Scientific Research*, *3*(12), 129–137. https://doi.org/10.7439/ijasr.v3i12.4410

ARK INVEST. (2018). Big Ideas 2018: Disruptive Innovation. Retrieved March 6, 2025, from https://research.ark-invest.com/hubfs/1_Download_Files_ARK-Invest/Infographics/BigIdeas2018-ARKInvest.pdf?hsCtaTracking=37c67fc6-1932-4b42-887c-ba1332a0e7a9%7C4a9f618a-acf9-428b-a7ab-11965014a86b

Arndt, C., Farmer, W., Strzepek, K., & Thurlow, J. (2012). Climate change, agriculture and food security in Tanzania. *Review of Development Economics*, *16*(3), 378–393. https://doi.org/10.1111/j.1467-9361.2012.00669.x

Barbashov, N. N., Shanygin, S. V., & Barkova, A. A. (2022). Agricultural robots for fruit harvesting in horticulture application. *IOP Conference Series: Earth and Environmental Science*, *981*, 032009, pp. 1–5. https://doi.org/10.1088/1755-1315/981/3/032009

Beghin, J. (2015). Assessing food security in Tanzania in the next decade. *Agricultural Policy Review, Winter*, 1–3.

Benedikt, C., & Osborne, M. A. (2017). How susceptible are jobs to computerisation? *Technological Forecasting and Social Change, 114*, 254–280. https://doi.org/10.1016/j.techfore.2016.08.019

Berenstein, R. (2019). The use of agricultural robots in crop spraying/fertilizer applications. In J. Billingsley (Ed.), *Robotics and Automation for Improving Agriculture* (pp. 109–136). Cambridge, UK: Burleigh Dodds Science Publishing Limited.

Berkowsky, R. W., Sharit, J., & Czaja, S. J. (2017). Factors predicting decisions about technology adoption among older adults. *Innovation in Aging, 2*(1), igy002. https://doi.org/10.1093/geroni/igy002

Betschart, S. (2019). Drones for agriculture in Tanzania. *Landscape Archteture Frotieres, 7*(2), 146–152. https://doi.org/10.15302/J-LAF-20190215

Bhimanpallewar, R., & Narasingarao, M. (2020). AgriRobot: Implementation and evaluation of an automatic robot for seeding and fertiliser microdosing in precision agriculture. *International Journal of Agricultural Resources, Gorvanance and Ecology, 16*(1), 33–50. https://doi.org/10.1504/IJARGE.2020.107064

Borhara, K., Pokharel, B., Bean, B., Deng, L., & Wang, S.-Y. S. (2020). On Tanzania's precipitation climatology, variability, and future projection. *Climate, 8*(2), 34, pp. 1–18. https://doi.org/10.3390/cli8020034

Braun, V., & Clarke, V. (2006). Using thematic analysis in psychology. *Applied Qualitative Research in Psychology, 3*(2), 77–101. https://doi.org/10.1191/1478088706qp063oa

Carbonero, F., Ernst, E., & Weber, E. (2018). Robots Worldwide: The Impact of Automation on Employment and Trade (No. 36). Research Department Working Paper. Geneva, Switzerland: International Labour Organization.

Centre for Coordination of Agricultural Research and Development for Southern Africa, & World Bank Group. (2022). Digital Agriculture Country Study Annex: Tanzania. Retrieved March 6, 2025, from www.ccardesa.org/sites/default/files/knowledge-products/CCARDESADigital AgricultureCountyStudy-Tanzania.pdf

Chan, T., & Feron, E. (2022). Building the robots of our dreams. In R. Attias (Ed.), *Robotics Impact* (pp. 38–39). Riyadh, Saudi Arabia: FII Institute.

Chauvin, M. (2022). Agriculture Robots Market Size is to Hit US$ 15.67 billion by 2028, and Grow at CAGR of 19.71% Over the Forecast Period 2022-2028. Retrieved March 6, 2025, from www.researchgate.net/publication/363367600_Agriculture_Robots_market_Size_is_to_Hit_US_1567_billion_by_2028_and_Grow_at_CAGR_of_1971_Over_the_Forecast_Period_2022-2028

Cheng, C., Fu, J., Su, H., & Ren, L. (2023). Recent advancements in agriculture robots: Benefits and challenges. *Machines, 11*(1), 48, pp. 1–24. https://doi.org/10.3390/machines11010048

Dahlin, E. (2019). Are robots stealing our jobs? *Socius: Sociological Research for a Dynamic World, 5*, 2378023119846249, pp. 1–14. https://doi.org/10.1177/2378023119846249

Dasgupta, S. (2020). Introduction. In F. Bárcia de Mattos, S. Dasgupta, X. Jiang, D. Kucera, & A. F. Schiavone (Eds.), *Robotics and Reshoring Employment Implications for Developing Countries* (pp. 1–23). Geneva, Switzerland: International Labour Organization.

Daum, T., Baudron, F., Birner, R., Qaim, M., & Grass, I. (2023). Addressing agricultural labour issues is key to biodiversity-smart farming. *Biological Conservation, 284*(June), 110165, pp. 1–14. https://doi.org/10.1016/j.biocon.2023.110165

Dauth, W., Findeleisen, S., Südekum, J., & Wößner, N. (2017). *German Robots: The Impact of Industrial Robots on Workers – IAB-Discussion Paper No. 30/2017*. Nürnberg, Germany: Institut für Arbeitsmarkt- und Berufsforschung.

De Backer, K., DeStefano, T., Menon, C., & Suh, J. R. (2018). Industrial Robotics and the Global Organisation of Production (No. 2018/03). OECD Science, Technology and Industry Working Papers. Paris, France: OECD Publishing.

De Vries, G. J., Gentile, E., Miroudot, S., & Wacker, K. (2020). The Rise of Robots and the Fall of Routine Jobs (No. 619). Mandaluyong City, Philippines: Asian Development Bank.

Di Gennaro, S. F., Rizza, F., Badeck, F. W., Berton, A., Delbono, S., Gioli, B., … & Matese, A. (2018). UAV-based high-throughput phenotyping to discriminate barley vigour with visible and near-infrared vegetation indices. *International Journal of Remote Sensing, 39*(15–16), 5330–5344. https://doi.org/10.1080/01431161.2017.1395974

Doering, O., & Sorensen, A. (2018). The land that shapes and sustains us. In J. Eise & K. A. Foster (Eds.), *How to Feed the World* (pp. 46–58). Washington, DC: Island Press.

Fahmida-Islam, S., Uddin, M. S., & Bansal, J. C. (2022). Harvesting robots for smart agriculture. In M. S. Uddin & J. C. Bansal (Eds.), *Computer Version and Machine Learning in Agriculture, Volume 2* (pp. 1–13). Singapore: Springer.

Flessner, M. L., Burke, I. C., Dille, J. A., Everman, W. J., Vangessel, M. J., Tidemann, B., … & Sikkema, P. H. (2021). Potential wheat yield loss due to weeds in the United States and Canada. *Weed Technology, 35*(6), 916–923. https://doi.org/10.1017/wet.2021.78

Food and Agriculture Organization of the United Nations. (2015). *Climate Change and Food Security: Risks and Responses*. Food and Agriculture Organization of the United Nations. https://doi.org/10.1080/14767058.2017.1347921

Food and Agriculture Organization of the United Nations (FAO). (2022). *The State of Food and Agriculture 2022: Leveraging Automation in Agriculture for Transforming Agrifood Systems*. Rome, Italy: Food and Agriculture Organization.

Fukase, E., & Martin, W. (2020). Economic growth, convergence, and world food demand and supply. *World Development, 132*, 104954, pp. 1–12. https://doi.org/10.1016/j.worlddev.2020.104954

Gaspar, R., & Harris, N. (2020). The Fate of Job Creation in the Philippines Amid the Automation Revolution: A Firm-Level Analysis (No. 1081). ADBI Working Paper. Tokyo, Japan: Asian Development Bank Institute.

Graetz, G., & Michaels, G. (2018). Robots at work. *The Review of Economics and Statistics, 100*(5), 753–768. https://doi.org/10.1162/rest_a_00754

Harmanda, T. T., Hazim, M., Wulandari, W., R Akbar, A., Wahjuni, S., & Priandana, K. (2019). Development of a seed-planter wheeled robot prototype. *IOP Conference Series: Earth and Environmental Science, 299*, 012055. https://doi.org/10.1088/1755-1315/299/1/012055

Hassan, M. U., Ullah, M., & Iqbal, J. (2016). Towards autonomy in agriculture: Design and prototyping of a robotic vehicle with seed selector. In M. A. Khan (Ed.), *2016 2nd International Conference on Robotics and Artificial Intelligence, ICRAI 2016. 01-02 November, Rawalpindi, Pakistan* (pp. 37–44). New York, NY: IEEE. https://doi.org/10.1109/ICRAI.2016.7791225

Hayashi, S., Yamamoto, S., Tsubota, S., Ochiai, Y., Kobayashi, K., Kamata, J., … & Peter, R. (2014). Automation technologies for strawberry harvesting and packing operations in Japan. *Journal of Berry Research, 4*(1), 19–27. https://doi.org/10.3233/JBR-140065

He, X., Ding, Y., Zhang, D., Yang, L., Cui, T., & Zhong, X. (2019). Development of a variable-rate seeding control system for corn planters Part I: Design and laboratory experiment. *Computers and Electronics in Agriculture*, *162*, 318–327. https://doi.org/10.1016/j.compag.2019.04.012

Husti, I. (2019) Possibilities of using robots in agriculture. *Hungarian Agricultural Engineering*, *35*, 59–67. https://doi.org/10.17676/HAE.2019.35.59

Hutsol, T., Kutyrev, A., Kiktev, N., & Biliuk, M. (2023). Robotic technologies in horticulture: Analysis and implementation prospects. *Agricultural Engineering*, *27*(1), 113–133. https://doi.org/10.2478/agriceng-2023-0009

Ing, L. Y., & Grossman, G. M. (2023). Introduction. In L. Y. Ing & G. M. Grossman (Eds.), *Robots and AI: A New Economic Era* (pp. 1–14). Oxon, UK: Routledge.

IPCC. (2014). *Climate Change 2014: Impacts, Adaptation, and Vulnerability. Part A: Global and Sectoral Aspects*. Cambridge, UK: Cambridge University Press.

Israel, B. (2022). Joint ventures for SMEs competitiveness and inclusive growth: A comparative analysis of SMEs in Mbeya, Tanzania. *E-Journal of Humanities, Arts and Social Sciences*, *3*(8), 337–353. https://doi.org/10.38159/ehass.2022385

Kamugisha, P. P., Leonard, A., & Mhanga, S. F. (2020). Investment Analysis of sunflower farming and prospects of raising household income in Iramba District, Tanzania. *International Journal of Environment, Agriculture and Biotechnology*, *5*(4), 1062–1069. https://doi.org/10.22161/ijeab.54.27

Khadatkar, A., Pandirwar, A. P., & Paradkar, V. (2023). Design, development and application of a compact robotic transplanter with automatic seedling picking mechanism for plug-type seedlings. *Scientific Reports*, *13*, 1883, pp. 1–12. https://doi.org/10.1038/s41598-023-28760-4

Kihara, J., Kizito, F., Jumbo, M., Kinyua, M., & Bekunda, M. (2020). Unlocking maize crop productivity through improved management practices in Northern Tanzania. *African Journal of Food, Agriculture, Nutrition and Development*, *20*(7), 17095–17112. https://doi.org/10.18697/ajfand.95.17965

Kim, G. H., Kim, S. C., Hong, Y. K., Han, K. S., & Lee, S. G. (2012). A robot platform for unmanned weeding in a paddy field using sensor fusion. In *IEEE International Conference on Automation Science and Engineering, August 20–24 2012, Seoul, South Korea* (pp. 904–907). New York, NY: IEEE. https://doi.org/10.1109/CoASE.2012.6386466

Kumar, P., & Ashok, G. (2021). Design and fabrication of smart seed sowing robot. *Materials Today: Proceedings*, *39*(Part 1), 354–358. https://doi.org/10.1016/j.matpr.2020.07.432

Linaza, M. T., Posada, J., Bund, J., Eisert, P., Quartulli, M., Döllner, J., … & Lucat, L. (2021). Data-driven artificial intelligence applications for sustainable precision agriculture. *Agronomy*, *11*(6), 1227, pp. 1–14. https://doi.org/10.3390/agronomy11061227

Lobulu, J., Shimelis, H., Laing, M., & Mushongi, A. A. (2019). Maize production constraints, traits preference and current Striga control options in western Tanzania: farmers' consultation and implications for breeding. *Acta Agriculturae Scandinavica Section B: Soil and Plant Science*, *69*(8), 734–746. https://doi.org/10.1080/09064710.2019.1652680

Lowenberg-DeBoer, J., Huang, I., Grigoriadis, V., & Blackmore, S. (2019). Economics of robots and automation in field crop production. *Precision Agriculture*, *21*, 278–299. https://doi.org/10.1007/s11119-019-09667-5

Luccio, M. (2022). Satellite-driven framing. *GPS World*, *33*(1), 20–27.

Luzi-Kihupi, A., Killenga, K., & Bonsi, C. (2015). A review of maize, rice, tomato and banana research in Tanzania. *Tanzania Journal of Agricultural Sciences*, *14*(1), 1–20.

Lyimo, N. G. (2005). Improving Farmers' Access to and Management of Disease Resistant Cultivars in the Southern Highlands of Tanzania. Retrieved March 6, 2025, from Crop Protection Programme website: https://assets.publishing.service.gov.uk/media/57a08c81ed915d622c0013bf/R8220_FTR.pdf

MacLaren, C., Storkey, J., Menegat, A., Metcalfe, H., & Dehnen-Schmutz, K. (2020). An ecological future for weed science to sustain crop production and the environment: A review. *Agronomy for Sustainable Development*, *40*(4), 24, pp. 1–29. https://doi.org/10.1007/s13593-020-00631-6

Magezi, E. F., Nakano, Y., & Sakurai, T. (2021). Determinants of mechanization in rice production in Tanzania: Evidence from panel data. *Japanese Journal of Agricultural Economics*, *23*, 77–82. https://doi.org/10.18480/jjae.23.0_77

Mahmud, M. S. A., Abidin, M. S. Z., Emmanuel, A. A., & Hasan, H. S. (2020). Robotics and automation in agriculture: Present and future applications. *Applications of Modelling and Simulation*, *4*(April), 130–140.

Manyika, J., Lund, S., Chui, M., Bughin, J., Woetzel, J., Batra, P., … & Sanghvi, S. (2017). Jobs Lost, Jobs Gained: Workforce Transitions in a Time of Automation. Retrieved March 6, 2025, from McKinsey Global Institute website: www.mckinsey.com/featured-insights/future-of-organizations-and-work/jobs-lost-jobs-gained-what-the-future-of-work-will-mean-for-jobs-skills-and-wages

Markets and Markets. (2023). Agricultural Robots Market by Type (Unmanned Aerial Vehciles/Drones, Milking Robots, Driverless Tractors, Automated Harvesting Systems), Farming Environment (Indoor and Outdoor), End-use Application and Region–Global Forecast to 2028. Retrieved March 6, 2025, from www.marketsandmarkets.com/Market-Reports/agricultural-robot-market-173601759.html

Martin, T., Gasselin, P., Hostiou, N., Feron, G., Laurens, L., Purseigle, F., & Ollivier, G. (2022). Robots and transformations of work in farm: A systematic review of the literature and a research agenda. *Agronomy for Sustainable Development*, *42*(4), 66, pp. 1–20. https://doi.org/10.1007/s13593-022-00796-2

Mason-D'Croz, D., Bogard, J. R., Sulser, T. B., Cenacchi, N., Dunston, S., Herrero, M., & Wiebe, K. (2019). Gaps between fruit and vegetable production, demand, and recommended consumption at global and national levels: an integrated modelling study. *The Lancet Planetary Health*, *3*(7), e318–e329. https://doi.org/10.1016/S2542-5196(19)30095-6

McAllister, W., Whitman, J., Varghese, J., Axelrod, A., Davis, A., & Chowdhary, G. (2020). Agbots 2.0: Weeding denser fields with fewer robots. In M. Toussaint, A. Bicchi, & T. Hermans (Eds.), *Robotics: Science and Systems XVI 2020. July 12-16. Corvalis, Oregon, USA* (pp. 1–9). Cambridge, MA: MIT Press. https://doi.org/10.15607/RSS.2020.XVI.062

McNulty, P. B., & Grace, P. M. (2009). *Agricultural Mechanization and Automation*. Paris, France: UNESCO: Encyclopedia of Life Support Systems.

Meyer, J. (2008). *The Adoption of New Technologies and the Age Structure of the Workforce* (No. 08–045). Mannheim, Germany: Centre for European Economic Research. https://doi.org/10.2139/ssrn.1210162

Mkonda, M. Y., & He, X. (2016). Efficacy of transforming agriculture for survival to commercial agriculture through "Kilimo Kwanza" initiative in Tanzania. *Natural Resources and Conservation*, *4*(4), 43–50. https://doi.org/10.13189/nrc.2016.040401

Mlilile, B. B., Kamugisha, P., & Chamwali, L. (2022). Effect of cropping pattern and agronomic practice on maize productivity among smallholder farmers in Kilosa District, Tanzania. *International Journal of Agronomy and Agricultural Research*, *21*(6), 57–67.

Msongaleli, B. M., Rwehumbiza, F., Tumbo, S. D., & Kihupi, N. (2015). Impacts of climate variability and change on rainfed sorghum and maize: Implications for food security policy in Tanzania. *Journal of Agricultural Science*, *7*(5), 124–142. https://doi.org/10.5539/jas.v7n5p124

Mwakisisile, A. J., & Mushi, A. R. (2019). Mathematical model for Tanzania population growth. *Tanzania Journal of Science*, *45*(3), 346–354.

Naresh, R. K., Narwal, E., & Kumar, L. (2021). Agricultural robotics and drones. In R. K. Naresh, S. Kumar, S. K. Gupta, & J. Choudhary (Eds.), *Artificial Intelligence in Indian Agriculture* (pp. 62–96). New Delhi, India: Jaya Publishing House.

Nath, D. (2023). Smart farming: Automation and robotics in agriculture. In A. Gehlot, M. Sharma, V. Hegde, P. Singh, & S. Biswas (Eds.), *Recent Trends in Agriculture (Volume–9)* (pp. 281–310). Delhi, India: Integrated Publications.

Nord, J. H., Koohang, A., & Paliszkiewicz, J. (2019). The Internet of Things: Review and theoretical framework. *Expert Systems with Applications*, *133*, 97–108. https://doi.org/10.1016/j.eswa.2019.05.014

Nyaligwa, L. M., Masuki, K. F., & Karwani, G. M. (2022). Variation in nutrient use efficiency under varying soil conditions in maize growing areas in Northern Zone Tanzania-East Africa. *International Journal of Current Research*, *14*(3), 20932–20936. https://doi.org/10.24941/ijcr.43100.03.2022

Nyembo, L. O., Mwabumba, M., Jahangeer, J., & Kumar, V. (2022). Historical and projected spatial and temporal rainfall status of Dar es Salaam, Tanzania, from 1982 to 2050. *Frontiers in Environmental Science*, *10*, 1025760, pp. 1–12. https://doi.org/10.3389/fenvs.2022.1025760

OECD. (2018). Putting Faces to the Jobs at Risk of Automation. Retrieved March 6, 2025, from Policy Brief on the Future of Work website: www.oecd.org/en/publications/putting-a-face-behind-the-jobs-at-risk-of-automation_5ded25f0-en.html

Oerke, E.-C. (2006). Crop losses to pests. *Journal of Agricultural Science*, *144*(1), 31–43. https://doi.org/10.1017/S0021859605005708

Otani, T., Itoh, A., Mizukami, H., Murakami, M., Yoshida, S., Terae, K., … & Takanishi, A. (2023). Agricultural robot under solar panels for sowing, pruning, and harvesting in a synecoculture environment. *Agriculture*, *13*(1), 18, pp. 1–22. https://doi.org/10.3390/agriculture13010018

Ottoni, B., E Oliveira, P. R., Estrela, L., Santos, A. T., & Barreira, T. (2022). Automation and job loss: The Brazilian case. *Nova Economia*, *32*(1), 157–180. https://doi.org/10.1590/0103-6351/6367

Presidente, G., & Massimiliano, C. (2022). Robots for Economic Development. Retrieved March 6, 2025, from Centre for Policy Research website: https://cepr.org/voxeu/columns/robots-economic-development

Pritchard, J. C. (2010). Animal traction and transport in the 21st century: Getting the priorities right. *Veterinary Journal*, *186*(3), 271–274. https://doi.org/10.1016/j.tvjl.2010.08.004

Qingchun, F., Xiu, W., Wengang, Z., Quan, Q., & Kai, J. (2012). New strawberry harvesting robot for elevated-trough culture. *International Journal of Agricultural and Biological Engineering*, *5*(2), 1–8.

Reddy, N. V., Reddy, A. V. V. V., Pranavadithya, S., & Kumar, J. J. (2016). A critical reveiw on agricultural. *International Journal of Mechanical Engineering and Technology*, *7*(4), 183–188.

Reiser, D., Sehsah, E.-S., Bumann, O., Morhard, J., & Griepentrog, H. W. (2019). Development of an autonomous electric robot implement for intra-row weeding in vineyards. *Agriculture*, *9*(1), 18, pp. 1–12. https://doi.org/10.3390/agriculture9010018

Roldán, J. J., del Cerro, J., Garzón-Ramos, D., Garcia-Aunon, P., Garzón, M., León, J. de, & Barrientos, A. (2018). Robots in agriculture: State of art and practical experiences. In A. J. R. Neves (Ed.), *Service Robots* (pp. 67–90). London, UK: IntechOpen.

Saengprachatanarug, K., Chaloemthoi, C., Kamwilaisak, K., Kasemsiri, P., Chaun-Udom, S., & Taira, E. (2018). Effect of metering device arrangement to discharge consistency of sugarcane billet planter. *Engineering in Agriculture, Environment and Food*, *11*(3), 139–144. https://doi.org/10.1016/j.eaef.2018.03.002

Sahoo, P. K., Kushwaha, D. K., Pradhan, N. C., Makwana, Y., Kumar, M., Jatoliya, M., … & Mani, I. (2021). Robotics application in agriculture. In R. Prasad (Ed.), *55th Annual Convention of Indian Society of Agricultural Engineers on Challenges and Technological Solutions for Ensuring Food, Water and Energy Security, International Symposium, November 23–25, Patna, Bihar, India* (pp. 60–76). New Delhi, India: Indian Society of Agricultural Engineers.

Saiz-Rubio, V., & Rovira-Más, F. (2020). From smart farming towards agriculture 5.0: A review on crop data management. *Agronomy*, *10*(2), 207, pp. 1–21. https://doi.org/10.3390/agronomy10020207

Sanchez, J., & Gallandt, E. R. (2021). Functionality and efficacy of Franklin Robotics' Tertill™ robotic weeder. *Weed Technology*, *35*(1), 166–170. https://doi.org/10.1017/wet.2020.94

Sarri, D., Lombardo, S., Lisci, R., Pascale, V., & Vieri, M. (2020). AgroBot Smash a robotic platform for the sustainable precision agriculture. In A. Coppola, G. C. Di Renzo, G. Altieri, & P. D'Antonio (Eds.), *Innovative Biosystems Engineering for Sustainable Agriculture, Forestry and Food Production: International Mid-Term Conference 2019 of the Italian Association of Agricultural Engineering (AIIA)* (pp. 793–801). Cham, Switzerland: Springer.

Scalera, L., Boscariol, P., Carabin, G., Vidoni, R., & Gasparetto, A. (2020). Enhancing energy efficiency of a 4-DOF parallel robot through task-related analysis. *Machines*, *8*(1), 10, pp. 1–14. https://doi.org/10.3390/machines8010010

Shiigi, T., Kondo, N., Kurita, M., Ninomiya, K., Rajendra, P., Kamata, J., … & Kohno, Y. (2008). Strawberry harvesting robot for fruits grown on table top culture. In *American Society of Agricultural and Biological Engineers Annual International Meeting 2008, 29 June–2 July, Providence, Rhode Island* (pp. 3139–3148). St. Joseph, MI: American Society of Agricultural and Biological Engineers (ASABE).

Snyder, H. (2019). Literature review as a research methodology: An overview and guidelines. *Journal of Business Research*, *104*, 333–339. https://doi.org/10.1016/j.jbusres.2019.07.039

Sori, H., Inoue, H., Hatta, H., & Ando, Y. (2018). Effect for a paddy weeding robot in wet rice culture. *Journal of Robotics and Mechatronics*, *30*(2), 198–205. https://doi.org/10.20965/jrm.2018.p0198

Sparrow, R., & Howard, M. (2021). Robots in agriculture: Prospects, impacts, ethics, and policy. *Precision Agriculture*, *22*(3), 818–833. https://doi.org/10.1007/s11119-020-09757-9

Sunitha, K. A., Suraj, G. S. G. S., Sowrya, C. H. P. N., Sriram, G. A., Shreyas, D., & Srinivas, T. (2017). Agricultural robot designed for seeding mechanism. *IOP Conference Series: Materials Science and Engineering*, *197*, 012043, pp. 1–6. https://doi.org/10.1088/1757-899X/197/1/012043

Tilman, D., Balzer, C., Hill, J., & Befort, B. L. (2011). Global food demand and the sustainable intensification of agriculture. *Proceedings of the National Academy of Sciences of the United States of America (PNAS)*, *108*(50), 20260–20264. https://doi.org/10.1073/pnas.1116437108

Tripodi, P., Massa, D., Accursio, V., & Cardi, T. (2018). Sensing technologies for precision phenotyping in vegetable crops: Current status and future challenges. *Agronomy*, *8*(4), 57, pp. 1–24. https://doi.org/10.3390/agronomy8040057

United Nations Conference on Trade and Development (UNCTAD). (2016). *Robots and Industrialization in Developing Countries* (No. 60). Geneva, Switzerland: United Nations Conference on Trade and Development.

United Nations Department of Economic and Social Affairs. (2022). World Population Prospects 2022: Summary of Results. Retrieved March 6, 2025, from United Nations Department of Economic and Social Affairs, Population Division website: www.un.org/development/desa/pd/sites/www.un.org.development.desa.pd/files/undesa_pd_2022_wpp_key-messages.pdf

United Republic of Tanzania (URT): Ministry of Agriculture. (2019). National Rice Development Strategy Phase II (NRDS II), 2019-2030. Retrieved March 6, 2025, from www.kilimo.go.tz/uploads/dasip/NATIONAL_RICE_DEVELOPMENT_STRATEGY_PHASE_II.pdf

United Republic of Tanzania (URT): Ministry of Agriculture. (2022). *Building A Better Tomorrow: Youth Initiative For Agribusiness (BBT-YIA) 2022–2030*. Dar es Salaam, Tanzania: United Republic of Tanzania: Ministry of Agriculture.

United Republic of Tanzania (URT): Ministry of Finance and Planning. (2021). *National Five Year Development Plan 2021/22–2025/26: Realising Competitiveness and Industrialization for Human Development*. Dar es Salaam, Tanzania: The United Republic of Tanzania: Ministry of Finance and Planning.

United Republic of Tanzania (URT): Ministry of Works Transport and Communication. (2016). National Information and Communication Technology Policy. Retrieved March 6, 2025, from www.ega.go.tz/uploads/publications/sw-1574848612-SERA2016.pdf

United Republic of Tanzania (URT). (2018). National Population Projections. Retrieved March 6, 2025, from www.nbs.go.tz/nbs/takwimu/census2012/Projection-Report-20132035.pdf

United Republic of Tanzania (URT). (2021a). 2020 Tanzania in Figures. Retrieved March 6, 2025, from www.nbs.go.tz/nbs/takwimu/references/2020_Tanzania_in_Figure_English.pdf

United Republic of Tanzania (URT). (2021b). National Sample Census of Agriculture 2019/20 – Main Report. Retrieved March 6, 2025, from www.nbs.go.tz/nbs/takwimu/Agriculture/2019-20_Agri_Census_Main_Report.pdf

United Republic of Tanzania (URT). (2023). Drafted National ICT Policy, 2023. Retrieved March 6, 2025, from www.mawasiliano.go.tz/uploads/documents/sw-1693455522-DOCUMENTTOUPLOADDRAFTAUGUSTNICTP.pdf

United Republic of Tanzania (URT), & National Bureau of Statistics [Tanzania]. (2022). *Integrated Labour Force Survey 2020/21: Analytical Report*. Dodoma, Tanzania: National Bureau of Statistics (NBS) [Tanzania].

Utstumo, T., Urdal, F., Brevik, A., Dørum, J., Netland, J., Overskeid, Ø., … & Gravdahl, J. T. (2018). Robotic in-row weed control in vegetables. *Computers and Electronics in Agriculture*, *154*, 36–45. https://doi.org/10.1016/j.compag.2018.08.043

Valle, S. S., & Klenzle, J. (2020). Agriculture 2.0: Agricultural robotics and automated equipment for sustainable crop production. Retrieved March 6, 2025, from Integrated Crop Management Vol. 24 website: www.fao.org/3/cb2186en/cb2186en.pdf

Van-Evert, F. K., Van Der Heijden, G. W. A. M., Lotz, L. A. P., Polder, G., Lamaker, A., De Jong, A., … & Van Der Zalm, T. (2006). A mobile field robot with vision-based detection of volunteer potato plants in a corn crop. *Weed Technology*, *20*(4), 853–861. https://doi.org/10.1614/wt-05-132.1

Van Dijk, M., Morley, T., Rau, M. L., & Saghai, Y. (2021). A meta-analysis of projected global food demand and population at risk of hunger for the period 2010–2050. *Nature Food*, *2*, 494–501. https://doi.org/10.1038/s43016-021-00322-9

World Bank Group. (2016). *World Development Report 2016: Digital Dividends*. Washington, DC: World Bank Publications.

World Economic Forum. (2017). The Future of Jobs and Skills in Africa: Preparing the Region for the Fourth Industrial Revolution. Retrieved March 6, 2025, from Reports website: www.weforum.org/publications/the-future-of-jobs-and-skills-in-africa-preparing-the-region-for-the-fourth-industrial-revolution

Xiong, W., & Tarnavsky, E. (2020). Better agronomic management increases climate resilience of maize to drought in Tanzania. *Atmosphere*, *11*(9), 982, pp. 1–18. https://doi.org/10.3390/atmos11090982

Xiong, Y., Ge, Y., Grimstad, L., & From, P. J. (2020). An autonomous strawberry-harvesting robot: Design, development, integration, and field evaluation. *Journal of Field Robotics*, *37*(2), 202–224. https://doi.org/10.1002/rob.21889

Yam, K. C., Tang, P. M., Jackson, J. C., Su, R., & Gray, K. (2023). The rise of robots increases job insecurity and maladaptive workplace behaviors: Multimethod evidence. *Journal of Applied Psychology*, *108*(5), 850–870. https://doi.org/10.1037/apl0001045

Zhou, H., Wang, X., Au, W., Kang, H., & Chen, C. (2022). Intelligent robots for fruit harvesting: Recent developments and future challenges. *Precision Agriculture*, *23*(5), 1856–1907. https://doi.org/10.1007/s11119-022-09913-3

Zhu, H., Zhang, Y., Mu, D., Bai, L., Zhuang, H., & Li, H. (2022). YOLOX-based blue laser weeding robot in corn field. *Frontiers in Plant Science*, *13*, 1017803, pp. 1–16. https://doi.org/10.3389/fpls.2022.1017803

14

CIRCULAR MATERIAL FLOWS, THE TWIN TRANSITION OF MANUFACTURING, AND THE FUTURE OF LABOUR

Insights from a Case Study of the Peniche Ocean Watch Initiative

Robin Teigland, Mikael Wiberg, Jon Erik Borgen, Mafalda de Freitas, Johan Landberg, Mohammad Rouhi, Karoline Teigland, and Woodrow Wiest

14.1 Introduction

In recent years, ocean plastics have emerged as a critical concern that transcends geographical boundaries and industrial and societal sectors. The Anthropocene era, marked by humanity's transformative impact on the planet, has witnessed the rapid rise of modern societies, technological advancements, and mass production practices. However, as the Anthropocene evolves, its defining characteristics are becoming increasingly entwined with the consequences of these very advancements. Notably, the relentless onslaught of the climate crisis, global warming, and the pervasive presence of ocean plastics are reshaping the narrative of this era (Ashton, 1997; Cressey, 2016; Sörlin, 2017). Here we define ocean plastics as both (1) ocean-bound plastic that has been defined as abandoned plastic waste located within 50 km from shores and is at risk of ending up in the ocean due to inefficient or nonexistent waste management practices and (2) plastic waste that is used in ocean-based industries, for example, fishing nets that may be disposed of through landfilling or incineration or that may be abandoned at sea or on land.

Ocean plastics, a manifestation of the challenges borne from our industrial world, have assumed a prominent place on the global agenda. In this chapter, we address the multifaceted dimensions of this issue, encompassing environmental, socio-economic, and technological aspects, with a focus on the urgent need for concerted action. While the problem of ocean plastics is already dire, projections indicate that its magnitude is poised to escalate exponentially in the near future. The oceans that connect the continents around the world, sometimes referred to

DOI: 10.4324/9781003391333-17

as a modern-day "no man's land", raise pressing questions around responsibility and accountability. Who bears the responsibility for addressing the consequences of plastic pollution, and how can the costs be equitably shared? This dilemma is further complicated by the far-reaching repercussions that stretch beyond the scope of marine ecosystems alone.

The challenges posed by ocean plastics extend their influence across diverse sectors. Coastal communities, traditionally reliant on fishing and supporting industries, such as packaging and shipyards, confront the threat of diminishing livelihoods and smaller tax bases. Further, the hopes that the tourism sector would provide new livelihoods are now being dashed as coastal areas are often plagued by polluted beaches or rising tides washing beaches away, while harmful algae blooms and other bacteria-infested pollution proliferate in the water. Moreover, the nasty tentacles of this issue reach far inland, affecting the agricultural industry through rising sea levels and temperature shifts.

In juxtaposition to the complexities and uncertainties, one undeniable truth emerges – ocean plastics are indeed everyone's problem. The global nature of the climate crisis underlines the inextricable interconnectedness of all nations and societies. Escaping the consequences of environmental degradation and plastic pollution is not an option; it is a challenge that demands collective action on a global scale.

Amidst the challenges, a glimmer of opportunity is emerging. This chapter recognises the potential of the labour market to harness innovation, entrepreneurship, and technological advancements to not only mitigate the impact of ocean plastics but also to transform the socio-economic landscape of coastal communities. The sheer scale of the problem opens doors to novel business models and technologies that can catalyse positive change. A pertinent avenue for exploration is the role of digital transformation and the "twin transition" – a symbiotic progression towards ecological sustainability and economic prosperity enabled through digital technologies.

To explore this idea, we present and discuss the case of the Peniche Ocean Watch Initiative. This initiative was founded by three of this chapter's authors in 2018 in Portugal in order to develop a "blue circular economy" model, that is, a circular economy model grounded in ocean resources. Through efforts to develop its microfactory concept encompassing the digital transformation of manufacturing, the Peniche Ocean Watch Initiative has enabled the re-routing and re-imagining of ocean plastics into valuable materials while closing the loop through the creation of new opportunities for the labour market.

In essence, this chapter embarks on a comprehensive exploration of the multifaceted challenge posed by ocean plastics. It navigates the intricate interplay of environmental concerns, socio-economic impacts, and technological innovations, all the while advocating for a collective and global response to this defining issue of our time. As we stand at the precipice of a critical juncture, the solutions we devise and the actions we take will undoubtedly shape the course of the Anthropocene era for generations to come.

14.2 Ocean Plastics: A Brief Background

Ocean plastics serve as a poignant symbol of how industrial development and globalisation have led to long-term unintended consequences for society and the environment. While the first plastics can be traced back to 1855 when celluloid was made from cellulose, a natural polymer in plants, it was not until the 1950s and 1960s that plastic production really started booming. This initial growth was characterised by consumer goods such as plastic bottles, containers, and other disposable products becoming ubiquitous in the Western world. A second boom for plastics then emerged on a global level in the late 1990s due to a combination of factors. New types of plastics were developed, such as polyethylene terephthalate (PET) for beverage bottles and expanded polystyrene (EPS) for packaging and insulation. On the supply side, plastic became the option of first choice for packaging and goods as supply chains became more globally integrated and transportation distances increased due to plastic's relative lightweight and durability compared to other materials such as glass, metal, or wood. Additionally, increased industrialisation combined with falling prices of energy, petroleum, and petrochemicals led to economies of scale and the mass production of plastic. As a result, annual plastics production has increased from two million tonnes in 1950 to over 413 million tonnes in 2023 and is expected to further increase to 1480 million tonnes by 2050 (Plastics Europe, 2022; Statista, 2024). Today the global plastics industry is highly concentrated with multinationals such as BASF SE, Celanese Corporation, Dow Inc., DuPont de Nemours, Inc., and Sumitomo Chemical Co. Ltd., as well as a few medium and small regional players (Grand View Research, 2023).

On the demand side, increasing urbanisation and fast-paced lifestyles together with mass marketing by fast-moving consumer goods multinationals has led to the demand for convenience products while globalisation has led to greater purchasing power of an expanding middle class in emerging economies and thus an increasing demand for consumer goods, predominantly made of plastic. As a result, plastic has become integral in our everyday lives and in just about every industry.

Our linear economy continues to prioritise the mass production, consumption, and disposal of goods, with neither accountability nor consideration of the long-term environmental impact, while a disposable culture emphasises convenience and disposability over durability and reusability. Despite recent advances within sustainability, around 90% of global plastic production is still from fossil-based raw material as manufacturers prefer virgin plastic due to its relatively low price and high quality and reliability (World Economic Forum, 2016). In 2021, bio-based/bioattributed plastics accounted for only 1.5% of world plastics production while around 8% were from post-consumer recycled plastics (Plastics Europe, 2022). Of note is that only around 9% of plastics produced since 1950 have been recycled

(Geyer, Jambeck, & Law, 2017), and one challenge to recycling is that plastics not only are produced with numerous potentially hazardous chemical compounds, but they also can absorb contaminants throughout their life cycle (Carmona et al., 2023; Plastics Europe, 2022).

As many plastics take hundreds of years to degrade, between 75 and 199 million tonnes are estimated to be now in our oceans with a further 8 to 14 million tonnes entering annually (Oceana, 2022; Sebille, 2016; Wakefield, 2022). The Great Pacific Garbage Patch, the largest of many accumulation zones, spans an area three times the size of France and weighs as much as 500 jumbo jets, and studies find that fishing gear, such as nets, lines, and traps, comprise 20–50% of the patch (Lebreton et al., 2018). Microplastics, defined as less than five millimetres in size, are now everywhere – from polystyrene fragments and polyethylene in the Mariana Trench, which holds the Earth's deepest known oceanic point – the Challenger Deep. Further, some studies are reporting 94,000 particles per litre in our drinking water and microplastics in our lungs and breast milk (World Health Organization, 2019).

In many countries, not only is the recycling infrastructure inadequate, but there is little monetary or other incentive for individuals or organisations to recycle, which is further compounded by the low level of awareness of the environmental, health, and societal effects of plastic pollution. Plastic pollution harms ecosystems and wildlife, and 90% of damage to marine wildlife is due to plastic waste while 700 marine species are threatened by plastic pollution (Chatziparaskeva, Papamichael, & Zorpas, 2022). Plastics leach harmful chemicals into the environment in addition to transferring additives, lethal metals, and other contaminants, for example, organic chemicals such as persistent organic pollutants (POP) that are toxic to animals and humans by consumption. Plastic pollution imposes significant economic costs, including clean-up expenses, damage to tourism, and impacts on fisheries and aquaculture, and the annual cost of marine litter is estimated to be around US$2.5 trillion (Chatziparaskeva et al., 2022).

14.3 Sustainability on the Agenda, but What about Circularity?

Currently, governments and practitioners alike are looking for more sustainable approaches to tackle the negative spiral brought on by the linear economy, such as that presented earlier. Initiatives such as sustainable development, ecosystems, environmental stewardship, corporate social responsibility, Environmental, Social, and Governance (ESG), green and blue transitions, and twin transitions are being developed and implemented to help fulfil the United Nations Sustainable Development Goals (United Nations, 2024). A central, recurring element in many initiatives is the concept of "circularity" – spanning from circular economy models, for example, Zeiss, Ixmeier, Recker, and Kranz (2021), circular material flows (MF theory) (Bucknall, 2020) and recirculation of natural resources (Chen, 2009) to circularity and waste management, for example, Cobo, Dominguez-Ramos, and Irabien (2018).

Unfortunately, while sustainability is seemingly on almost everyone's agenda, most efforts pertain to merely sustaining the status quo. For instance, we recognise the significant issues related to CO_2 emissions from fossil fuelled cars, but rather than critically questioning the use of cars and whether individuals should own a car, we seek instead to find alternative fuel sources. Ethanol was an up-and-coming candidate just a decade ago, and now batteries for electric cars are on the agenda. Thus, a life cycle or a holistic perspective is rarely taken. Indeed, few are aware or wish to acknowledge that for every tonne of mined lithium, 1.9 tonnes of water are required, with the added emission of 15 tonnes of CO_2 in the process (Crawford, 2022; Katwala, 2018). Mining lithium, cobalt, and nickel requires hazardous chemicals and extensive manual labour (sometimes even child labour) in areas where water is scarce, and runoff contaminates underground water sources (McKie, 2021). Conversely, China, where around 77% of all batteries are produced, uses coal as its primary energy source (Crawford, 2022).

Moreover, electric cars are generally heavier than their counterparts due to their battery packs. The average electric car weighs 1.9 tonnes with the largest SUVs strikingly heavy, for example, Mercedes EQV at 2.96 tonnes, Audi e-tron 55 at 2.72 tonnes (Kane, 2021). It is no wonder that some have labelled this development "the green paradox" (Larsson & Hatzigeorgiou, 2022). Meanwhile, cars on the road continue to grow, requiring ever more resources. In 2020, of the 56 million new cars sold globally, 56% or 30.1 million were SUVs (of which 29.6 million were fossil fuel and 1.1 million electric), a sixfold increase in just nine years (Bekker, 2023; Carlier, 2023). To build these cars, extensive global supply chains providing the 30,000 parts for an average car have been created with little transparency (DataInterchange, 2021). Indeed, Renault was the only company as of 2022 requesting that members of its supply chain set targets aligned with the Paris Agreement (Wood, 2022). When it comes to end of life, while around 80% of automobile content by weight is recycled (LeBlanc, 2019), only 25–30% of a new automobile is made from recycled materials, meaning that 70–75% is still virgin materials extracted from the earth (Renault Group, 2022). The sustainability goals set by some of the globe's largest auto manufacturers could be claimed to not even be that inspiring, for example, Volvo – 35% recycled materials by 2030, Mercedes – 40% recycled materials by 2030, and BMW – an aim to use 50% recycled materials but with no year designated (BMW Group, 2024; Mercedes-Benz Group, 2024; Volvo, 2024).

Thus, it appears that our common approach is merely "to treat the symptom and not the disease" as we continue our journey towards resource depletion. Perhaps this is why, as noted by the 2023 Circularity Gap Report, only 7.2% of the world is circular as of 2023, a number that has declined from 9.1% in 2018 due to increasing raw material extraction, build-up of material stocks, and low levels of end-of-use processing and cycling (Circle Economy Foundation, 2023; Larsson, 2021). Thus, researchers are increasingly realising that to truly reach a circular economy, a systems-level transformation must be achieved (Despeisse et al., 2017), in which our dominant linear models of production and consumption and belief systems are challenged.

14.4 Re-routing the Tide for Community Resilience: Re-imagining Waste as a Valuable Resource through the Twin Transformation of Manufacturing

Moving forward, we need to take a more holistic perspective and find alternatives to challenge and break the "take→make→use→waste" linear material flow. It is not only about the plastic materials, the waste, and the pollution, but it is also about the larger system in which plastics are embedded – that is the material practice surrounding these materials – ranging from the sourcing of material to the production facility to the distribution channels, to the customer, and to their final destination. We think about this not only as a "call to action" but also as a "call to re-imagine and re-route". It is meaningless to just act if we do not also change the underlying system – so that new material practices can be established, including means for repurposing, and reusing, and maybe even repairing the things we make.

However, material practices are not easily changed. According to Giddens' (1984) structuration theory, structures are established over time, through patterns of practices, which in return are maintained and adapted through the exercise of agency. What we repeatedly do forms our practices, and over time these practices form structures that are exceptionally difficult to change. Accordingly, to change or "re-imagine" current practices, including "re-routing" established material flows, is not something that can occur quickly nor only because new rules, laws, regulations, or policies are implemented. Instead, it changes through the exercise of agency that is through actions taken by individuals, repeatedly and over time. We can lead by example, but for large-scale change to occur, we need to repeatedly act and approach materials in alternative ways – to exercise agency, to form new practices over time, and to form new structures that govern material flows. Thus, to help us on this transformation, we are following these principles in the establishment of new material practices, and, in particular, using the case of ocean plastics to create a sense of urgency. The trajectory of ocean plastics and its direct and indirect effects on the environment and coastal communities presents an unparalleled opportunity for change.

Currently about 40% of the global population lives within 100 kilometres from the coast (Burke et al., 2001). The ocean and its living resources are the primary source of food, livelihood, community, and even identity for hundreds of millions of people across the globe. For centuries, traditions and cultural norms around fishing practices have been followed, ensuring not only that the collective resource was conserved and replenished but also creating a collective spirit and sense of community. However, similar to many other industries, industrialisation and globalisation have, since the 1950s, brought about a disassociation between the development of a modern industry and the development of those traditionally involved in the industry. Within the fishing industry, industrialisation has led to significant efficiency through new technologies such as radar, sonar, and electronic navigation systems while global policies opened waters for large-scale fishing fleets. As a result, demersal (bottom) trawl nets have destroyed coral reefs, and large-scale fishing fleets and illegal fishing have overfished waters across the globe. It is estimated that nearly 90% of global fish stocks are overexploited, depleted, fully exploited, or in recovery from exploitation (Kituyi, 2018). In recent years, fishing bans and regulations in areas across the globe have cut off the livelihoods of not only the fishermen but also those working in supporting jobs such as boat building, gear manufacturing, and packaging. Furthermore, the ocean is also threatened by climate change and industrialisation in other sectors that have led to effects such as increased algae growth due to fertiliser runoff and migrating fish due to warmer waters.

For coastal communities, the effects of industrialisation and globalisation have been devastating. For example, the Atlantic Northwest cod industry collapsed in the early 1990s, and 35,000 fishermen and plant workers lost their jobs (Gien, 2000). Today West-African fisheries have declined by around 50% in the past 30 odd years (Vince, 2022). A 2011 study found that 99% of all fishermen in the world were small-scale fishers (Shester & Micheli, 2011); however, only a small percentage of the world's fishers and fishing communities actually have benefited from industrialisation and globalisation. As a result, coastal communities have become increasingly poor (Campbell, Whittingham, & Townsley, 2006). For example, in the UK, these communities have higher rates of unemployment, poorer health, and lower wages and lag in digitalisation while experiencing a brain drain and other demographic challenges as younger residents leave for cities while the number of pensioners grows (Ward, Cromarty, Garratt, & Barton, 2022). At the individual level, there is a sense of lost identity and hopelessness in addition to addiction, such as gambling and alcoholism. Coastal communities have become trapped in a cycle of disadvantage as they are unattractive for investment and do not have access to the resources or power needed to tap into new opportunities. One study in the UK revealed that individuals in coastal communities were around 44% less likely to start a business, and those individuals who did start a business were 24% more likely to go into insolvency than their counterparts in non-coastal communities (Carpenter & Balata, 2018).

Recent years have led to an increase in tourism due to economic development and changing consumer values, deregulation, and low-fare airlines combined with digitalisation (OECD, 2016). While tourism may create jobs and bring income, highly seasonal tourism leads not only to a low-level of local services during the off-season but also to difficulties in providing the necessary health and social care for locals year-round. Even anti-social behaviours of visitors and pollution can further worsen the situation for the locals. Finally, tourism brings jobs that tend to be relatively low skilled, low paid, and highly seasonal, leading to a highly transient and seasonal workforce that does little to build the skill base and resilience of the local community nor enable a coastal community to maintain strides with urban areas when it comes digitalisation.

14.5 Peniche Ocean Watch Initiative: Driving Change through Engaged Scholarship

By devising effective strategies to mitigate these environmental and socio-economic repercussions, we can pave the way for a more equitable and sustainable future. Together the first co-author and an international team of practitioners and researchers under the umbrella of the Peniche Ocean Watch Initiative are currently developing the concept of a blue circular economy model in Peniche, Portugal.

Peniche lies 95 kilometres northwest of Lisbon and is one of the largest traditional fishing ports in Portugal. Gillnet fishing is the second most common fishing practice in Peniche, with 40 boats operating from the Peniche port. The environmental challenge is that gillnets are used only once or twice, and while some nets are lost or dumped at sea, every year more than 40,000 kilos of discarded gillnets are dumped in the Peniche harbour, before ultimately ending up in landfills or burned at incineration sites. The environmental impact is alarming as burning just one tonne of fishing nets releases 2.9 tonnes of CO_2 emissions (QMRE, 2023).

To solve this unsustainable practice and close the loop of plastic production while enabling a more resilient community through jobs and digitalisation, a systems-level transformation must be achieved. Peniche Ocean Watch's vision since its start in 2018 is to digitally transform manufacturing through developing a circular model based on its "microfactory" concept. The primary idea behind the microfactory concept is that a local industrial waste stream, for example, plastic, is collected and recycled into a secondary raw material that is then fed into a large-scale additive manufacturing machine that produces large products on demand for the local market – *all within the walls of the same production facility*. The microfactory concept can then be "scaled" out through creating a global network of microfactories connected through a digital platform on the Internet. This solution would enable firms to manufacture their products from local waste streams on demand and close to a local market, without lengthy transportation times or the risk of being exposed to supply chain shocks.

Since 2018, the Peniche Ocean Watch team has been developing the microfactory concept together with local fishermen and other community members. To move towards the circular model, the company Circular Ocean Lda was founded under the Peniche Ocean Watch Initiative to collect, sort, clean, and shred discarded gillnets in Peniche. Sorting and cleaning are a manually labour-intensive process as it requires handiwork of individuals to ensure a clean, monomaterial, that is, comprising only one plastic type. The gillnets are made from polyamide 6 (PA6 – nylon), while the ropes are made from other plastic types and therefore need to be removed. Further, other objects such as fishhooks, fish, seaweed, and other biomaterial must also be removed before the nets are washed. Once the nets are dry, they are shredded and then compounded into pellets and filaments for manufacturing under the name of PENYLON™. To date, Peniche Ocean Watch has recycled around 90 tonnes of fishing nets, preventing the emission of 232 tonnes of CO_2.

While the goal of the microfactory concept is to produce products in Peniche from the PENYLON material for the local market, initial attempts by Peniche Ocean Watch to complete the circle were unsuccessful. Portugal did not have the design or additive manufacturing skills nor was there an interest from the local market for such sustainable, innovative products. Thus, to complete the circle, some team members founded Ekbacken Studios AB in Sweden to produce high design furniture from the PENYLON material using large-scale additive manufacturing. However, as Ekbacken Studios was a start-up, it was difficult to arrange financing for the purchase of large-scale additive manufacturing machines to produce in-house. As a result, Circular Ocean and Ekbacken Studios partnered with Research Institutes of Sweden (RISE), Artex AB, and The Industry AB to gain access to their production equipment and facilities. Ekbacken Studios also designed its products such that at the end of their life, they could be returned, shredded, pelletized, and then printed once again, thereby closing the loop. Of significance is that IVL – the Swedish Environmental Research Institute calculated that even with the transportation of the PENYLON material to Sweden from Portugal, there is a remarkable approximate 90% reduction in CO_2 compared to manufacturing with virgin plastic.

In addition to the above, the team's efforts have resulted in two interdisciplinary innovation research projects: OCEAN-LSAM in 2022 and SuRF-LSAM in 2023, under Sweden's Produktion2030 Strategic Innovation Program financed by Vinnova – Sweden's Innovation Agency, the Swedish Energy Agency, and the Swedish Research Council for Sustainable Development. The overarching objective of these projects is to turn the network of microfactories concept into reality in Portugal and Sweden by the year 2027, with the further aim to replicate and implement the microfactory concept in coastal communities worldwide, while empowering local communities with entrepreneurial mindsets and stimulating their local economies.

Thus, this "blue circular economy" model re-imagines the traditional linear model of centralised production that overproduces a standardised product to reduce unit costs through economies of scale for global transportation. Peniche Ocean Watch's novel solution enables the production of customised or smaller quantities of products on demand using local recycled materials for delivery to local buyers. Products will then be both easily traceable and returnable to the microfactory for further recycling and remanufacturing into new products for the local market. Further, through the digital platform, a company, for example, in Sweden can sustainably meet the demands of customers in Portugal as it can design a customised product for local production in Portugal, thereby not only reducing transportation costs but also delivery times.

Regarding labour, throughout this circular flow enabled by the microfactory concept, we have found that new forms of labour have been created – from more manual routine to more highly skilled, non-routine work. The beginning of the circular material process requires (1) extensive manual labour due to the physical collection and transportation of the heavy fishing nets, (2) fine motor skills required in the sorting and cleaning process, and (3) machine operation skills to run the shredding machine. To facilitate this, Circular Ocean has created several jobs in its microfactory in Peniche: three full-time jobs for the overseeing and running of the microfactory as well as two part-time jobs and hourly work for around ten additional individuals through a partnership with CERCIPeniche – a social rehabilitation centre that provides inclusive work opportunities for individuals who have difficulty entering or remaining in the workforce. Results from Circular Ocean's efforts have proven promising, as all those involved in the process report that both their work in the microfactory creates a real sense of meaning and purpose. Furthermore, this local collaboration with the community has enabled Circular Ocean to expand its activities to nearby fishing ports, despite inter-port rivalry, as members of other communities understand that these circular model activities are indeed beneficial for the community at the collective level.

Moving through the circular model from material preparation to material compounding and production, a higher level of cognitive and non-routine skills in several areas are required, especially as several technological challenges exist (Rouhi, Landberg, Wiest, Teigland, & Teigland, 2023). Firstly, material science skills are needed to create the right "recipe" for compounding the shredded nets into a material suitable for additive manufacturing. For example, decisions need to be made related to which fillers/stabilisers should be compounded with the pure nylon material and in what percentages, depending on the final product use case. Furthermore, digital design skills are required to design a product suitable for large-scale additive manufacturing using the compounded material, while digital twin/simulation skills using artificial intelligence are required to improve the design's feasibility for additive manufacturing. By simulating the printing process in advance, mistakes due to parameters such as printing speed and printing nozzle temperature can be avoided, thereby minimising the amount of wasted material, energy, and time during manufacturing. Compounding and large-scale additive manufacturing machine operators are also needed to run the machines as well as individuals involved in logistics within the microfactory. Further, higher level cognitive skills will also be required in order to create a global network of microfactories, as a digital platform needs to be created and maintained that enables the sharing of knowledge, data, and files among the microfactories as well as material sourcing and product traceability.

With the aim to create a microfactory in Portugal by 2026, the Peniche Ocean Watch Initiative will create both manual and cognitive jobs comprising more routine to less routine tasks. As a result, this localised approach of microfactories can be instrumental in not only combatting ocean plastics but also contributing to local economies by offering a blueprint for fostering community-level resilience and sustainable employment opportunities.

14.6 Implications and New Directions

Reflecting on the discussion in this chapter, we find that when we move in the direction of a blue circular economy model of manufacturing, there are also implications for how work is conducted – where, by whom, through which division of labour, and along which process. As noted in this chapter, if we start with the concept of microfactories, we envision not just one microfactory in one location but the establishment of global networks of microfactories, which clearly signifies a transformation in the way we approach manufacturing. We can move from centralised mass production using virgin materials for inventory to the decentralised, local production of on-demand goods using locally collected and recycled materials, that is, "close to the market, but also close to the material". This decentralisation has the potential to revitalise local economies by creating all types of jobs and reducing the dependence on centralised and automated manufacturing hubs. As such, the microfactory concept is not only about reshaping and repurposing materials, but it is also about completely reshaping assembly lines, distribution chains, and even local economies. We can also see how the establishment of networks of microfactories enables new sustainable practices since these networks can drastically reduce the carbon footprint associated with traditional supply chains as the proximity of microfactories to consumers minimises transportation emissions and fosters sustainability. This decentralised model can serve as a blueprint for reducing global reliance on long-distance shipping and, consequently, mitigating the environmental impact of transportation.

Another aspect has bearing for the development of a global circular economy. The use of collected waste materials as inputs for microfactories promotes one of the fundamental principles of a circular economy – to re-imagine materials for new purposes. To recycle and repurpose is key to the circular economy. This approach not only reduces waste but also reduces the demand for virgin resources. This shift towards circularity aligns with global efforts to combat resource depletion and environmental degradation. By relying on recycled materials, businesses can reduce their dependence on fluctuating commodity and raw material prices. This not only enhances stability but also contributes to resource security and resilience.

The microfactory concept also presents an opportunity to redefine work and job opportunities. It fosters the creation of new roles associated with materials collection, recycling, microfactory operation, and digital platform management. This diversification of job profiles also enhances inclusion and social sustainability by addressing unemployment and offering meaningful work. Our proposed transition to microfactories and sustainable practices imbues work with a sense of purpose. Employees in these settings often find their roles deeply connected to a feeling of "doing good" for nature – an ethical way of being and living as well as adding to community well-being. People find it meaningful to engage, on a personal level, as well as in relation to doing small but important work for a more sustainable future. This sense of purpose contributes to social justice by offering people opportunities to engage in meaningful, socially responsible work, while also giving them an opportunity to engage in a concrete action for a more sustainable planet.

While the microfactory concept may be small by definition, it can deliver fundamental impact in terms of the three areas of sustainability:

- **Economic impact:** The growth of microfactories and the networks enabling them can stimulate local economies, increase resilience by reducing dependence on imported goods, and potentially lower costs of goods through efficient resource utilisation and elimination of extensive transportation costs.
- **Environmental impact:** The use of recycled materials, on-demand production, and reduced transportation distances can result in a significantly decreased environmental footprint, extending beyond immediate production to resource conservation and waste reduction.
- **Social impact:** The emergence of new job opportunities, coupled with a sense of purpose, contributes to social well-being, while empowering communities and supporting a more equitable distribution of wealth and resources.

Thus, the microfactory concept, the utilisation of recycled materials, and the reconfiguration of labour might come with far-reaching implications. They extend into the realms of environmental sustainability, economic resilience, and social justice. This innovative approach to manufacturing holds the potential to transform industries, reshape labour markets, and create a more sustainable and equitable future. As we progress towards these goals, we need to remain mindful of the potential challenges and continue to refine and adapt our strategies to ensure the long-term success of this transformative vision. In the next section we take this as our point of departure for thinking about what this means in terms of a gateway to an alternative future.

14.7 Towards an Alternative Future

In this chapter, we have addressed ocean plastics from a standpoint of constructive progress. Rather than just acknowledging and underscoring the existing problems regarding this material in our ecosystem, we have examined an alternative path for moving forward. We have personally engaged in how these materials are approached and re-imagined. Our team works with the local community and local stakeholders and engages them in these new material practices, and we do it repeatedly – over time. Instead of seeking to sell the idea of microfactories to the local communities, we work from within, together with, and through the materials – as change agents – to "exercise agency", to form new socio-material practices, and accordingly new ways of doing, working, and living – over time. Accordingly, our approach neither seeks "quick fixes" nor aims to achieve radical change. Instead, we take a long view – to slowly but steadily re-imagine existing practices into something more sustainable.

In this chapter, we have also presented an empirical and action-oriented case where we work as engaged scholars to realise the concept of "microfactories" as a new form of manufacturing enabled through a twin transition. Here, the focus is on the small scale, on the "close to the material" practice of cleaning fishing nets with our own bare hands, working with local communities, and building a network of actors, rather than huge, automated factory plants operating based on the economies of scale principle. Location is key, and so is the closeness to the local community.

There are also interesting side effects and implications for research methods and approaches here. Staying close to the *place*, the *community*, and *the material at hand* leads to an engaged and responsible way of working. It is sustainable, not only from a temporal viewpoint, but, more importantly, from an ethical and social viewpoint. When people are engaged in this alternative system, they can feel that their actions matter, they can feel a sense of belonging, and they can find their jobs meaningful. The small actions taken in cleaning a fishing net correspond directly to helping our oceans.

Leaving the micro-level for a second, we can also say that this shift towards engaged and sustainable ways of working – doing something meaningful while contributing to sustainable development – provides benefits for the future labour market around the world. Instead of travelling into huge megacities to spend the day in a factory or an office, work can be locally situated – for the locals. As such, this project also has real-life practical implications.

Now, as we re-imagine and re-route our approach towards a new theory of circular economy, we must at the same time confront and challenge the dominant linear model of "take→make→use→waste" that has led to the proliferation of ocean plastics and other material waste. This transition demands a fundamental shift towards the establishment of local circular material ecosystems, which are not only ecologically sound but also socially just as we have pinpointed in this chapter. But how should this transition happen? What are the key concerns for making this shift?

Firstly, we advocate for the need to break existing material flows, and accordingly we challenge established manufacturing principles and practices. The linear approach has been built around a one-way journey for materials, leading to their eventual disposal as waste or other forms of footprints. By truly embracing circularity, we disrupt this one-directional flow, and we recognise how materials can be valuable resources that can be re-routed to circulate within a circular material system. Secondly, we emphasise the importance of breaking existing material practices. This means re-imagining how we interact with materials, who the stakeholders are, and how they are engaged in these material practices. We propose an approach that joins and challenges these networks of materials and stakeholders, aligns interests, and facilitates change from within. This approach recognises the interconnectedness of materials and the stakeholders involved in these systems.

Furthermore, our commitment to social justice as part of our striving for a better future – for everyone – is indeed integral to this transition. We acknowledge that the burden of plastic pollution disproportionately affects developing countries. Therefore, any shift towards a circular material ecosystem must be inclusive and "scalable" across these regions. This implies not only mitigating the adverse effects of existing waste but also providing opportunities for economic development and improved living conditions. This is also the case at the local level. Our approach is about engaging rather than pushing for additional separations between those who are privileged and those who suffer. In this context, our microfactory concept serves as a promising example. By working closely with local communities, engaging in hands-on material practices, and building networks of actors, such as local stakeholders, we not only address the ecological challenges but also foster social and economic well-being. This approach can be adapted and scaled to regions facing similar environmental and social dilemmas.

Ultimately, our vision of a circular material ecosystem is a slow process with a clear goal cantered on a long-term commitment to re-imagine existing practices into something more sustainable. By staying close to the geographical place, the community, and the materials at hand, we promote engaged and responsible ways of working that are not only temporally sustainable but, more crucially, also ethically and socially responsible. This shift towards engaged and sustainable ways of working is not limited to our specific empirical case but holds promise for the future labour market worldwide. Instead of feeding the urban megacities, this new paradigm of local circular material ecosystems allows people to find meaningful employment within their local communities. It enables individuals to see the direct impact of their actions on the environment, fostering a sense of purpose and belonging while simultaneously contributing to a more sustainable planet and way of living.

14.8 Conclusion

As we now move to the conclusion, we suggest that our chapter advocate a shift from the linear "take→make→use→waste" model to local circular material ecosystems. By breaking existing material flows and practices and prioritising social justice, we chart a heading towards a more sustainable and equitable future. This journey not only puts us "hands-on" in direct contact with the materials and as such revitalises our relationship with the environment, but it also offers a transformative vision for the global labour market and for thinking about a more inclusive and engaged future – for everyone.

The notion that ocean plastics could morph into the source of digital transformation of manufacturing and more meaningful work is not a mere speculation but a tangible prospect rooted in the urgency of the issue. The scale of plastic pollution necessitates an expansive and diversified workforce to tackle its myriad facets – from clean-up and collection efforts across coastlines to the development of advanced mechanical and chemical recycling technologies and waste management strategies to AI-enabled design and manufacturing. In this regard, our example can serve as an inspiration for the potential for large-scale job creation in response to environmental challenges.

Thus, the compelling narrative of ocean plastics resonates far beyond its explicit presence in the text. The urgency of this issue and its manifold ramifications warrant a comprehensive exploration that navigates the interplay of environmental, socio-economic, and technological factors. Through a concerted effort to reshape the labour market, leverage innovative solutions, and acknowledge the urgency of addressing this challenge, we can steer the course of the Anthropocene towards a more sustainable and resilient trajectory. To break existing linear material flows is by no means a "one man's job". On the contrary, the existing material flows are upheld, protected, and fuelled by strong stakeholders and their established business models, tempting incentive structures, and expensive developed and installed technologies. Accordingly, to break or redirect these flows is a matter of finding alternative models, new opportunities for more sustainable collaborations, and alternative ways of using technologies. The future is accordingly not only about *reducing* omissions but fundamentally reimagining what we do and how we do it – together. The future of labour is accordingly about togetherness, to collaborate and co-create across different expertise areas, across different domains, and across different business models, but towards a shared goal – to make the world a better place. The future of labour is rich from the viewpoint of how we need to re-imagine what we do, who should do it, and who should pay for the work that needs to be done. And there is plenty of work to be done in order to re-route and re-imagine current (material) practices. As we uncover the intricate layers of the ocean plastics phenomenon, we invite the reader of this chapter to embark on their own journey of discovery, realisation, and transformation – a journey that holds the promise of a better, cleaner, and more interconnected future.

Conflict of Interest

The first, third, and seventh authors are the co-founders of the Peniche Ocean Watch Initiative, Circular Ocean Lda, and Ekbacken Studios AB.

Acknowledgements

The authors would like to acknowledge Produktion2030 – a strategic innovation programme supported by Vinnova, the Swedish Energy Agency and the Swedish Research Council for Sustainable Development for their valuable co-financing of the OCEAN-LSAM and SuRF-LSAM projects as well as the Swedish Internet Foundation for their generous funding of this research.

References

Ashton, T. S. (1997). *The Industrial Revolution 1760–1830* (2nd ed.). Oxford, UK: Oxford University Press.

Bekker, H. (2023). 2022 (Full Year) International: Worldwide Car Sales. Retrieved March 6, 2025, from Car Sales Statistics website: www.best-selling-cars.com/international/2022-full-year-international-worldwide-car-sales

BMW Group. (2024). Sustainability. Retrieved February 24, 2024, from www.bmwgroup.jobs/nordics/en/sustainability.html

Bucknall, D. G. (2020). Plastics as a materials system in a circular economy. *Philosophical Transactions of the Royal Society A: Mathematical, Physical and Engineering Sciences*, *378*(2176), 20190268. https://doi.org/10.1098/rsta.2019.0268

Burke, L., Kura, Y., Kassem, K., Revenga, C., Spalding, M. D., & McAllister, D. (2001). *Pilot Analysis of Global Ecosystems: Coastal Ecosystems*. Washington, DC: World Resources Institute.

Campbell, J., Whittingham, E., & Townsley, P. (2006). Responding to coastal poverty: Should we be doing things differently or doing different things? In C. T. Hoanh, T. P. Tuong, J. W. Gowin, & B. Hardy (Eds.), *Environment and Livelihoods in Tropical Coastal Zones: Managing Agriculture-Fishery-Aquaculture Conflicts* (pp. 274–292). Oxon, UK: CABI.

Carlier, M. (2023). Sport Utility Vehicles Worldwide–Statistics & Facts. Retrieved March 6, 2025, from Statista website: www.statista.com/topics/6185/suv-market-worldwide/#topicOverview

Carmona, E., Rojo-Nieto, E., Rummel, C. D., Krauss, M., Syberg, K., Ramos, T. M., … & Almroth, B. C. (2023). A dataset of organic pollutants identified and quantified in recycled polyethylene pellets. *Data in Brief*, *51*, 109740, pp. 1–7. https://doi.org/10.1016/j.dib.2023.109740

Carpenter, G., & Balata, F. (2018). Coastal Communities in the UK: A Vision for Starting Up, Not Shutting Down. Retrieved March 6, 2025, from New Economics Foundation website: https://neweconomics.org/uploads/files/coastalinsolvency_startingup.pdf

Chatziparaskeva, G., Papamichael, I., & Zorpas, A. A. (2022). Microplastics in the coastal environment of Mediterranean and the impact on sustainability level. *Sustainable Chemistry and Pharmacy*, *29*, 100768, pp. 1–15. https://doi.org/10.1016/j.scp.2022.100768

Chen, J. Z. (2009). Material flow and circular economy. *Systems Research and Behavioral Science*, *26*(2), 269–278. https://doi.org/10.1002/sres.968

Circle Economy Foundation. (2023). Circularity Gap Report 2023. Retrieved March 6, 2025, from www.circularity-gap.world/2023

Cobo, S., Dominguez-Ramos, A., & Irabien, A. (2018). From linear to circular integrated waste management systems: A review of methodological approaches. *Resources, Conservation and Recycling*, *135*, 279–295. https://doi.org/10.1016/j.resconrec.2017.08.003

Crawford, I. (2022). How Much CO2 Is Emitted by Manufacturing Batteries? Retrieved March 6, 2025, from MIT Climate Portal website: https://climate.mit.edu/ask-mit/how-much-co2-emitted-manufacturing-batteries

Cressey, D. (2016). Bottles, bags, ropes and toothbrushes: The struggle to track ocean plastics. *Nature*, *536*(7616), 263–265. https://doi.org/10.1038/536263a

DataInterchange. (2021). Overcoming Supply Chain Visibility Issues in the Automotive Industry. Retrieved March 6, 2025, from https://datainterchange.com/supply-chain-visibility-issues

Despeisse, M., Baumers, M., Brown, P., Charnley, F., Ford, S. J., Garmulewicz, A., … & Rowley, J. (2017). Unlocking value for a circular economy through 3D printing: A research agenda. *Technological Forecasting and Social Change*, *115*, 75–84. https://doi.org/10.1016/j.techfore.2016.09.021

Geyer, R., Jambeck, J. R., & Law, K. L. (2017). Production, use, and fate of all plastics ever made. *Science Advances*, *3*(7), e1700782, pp. 1–5. https://doi.org/10.1126/sciadv.1700782

Giddens, A. (1984). *The Constitution of Society: Outline of the Theory of Structuration*. Berkeley, CA: University of California Press.

Gien, L. T. (2000). Land and sea connection: The East Coast fishery closure, unemployment and health. *Canadian Journal of Public Health*, *91*(2), 121–124. https://doi.org/10.1007/BF03404926

Grand View Research. (2023). Plastic Market Size, Share & Trends Analysis Report By Product (PE, PP, PU, PVC, PET, PS), By Application (Injection molding, blow molding, roto molding, compression molding), By End-use, By Region, and Segment Forecasts, 2024 – 2030. Retrieved March 6, 2025, from www.grandviewresearch.com/industry-analysis/global-plastics-market

Kane, M. (2021). Electric Cars From Heaviest to Lightest. Retrieved March 6, 2025, from InsideEVs website: https://insideevs.com/news/527966/electric-cars-from-heaviest-lightest

Katwala, A. (2018). The Spiralling Environmental Cost of Our Lithium Battery Addiction. Retrieved March 6, 2025, from Wired website: www.wired.co.uk/article/lithium-batteries-environment-impact

Kituyi, M. (2018). 90% of Fish Stocks Are Used Up–Fisheries Subsidies Must Stop. Retrieved March 6, 2025, from United Nations Conference on Trade and Development (UNCTAD) website: https://unctad.org/news/90-fish-stocks-are-used-fisheries-subsidies-must-stop

Larsson, A. (2021). Circular value: A scoping review of the circular economy's effects on value-creation. *Scientific Journal of Research & Reviews*, *3*(1), 10.33552/SJRR.2021.03.000555, pp. 1–9. https://doi.org/10.33552/SJRR.2021.03.000555

Larsson, A., & Hatzigeorgiou, A. (2022). The Green Paradox—The Pitfalls of Green Energy and How to Overcome Them. Retrieved March 6, 2025, from Newsweek website: www.newsweek.com/green-paradox-pitfalls-green-energy-how-overcome-them-opinion-1715865

LeBlanc, R. (2019). 20 Auto Recycling Facts and Figures. Retrieved March 6, 2025, from Live About website: www.liveabout.com/auto-recycling-facts-and-figures-2877933

Lebreton, L., Slat, B., Ferrari, F., Sainte-Rose, B., Aitken, J., Marthouse, R., … & Reisser, J. (2018). Evidence that the Great Pacific Garbage Patch is rapidly accumulating plastic. *Scientific Reports*, *8*(1), 4666. https://doi.org/10.1038/s41598-018-22939-w

McKie, R. (2021). Child Labour, Toxic Leaks: The Price We Could Pay For a Greener Future. Retrieved March 6, 2025, from The Guardian website: www.theguardian.com/environment/2021/jan/03/child-labour-toxic-leaks-the-price-we-could-pay-for-a-greener-future

Mercedes-Benz Group. (2024). Core Element of Our Sustainable Business Strategy: Ambition 2039. Retrieved March 6, 2025, from https://group.mercedes-benz.com/responsibility/sustainability/climate-environment/ambition-2039-our-path-to-co2-neutrality.html

Oceana. (2022). Plastic Is a Growing Threat to Our Future. Retrieved March 6, 2025, from https://usa.oceana.org/wp-content/uploads/sites/4/263943_FactSheet_v2-1.pdf

OECD. (2016). *OECD Tourism Trends and Policies 2016*. Paris, France: OECD Publishing.

Plastics Europe. (2022). Plastics–The Facts 2022. Retrieved March 6, 2025, from https://plasticseurope.org/knowledge-hub/plastics-the-facts-2022

QMRE. (2023). Carbon Emissions and Plastic Waste. Retrieved March 6, 2025, from www.qmre.ltd/carbon-emissions-and-plastic-waste

Renault Group. (2022). The Future is Neutral: The Circular Economy Is Stepping Into a New Era! Retrieved March 6, 2025, from Newsroom Renault Group website: https://media.renaultgroup.com/the-future-is-neutral-the-circular-economy-is-stepping-into-a-new-era

Rouhi, M., Landberg, J., Wiest, W., Teigland, K., & Teigland, R. (2023). Large scale additive manufacturing of recycled polymer composites. In M. Maiaru, B. Bednarcyk, E. J. Pineda, & G. M. Odegard (Eds.), *38th Technical Conference of the American Society for Composites, ASC 2023, September 17-20, Greater Boston, Massachusetts, USA* (pp. 2405–2411). Lancaster, PA: DEStech Publications.

Sebille, E. van. (2016). How Much Plastic Is There in the Ocean? Retrieved March 6, 2025, from World Economic Forum website: www.weforum.org/agenda/2016/01/how-much-plastic-is-there-in-the-ocean

Shester, G. G., & Micheli, F. (2011). Conservation challenges for small-scale fisheries: Bycatch and habitat impacts of traps and gillnets. *Biological Conservation*, *144*(5), 1673–1681. https://doi.org/10.1016/j.biocon.2011.02.023

Sörlin, S. (2017). *Antropocen – En essä om människans tidsålder [Anthropecene – An Essay on the Age of Man]*. Stockholm, Sweden: Weyler förlag.

Statista. (2024). Annual Production of Plastics Worldwide from 1950 to 2023. Retrieved March 6, 2025, from www.statista.com/statistics/282732/global-production-of-plastics-since-1950

United Nations. (2024). The 17 Goals. Retrieved March 6, 2025, from https://sdgs.un.org/goals

Vince, G. (2022). How the World's Oceans Could Be Running Out of Fish. Retrieved March 6, 2025, from BBC Future website: www.bbc.com/future/article/20120920-are-we-running-out-of-fish

Volvo. (2024). Sustainability. Retrieved March 6, 2025, from www.volvocars.com/intl/v/sustainability/circular-economy

Wakefield, F. (2022). Top 25 Recycling Facts and Statistics for 2022. Retrieved March 6, 2025, from World Economic Forum website: www.weforum.org/agenda/2022/06/recycling-global-statistics-facts-plastic-paper

Ward, M., Cromarty, H., Garratt, K., & Barton, C. (2022). *The Future of Coastal Communities* (No. CDP 2022/0153). London, UK: The House of Commons Library.

Wood, R. (2022). Why the Automotive Industry is Pointing Headlights At Suppliers in the Race to Cut Carbon Emissions. Retrieved March 6, 2025, from Emitwise website: https://emitwise.com/resources/blog/automotive-industry-suppliers-cut-carbon-emissions

World Economic Forum. (2016). *The New Plastics Economy: Rethinking the Future of Plastics*. Cologny, Switzerland: World Economic Forum.

World Health Organization. (2019). *Microplastics in Drinking Water*. Geneva, Switzerland: World Health Organization.

Zeiss, R., Ixmeier, A., Recker, J., & Kranz, J. (2021). Mobilising information systems scholarship for a circular economy: Review, synthesis, and directions for future research. *Information Systems Journal*, *31*(1), 148–183. https://doi.org/10.1111/isj.12305

15
CONCLUSION

Understanding the Labour Landscape of Tomorrow

Anthony Larsson and Andreas Hatzigeorgiou

15.1 Introduction

The introductory chapter of this volume posited the following question:

> What promises and dangers does the future labour landscape hold for us? What can be done in order to make it flourish and become more innovative, successful, and sustainable? Conversely, what threats or difficulties can we expect, and could (or should) anything be done in order to avert these dangers? What changes should the labour landscape undertake to accommodate for changed working habits and the onslaught of artificial intelligence (AI)? Are we indeed witnessing the end of the current labour landscape as we know it?

In discerning the answers to these questions, this volume has analysed various aspects of the labour landscape of tomorrow throughout 13 chapters by experts in the field from both academia and the industry. Looking at the possible future impact of digital transformation, artificial intelligence (AI) and new potential strategies and approaches, this book has been structured into three overarching sections of the labour landscape expected to be impacted by the future digital advancements. The themes were:

1 The Future of Society and Economy
   These chapters focussed on how future technologies and practices have impacted and will continue to impact the labour landscape on a socio-economic level.

DOI: 10.4324/9781003391333-18

2 The Future Way of Working
These chapters discussed the changing nature of labour as a result of AI, technology, and the digital transformation and the conditions under which work may be done in the future.
3 New Uses of AI and Technology in Labour
These chapters discussed how AI and technology is used to impact and change the types of work as such.

This chapter seeks to provide an overview of the situation, a brief summary of the discussions carried across the chapters of this book, and a final synthesis of the findings on what the future labour landscape may offer.

15.2 The Current State of Digitalisation and AI

Admittedly, "technology" is a wide concept that is often given particular designations depending on what purpose it servers, but used here pertains to any kind of technological development that impacts the labour landscape (Baier, Berger, Kreuzer, Oberländer, & Röglinger, 2023). Digitalisation, the digital transformation of labour, and the development of generative AI are often described as "disruptive" because it fundamentally changes how individuals sustain themselves and determines who continues to work in their trained fields. Essentially, the convergence of digital technologies, AI, and new approaches are reshaping the future labour landscape (Marku, Castriotta, Guardo, & Loi, 2021; Schaffers, Vartiainen, & Bus, 2020).

Digital transformation in business is typically a complex and challenging process to fully implement. As technology advances at a rapid pace, organisations face constant pressure to keep up or risk being left behind. Today, most organisations encounter two primary challenges when it comes to digital transformation. First, they must prioritise digitalisation on their strategic roadmap. Second, they must develop the agility to adopt new technologies before they become obsolete. There is no doubt that digital technologies are reshaping organisations fundamentally. To succeed and remain competitive, businesses need a coherent, viable strategy, employers must plan for reskilling their workforce, and individuals must stay informed, motivated, and ready to adapt to rapid changes.

AI has not only evolved extensively in concept throughout the first decades of the twenty-first century, but its practical application has also seen a considerable upswing in the labour environment, raising serious questions about what the future labour landscape will look like and to what extent we as humans will be required to perform certain tasks (Agarwal, Swami, & Malhotra, 2024; Reynolds, 2021). To this end, the changes that AI and other types of digital/technological developments bring forth not only impacts the workers and employees, but also governments, as they need to prepare citizens for a digital future while addressing challenges such as inequality, wage deflation, and potential social unrest caused by the transformation of society and the labour market. Already now, there is scientific research that shows that there are difficulties associated with the ongoing requirement for upskilling and/or reskilling as an adaptive reaction to these technological changes (Cramarenco, Burcă-Voicu, & Dabija, 2023).

A recurrent theme in the contemporary discourse is to what extent digitalisation and AI reduce and/or eliminate jobs, and what opportunities it may provide to make labour easier and more effective in others areas, and possibly even give rise to new types of job opportunities (Kavathatzopoulos, 2024; Zarkadakis, 2015). Some scholars strongly argue that the digital automation is undermining human labour, leading to widespread redundancy in many processes and tasks in the future (Stefano, 2019). For instance, Budhwar et al. (2022, p. 1086) argue that "AI and other automation technologies always need to adhere to privacy, legal, moral and ethical principles", which means that the heuristics used may be fickle and that the businesses would thus need to adapt to the AI's mode of operation rather than vice versa. Others take on a more optimistic view, suggesting that AI has been long demonised by scaremongers and that it will in fact offer improved work conditions and opportunities for mankind (Atkinson, 2018).

What then can we say about the true face of AI and digitalisation? The reality is that the future in this area remains uncertain. As witnessed above, predictions in this area have been, and remain, fragmented and often even contradictory. Many fundamental questions remain unanswered: How will the automation of work impact the very foundation of the welfare state? How does the future of labour affect people's economy? Is it really possible to reskill all workers? These and many other essential issues have been explored within this book. Hence, a summarising commentary of the chapters will follow.

15.3 Chapter Discussion

15.3.1 The Future of Society and Economy

The book starts with a historical treatise by Ashworth ("Innovation and Destruction: Technology, Ecology, and the Future of Social Labour") about how technological innovation has been propelled in the past through various ideologies and schools of thought stemming from the Industrial Revolution. Ashworth dissects the mainstream arguments of the impact of new technology and its bearing on human labour. He then examines various concepts that developed during the Industrial Revolution and finally concluding with a discussion on what the development has meant for the future of labour and how the way was paved for the current debate on labour, AI, and ecology. To this end, he contends machines are inherently designed to be better, faster and more efficient than humans when it comes to performing certain tasks and that society today judges humans based on standards dictated by computers, rather than having humans assess computers according to a human standard.

Castronova's chapter ("Smart Money") sought to understand the significance of "smart money", for example, money designed with specific goals in mind, and what ramifications that has on markets, society, and people by and large, and how smart money may alter interactions in markets and elsewhere in society. Castronova posits that money is in a sense autonomous because it emerges from a mutual concept of value independently shared by large numbers of people, and that money (and the value it represents) is not "invented" as such, but rather emerges through progression. He contrasts the use of "smart" money with "dumb" money, where the former, enabled by technological advancements, has clear goals and takes on different characteristics and is useful for specific purposes, whereas the latter is the kind of traditional money that can be used for anything. The chapter concluded that smart money carries a lot of risk, and may appear threatening in many instances, while also deducing that smart money is also a sign of the times, since there are not many other types of currencies that could be used to which one could not apply "smart" technology.

Kotkin and Toplansky's chapter ("AI and the Future of Society and Economy") examined the context of which the adoption of the different types of AI would affect the global economy and society. The chapter considered various areas such as business strategies global employment, education of youth, distribution of wealth, and policy choices. The chapter discussed AI's ability to improve decision-making, its potential to disrupt existing business models, and its potential to create new jobs and industries. However, the authors also warn of the potential negative consequences of AI, such as job displacement, increased inequality, and the erosion of privacy. The authors discuss the concerns raised by AI's creators and promoters regarding its potential risks, such as the dangers linked to the rise of artificial general intelligence (AGI) and the concentration of power in the hands of a few powerful companies. The authors conclude by emphasising the need for regulation and ethical considerations to ensure that AI is developed and used responsibly, while cautioning people from making themselves too dependent on AI, as not to erode human creativity, empathy, and personal expression.

Chapter 5 by Michael Lind ("Work and Workers in the Age of AI: The Influence of Technology, Trade, and Institutions") takes on the insights of the neo-Schumpeterian school of economics, identifying three major factors/variables that shape the impact of a new technology like AI on the employment structure of a country. The first factor looks at the relationship between the country and the current stage of the new techno-economic paradigm, moving from invention through innovation to diffusion of the new technology. The second factor is the relationship of a specific national or local economy to the world economy. The third factor pertains to national political and economic institutions, particularly labour market institutions. While AI has the potential to disrupt and transform economies, its effects will vary significantly depending on the specific context of each country. The key to understanding AI's impact is to examine these factors in detail and consider how they interact with each other. Lind contends that while liberal democracies have historically been superior in promoting innovation, recent examples show that authoritarian regimes can also excel in this area. Domestic labour market institutions also play a crucial role in determining how the gains from AI are distributed. Ultimately, Lind prognosticates that there will be digital democracies and digital dictatorships and that these nations will specialise in different exports and that they will consist of both high-wage and low-wage countries. He concludes that technological innovation will continue to transform all societies, but that this transformation will look different in different places.

Chapter 6 by Bent Greve ("AI and Welfare States: Curse, Solutions or Both?") discusses the impact of AI on welfare states by delving deeper into a number of elements that may influence this development. Greve argues that AI will influence not only the number of jobs, but also change qualifications needed in many different jobs, indicating the need for life-long learning in order to remain relevant on the labour market. Greve contends that AI could lead to job losses, especially in routine tasks, but also impact non-routine jobs. While new jobs may emerge, the overall impact on employment is uncertain. Likewise, AI can improve efficiency and consistency in public administration but it also poses risks of bias. AI can be used for tasks like tax administration and benefits eligibility determination. To this end, AI can enhance healthcare services through data analysis and automation but may also increase costs. It can improve efficiency in areas like medical consultations and drug development. AI may also help increase tax revenue but also poses challenges due to tax avoidance and global economic factors. Greve concludes that the impact of AI on welfare states is complex and multifaceted, presenting both opportunities and challenges for governments and individuals. As such, Greve's chapter emphasises the need for careful consideration of the potential benefits and drawbacks of AI in welfare systems and the importance of addressing ethical and social implications.

15.3.2 The Future Way of Working

Chapter 7 by Christos Makridis ("Interactions Reimagined: The Impact of Hybrid Work on Team Communication and Coordination") discusses the rise of hybrid work and its impact on the modern workplace. Makridis shows how the degree of coordination within an occupation is correlated with hourly wages, employment, and productivity, and how generative AI tools have the potential to reduce the barriers to coordinating complex work. After reviewing these patterns, this chapter explores the implications for employee productivity while evaluating the role of communication in the coordination of complex tasks in the workplace. Makridis's point of departure is that pandemic accelerated the shift towards remote work, leading to a significant increase in hybrid work arrangements. While this offers flexibility and benefits for both employers and employees, it also presents challenges such as communication difficulties and potential productivity issues.

The pandemic forced businesses to adopt remote work, and many have continued to use hybrid models since then. These offer flexibility and can improve work–life balance, but it can also lead to communication issues and reduced productivity in some cases. To this end, effective communication is crucial for productivity in hybrid work. Technology has advanced to support remote communication, but it requires intentional efforts and best practices. Makridis exemplifies with a case study of a company, BRAC, and its experience in order to highlight the challenges and opportunities of transitioning to remote work, including the importance of technology adoption and maintaining organisational culture. Makridis concludes that there is a need for proactive measures and collaboration to leverage the opportunities presented by hybrid work and mitigate its potential challenges.

Grafström's chapter ("Young Workers Want To Be in the Office: An Investigation Based on Swedish Survey Data") seeks to discern if the preference for working from home (WFH) is different among different age cohorts, with a special interest in young workers attitudes. The chapter analyses the result from a web-based survey involving 1,769 Swedish workers, among whom 1,000 were classified as office workers. While younger respondents initially showed a preference for WFH, they later expressed a stronger desire to work in a physical office. Older respondents, on the other hand, consistently preferred WFH. Factors such as the desire to separate work and home life, social interaction, and communication with colleagues influenced respondents' decisions about WFH. The availability of remote work options varied across age groups, with older respondents having more flexibility in this regard. With the caveat that attitudes and preferences are dynamic and may change over time, Grafström concludes that age plays a significant role in determining WFH preferences. As such, there is a need for flexible office solutions in this regard since there is no universal solution that will appeal to everyone.

Chapter 9 by Miriam Cherry ("The Possible Futures for Gig Work: Digital Platform Labour and Its Regulation") looks at the legal developments concerning the employment status of digital platform workers/gig workers, and how the hitherto rulings have given contradictory messages from legal systems around the world, and particularly so in the United States and the European Union. The gig economy has faced significant challenges in balancing labour rights and platform growth. Despite the widespread use of digital platforms, workers often lack basic labour protections due to ambiguous employment relationships. This has led to extensive litigation and varying regulatory outcomes across different legal systems. Courts have struggled to classify these relationships as employee or independent contractor, leading to inconsistent regulations. Cherry argues that the global nature of digital platforms has made it difficult for national governments to regulate effectively. The European Union's Platform Work Directive aims to address this by establishing a presumption of employment status for platform workers. The International Labor Organization (ILO) is developing an international standard on platform work to provide a global framework for regulating the gig economy. Cherry concludes by extending hope that the gig economy of tomorrow finds a balance between worker rights and platform growth, where international collaboration and standardised regulations are essential for ensuring fair treatment of gig workers.

15.3.3 New Uses of AI and Technology in Labour

Chapter 10 by Charlotte Mattfolk and Siri Wikander ("AI and the Future of Work: How Organisational Structures and the Role of Humans Transform in the Age of AI") explores how significant societal and organisational changes, particularly in how we build, manage, and collaborate within organisations. It focusses on blending technological advancements with a human-centric approach. Through structured interviews, workshops, and literature reviews, the study highlights the evolving relationship between humans and AI. Mattfolk and Wikander argue that both climate change and AI are driving new ways of thinking about society, organisations, and the economy. Current structures, optimised for the industrial era, are inadequate for today's digital infrastructure. AI's ability to generate content and eventually achieve AGI will challenge mankind's understanding of human cognition and organisational dynamics. The authors argue that AI offers powerful tools to enhance efficiencies, insights, and innovation. However, organisations struggle to grasp its potential, especially as AI development is resource-intensive and controlled by a few. The gap between AI-proficient companies and those lagging behind is widening. Mattfolk and Wikander discuss the growing impact of AI and digitalisation on communication, human development, and organisational systems, highlighting key trends and challenges. The authors advocate for transitioning from hierarchical structures to fluid networks that prioritise skills over roles and value set to tasks rather than roles, while also discussing the transition to "economies of data". There, value exponentially grows with data accumulation, emphasising user involvement and service-oriented business models, where "intelligence" is at the core of every company. The authors conclude that AI could enable a more decentralised, human-centric, and ethical approach to work, fostering a future where both individual and collective growth are prioritised. By the same token, it challenges us to reflect on what tasks humans truly want to engage in while AI handles the rest.

Chapter 11 by Ling Koay ("The Rise of Cyborg Marketers: A Marketer's Guide to Survive and Thrive in the Era of AI") discusses the impact of technology, particularly generative AI, on marketing. Koay highlights the paradox of technological advancement, where innovation can lead to both benefits and concerns about losing control, emphasising the importance of considering ethical boundaries and potential consequences of unchecked technological progress. Exploring the role of creativity in marketing and the need for marketers, Koay introduces the concept of "cyborg marketers", which seeks to combine human skills with digital tools, in particular regard to particularly AI and data analytics.

Koay contends that marketers need to master creativity, leverage AI effectively, and adapt to the rapidly changing marketing landscape.

Chapter 12 by Mohammad Amir Anwar ("Value Chains of AI: Data Training Firms, Platforms, and Workers") explores the role of human labour in the development of AI. It highlights that while AI is becoming increasingly prevalent, many people still do not understand how it works. Anwar argues that AI systems require vast amounts of training data, which is often provided by human workers in developing countries, or the "Global South". This process, known as "data work", is essential for AI development. Anwar uses the value chains framework to examine the different actors involved in this process, including data training firms, labour platforms, and workers. The chapter discusses how platforms connect businesses with human workers who do small tasks to train AI systems. These tasks are called "microwork" or "crowdwork" and can be done from anywhere with an Internet connection. This creates a global network of workers, with a majority located in developing countries. Yet, Anwar argues that the vast majority of profits generated by work yielded by these data workers do not befall to the workers themselves but rather to various firms and shareholders. Hence, participation in global value chains per se does not necessarily provide a pathway for less affluent individuals and regions to move up the value chains and capture more of the economic value. For this reason, Anwar concludes that there needs to be a new way of ensuring more transparency among these value chains in addition to holding these firms more accountable.

Chapter 13 by Proscovia Kamugisha ("Re-skilling Human Capital for Inclusive Economic Growth in the Face of Emerging Agricultural Automation in Africa: The Tanzania Perspective") looks at the displacement of human jobs in Tanzania, where a large proportion of national labour force is employed in agriculture whose tasks are manual. Kamugisha's chapter uses a semi-structured review and content analysis, tracing history of agricultural automation from early mechanisation to modern-day robotics and AI. The text analyses the current status of agricultural automation in Tanzania, noting limited adoption but growing interest and initiatives. It discusses the potential threats to jobs, particularly for low-skilled workers, and emphasises the need for education and skill development to mitigate these risks. Kamugisha explores the potential benefits of agricultural automation, such as increased productivity and reduced costs, while discussing the potential for spill-over effects from farms to other, surrounding farming communities. The chapter concludes that while agricultural automation can increase productivity, it also poses a threat to jobs, particularly in the agriculture sector. The displacement of human jobs could exacerbate the country's unemployment problem among low-skilled agricultural labour. The text emphasises the need for upgraded education systems to prepare the workforce for the future, with a recommendation to focus on vocational skills development at primary and secondary levels to provide alternative employment opportunities.

Chapter 14 by Robin Teigland et al. ("Circular Material Flows, the Twin Transition of Manufacturing, and the Future of Labour: Insights from a Case Study of the Peniche Ocean Watch Initiative") analyses the "twin transition" of manufacturing and the future of labour within the context of the circular economy and ocean plastics. Specifically, Teigland et al. explore the concept of a "blue circular economy" model as a solution to address the challenges posed by ocean plastics, emphasising the need to shift from a linear economy to a circular model, focussing on material practices and repurposing waste. The Peniche Ocean Watch Initiative in Portugal serves as a case study for implementing a blue circular economy model. This initiative focusses on recycling discarded fishing nets and using them to create new products through additive manufacturing. It aims to create jobs, promote local economic development, and reduce the environmental impact of plastic pollution. The authors underscore the importance of collaboration, innovation, and digital transformation in achieving a circular economy. The text concludes by advocating for a shift towards a circular material ecosystem, calling upon the need to break existing material flows and practices, prioritising social justice, and engaging in collaborative efforts. In bringing about a shift towards a new economy, the authors emphasise the potential of such as system being one that may create a more sustainable and equitable future, fostering economic development, social well-being, and environmental preservation.

15.4 Findings

This anthology sought to explore some overarching themes in which AI, digitalisation, digital transformation, and future technology and practices can be expected to impact the labour landscape in the future in the decades to come. In doing this, the book was structured up into three overarching themes. The findings in each theme can be summarised in the forthcoming section.

15.4.1 The Future of Society and Economy

These chapters focussed on how future technologies and practices have impacted and will continue to impact the labour landscape on a socio-economic level. A synthesis of the findings in the chapters of this section tells a narrative of the transformative impact of technological advancements, in particular regard to AI, not only on the labour market, but also on the economic systems and societal structures.

These chapters collectively highlight the dual nature of technological progress. On the one hand, AI and other innovations have the potential to enhance productivity, create new industries, and improve efficiency in both private and public sectors. For instance, AI-driven tools can streamline processes in healthcare and public administration, automate routine tasks, and introduce "smart money" with specialised economic functions. These changes can optimise decision-making, enable more precise financial systems, and address complex problems with unprecedented speed and accuracy.

On the other hand, the authors emphasise the risks and disruptions that accompany this progress. The widespread adoption of AI could lead to significant job displacement, especially in routine tasks, and alter the qualifications required for many roles, necessitating a shift towards life-long learning. AI's potential to widen economic inequality and concentrate power in the hands of a few companies or authoritarian states is another concern. Moreover, as AI becomes more integrated into society, it raises ethical questions around privacy, bias, and the erosion of human qualities such as creativity, empathy, and personal expression.

A key insight shared across the chapters is the importance of context in determining the impact of AI. Technological advancement does not affect all societies uniformly. Factors such as a country's stage of economic development, its position in the global economy, and the strength of its political and labour market institutions significantly shape how AI and related technologies are adopted and utilised. This variance could lead to a future where digital democracies and digital autocracies coexist, each leveraging technology in distinct ways to maintain their economic positions.

The key takeaway from this section is that while technological innovation of the labour market holds promise for economic growth and societal improvement, it also requires careful management and regulation to avoid exacerbating existing inequalities and societal divisions. The chapters in this section call for a balanced approach that indeed recognises the benefits of AI, but also remains vigilant about its inherent risks. Policymakers should thus be urged to adopt strategies that ensure inclusive access to the gains of technology, support those displaced by automation, and safeguard human values in an increasingly automated world. By doing so, society can navigate the complexities of the technological future and shape an economy that serves the broader public interest.

15.4.2 The Future Way of Working

These chapters focussed on the changing nature of labour as a result of AI, technology, and the digital transformation and the conditions under which work may be done in the future. A synthesis of the findings presented in the chapters of this section uncovers the evolving nature of work in response to technological advancements, changing worker preferences, and the challenges of regulating emerging work models.

A central theme is the shift towards greater flexibility in the workplace, driven in part by the COVID-19 pandemic, which has reshaped work dynamics through the adoption of hybrid and remote work arrangements. While this shift has provided new opportunities for productivity and work–life balance, it has also introduced complexities that the labour market must address. For instance, there is the case of "hybrid work", which combines remote and in-office work. In recent years, this has become a prominent model, as it offers flexibility to both employers and employees. However, this flexibility comes with challenges, particularly around maintaining effective communication and coordination among staff members and teams. For organisations to maximise productivity in a hybrid setting, they need to invest in technology and cultivate intentional communication practices to bridge the gaps that can arise from remote work. This approach can help balance the benefits of flexibility with the need for cohesion and productivity.

Simultaneously, worker preferences regarding remote and in-office work are not uniform. Demographic factors, such as age, significantly influence these preferences. In particular younger workers, who are often eager, at least initially, to favour remote work for its flexibility, may eventually express a desire to return to the office for social interaction and clearer boundaries between work and home life. Older workers, however, tend to value the flexibility of remote work more consistently. This diversity in preferences underscores the need for adaptable workplace policies that can cater to different needs and provide a balance between autonomy and the benefits of in-person interaction.

In parallel, the growth of the gig economy has introduced new challenges related to labour protections and employment status. The ambiguous nature of gig work relationships has led to inconsistent legal interpretations and regulations, making it difficult to secure basic rights for platform workers. Addressing these challenges requires coordinated international efforts to establish regulatory frameworks that balance the growth of digital platforms with fair labour standards. The European Union's initiatives and the ILO's efforts to set global standards are steps towards achieving a more equitable environment for gig workers.

Overall, chapters in this section reveal that the future of work is shaped by the need to balance flexibility with structure. The labour market must adapt to hybrid work models while ensuring that workers remain engaged and productive. At the same time, it must accommodate diverse preferences to create inclusive and satisfying work environments. For the gig economy, finding a regulatory balance is essential to ensure fair treatment for workers while fostering innovation and growth. Ultimately, the successful evolution of the workplace will depend on the ability to navigate these complexities through adaptable strategies, technological integration, and collaborative regulation.

15.4.3 New Uses of AI and Technology in Labour

These chapters focussed how AI and technology is used to impact and change the types of work as such. A synthesis of the findings presented in the chapters of this section reveal a unifying theme of the need for balance between embracing technological advances and addressing their societal implications, particularly with respect to equity, organisational structure, and employment.

AI is driving a shift from traditional hierarchical structures to more fluid, skill-oriented networks. This transformation aims to make the labour market more agile and better suited to the complexities of the digital age. The rise of AI is seen as a catalyst for new ways of thinking about work and economic value, moving away from industrial-era frameworks. In particular, the concept of "intelligence" becomes central to modern businesses, enabling new insights, efficiencies, and innovations. However, this shift also requires a fundamental reimagining of roles and collaboration, blending technological tools with human strengths.

To this end, the expansion of AI raises important ethical concerns, particularly around transparency, control, and the fair distribution of benefits. AI development often relies on hidden human labour, especially in the form of "data work" in the Global South, where workers perform essential tasks like data labelling and training for low wages. Despite their vital role in the AI ecosystem, these workers remain marginalised, while the economic gains are concentrated among firms and shareholders. Addressing this imbalance requires more transparency and accountability, ensuring that those contributing to AI's development benefit more equitably from its economic rewards.

Automation poses risks to employment, especially in sectors like agriculture where manual labour is prevalent. As robots and machines take over routine tasks, there is a pressing need to reskill the workforce to adapt to new roles and opportunities in a more automated world. Educational systems must evolve to equip individuals with the skills required for emerging industries, ensuring that workers can transition into more resilient and adaptive roles. This is particularly critical in regions with a high dependency on low-skilled labour, where job losses could exacerbate social inequalities if not managed through targeted upskilling efforts.

The shift towards sustainable economic models, like the circular economy, offers a path to mitigate some of the disruptions caused by automation. By reimagining value creation through recycling and repurposing materials, industries can promote both environmental stewardship and local job creation. This approach, illustrated by the blue circular economy model, highlights the potential for technological innovation to support more sustainable and inclusive growth. This could help facilitate the creation of economic systems that are efficient, equitable, and aligned with the broader social and environmental goals.

Hence, AI and automation can enable a more efficient, innovative, and sustainable future if their integration into society is managed thoughtfully. The key is to foster a human-centred approach to technological change, ensuring that the benefits of AI are widely shared and that those who are vulnerable to displacement are provided with opportunities for growth and adaptation. Achieving this requires rethinking organisational and/or labour structures, promoting ethical frameworks, and investing in education and reskilling. Ideally, it would be possible to harness the potential of AI to create a more equitable future, where technology and human creativity work together to address the challenges the future labour market presents, while fostering collective and individual well-being.

15.5 Conclusion

In answering the questions set forth by the introductory chapter in identifying the promises and threats posed by the future labour market, and what lessons to be learned, this book identified and analysed three different facets in which the labour landscape would be affected by future advancements: (1) The Future of Society and Economy, (2) The Future Way of Working, and (3) New Uses of AI and Technology in Labour. This section will seek to synthesise the conclusions drawn by the studies presented in this volume.

It is undeniable that AI, digital transformation, and other technological advancements are reshaping the labour market, societal structures, and economic systems as we know them. The conclusion drawn from this book's studies is that one needs to emphasise the dual impact of technological progress: the potential for increased efficiency, innovation, and economic growth, alongside the challenges it poses to employment, equity, and societal stability. As AI and automation transform traditional work environments, a common theme is the need to balance technological integration with human-centred values, aiming for a future where technological gains are broadly accessible and the potential negative impacts, like job displacement and increased inequality, are mitigated.

It can be deduced that AI and digital technologies affect socio-economic structures. On the positive side, AI is perceived by its proponents as a driver of productivity and economic opportunities, with applications that streamline tasks in diverse sectors, from healthcare to finance. On the flipside, however, it raises concerns about the potential for job displacement, deepening economic divides, and concentration of power among tech giants or authoritarian regimes. The impact of AI varies greatly across different socio-political contexts, shaping divergent futures for digital democracies and autocracies. To counterbalance the risks, it would be prudent to consider regulatory measures to ensure that the technological advances are working to the advantage of a free and open society with checks and balances in place to ensure transparency and accountability that safeguards human values.

The way work is organised is also undergoing significant changes. For example, there has been a shift towards flexible work arrangements like remote and hybrid models. This shift was accelerated by the COVID-19 pandemic and has altered work dynamics permanently. While these models can enhance work–life balance, they also introduce challenges related to maintaining cohesion, communication, and productivity. Different demographics exhibit varying preferences for remote or in-office work, suggesting the need for adaptable workplace policies. At the same time, the gig economy has emerged as a major feature of the modern labour landscape, but it raises questions around labour rights and legal definitions, emphasising the need for coordinated international regulations and recognised judicial definitions.

Moreover, AI has prompted a shift from hierarchical models to more agile, skill-based networks, pushing companies to rethink roles and embrace a more dynamic, innovation-driven approach. However, these shifts also highlight ethical challenges, including the fair distribution of benefits. A significant portion of AI's development relies on low-paid workers in the Global South who perform "data work" that powers AI systems, while the economic rewards primarily flow elsewhere. Addressing this imbalance requires greater transparency of the distribution of gains. In addition, the rise of automation brings to pass the risk of significant job losses, particularly in sectors that rely on manual labour. This underscores the importance of reskilling and enabling educational adaptation to ensure a smooth transition for displaced workers.

In conclusion, the projected developments of the future labour landscape hold great potential for fostering productivity, innovation, and sustainable growth. However, they also carry risks of exacerbating imbalances, presenting opportunities for cynical use of power concentration and human right violations, and displacing workers. To harness these technologies effectively, it is crucial to adopt policies and strategies that prioritise the well-being of individuals and communities. This includes investing in reskilling and education, building adaptable and inclusive workplace policies, and developing frameworks that ensure transparency and equitability in the labour landscape of tomorrow. By navigating these complexities, society can leverage AI as a benign and benevolent force that benefits society by blending the strengths of human creativity with the efficiencies of digital tools, and fostering an economy that supports both the individual and collective well-being.

References

Agarwal, P., Swami, S., & Malhotra, S. K. (2024). Artificial intelligence adoption in the post COVID-19 new-normal and role of smart technologies in transforming business: A review. *Journal of Science and Technology Policy Management*, *15*(3), 506–529. https://doi.org/10.1108/JSTPM-08-2021-0122

Atkinson, R. D. (2018). "It is going to kill us!" and other myths about the future of artificial intelligence. *IUP Journal of Computer Sciences*, *12*(4), 7–56.

Baier, M.-S., Berger, S., Kreuzer, T., Oberländer, A. M., & Röglinger, M. (2023). What makes digital technology? A categorization based on purpose. *Communications of the Association for Information Systems*, *52*, 332–384. https://doi.org/10.17705/1CAIS.05215

Budhwar, P., Malik, A., De Silva, M. T. T., & Thevisuthan, P. (2022). Artificial intelligence–Challenges and opportunities for international HRM: A review and research agenda. *The International Journal of Human Resource Management*, *33*(6), 1065–1097. https://doi.org/10.1080/09585192.2022.2035161

Cramarenco, R. E., Burcă-Voicu, M. I., & Dabija, D.-C. (2023). The impact of artificial intelligence (AI) on employees' skills and well-being in global labor markets: A systematic review. *Oeconomia Copernicana*, *14*(3), 731–767.

Kavathatzopoulos, I. (2024). Artificial intelligence and the sustainability of thinking: How AI may destroy us, or help us. In T. T. Lennerfors & K. Murata (Eds.), *Ethics and Sustainability in Digital Cultures* (pp. 19–30). Oxon, UK: Routledge.

Marku, E., Castriotta, M., Guardo, M. C. Di, & Loi, M. (2021). Mapping innovation in the digital transformation Era: The role of technology convergence. In Information Resources Management Association (Ed.), *Research Anthology on Digital Transformation, Organizational Change, and the Impact of Remote Work* (pp. 761–779). Hershey, PA: IGI Global.

Reynolds, K. (2021). COVID-19 Increased the Use of AI. Here's Why It's Here to Stay. Retrieved March 6, 2025, from World Economic Forum website: www.weforum.org/agenda/2021/02/covid-19-increased-use-of-ai-here-s-why-its-here-to-stay

Schaffers, H., Vartiainen, M., & Bus, J. (2020). Introduction. In H. Schaffers, M. Vartiainen, & J. Bus (Eds.), *Digital Innovation and the Future of Work* (pp. 1–16). Gistrup, Denmark: River Publishers.

Stefano, V. De. (2019). "Negotiating the algorithm": Automation, artificial intelligence, and labor protection. *Comparative Labor Law & Policy Journal*, *41*(1), 15–46.

Zarkadakis, G. (2015). *In Our Own Image: Will Artificial Intelligence Save or Destroy Us?* London, UK: Rider.

AFTERWORD

Navigating the Future of Labour in an Age of Technological Disruption

In recent decades, the rapid pace of technological development has redefined the nature of work, catalysed by the digital revolution and artificial intelligence (AI). The chapters of this anthology delve deeply into this transformation, offering insights into how these forces shape the present and future of labour markets across industries and geographies. As we stand at this pivotal juncture, it becomes clear that while technological innovation promises remarkable opportunities, it also presents a number of profound challenges—economic, social, and ethical—that we must collectively address.

It is important to remember that the running theme throughout this volume, technology's relationship with labour, is neither static nor predetermined. Technological advances are not autonomous forces that render humans obsolete; rather, they have the potential to complement human labour, augment productivity, and create new forms of work. History has repeatedly shown that technological revolutions can increase prosperity, raise living standards, and create entirely new sectors of the economy. For example, the industrial revolution led to the decline of agricultural employment but simultaneously gave rise to manufacturing, eventually reshaping the global economy and labour market. Likewise, the digital revolution is rapidly transforming service sectors, giving birth to new jobs that were unthinkable just a few decades ago.

Yet, this transformation is not without dislocation. Automation and AI, in particular, are accelerating the erosion of routine, middle-skill jobs, leading to what has been termed the "hollowing out" of the labour market. Roles that involve repetitive tasks—whether in manufacturing, clerical work, or even some aspects of white-collar jobs—are being automated at a pace that outstrips the ability of many workers to adapt. This creates a bifurcation in the labour market: on one end, there are high-skill, high-wage jobs that require creativity, problem-solving,

DOI: 10.4324/9781003391333-19

and interpersonal skills, and on the other, low-skill, low-wage jobs that are less susceptible to automation but offer limited pathways for upward mobility.

The challenge, then, is not simply one of job displacement but of managing the transition in a way that promotes broad-based prosperity. This requires a concerted effort to equip workers with the skills needed to thrive in a digital economy. Education and workforce training must be reimagined to emphasise lifelong learning, adaptability, and the cultivation of uniquely human skills that machines are unlikely to replicate—such as empathy, leadership, and complex decision-making. Furthermore, policies that support worker mobility, income security, and access to high-quality education are essential to prevent the deepening of inequality in an increasingly polarised labour market.

International collaboration is crucial in addressing these challenges, as technological disruption does not respect national borders. Global supply chains and digital platforms make it clear that the future of work will be shaped by forces that transcend individual countries. As such, sharing best practices for labour market policies, education systems, and social safety nets will be vital to ensuring that the benefits of technological progress are distributed equitably, not just within nations but across them.

However, it is equally important to acknowledge that technology, while a driver of change, is not destiny. Public policy plays a critical role in shaping the labour market's evolution. We must remain vigilant against the false narrative that automation and AI will lead inevitably to a "jobless future". Instead, our focus should be on how we can guide technological development to ensure that it empowers workers, fosters inclusion, and improves the quality of life for all.

One significant lesson from history is that periods of technological upheaval often lead to a re-evaluation of labour's role in society. As AI and automation advance, we are presented with an opportunity to rethink not just how we work, but why we work. The traditional notion of employment as a source of financial security is increasingly giving way to broader considerations about meaning, purpose, and well-being. Some scholars have even called for bold experiments such as universal basic income or shorter workweeks as ways to ensure that the gains from technological progress are shared more evenly across society.

As an urbanist, having advised more than 300 cities and 50 national governments on strategies for city development and investment, I, after reading this book, particularly reflect on how the future of labour affects our cities. As cities become increasingly central to the technological transformation of work, their role as hubs of innovation, labour, and policy experimentation cannot be overstated. Urban centres mentioned within this book, such as Silicon Valley, Hollywood, Stockholm, and Peniche, exemplify how geography shapes the adoption and impact of technological advancements. These cities and places act as incubators for emerging industries, fostering ecosystems where businesses, workers, and policymakers converge to navigate the challenges and opportunities of the digital age. At the same time, the spatial divide between urban and rural areas underscores the uneven distribution of technological benefits, with rural regions often lagging behind in access to infrastructure, education, and job opportunities tied to the digital economy. Bridging this urban–rural divide will be critical to ensuring that the transformative power of technology does not exacerbate existing inequalities but instead serves as a unifying force in the global labour landscape.

As this book has shown, the future of labour is uncertain, daunting and even in some cases intimidating, but at the same time also full of potential and promise. The task ahead is to ensure that we harness that potential in ways that are effective, equitable, and sustainable. While technological change is inevitable, the shape of our future labour markets depends on the choices we make today—choices about how we train workers, design policies, and distribute the benefits of innovation. The road ahead is challenging, but by working together across sectors and borders, we can build a future of work that is not just automated, but human-centred, dignified, and prosperous for all.

In closing, let me offer a reflection: technological progress is often framed as a race, with countries and companies vying to outpace one another in innovation. However, the future of work should not be seen as a zero-sum competition. Rather, it is an opportunity for collective progress, where our shared goal is to create an economy—and a society—that works for everyone. With thoughtful leadership, investment in people, and a commitment to equity, we can ensure that the future of labour is one of possibility, not peril.

Greg Clark, Chair, Connected Places Catapult; Visiting Professor, Cities and Innovation, Strathclyde University; Chair, UK Government Secure Connected Places External Advisory Group; Chair, UK Cities Climate Investment Commission

INDEX

Note: Page numbers in **bold** refer to tables, and those in *italics* refer to figures.

Kolibri 360 GmbH
Ferdinand-Jühlke-Straße 7
99095 Erfurt, Deutschland
produktsicherheit@kolibri360.de